NEGIMA! 16

Ken Akamatsu

TRANSLATED BY
Toshifumi Yoshida

ADAPTED BY
Ikoi Hiroe

LETTERING AND RETOUCH BY
Steve Palmer

D1004705

DEL REY

BALLANTINE BOOKS • NEW YORK

A Del Rey Trade Paperback Original

Negima! volume 16 copyright © 2006 by Ken Akamatsu
English translation copyright © 2007 by Ken Akamatsu

Published in the United States by Del Rey Books, an imprint of The Random House Publishing Group, a division of Random House, Inc., New York.

DEL REY is a registered trademark and the Del Rey colophon is a trademark of Random House, Inc.

Publication rights arranged through Kodansha Ltd.

First published in Japan in 2006 by Kodansha Ltd., Tokyo

ISBN 978-0-345-49924-0

Printed in the United States of America

www.delreymanga.com

9 8 7 6 5 4 3 2 1

Translator—Toshifumi Yoshida
Adapter—Ikoi Hiroe
Lettering and retouch—Steve Palmer

Honorifics Explained

Throughout the Del Rey Manga books, you will find Japanese honorifics left intact in the translations. For those not familiar with how the Japanese use honorifics and, more important, how they differ from American honorifics, we present this brief overview.

Politeness has always been a critical facet of Japanese culture. Ever since the feudal era, when Japan was a highly stratified society, use of honorifics—which can be defined as polite speech that indicates relationship or status—has played an essential role in the Japanese language. When addressing someone in Japanese, an honorific usually takes the form of a suffix attached to one's name (example: "Asuna-san"), is used as a title at the end of one's name, or appears in place of the name itself (example: "Negi-sensei," or simply "Sensei!").

Honorifics can be expressions of respect or endearment. In the context of manga and anime, honorifics give insight into the nature of the relationship between characters. Many English translations leave out these important honorifics and therefore distort the feel of the original Japanese. Because Japanese honorifics contain nuances that English honorifics lack, it is our policy at Del Rey not to translate them. Here, instead, is a guide to some of the honorifics you may encounter in Del Rey Manga.

-*san*: This is the most common honorific and is equivalent to Mr., Miss, Ms., or Mrs. It is the all-purpose honorific and can be used in any situation where politeness is required.

-*sama*: This is one level higher than "-san" and is used to confer great respect.

-*dono*: This comes from the word "tono," which means "lord." It is an even higher level than "-sama" and confers utmost respect.

-*kun*: This suffix is used at the end of boys' names to express familiarity or endearment. It is also sometimes used by men among friends, or when addressing someone younger or of a lower station.

-chan: This is used to express endearment, mostly toward girls. It is also used for little boys, pets, and even among lovers. It gives a sense of childish cuteness.

Bozu: This is an informal way to refer to a boy, similar to the English terms "kid" and "squirt."

Sempai/Senpai: This title suggests that the addressee is one's senior in a group or organization. It is most often used in a school setting, where underclassmen refer to their upperclassmen as "sempai." It can also be used in the workplace, such as when a newer employee addresses an employee who has seniority in the company.

Kohai: This is the opposite of "sempai" and is used toward underclassmen in school or newcomers in the workplace. It connotes that the addressee is of a lower station.

Sensei: Literally meaning "one who has come before," this title is used for teachers, doctors, or masters of any profession or art.

Anesan (or *nesan*): A generic term for a girl, usually older, that means sister.

Ojōsama: A way of referring to the daughter or sister of someone with high political or social status.

-[blank]: This is usually forgotten in these lists, but it is perhaps the most significant difference between Japanese and English. The lack of honorific means that the speaker has permission to address the person in a very intimate way. Usually, only family, spouses, or very close friends have this kind of permission. Known as *yobisute*, it can be gratifying when someone who has earned the intimacy starts to call one by one's name without an honorific. But when that intimacy hasn't been earned, it can be very insulting.

A Word from the Author

Negima!, the new animated series, has made its TV debut. Negi and Asuna are back, more powerful than ever! Please check the official website for showtimes on your local station!

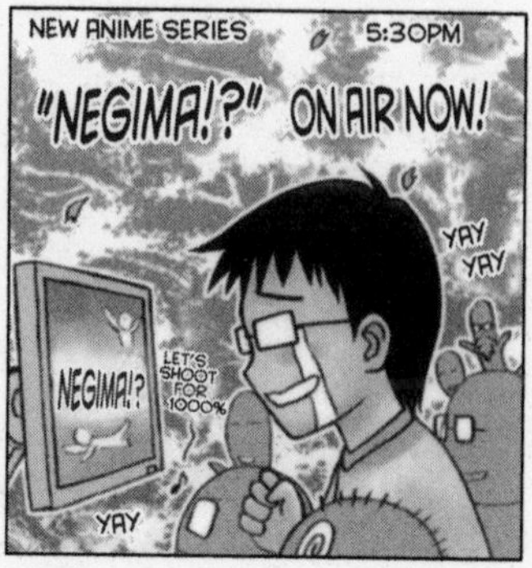
NEW ANIME SERIES
5:30PM
"NEGIMA!?" ON AIR NOW!
YAY
YAY
NEGIMA!?
LET'S SHOOT FOR 1000%
YAY

Now, for the manga version, I present *Negima!* volume 16! In the previous volume, Negi and his newly formed party fell into Chao's trap...but a true hero turns a dire situation into a chance to triumph! Negi's counterattack begins with his new and powerful partners!

The Mahora Festival episodes will come to a close in the next volume. Please continue to support this series in the future!

Ken Akamatsu
www.ailove.net

魔法先生ネギま!

MAGISTER NEGI MAGI

16

Ken Akamatsu

赤松健

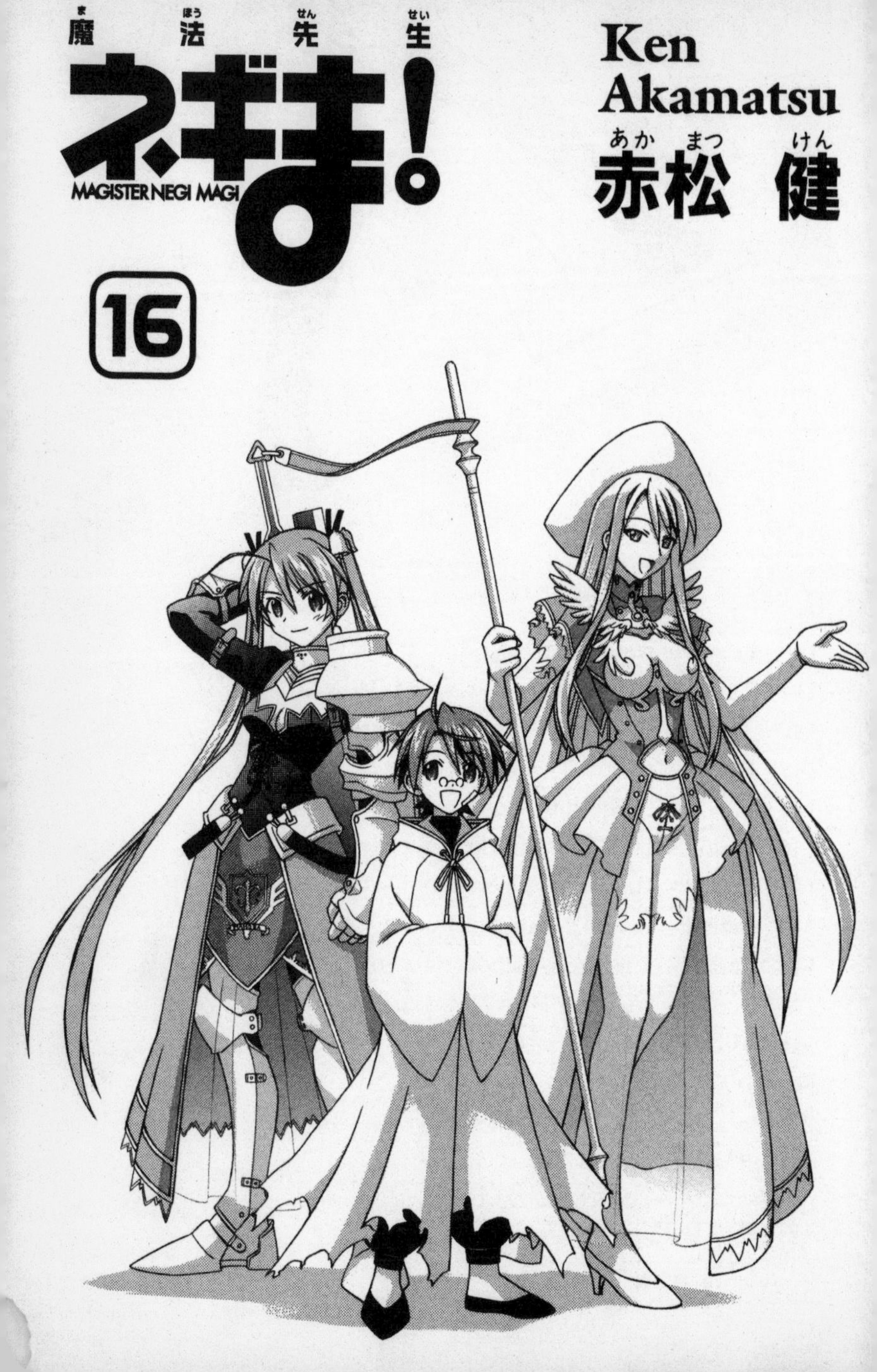

麻帆良祭実行委員会2003年6月22日認可／デザイン・イラスト・ハル
ACCESS BY MOBILE PHONE

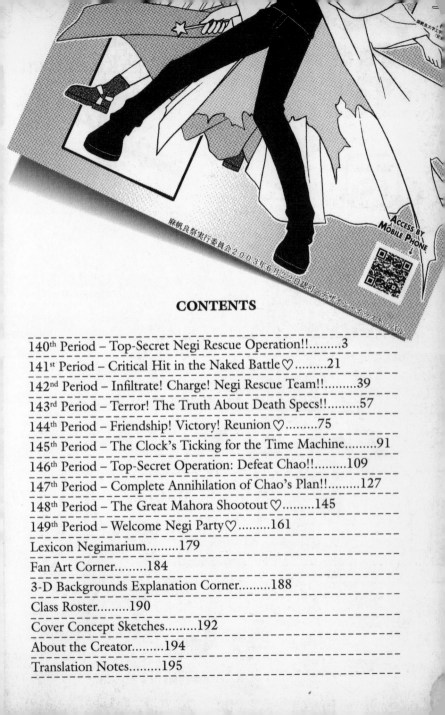

CONTENTS

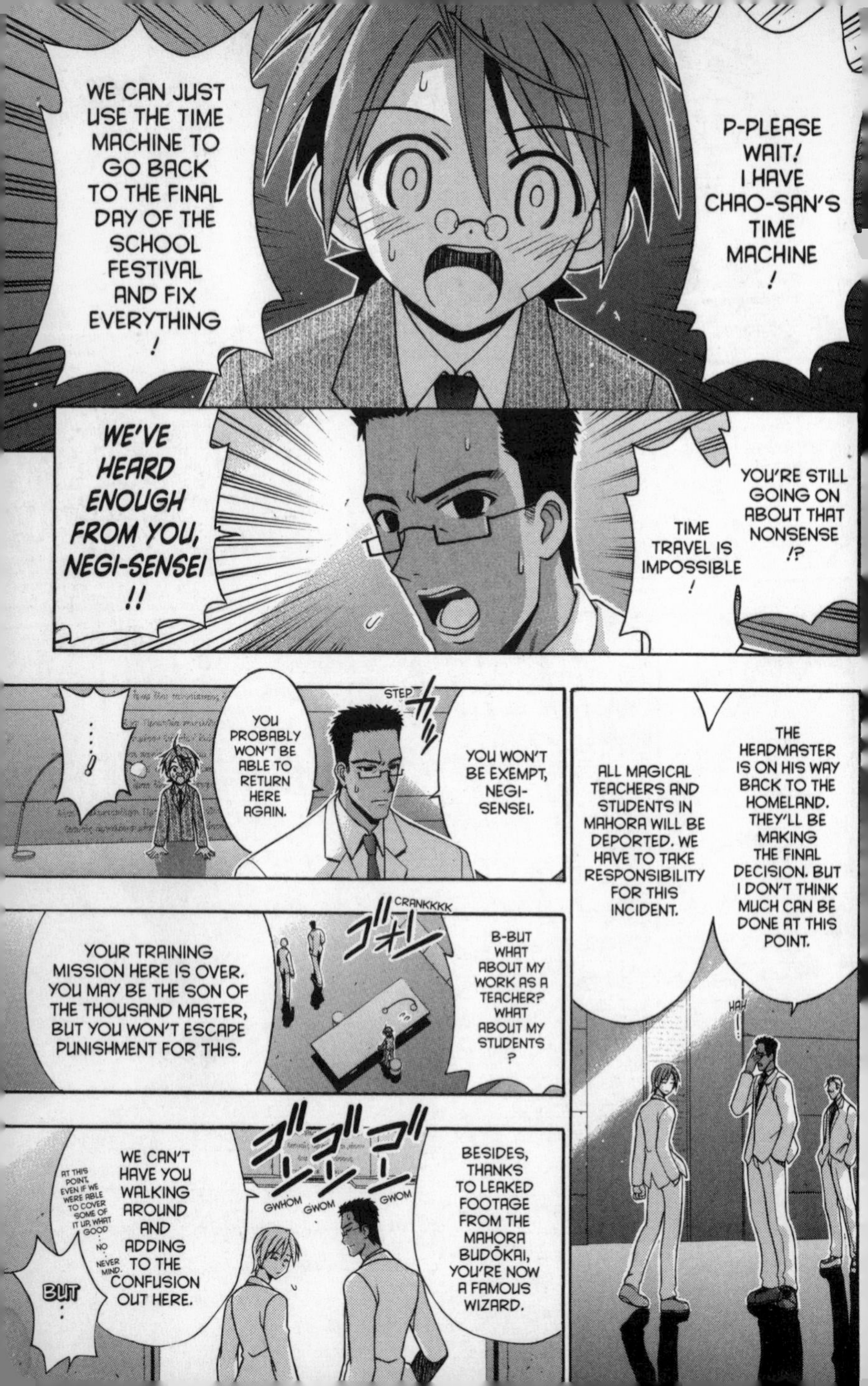
P-PLEASE WAIT! I HAVE CHAO-SAN'S TIME MACHINE!
WE CAN JUST USE THE TIME MACHINE TO GO BACK TO THE FINAL DAY OF THE SCHOOL FESTIVAL AND FIX EVERYTHING!
YOU'RE STILL GOING ON ABOUT THAT NONSENSE!?
TIME TRAVEL IS IMPOSSIBLE!
WE'VE HEARD ENOUGH FROM YOU, NEGI-SENSEI!!
THE HEADMASTER IS ON HIS WAY BACK TO THE HOMELAND. THEY'LL BE MAKING THE FINAL DECISION. BUT I DON'T THINK MUCH CAN BE DONE AT THIS POINT.
ALL MAGICAL TEACHERS AND STUDENTS IN MAHORA WILL BE DEPORTED. WE HAVE TO TAKE RESPONSIBILITY FOR THIS INCIDENT.
HAH
STEP
YOU WON'T BE EXEMPT, NEGI-SENSEI.
YOU PROBABLY WON'T BE ABLE TO RETURN HERE AGAIN.
......!
CRANKKKK
B-BUT WHAT ABOUT MY WORK AS A TEACHER? WHAT ABOUT MY STUDENTS?
YOUR TRAINING MISSION HERE IS OVER. YOU MAY BE THE SON OF THE THOUSAND MASTER, BUT YOU WON'T ESCAPE PUNISHMENT FOR THIS.
GWOM
GWOM
GWHOM
BESIDES, THANKS TO LEAKED FOOTAGE FROM THE MAHORA BUDŌKAI, YOU'RE NOW A FAMOUS WIZARD.
WE CAN'T HAVE YOU WALKING AROUND AND ADDING TO THE CONFUSION OUT HERE.
AT THIS POINT, EVEN IF WE WERE ABLE TO COVER SOME OF IT UP, WHAT GOOD... NO... NEVER MIND.
BUT...

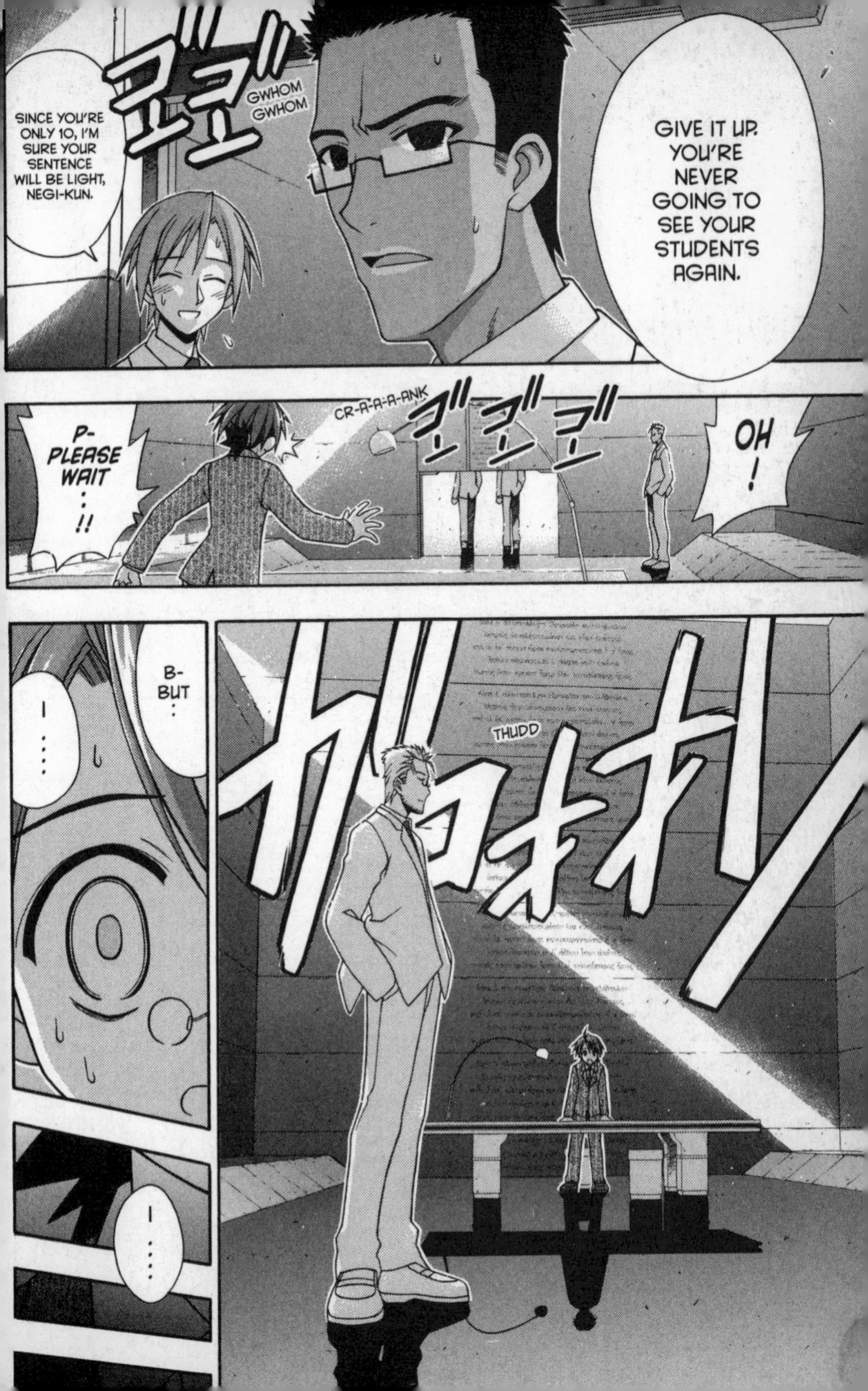
GIVE IT UP. YOU'RE NEVER GOING TO SEE YOUR STUDENTS AGAIN.
GWHOM GWHOM
SINCE YOU'RE ONLY 10, I'M SURE YOUR SENTENCE WILL BE LIGHT, NEGI-KUN.
OH!
CR-A-A-A-ANK
P-PLEASE WAIT...!!
THUDD
B-BUT...
I...
I...

BAD ENDING

SCHOOL FESTIVAL – CHAO EPISODE
ERMINE ENDING NO. 16

NEGI SPENDS THE NEXT SIX MONTHS AS AN ERMINE.
HE'LL NEVER RETURN TO MAHORA ACADEMY AGAIN.

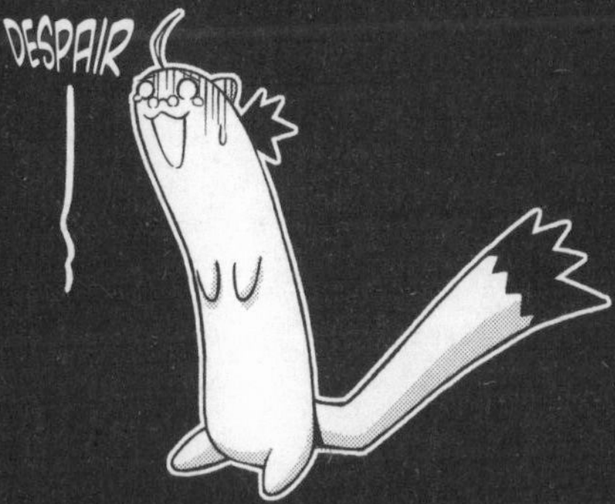
DESPAIR

TRY AGAIN ◀

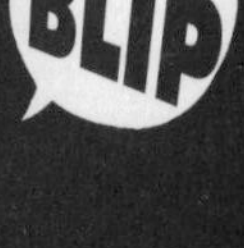
BLIP

STRATEGY TIPS: THINK ABOUT WHERE YOU MADE A MISTAKE. WAS IT A GOOD IDEA TO SPEND AN ADDITIONAL NIGHT IN EVA'S RESORT TO PLAN YOUR ATTACK? WAS IT A GOOD IDEA TO PARTICIPATE IN THE MAHORA BUDŌKAI WITHOUT TAKING PRECAUTIONS? PERHAPS ACCEPTING THE TIME MACHINE FROM CHAO IN THE FIRST PLACE WAS A BAD IDEA? RETURN TO YOUR LAST SAVE POINT AND TRY AGAIN. I'M SURE YOU'LL FIND THE ANSWER SOMEWHERE!

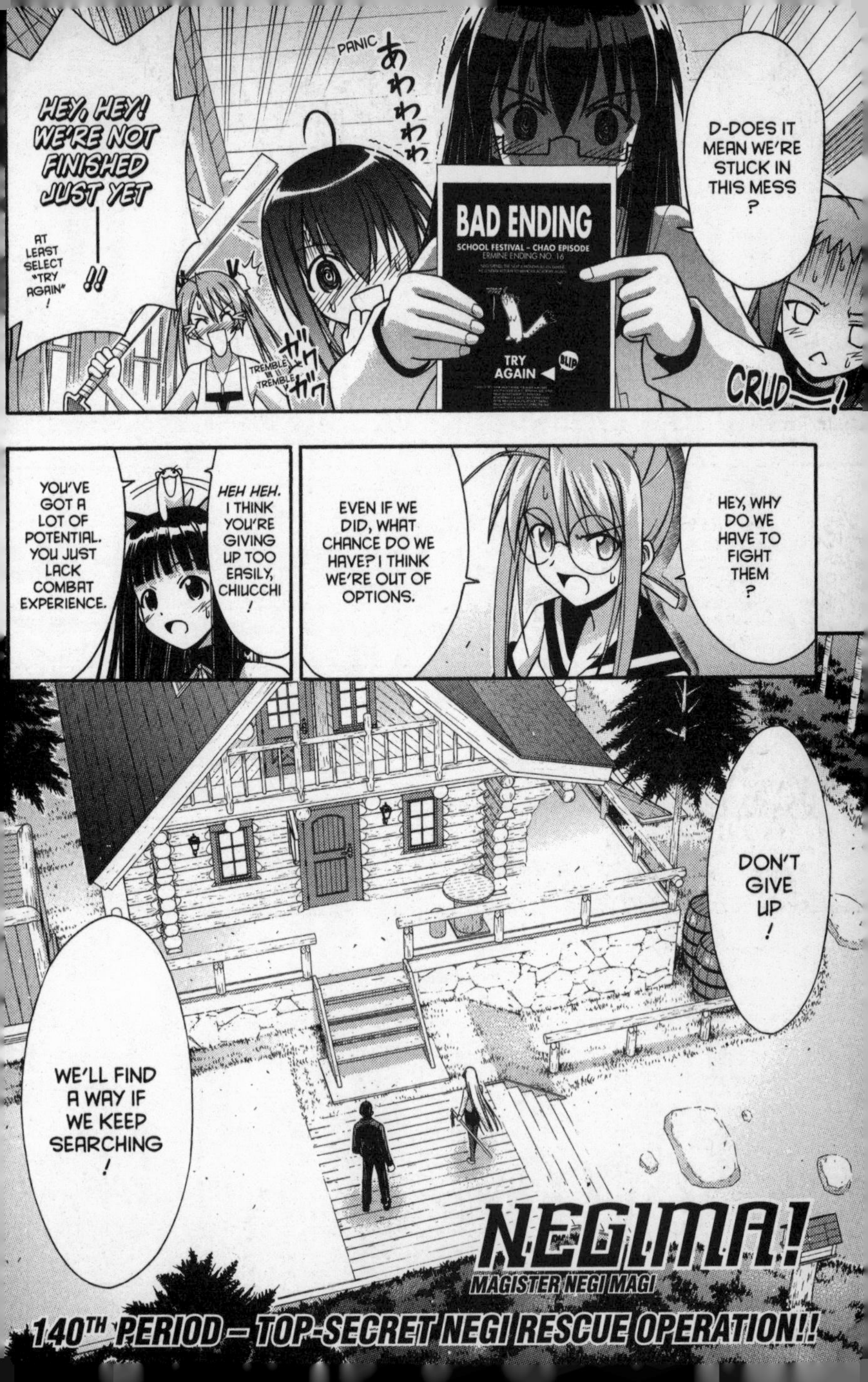
D-DOES IT MEAN WE'RE STUCK IN THIS MESS?
PANIC あわわわわ
BAD ENDING
SCHOOL FESTIVAL – CHAO EPISODE
ERMINE ENDING NO. 16
TRY AGAIN
BLIP
CRUD—!
HEY, HEY! WE'RE NOT FINISHED JUST YET—!!
AT LEAST SELECT "TRY AGAIN"!
TREMBLE TREMBLE ガクガク
HEY, WHY DO WE HAVE TO FIGHT THEM?
EVEN IF WE DID, WHAT CHANCE DO WE HAVE? I THINK WE'RE OUT OF OPTIONS.
HEH HEH. I THINK YOU'RE GIVING UP TOO EASILY, CHIUCCHI!
YOU'VE GOT A LOT OF POTENTIAL. YOU JUST LACK COMBAT EXPERIENCE.
DON'T GIVE UP!
WE'LL FIND A WAY IF WE KEEP SEARCHING!
NEGIMA!
MAGISTER NEGI MAGI
140TH PERIOD – TOP-SECRET NEGI RESCUE OPERATION!!

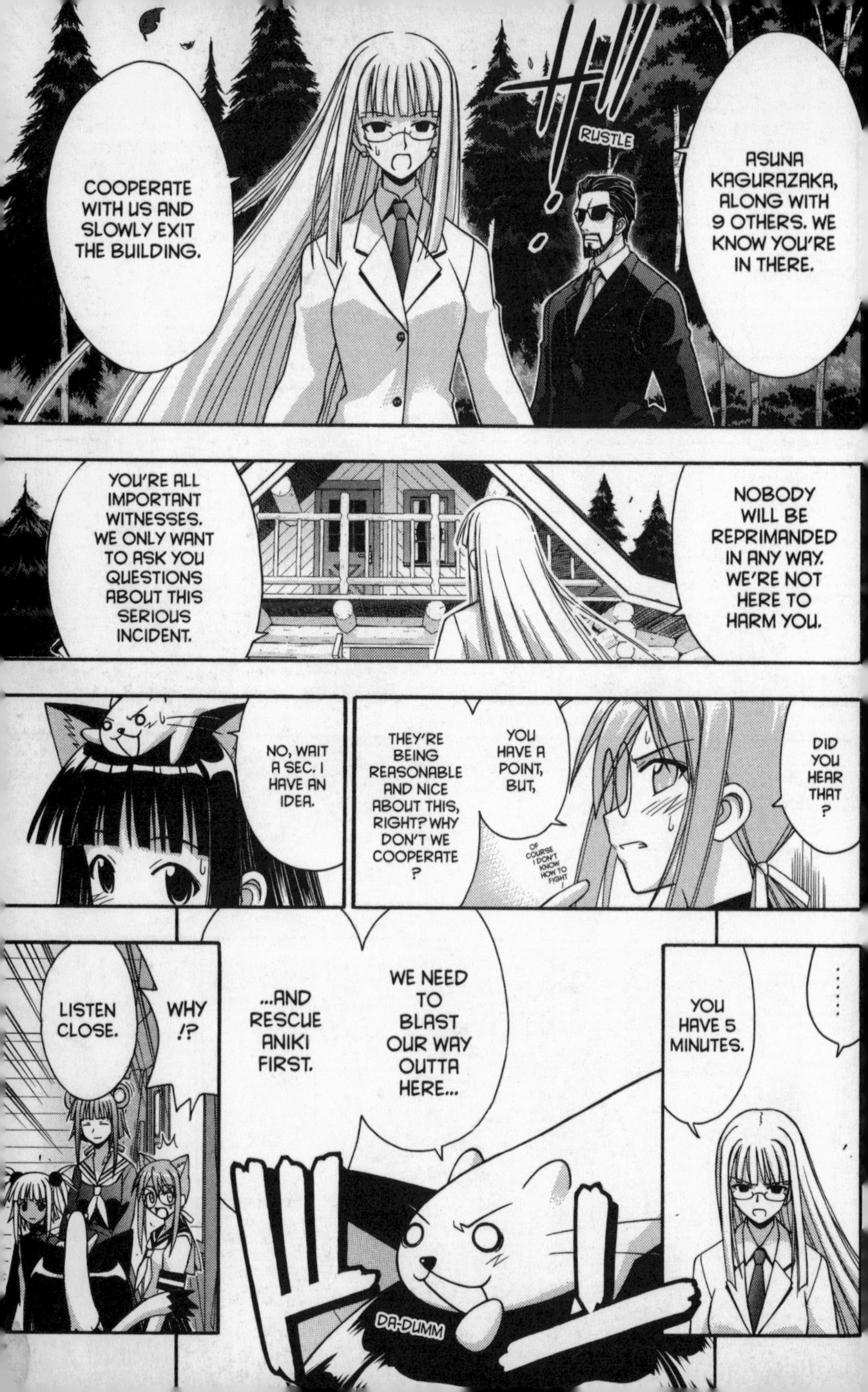
ASUNA KAGURAZAKA, ALONG WITH 9 OTHERS. WE KNOW YOU'RE IN THERE.
RUSTLE
COOPERATE WITH US AND SLOWLY EXIT THE BUILDING.
NOBODY WILL BE REPRIMANDED IN ANY WAY. WE'RE NOT HERE TO HARM YOU.
YOU'RE ALL IMPORTANT WITNESSES. WE ONLY WANT TO ASK YOU QUESTIONS ABOUT THIS SERIOUS INCIDENT.
DID YOU HEAR THAT?
YOU HAVE A POINT, BUT,
OF COURSE I DON'T KNOW HOW TO FIGHT!
THEY'RE BEING REASONABLE AND NICE ABOUT THIS, RIGHT? WHY DON'T WE COOPERATE?
NO, WAIT A SEC. I HAVE AN IDEA.
......
YOU HAVE 5 MINUTES.
WE NEED TO BLAST OUR WAY OUTTA HERE...
...AND RESCUE ANIKI FIRST.
DA-DUMM
WHY!?
LISTEN CLOSE.

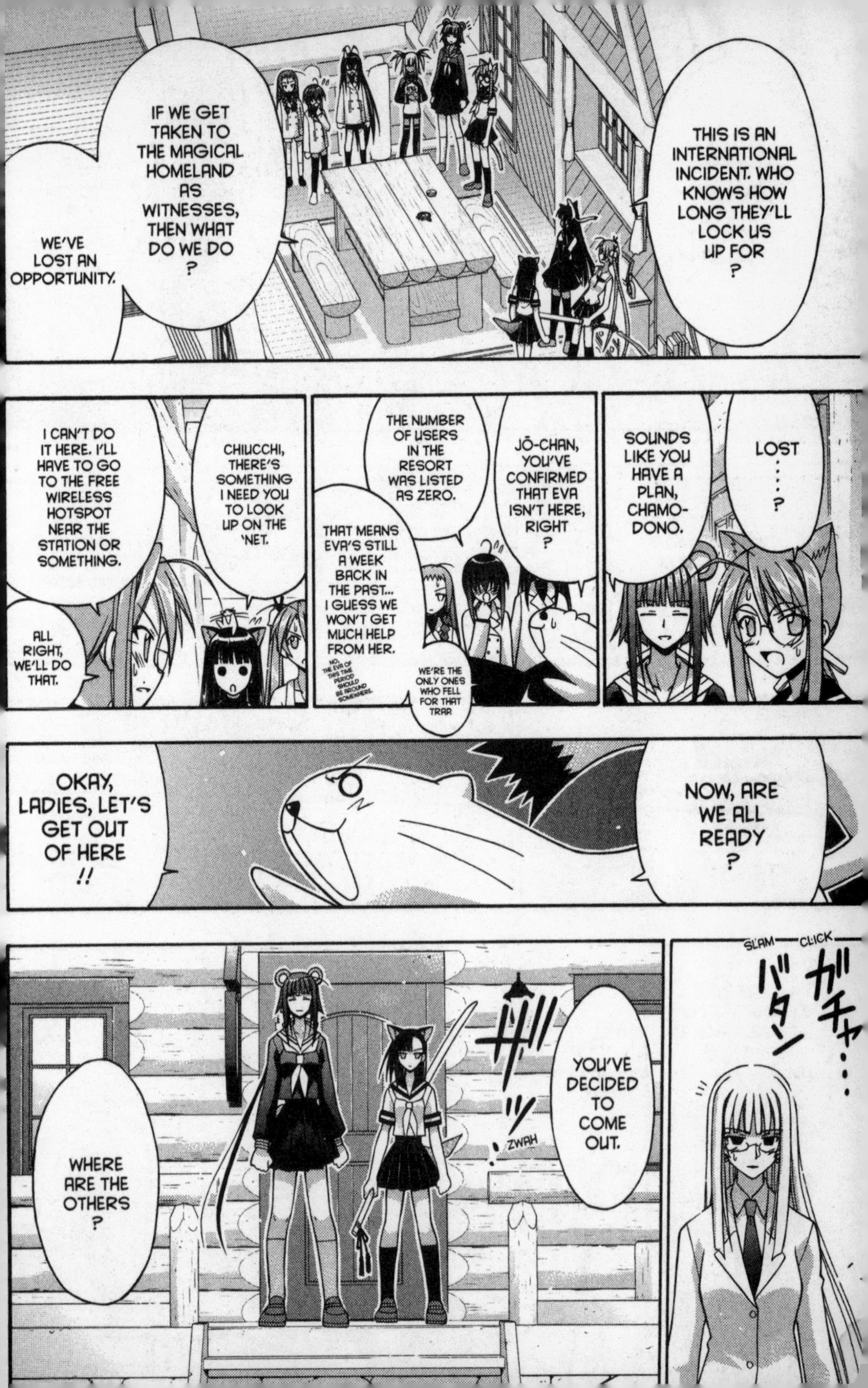
THIS IS AN INTERNATIONAL INCIDENT. WHO KNOWS HOW LONG THEY'LL LOCK US UP FOR?
IF WE GET TAKEN TO THE MAGICAL HOMELAND AS WITNESSES, THEN WHAT DO WE DO?
WE'VE LOST AN OPPORTUNITY.
LOST....?
SOUNDS LIKE YOU HAVE A PLAN, CHAMO-DONO.
JŌ-CHAN, YOU'VE CONFIRMED THAT EVA ISN'T HERE, RIGHT?
THE NUMBER OF USERS IN THE RESORT WAS LISTED AS ZERO.
THAT MEANS EVA'S STILL A WEEK BACK IN THE PAST... I GUESS WE WON'T GET MUCH HELP FROM HER.
WE'RE THE ONLY ONES WHO FELL FOR THAT TRAP.
NO, THE EVA OF THIS TIME PERIOD SHOULD BE AROUND SOMEWHERE.
CHIUCCHI, THERE'S SOMETHING I NEED YOU TO LOOK UP ON THE 'NET.
I CAN'T DO IT HERE. I'LL HAVE TO GO TO THE FREE WIRELESS HOTSPOT NEAR THE STATION OR SOMETHING.
ALL RIGHT, WE'LL DO THAT.
NOW, ARE WE ALL READY?
OKAY, LADIES, LET'S GET OUT OF HERE!!
ガチャ…
SLAM—CLICK
バタン
YOU'VE DECIDED TO COME OUT.
ザッ
ZWAH
WHERE ARE THE OTHERS?

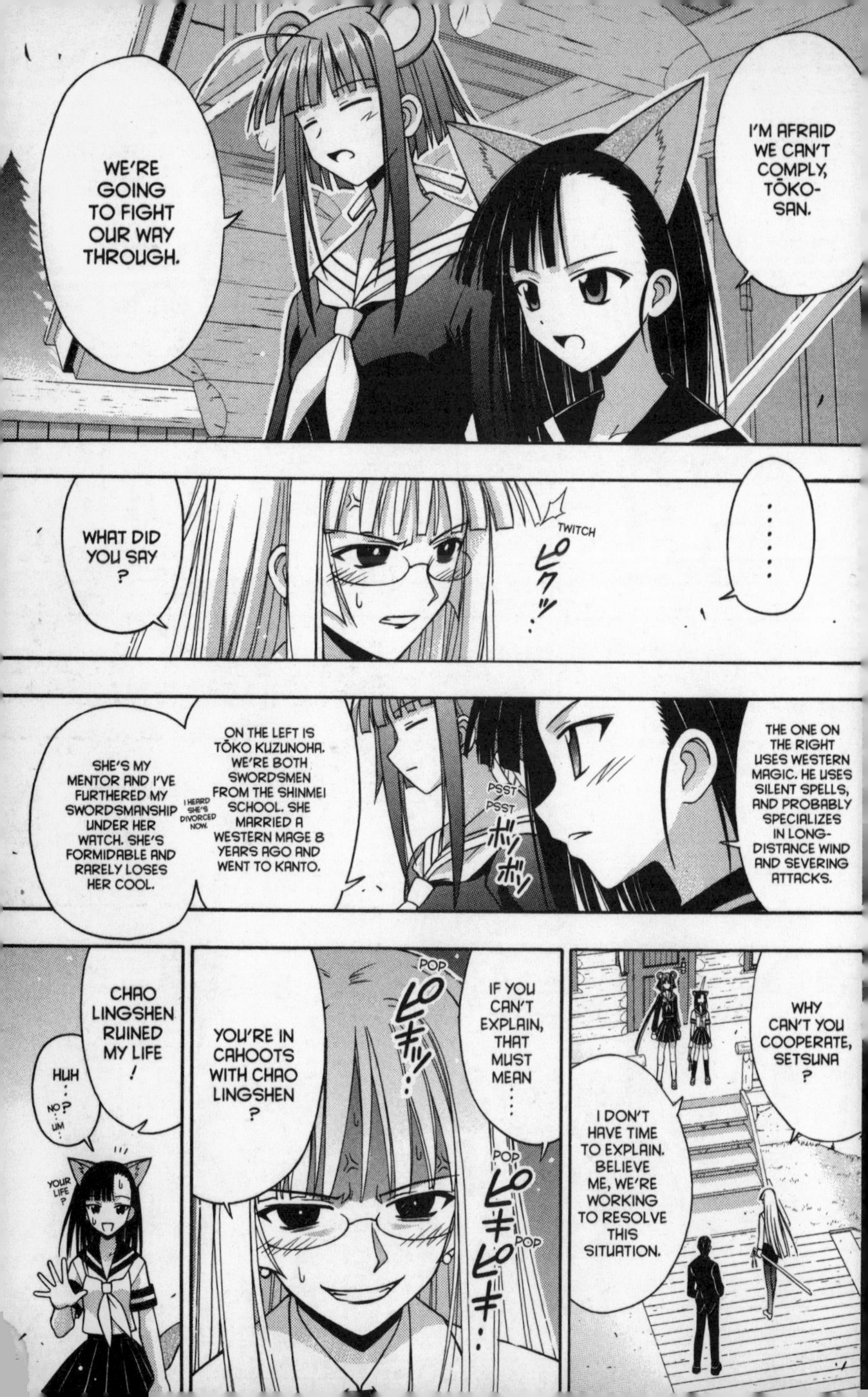
I'M AFRAID WE CAN'T COMPLY, TŌKO-SAN.
WE'RE GOING TO FIGHT OUR WAY THROUGH.
……
TWITCH
WHAT DID YOU SAY?
THE ONE ON THE RIGHT USES WESTERN MAGIC. HE USES SILENT SPELLS, AND PROBABLY SPECIALIZES IN LONG-DISTANCE WIND AND SEVERING ATTACKS.
PSST PSST
ON THE LEFT IS TŌKO KUZUNOHA. WE'RE BOTH SWORDSMEN FROM THE SHINMEI SCHOOL. SHE MARRIED A WESTERN MAGE 8 YEARS AGO AND WENT TO KANTO.
I HEARD SHE'S DIVORCED NOW.
SHE'S MY MENTOR AND I'VE FURTHERED MY SWORDSMANSHIP UNDER HER WATCH. SHE'S FORMIDABLE AND RARELY LOSES HER COOL.
WHY CAN'T YOU COOPERATE, SETSUNA?
I DON'T HAVE TIME TO EXPLAIN. BELIEVE ME, WE'RE WORKING TO RESOLVE THIS SITUATION.
IF YOU CAN'T EXPLAIN, THAT MUST MEAN……
POP
YOU'RE IN CAHOOTS WITH CHAO LINGSHEN?
POP
POP
CHAO LINGSHEN RUINED MY LIFE!
HUH… NO? UM…
YOUR LIFE?

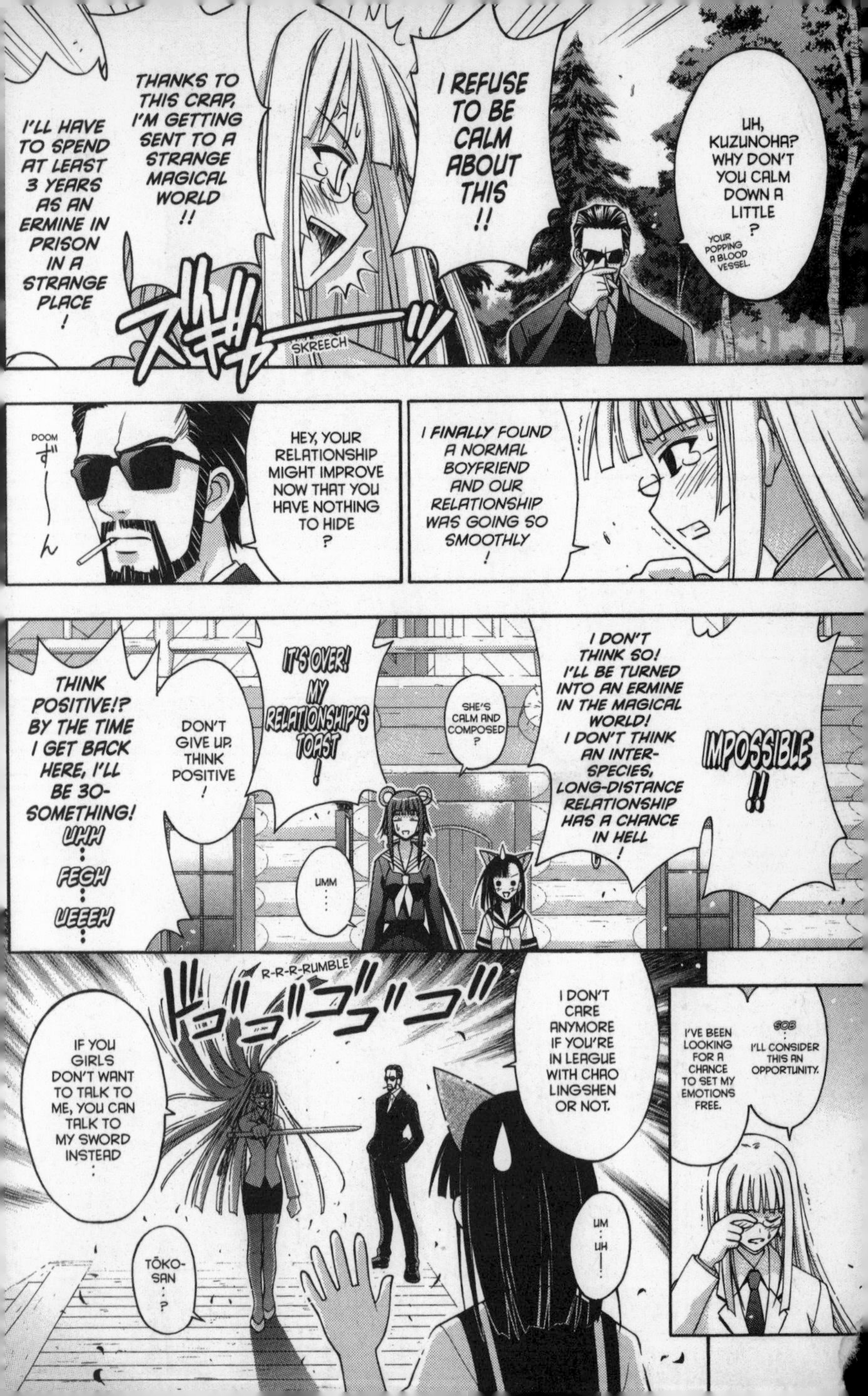
UH, KUZUNOHA? WHY DON'T YOU CALM DOWN A LITTLE?
YOUR POPPING A BLOOD VESSEL.
I REFUSE TO BE CALM ABOUT THIS!!
THANKS TO THIS CRAP, I'M GETTING SENT TO A STRANGE MAGICAL WORLD!!
I'LL HAVE TO SPEND AT LEAST 3 YEARS AS AN ERMINE IN PRISON IN A STRANGE PLACE!
SKREECH
I FINALLY FOUND A NORMAL BOYFRIEND AND OUR RELATIONSHIP WAS GOING SO SMOOTHLY!
HEY, YOUR RELATIONSHIP MIGHT IMPROVE NOW THAT YOU HAVE NOTHING TO HIDE?
DOOM
IMPOSSIBLE!!
I DON'T THINK SO! I'LL BE TURNED INTO AN ERMINE IN THE MAGICAL WORLD! I DON'T THINK AN INTER-SPECIES, LONG-DISTANCE RELATIONSHIP HAS A CHANCE IN HELL!
SHE'S CALM AND COMPOSED?
IT'S OVER! MY RELATIONSHIP'S TOAST!
UMM...
DON'T GIVE UP. THINK POSITIVE!
THINK POSITIVE!? BY THE TIME I GET BACK HERE, I'LL BE 30-SOMETHING! UHH... FEGH... UEEEH...
SOB
I'LL CONSIDER THIS AN OPPORTUNITY.
I'VE BEEN LOOKING FOR A CHANCE TO SET MY EMOTIONS FREE.
I DON'T CARE ANYMORE IF YOU'RE IN LEAGUE WITH CHAO LINGSHEN OR NOT.
R-R-R-RUMBLE
IF YOU GIRLS DON'T WANT TO TALK TO ME, YOU CAN TALK TO MY SWORD INSTEAD...
UM...UH!
TŌKO-SAN...?

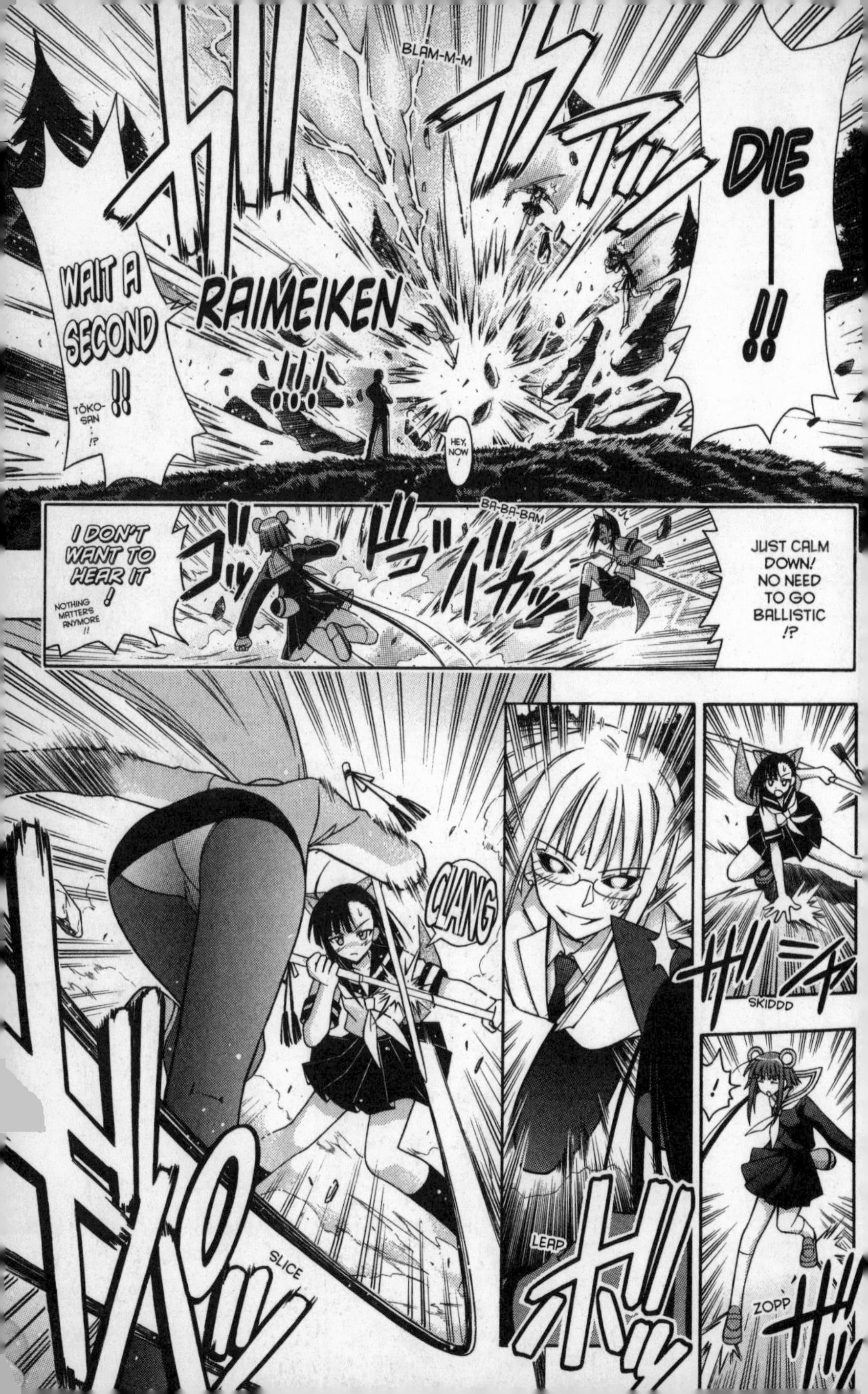
DIE—!!
BLAM-M-M
RAIMEIKEN!!!
HEY, NOW!
WAIT A SECOND!!
TŌKO-SAN...!?
JUST CALM DOWN! NO NEED TO GO BALLISTIC!?
BA-BA-BAM
I DON'T WANT TO HEAR IT!
NOTHING MATTER'S ANYMORE!!
SKIDDD
ZOPP
LEAP
CLANG
SLICE

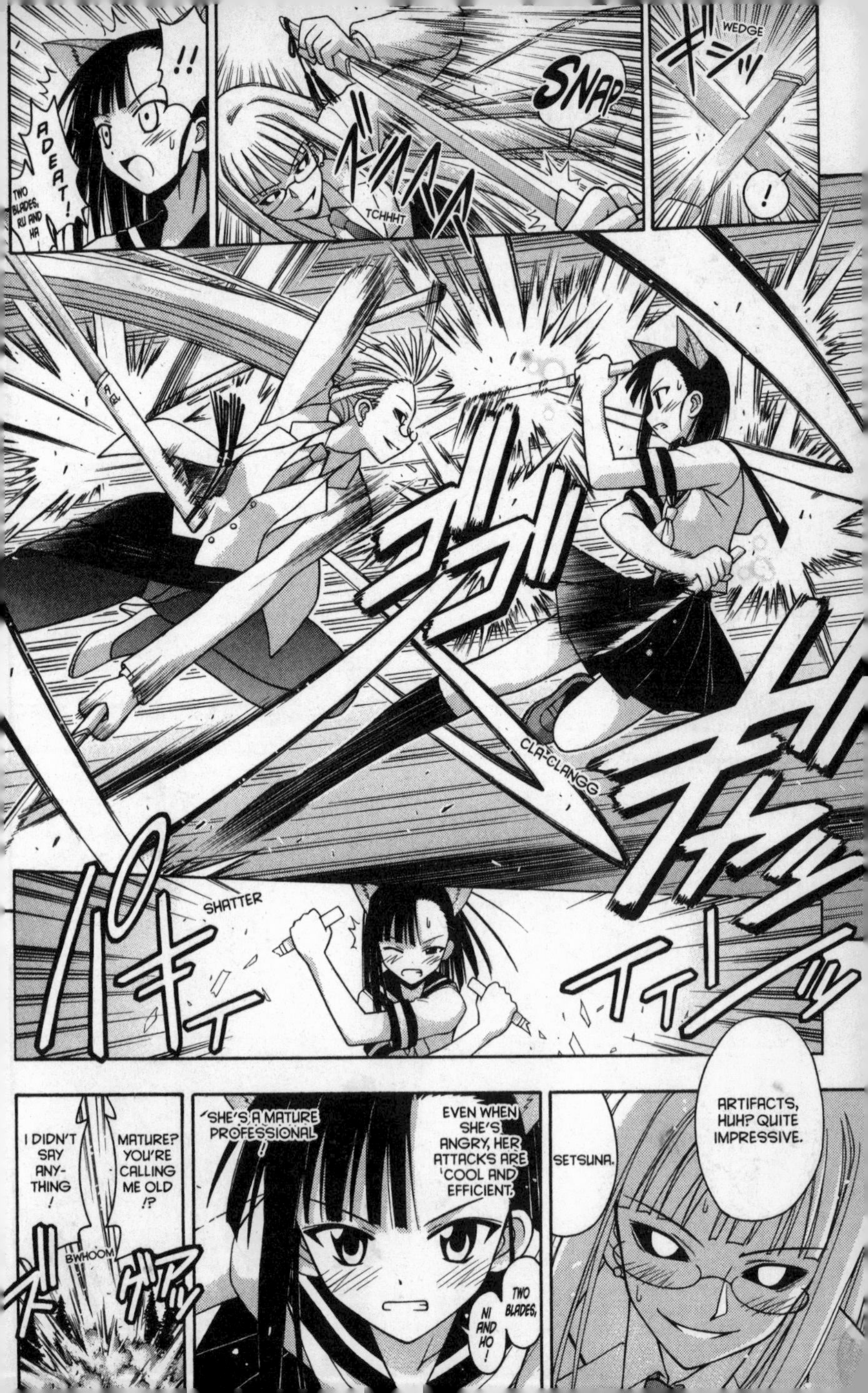
WEDGE
!
SNAP
TCHHHT
!!
ADEAT!
TWO BLADES, RU AND HA
CLA-CLANGG
SHATTER
ARTIFACTS, HUH? QUITE IMPRESSIVE.
SETSUNA.
TWO BLADES,
NI AND HO!
EVEN WHEN SHE'S ANGRY, HER ATTACKS ARE COOL AND EFFICIENT.
SHE'S A MATURE PROFESSIONAL!
MATURE? YOU'RE CALLING ME OLD!?
I DIDN'T SAY ANYTHING!
BWHOOM

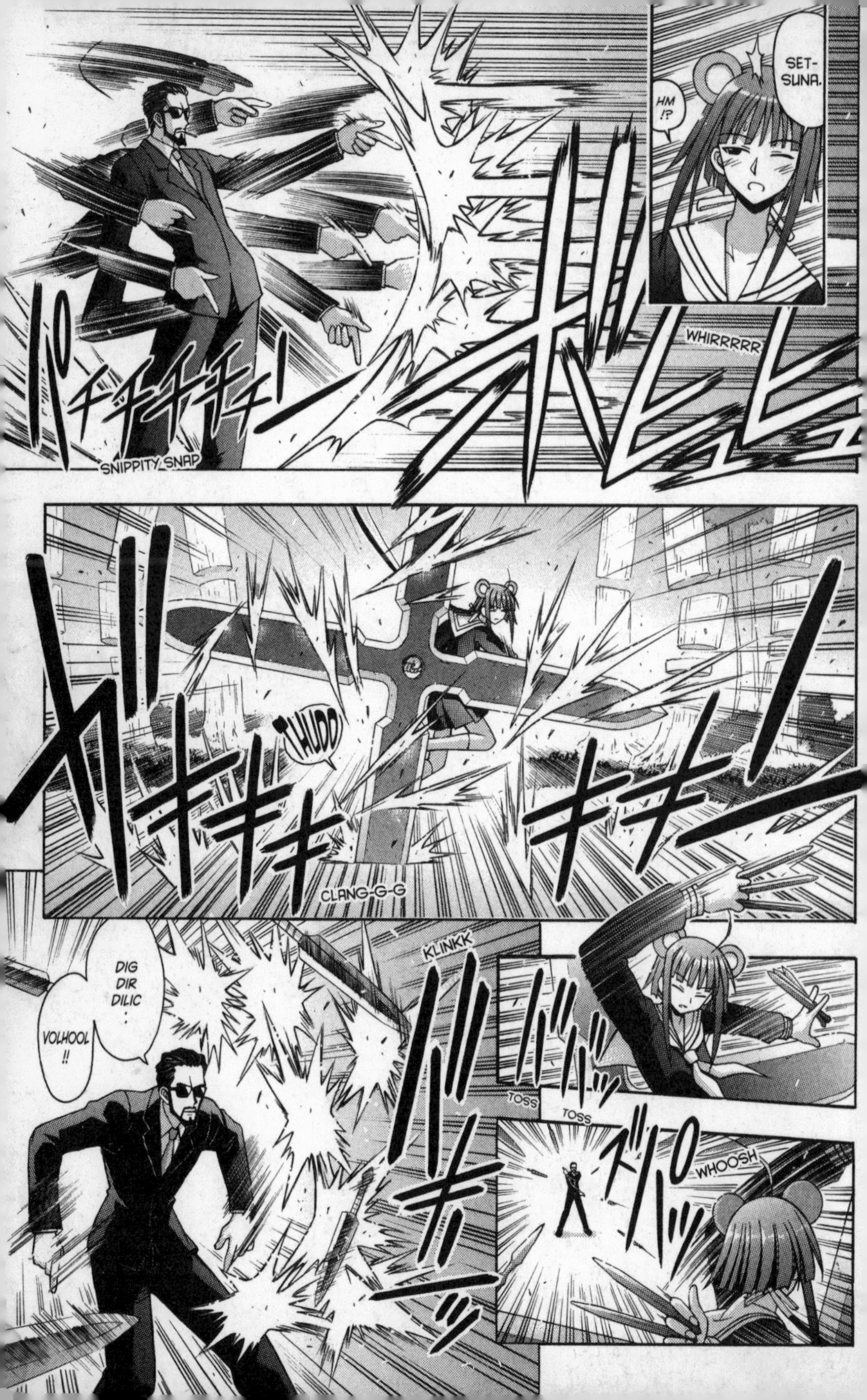
SET-SUNA.
HM!?
WHIRRRRR
パチチチチン
SNIPPITY SNAP
THUDD
CLANG-G-G
KLINKK
TOSS
TOSS
WHOOSH
DIG DIR DILIC VOLHOOL!!

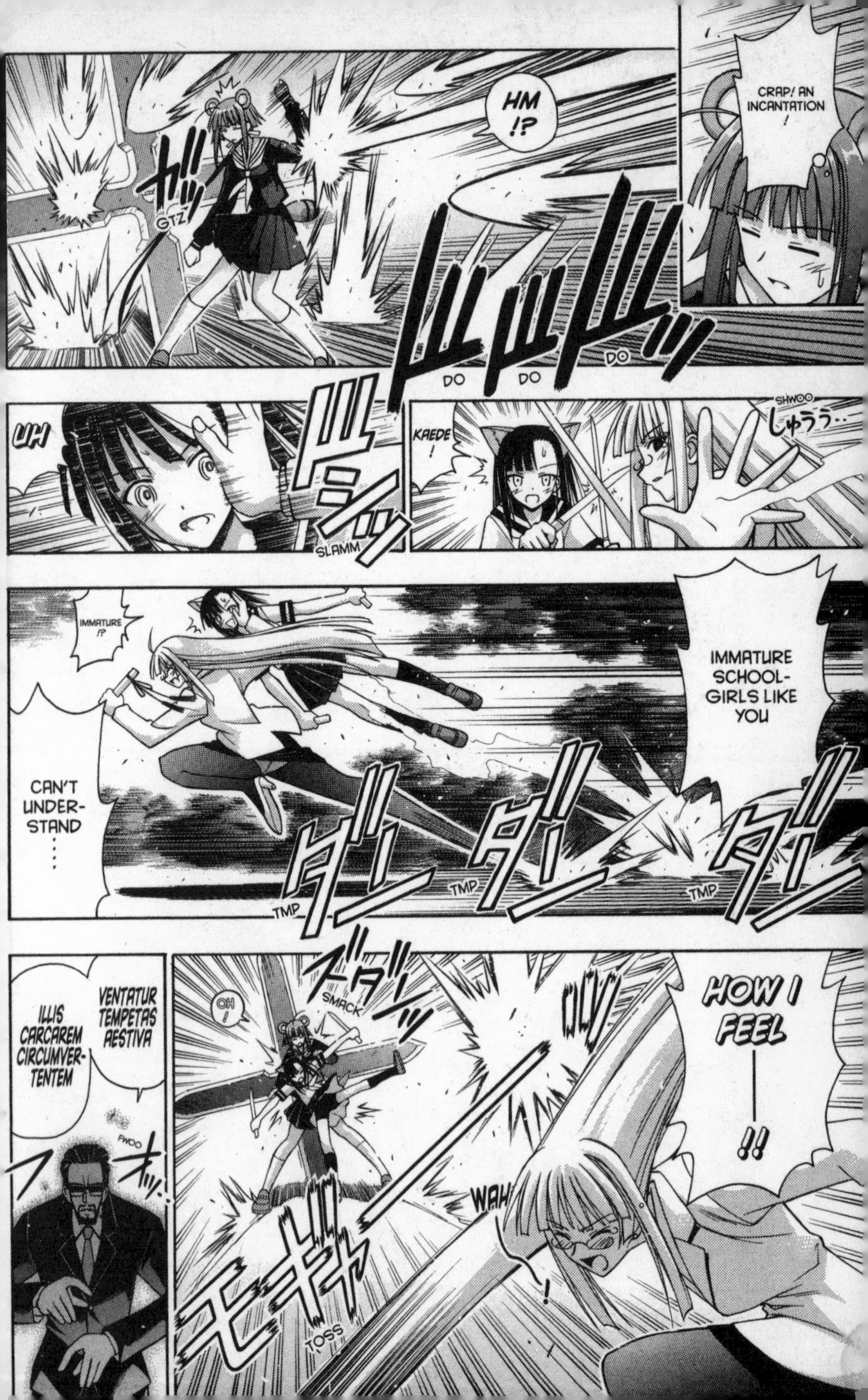
CRAP! AN INCANTATION !
HM !?
GTZ
DO
DO
DO
SHWOO
しゅううう‥
KAEDE !
SLAMM
UH
IMMATURE SCHOOL-GIRLS LIKE YOU
TMP
TMP
TMP
IMMATURE !?
CAN'T UNDER-STAND ....
HOW I FEEL — !!
WAH
!
SMACK
OH !
TOSS
VENTATUR TEMPETAS AESTIVA
ILLIS CARCAREM CIRCUMVER-TENTEM
FWOO

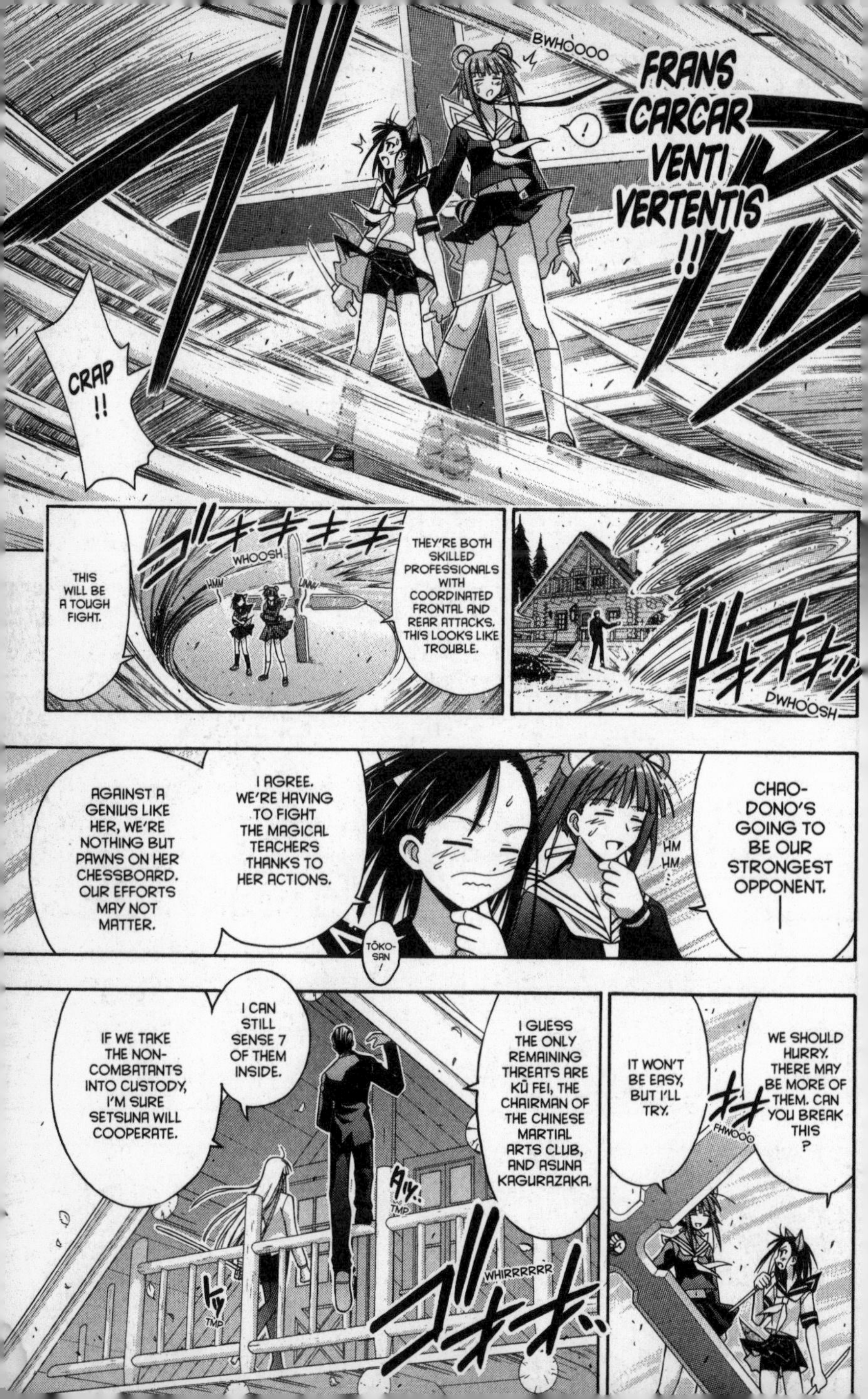
BWHOOOO
FRANS CARCAR VENTI VERTENTIS !!
!
CRAP !!
DWHOOSH
THEY'RE BOTH SKILLED PROFESSIONALS WITH COORDINATED FRONTAL AND REAR ATTACKS. THIS LOOKS LIKE TROUBLE.
WHOOSH
THIS WILL BE A TOUGH FIGHT.
CHAO-DONO'S GOING TO BE OUR STRONGEST OPPONENT.
HM HM
I AGREE. WE'RE HAVING TO FIGHT THE MAGICAL TEACHERS THANKS TO HER ACTIONS.
AGAINST A GENIUS LIKE HER, WE'RE NOTHING BUT PAWNS ON HER CHESSBOARD. OUR EFFORTS MAY NOT MATTER.
TŌKO-SAN!
WE SHOULD HURRY. THERE MAY BE MORE OF THEM. CAN YOU BREAK THIS?
FHWOOO
IT WON'T BE EASY, BUT I'LL TRY.
I GUESS THE ONLY REMAINING THREATS ARE KŪ FEI, THE CHAIRMAN OF THE CHINESE MARTIAL ARTS CLUB, AND ASUNA KAGURAZAKA.
I CAN STILL SENSE 7 OF THEM INSIDE.
IF WE TAKE THE NON-COMBATANTS INTO CUSTODY, I'M SURE SETSUNA WILL COOPERATE.
TMP
WHIRRRRRR
TMP

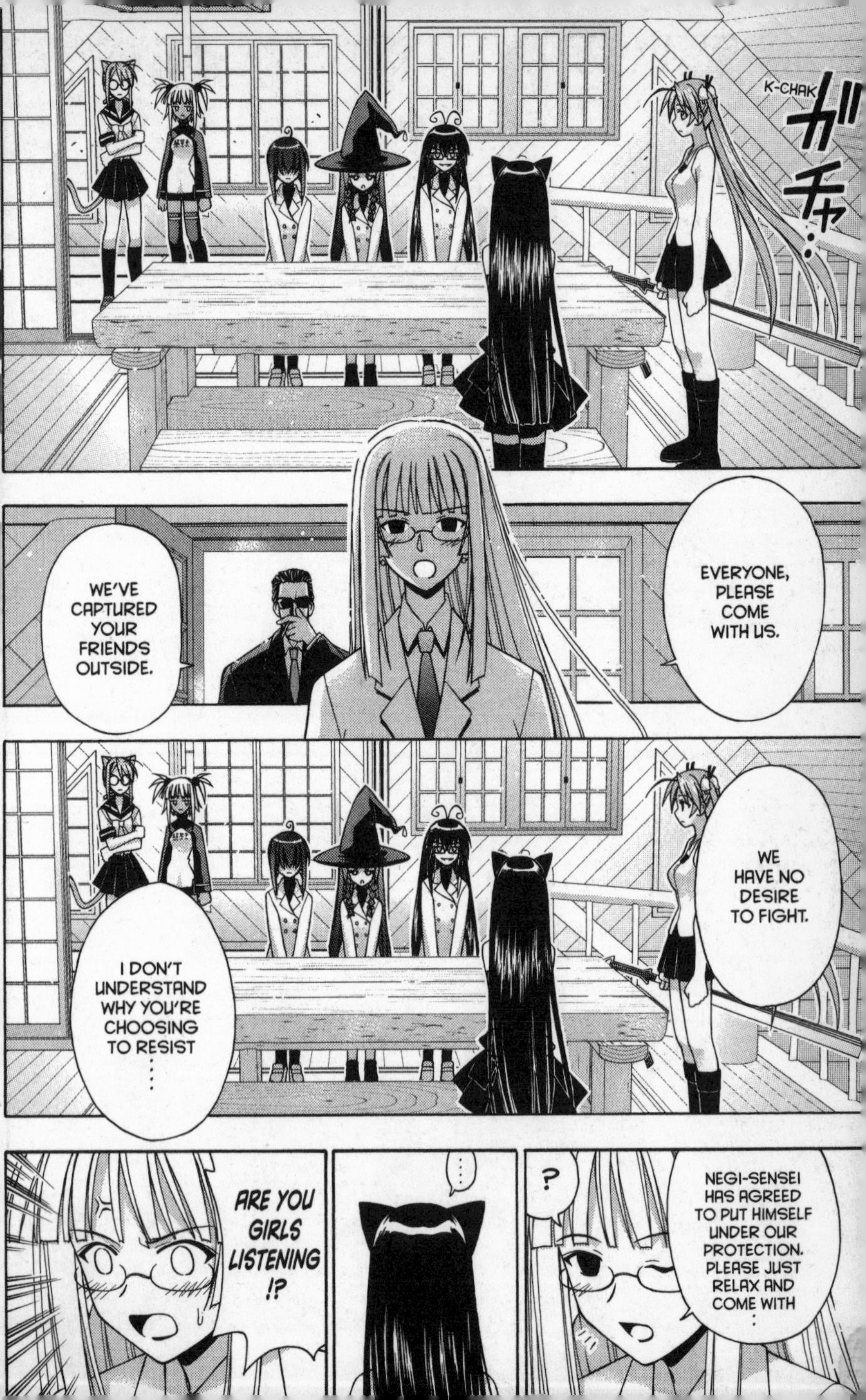
K-CHAK
ガチャ
EVERYONE, PLEASE COME WITH US.
WE'VE CAPTURED YOUR FRIENDS OUTSIDE.
WE HAVE NO DESIRE TO FIGHT.
I DON'T UNDERSTAND WHY YOU'RE CHOOSING TO RESIST ...
?
NEGI-SENSEI HAS AGREED TO PUT HIMSELF UNDER OUR PROTECTION. PLEASE JUST RELAX AND COME WITH :
...
ARE YOU GIRLS LISTENING !?

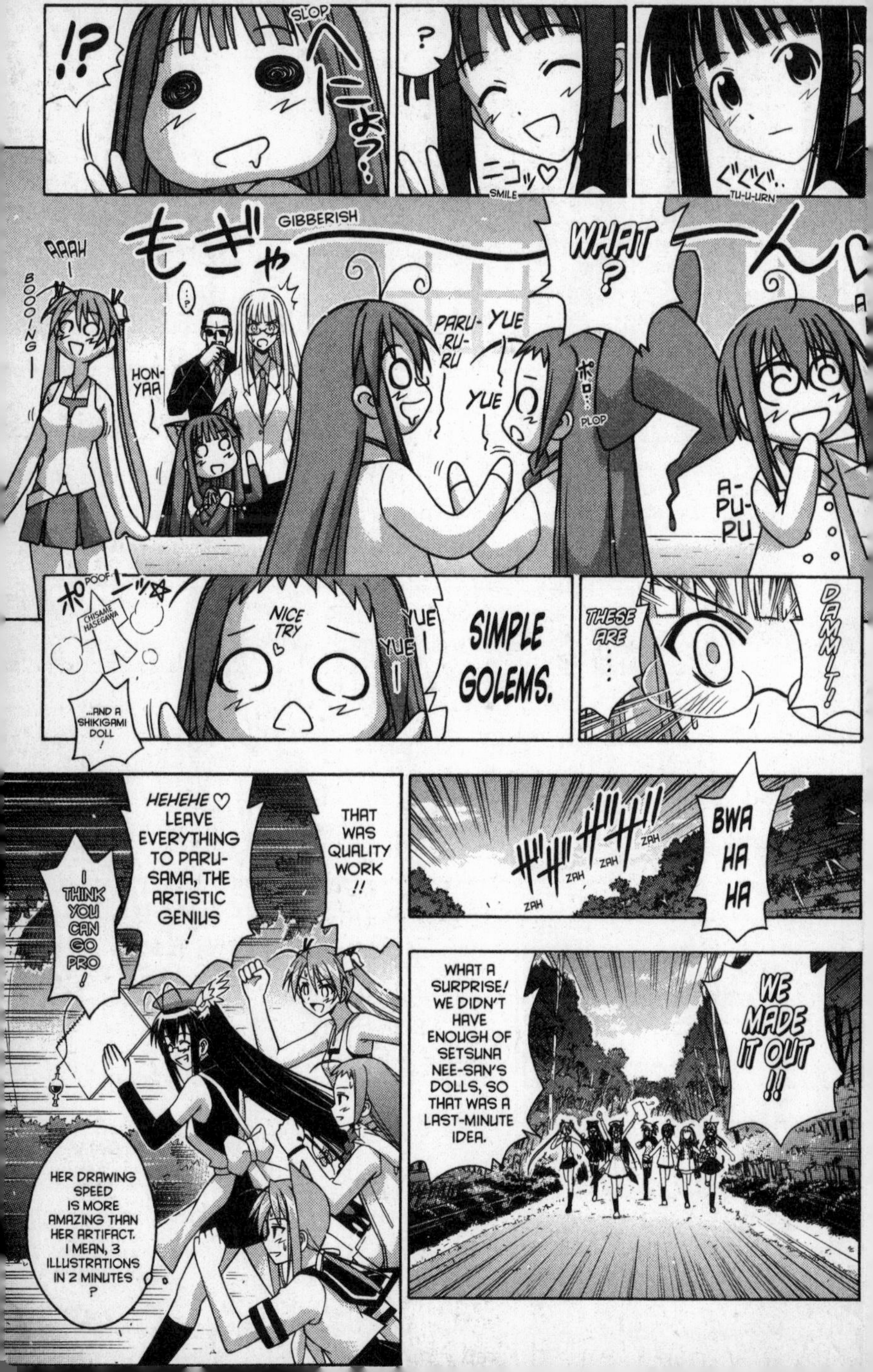

ぐぐぐ..
TU-U-URN
?
ニコッ♡
SMILE
!?
SLOP
へーよっ?
ーん♡
WHAT ?
A-PU-PU
PARU-RU-RU
YUE
YUE
ポロ..
PLOP
もぎゃ
GIBBERISH
...P
HON-YAA
AAAH
BOOOING
DAMMIT!
THESE ARE......
SIMPLE GOLEMS.
YUE YUE
NICE TRY ♡
ポーッ☆
POOF
CHISAME HASEGAWA
...AND A SHIKIGAMI DOLL!
BWA HA HA
ZAH ZAH ZAH ZAH
WE MADE IT OUT!!
WHAT A SURPRISE! WE DIDN'T HAVE ENOUGH OF SETSUNA NEE-SAN'S DOLLS, SO THAT WAS A LAST-MINUTE IDEA.
THAT WAS QUALITY WORK!!
HEHEHE ♡ LEAVE EVERYTHING TO PARU-SAMA, THE ARTISTIC GENIUS!
I THINK YOU CAN GO PRO!
HER DRAWING SPEED IS MORE AMAZING THAN HER ARTIFACT. I MEAN, 3 ILLUSTRATIONS IN 2 MINUTES?

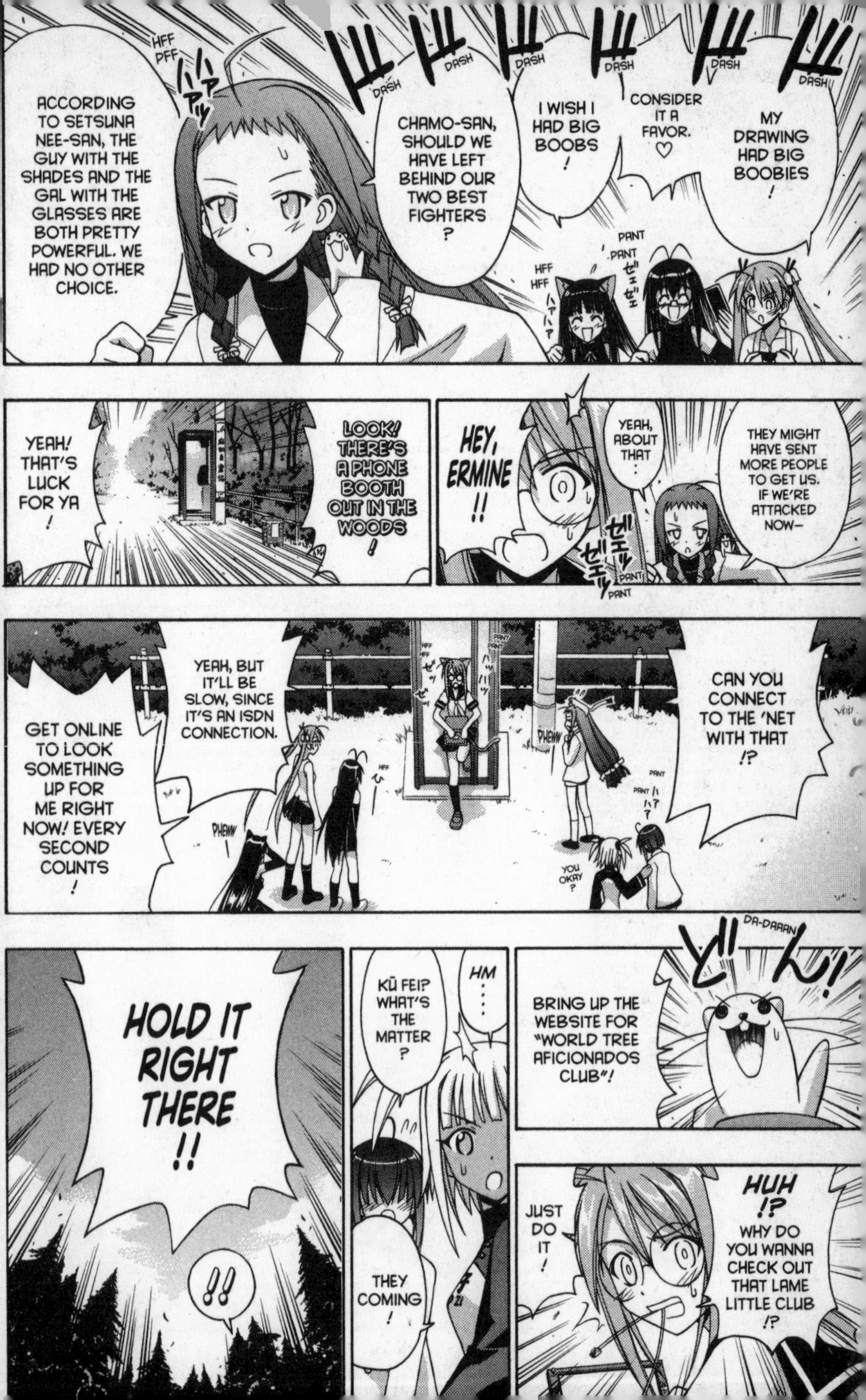
DASH
DASH
DASH
DASH
DASH
DASH
MY DRAWING HAD BIG BOOBIES!
CONSIDER IT A FAVOR. ♡
I WISH I HAD BIG BOOBS!
CHAMO-SAN, SHOULD WE HAVE LEFT BEHIND OUR TWO BEST FIGHTERS?
HFF PFF
ACCORDING TO SETSUNA NEE-SAN, THE GUY WITH THE SHADES AND THE GAL WITH THE GLASSES ARE BOTH PRETTY POWERFUL. WE HAD NO OTHER CHOICE.
PANT PANT
HFF HFF
THEY MIGHT HAVE SENT MORE PEOPLE TO GET US. IF WE'RE ATTACKED NOW—
YEAH, ABOUT THAT...
HEY, ERMINE!!
PANT PANT
LOOK! THERE'S A PHONE BOOTH OUT IN THE WOODS!
YEAH! THAT'S LUCK FOR YA!
CAN YOU CONNECT TO THE 'NET WITH THAT!?
PANT PANT
YOU OKAY?
YEAH, BUT IT'LL BE SLOW, SINCE IT'S AN ISDN CONNECTION.
HFF HFF
PANT PANT
PHEWW
HFF
GET ONLINE TO LOOK SOMETHING UP FOR ME RIGHT NOW! EVERY SECOND COUNTS!
PHEWW
DA-DARAN
BRING UP THE WEBSITE FOR "WORLD TREE AFICIONADOS CLUB"!
HUH!? WHY DO YOU WANNA CHECK OUT THAT LAME LITTLE CLUB!?
JUST DO IT!
HM...
KŪ FEI? WHAT'S THE MATTER?
THEY COMING!
HOLD IT RIGHT THERE!!
!!

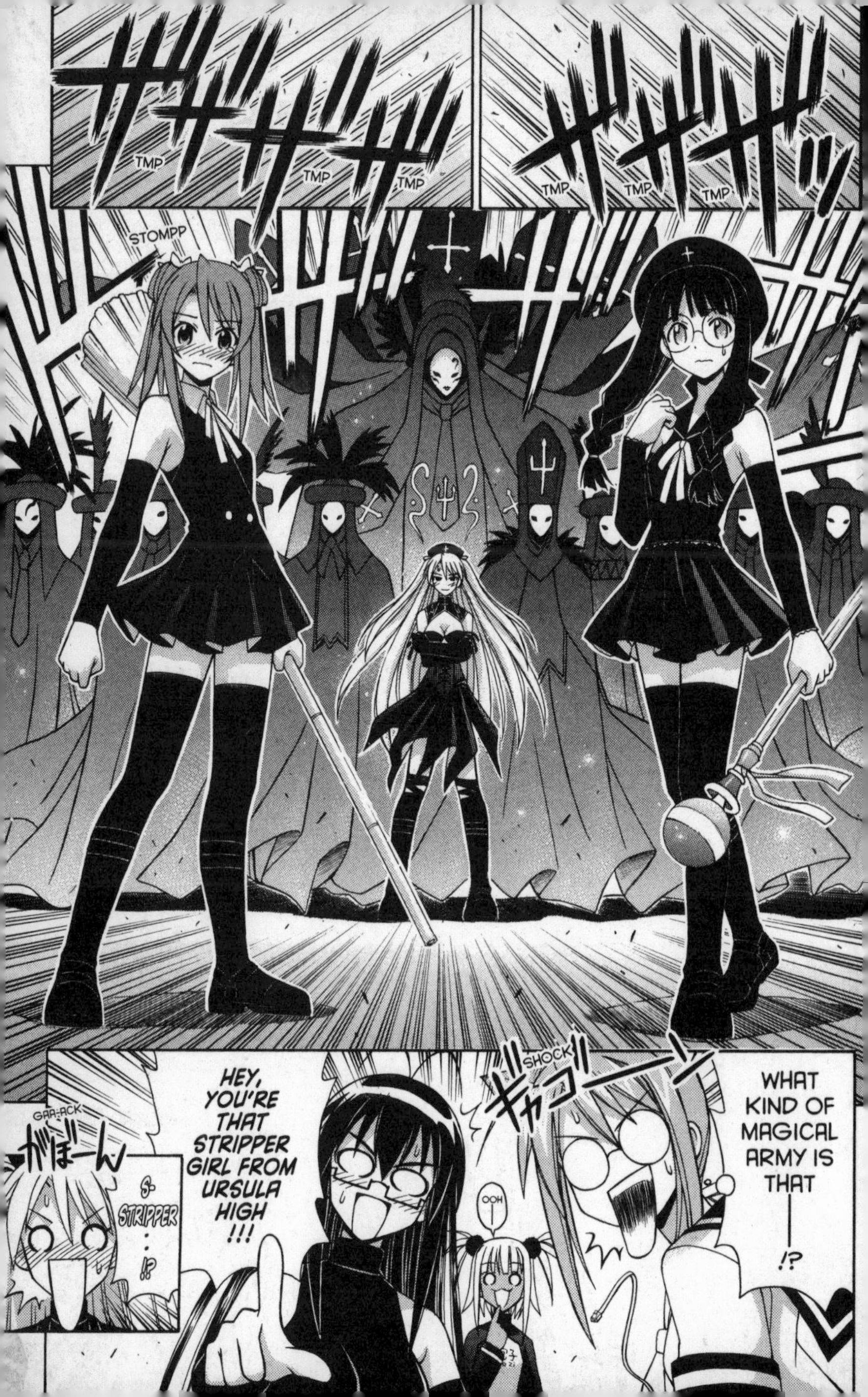

TMP
TMP
TMP
TMP
TMP
TMP
STOMPP
WHAT KIND OF MAGICAL ARMY IS THAT —!?
SHOCK
ギャゴーン
OOH
HEY, YOU'RE THAT STRIPPER GIRL FROM URSULA HIGH!!!
S-STRIPPER...!?
GAR-ACK
がぼーん

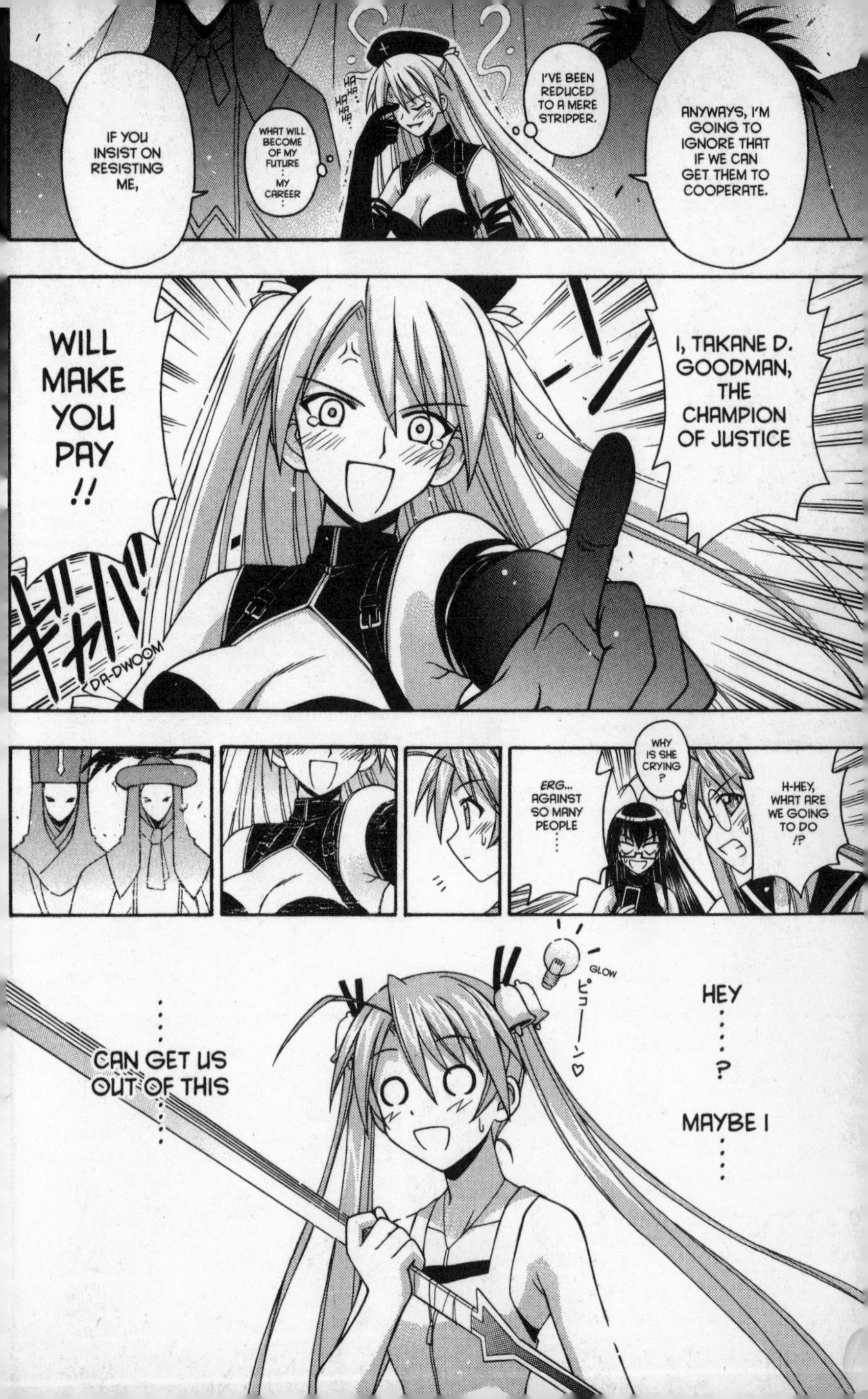
ANYWAYS, I'M GOING TO IGNORE THAT IF WE CAN GET THEM TO COOPERATE.
I'VE BEEN REDUCED TO A MERE STRIPPER.
HA HA HA HA HA
WHAT WILL BECOME OF MY FUTURE ... MY CAREER ...
IF YOU INSIST ON RESISTING ME,
I, TAKANE D. GOODMAN, THE CHAMPION OF JUSTICE
WILL MAKE YOU PAY !!
DA-DWOOM
H-HEY, WHAT ARE WE GOING TO DO !?
WHY IS SHE CRYING ?
ERG... AGAINST SO MANY PEOPLE ...
GLOW
ピコーン♡
HEY ... ?
MAYBE I ...
CAN GET US OUT OF THIS ...

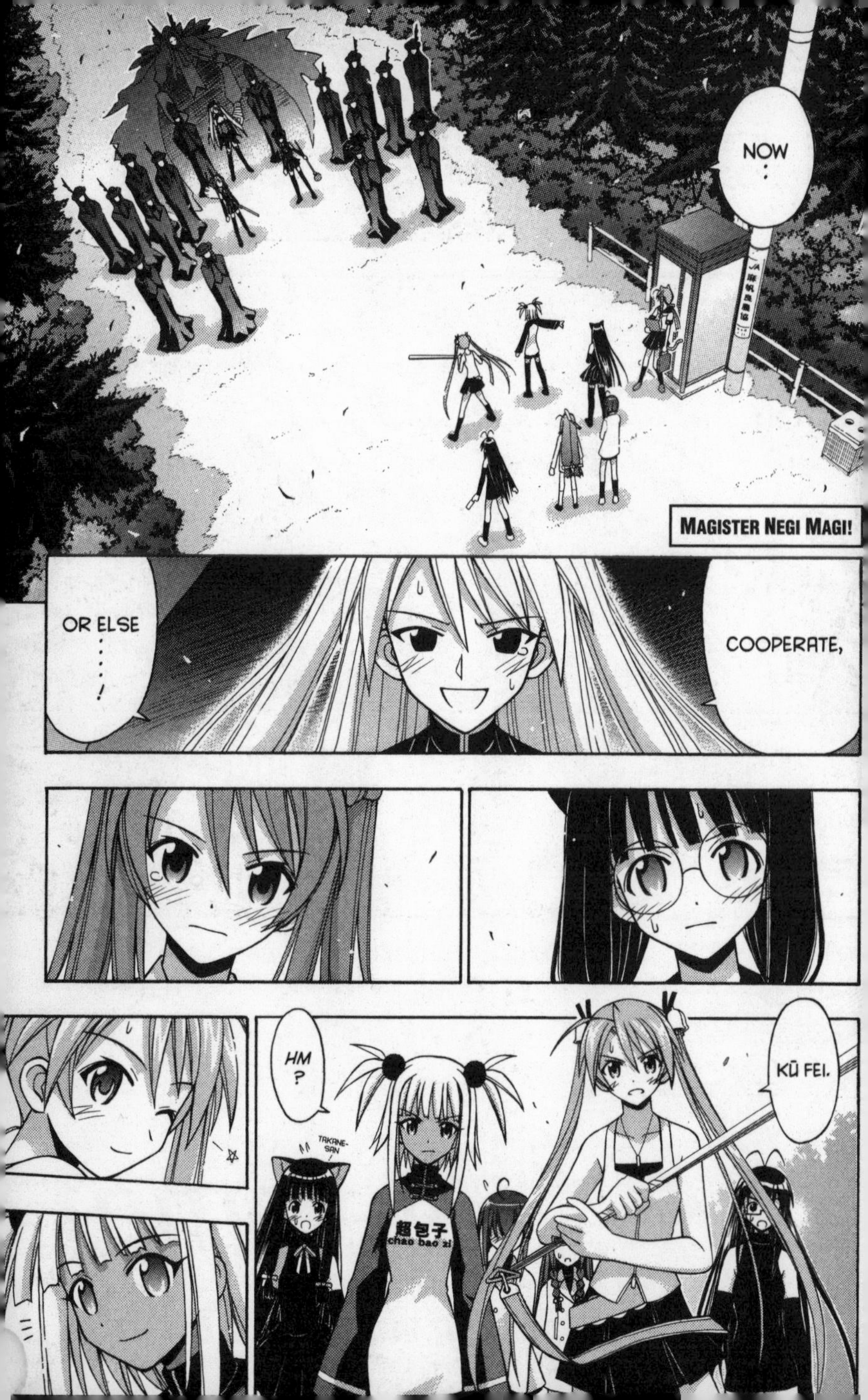
NOW...
MAGISTER NEGI MAGI!
COOPERATE,
OR ELSE....!
KŪ FEI.
HM?
TAKANE-SAN!

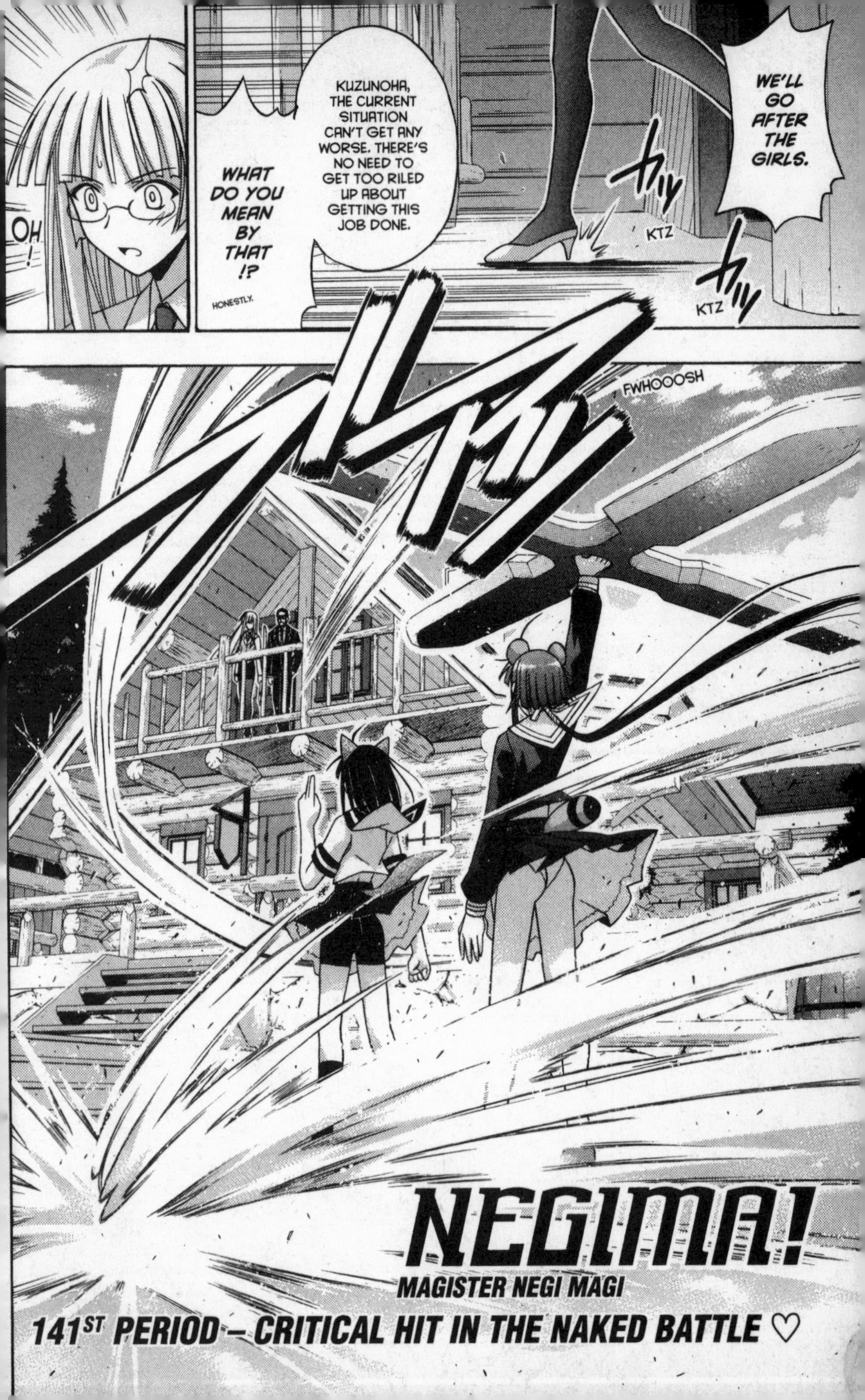
WE'LL GO AFTER THE GIRLS.
KTZ
KTZ
KUZUNOHA, THE CURRENT SITUATION CAN'T GET ANY WORSE. THERE'S NO NEED TO GET TOO RILED UP ABOUT GETTING THIS JOB DONE.
WHAT DO YOU MEAN BY THAT!?
HONESTLY.
OH!
FWHOOOSH
NEGIMA!
MAGISTER NEGI MAGI
141ST PERIOD – CRITICAL HIT IN THE NAKED BATTLE ♡

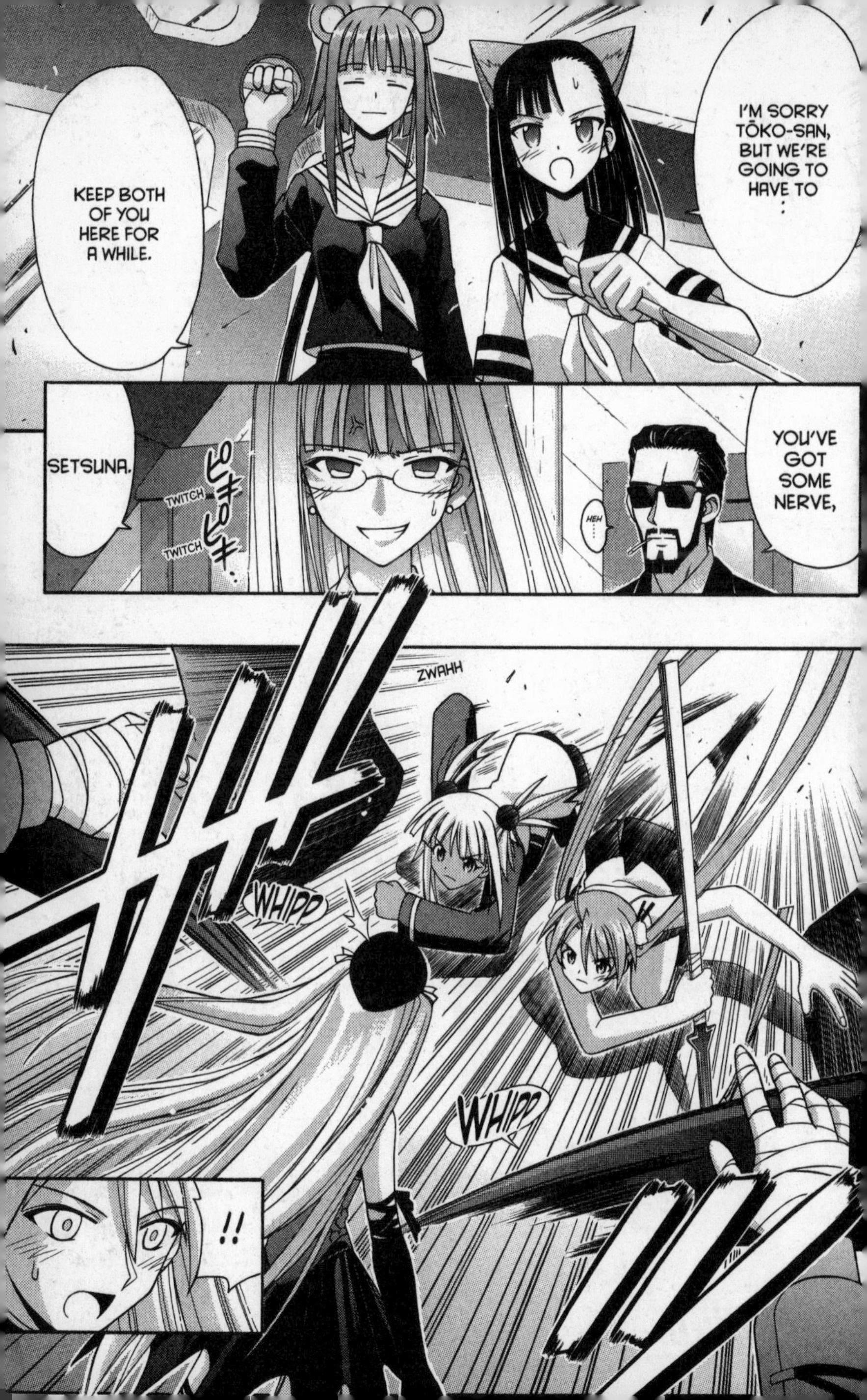
I'M SORRY TŌKO-SAN, BUT WE'RE GOING TO HAVE TO :
KEEP BOTH OF YOU HERE FOR A WHILE.
YOU'VE GOT SOME NERVE,
HEH ....
SETSUNA.
ピキッ
TWITCH
ピキ
TWITCH
ZWAHH
WHIPP
WHIPP
!!

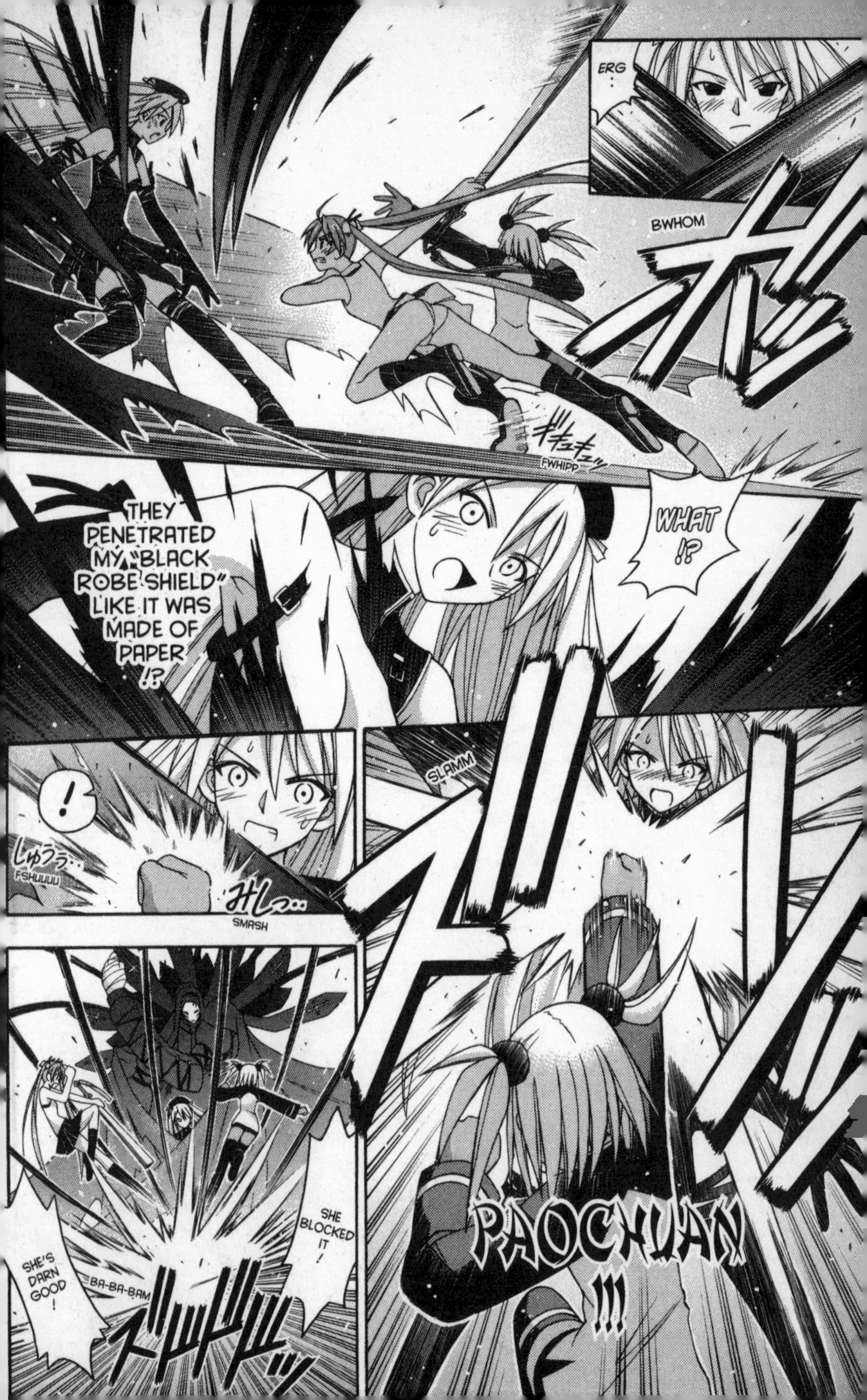

ERG
BWHOM
FWHIPP
WHAT!?
THEY PENETRATED MY "BLACK ROBE SHIELD" LIKE IT WAS MADE OF PAPER!?
SLAMM
PAOCHUAN!!!
!
FSHUUUU
SMASH
SHE BLOCKED IT!
SHE'S DARN GOOD!
BA-BA-BAM

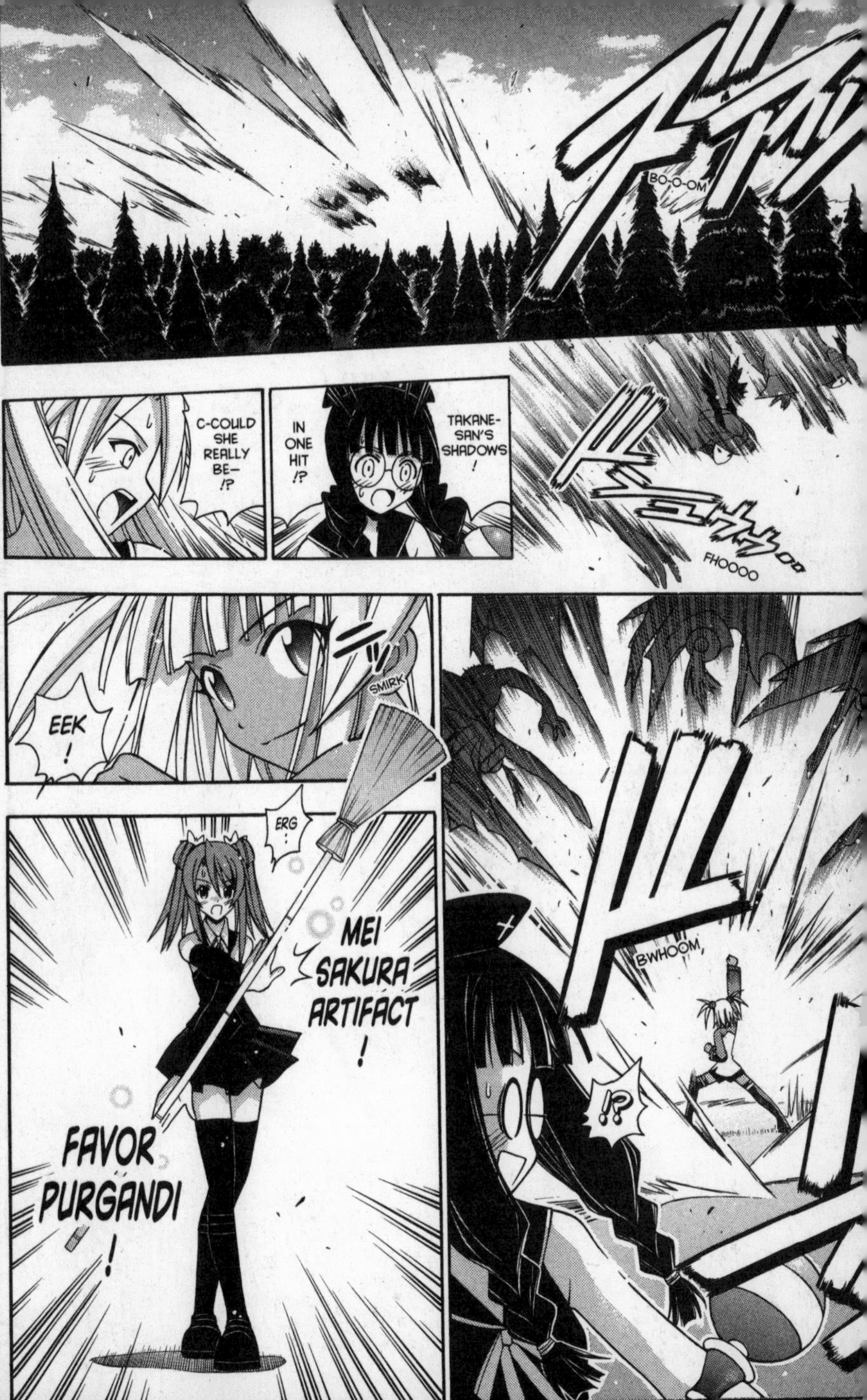
BO-O-OM
FHOOOO
TAKANE-SAN'S SHADOWS!
IN ONE HIT!?
C-COULD SHE REALLY BE—!?
BWHOOM,
!?
SMIRK
EEK!
ERG:
MEI SAKURA ARTIFACT!
FAVOR PURGANDI!

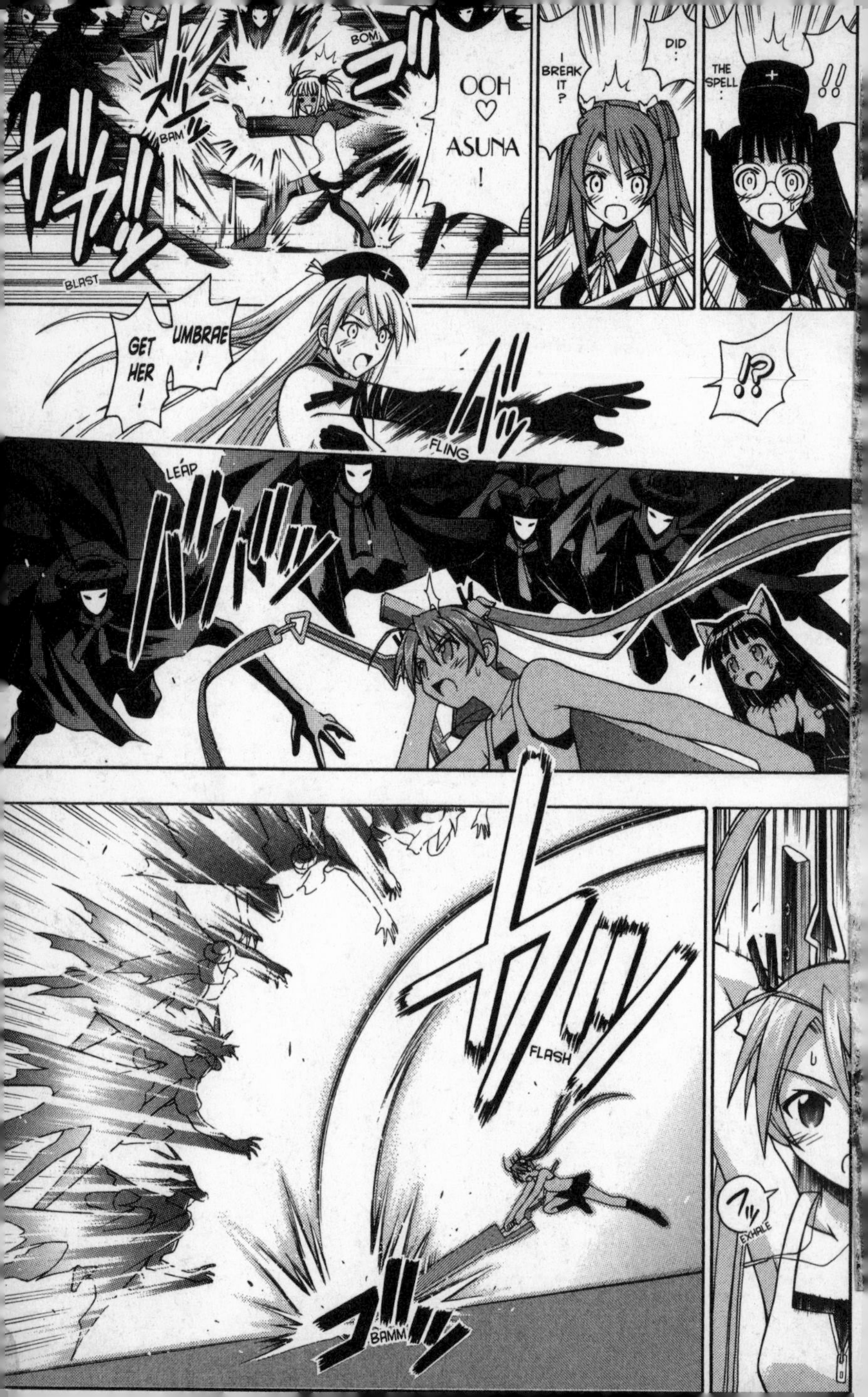
THE SPELL...
!!
DID...
I BREAK IT?
BOM
OOH ♡ ASUNA!
BAM
BLAST
!?
UMBRAE!
GET HER!
FLING
LEAP
EXHALE
FLASH
BAMM

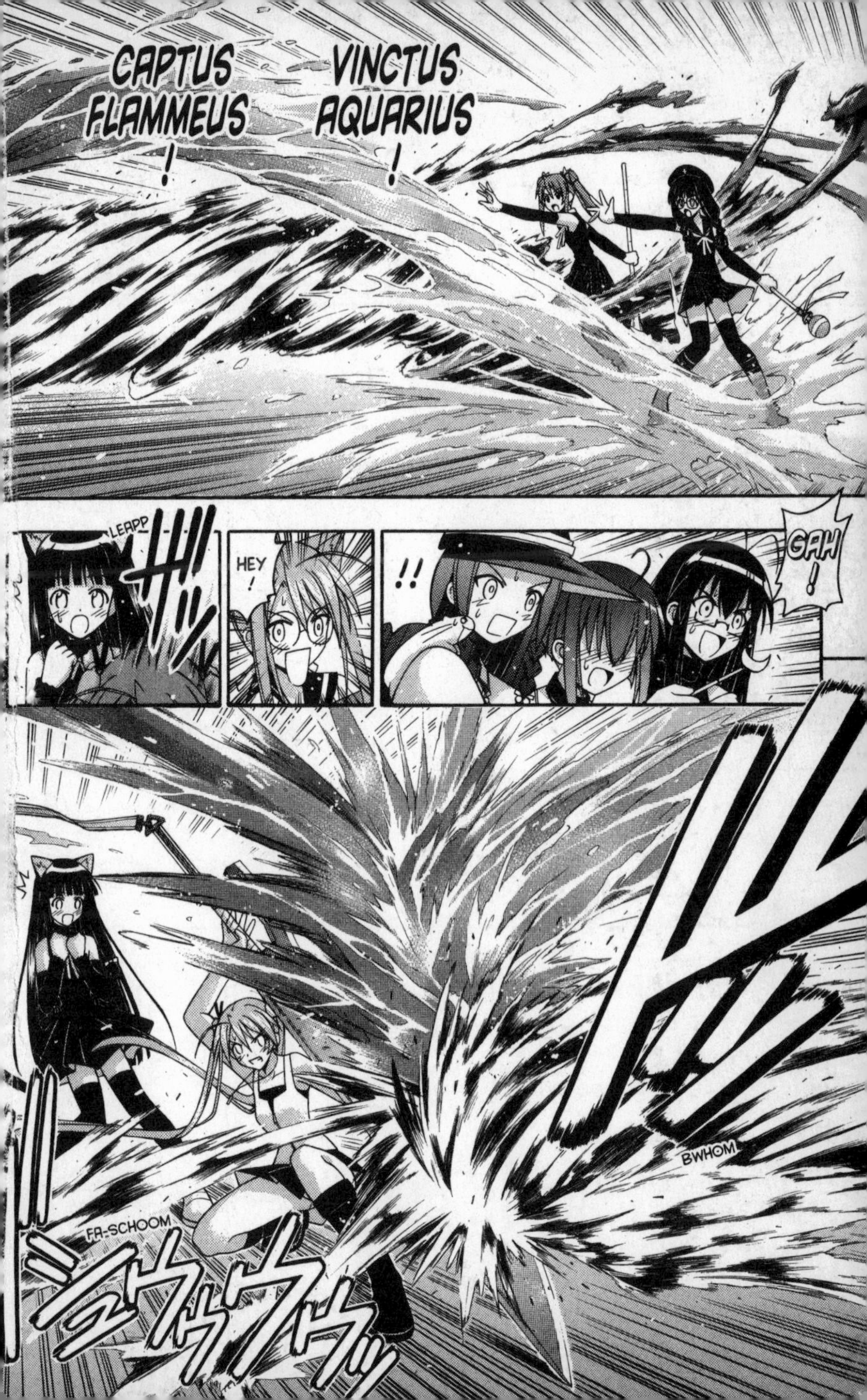
VINCTUS AQUARIUS !
CAPTUS FLAMMEUS !
GAH !
!!
HEY !
LEAPP
BWHOM
FA-SCHOOM

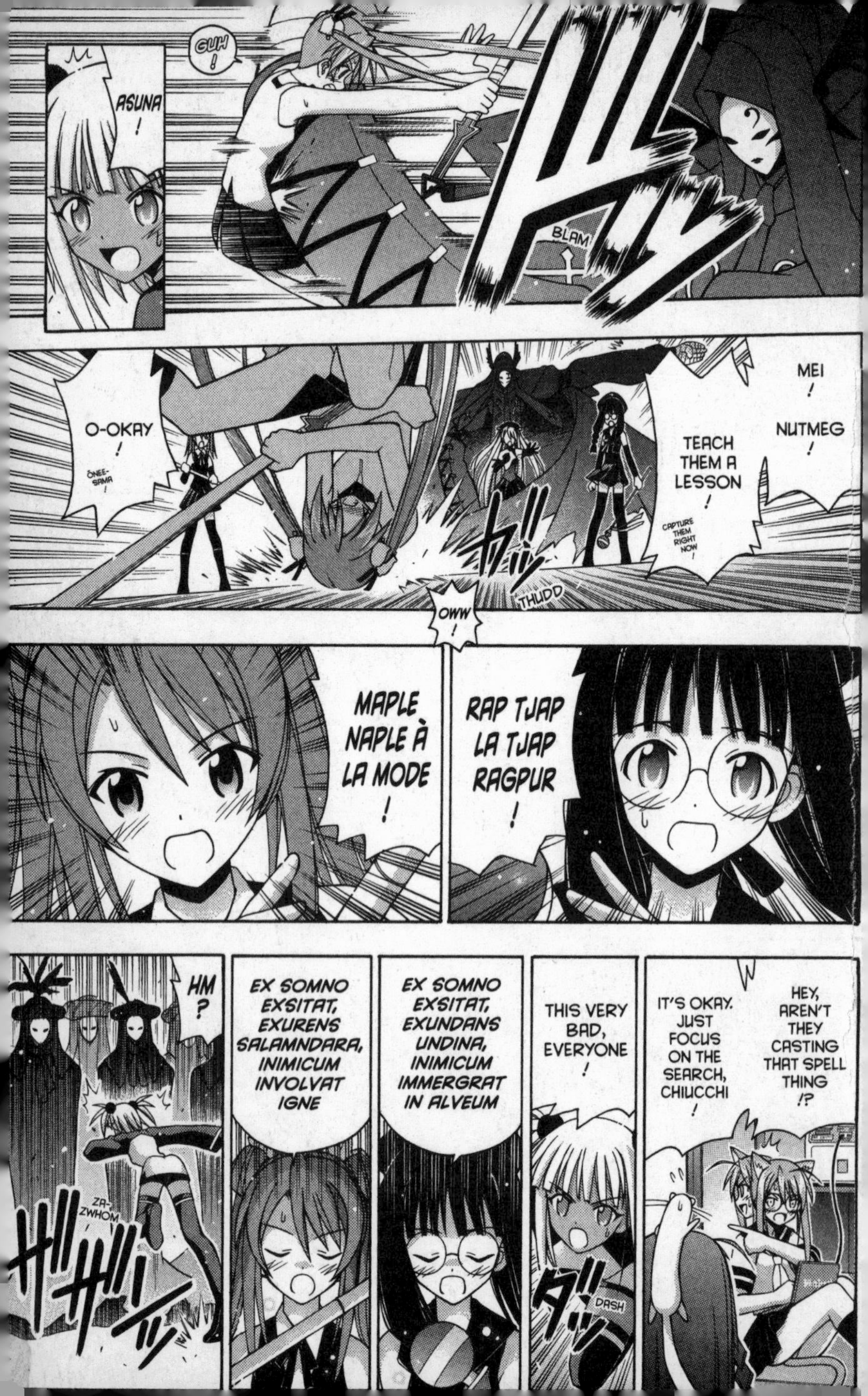
BLAM
GUH!
ASUNA!
MEI! NUTMEG!
TEACH THEM A LESSON!
CAPTURE THEM RIGHT NOW!
THUDD
O-OKAY!
ÔNEE-SAMA!
OWW!
RAP TJAP LA TJAP RAGPUR!
MAPLE NAPLE À LA MODE!
HEY, AREN'T THEY CASTING THAT SPELL THING!?
IT'S OKAY. JUST FOCUS ON THE SEARCH, CHIUCCHI!
THIS VERY BAD, EVERYONE!
DASH
EX SOMNO EXSITAT, EXUNDANS UNDINA, INIMICUM IMMERGRAT IN ALVEUM
EX SOMNO EXSITAT, EXURENS SALAMNDARA, INIMICUM INVOLVAT IGNE
HM?
ZA-ZWHOM

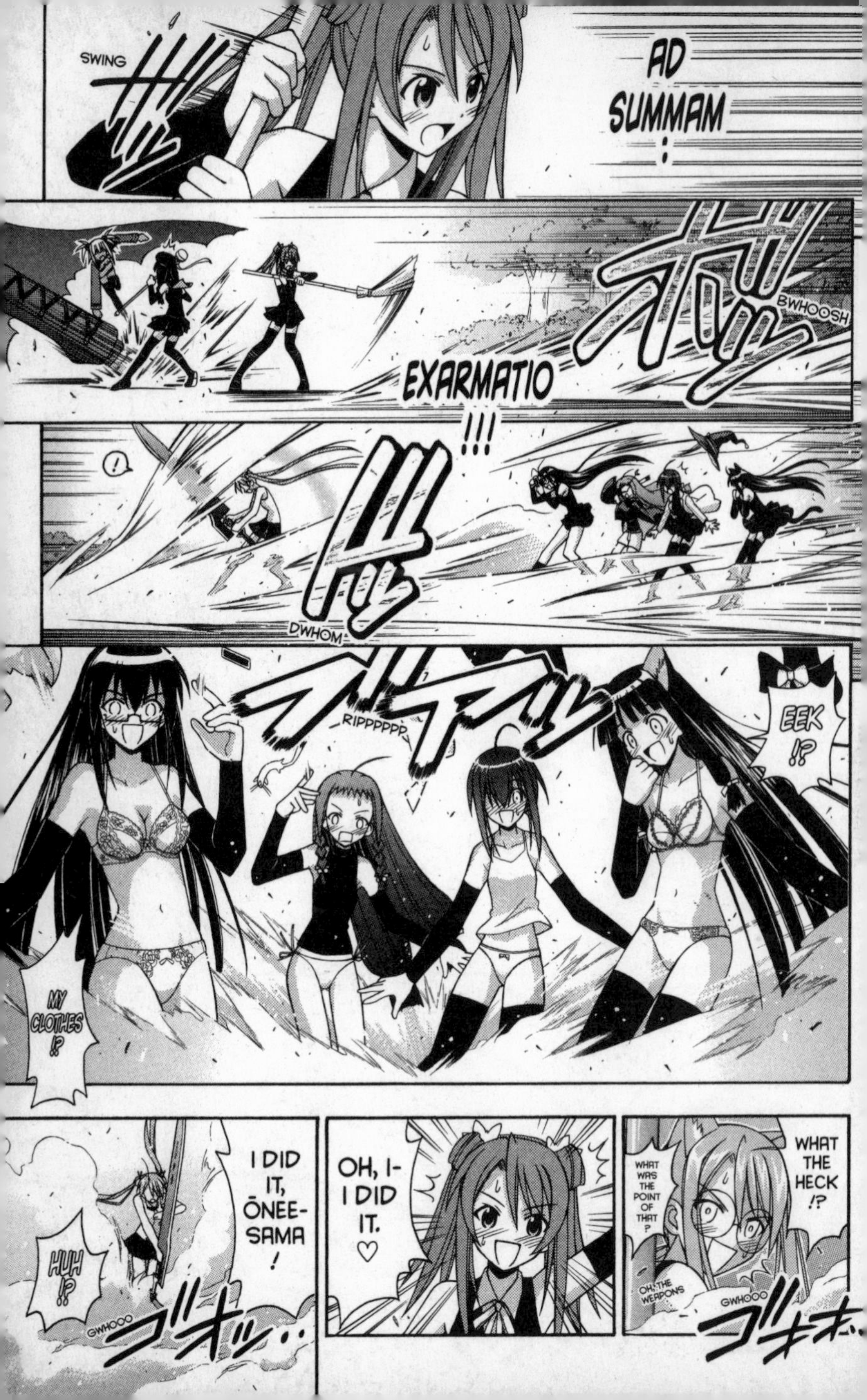
AD SUMMAM :
SWING
BWHOOSH
EXARMATIO !!!
!
DWHOM
EEK !?
RIPPPPPP
MY CLOTHES !?
WHAT THE HECK !?
WHAT WAS THE POINT OF THAT ?
OH, THE WEAPONS
GWHOOO
OH, I- I DID IT. ♡
I DID IT, ŌNEE-SAMA !
HUH !?
GWHOOO

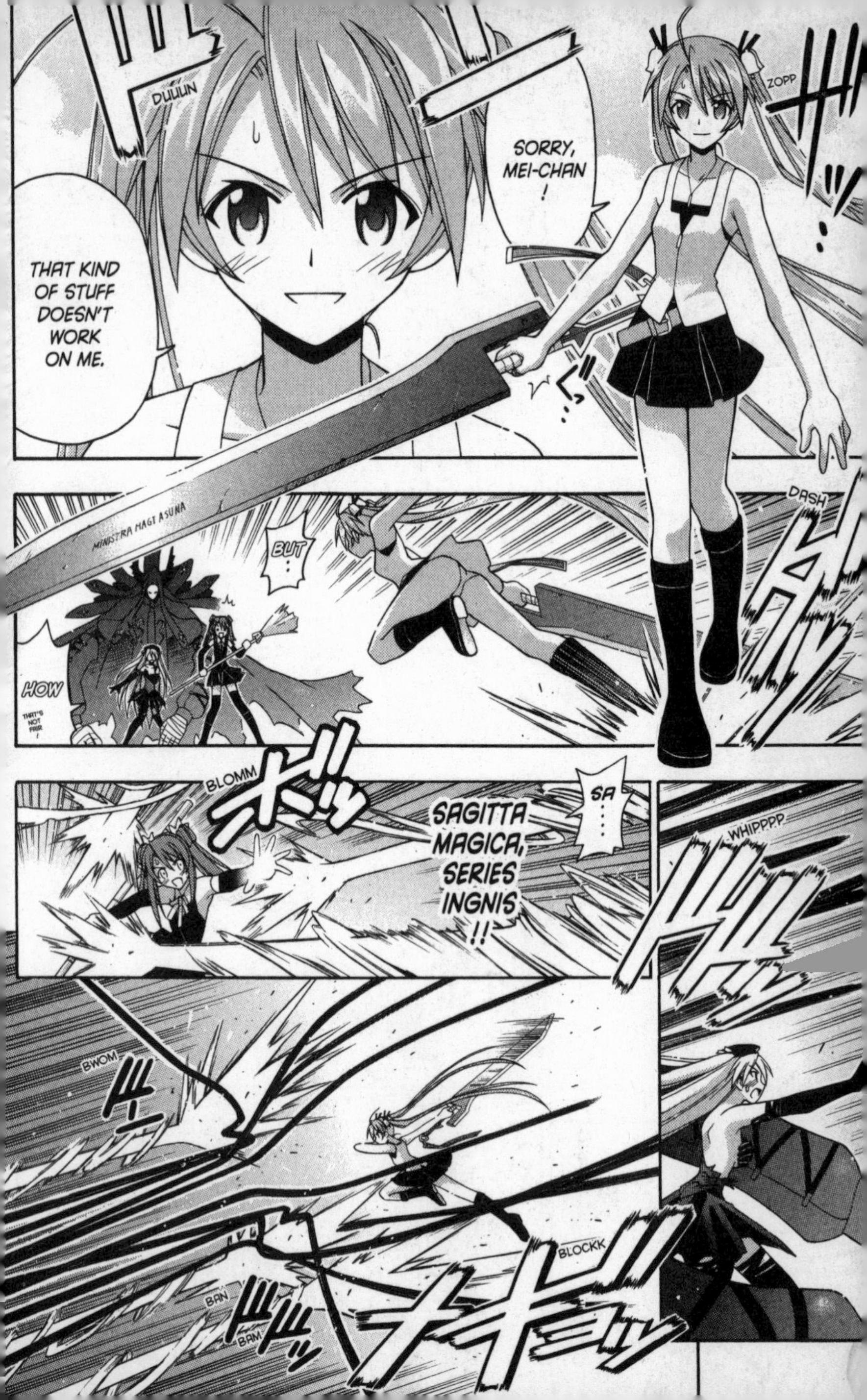
ZOPP
DUUUN
SORRY, MEI-CHAN!
THAT KIND OF STUFF DOESN'T WORK ON ME.
MINISTRA MAGI ASUNA
DASH
BUT...
HOW
THAT'S NOT FAIR!
WHIPPPP
SA...
SAGITTA MAGICA, SERIES INGNIS!!
BLOMM
BLOCKK
BWOM
BAN
BAM

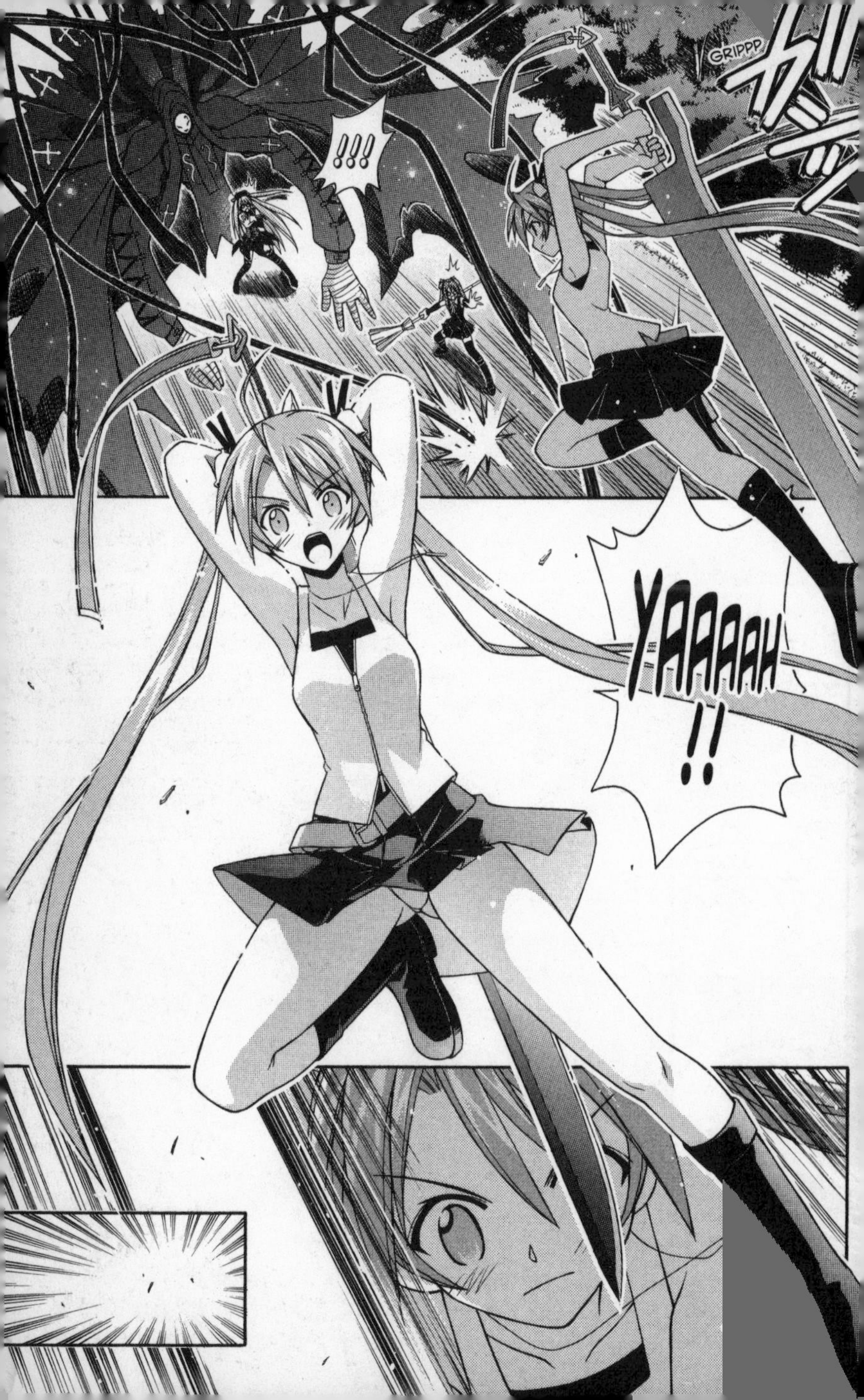
GRIPPP
!!!
YAAAAH !!

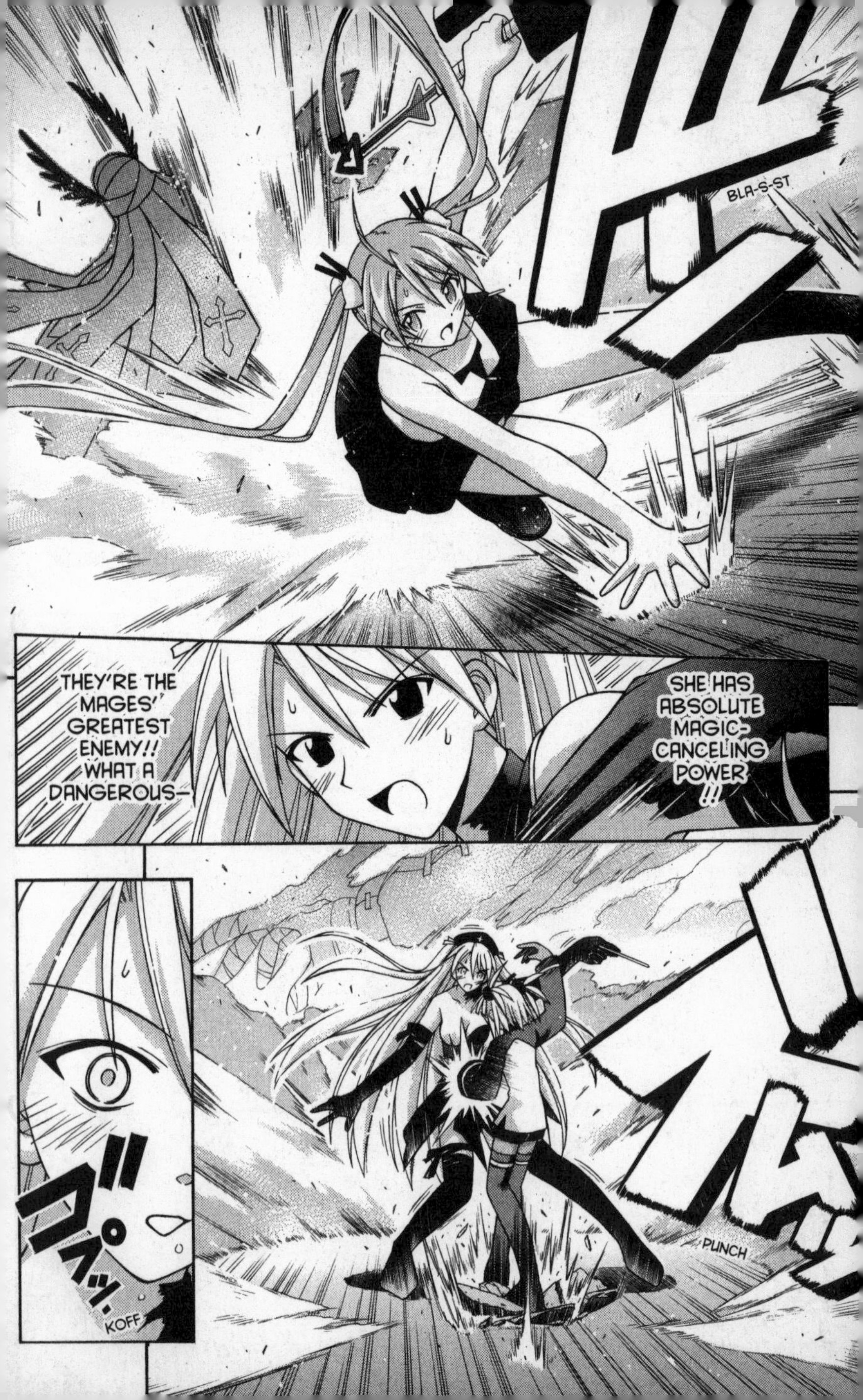
BLA-S-ST
SHE HAS ABSOLUTE MAGIC-CANCELING POWER!!
THEY'RE THE MAGES' GREATEST ENEMY!! WHAT A DANGEROUS—
PUNCH
KOFF

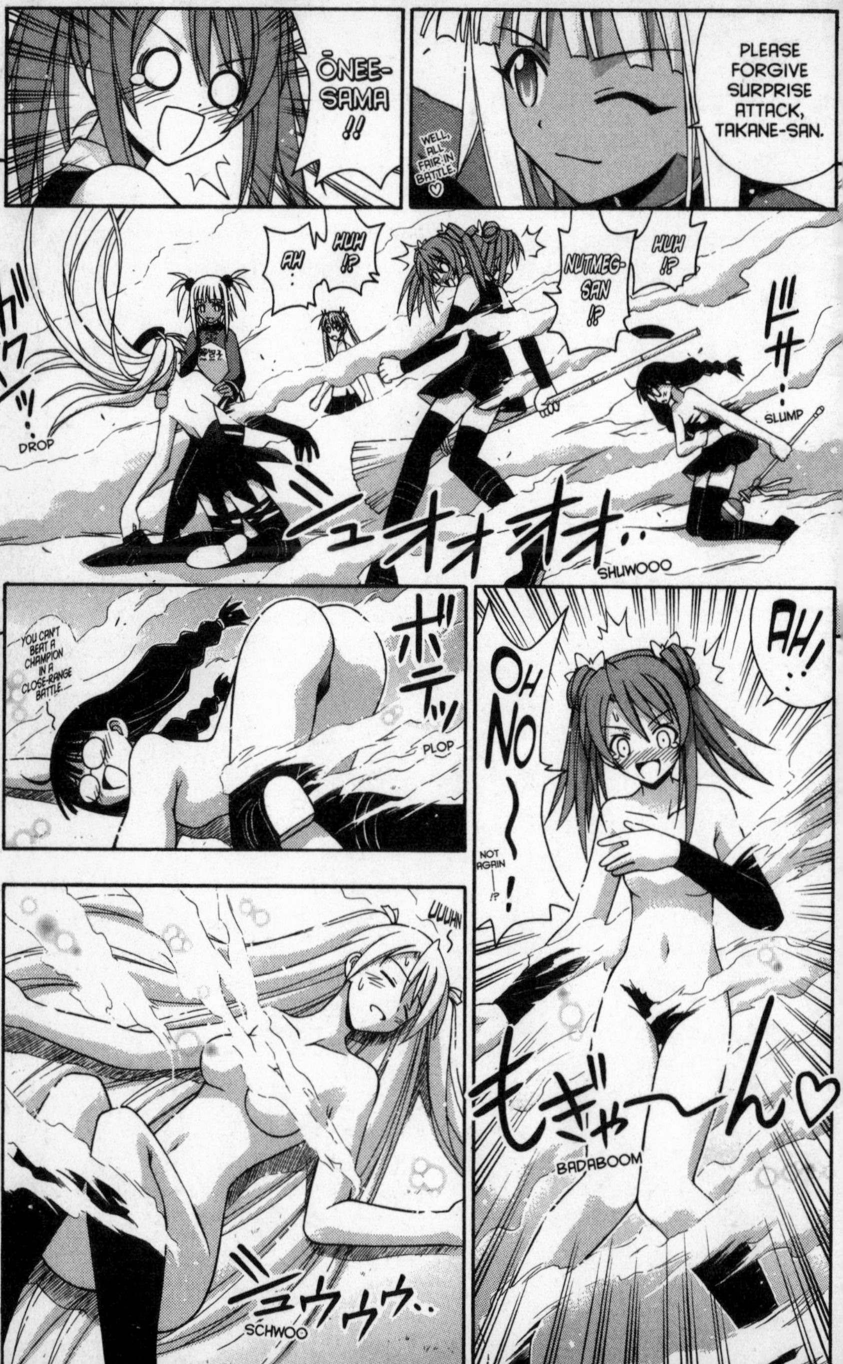

PLEASE FORGIVE SURPRISE ATTACK, TAKANE-SAN.
WELL, ALL FAIR IN BATTLE. ♡
ŌNEE-SAMA !!
HUH !?
NUTMEG-SAN !?
HUH !?
AH
ドサッ
SLUMP
ガクンッ
DROP
シュオオオオ‥
SHUWOOO
AH!
OH NO~!
NOT AGAIN!?
もぎゃ〜ん♡
BADABOOM
YOU CAN'T BEAT A CHAMPION IN A CLOSE-RANGE BATTLE...
ボテッ
PLOP
UUUHN
シュウウウ‥
SCHWOO

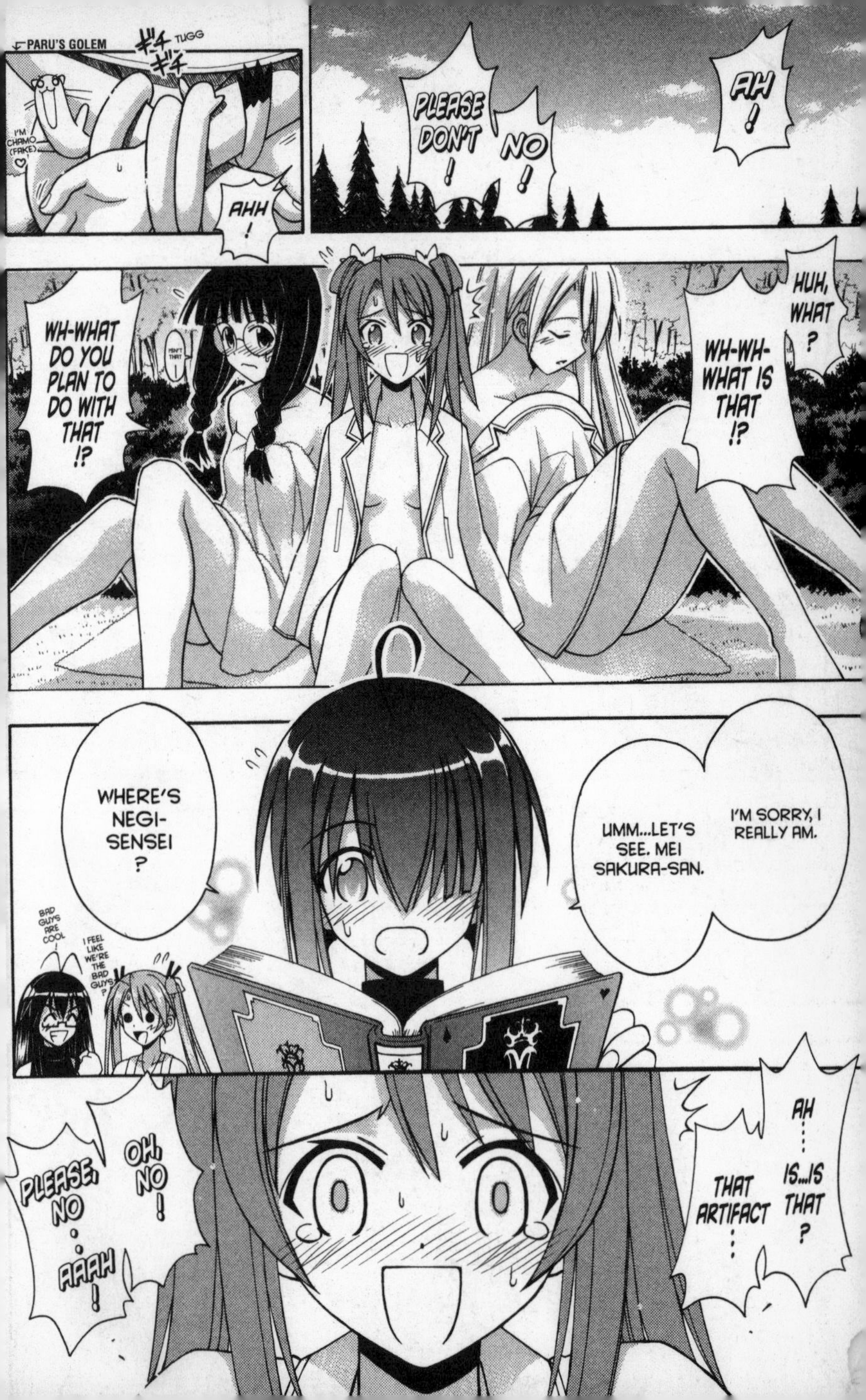
AH!
NO!
PLEASE DON'T!
PARU'S GOLEM
TUGG
I'M CHAMO (FAKE) ♡
AHH!
HUH, WHAT?
WH-WH-WHAT IS THAT!?
ISN'T THAT
WH-WHAT DO YOU PLAN TO DO WITH THAT!?
I'M SORRY, I REALLY AM.
UMM...LET'S SEE. MEI SAKURA-SAN.
WHERE'S NEGI-SENSEI?
I FEEL LIKE WE'RE THE BAD GUYS?
BAD GUYS ARE COOL!
AH...
IS...IS THAT
THAT ARTIFACT...?
OH, NO!
PLEASE, NO...AAAH!

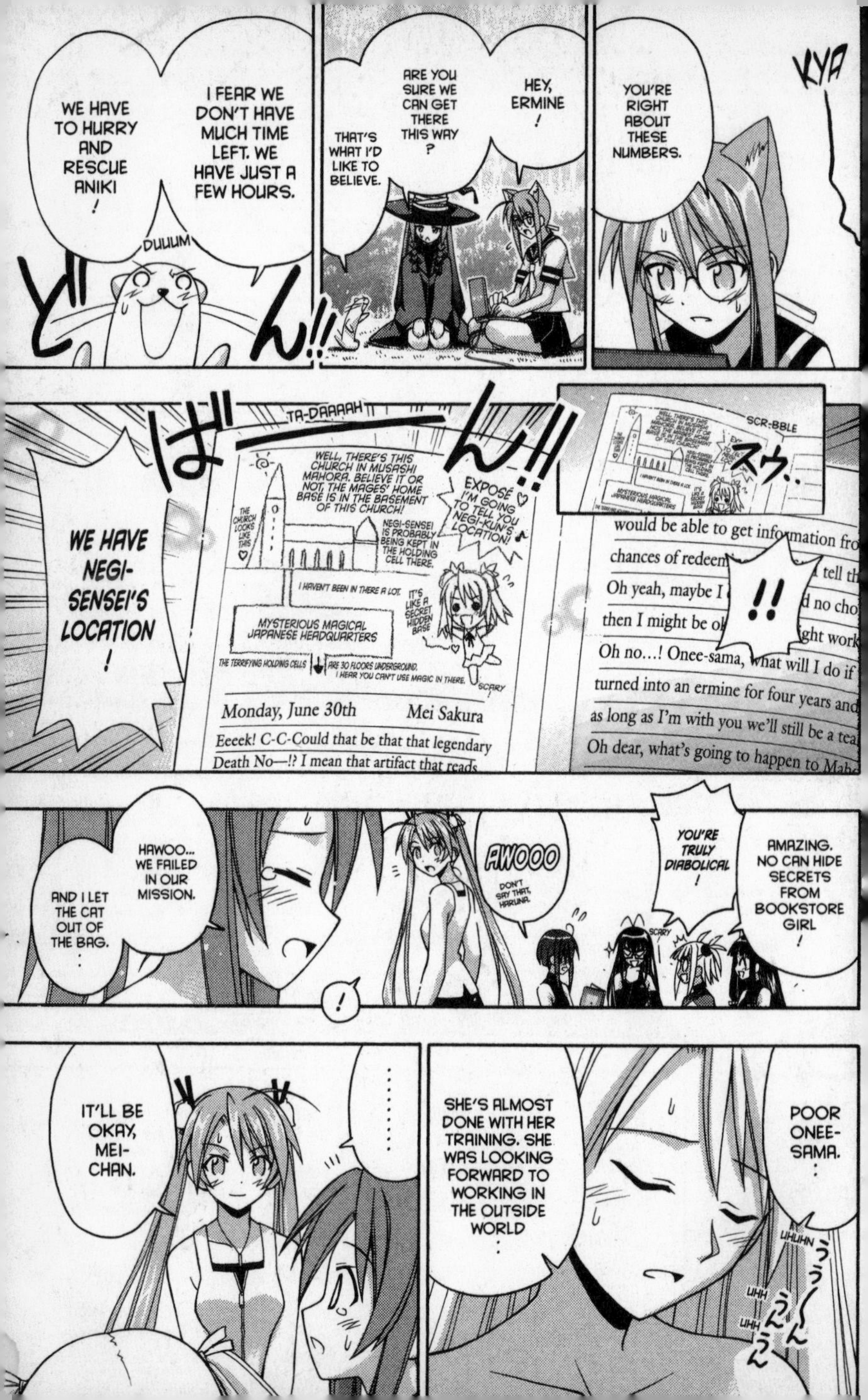
KYA
YOU'RE RIGHT ABOUT THESE NUMBERS.
HEY, ERMINE!
ARE YOU SURE WE CAN GET THERE THIS WAY?
THAT'S WHAT I'D LIKE TO BELIEVE.
I FEAR WE DON'T HAVE MUCH TIME LEFT. WE HAVE JUST A FEW HOURS.
WE HAVE TO HURRY AND RESCUE ANIKI!
DUUUM
どん!!
SCR-BBLE
スゥ..
would be able to get information fro
chances of redeem
tell th
Oh yeah, maybe I
d no cho
then I might be ok
ight work
Oh no…! Onee-sama, what will I do if
turned into an ermine for four years and
as long as I'm with you we'll still be a tea
Oh dear, what's going to happen to Mah
!!
ばーん!!
TA-DAAAAH
WELL, THERE'S THIS CHURCH IN MUSASHI MAHORA. BELIEVE IT OR NOT, THE MAGES' HOME BASE IS IN THE BASEMENT OF THIS CHURCH!
EXPOSÉ I'M GOING TO TELL YOU NEGI-KUN'S LOCATION!
THE CHURCH LOOKS LIKE THIS
NEGI-SENSEI IS PROBABLY BEING KEPT IN THE HOLDING CELL THERE.
I HAVEN'T BEEN IN THERE A LOT.
IT'S LIKE A SECRET HIDDEN BASE
MYSTERIOUS MAGICAL JAPANESE HEADQUARTERS
THE TERRIFYING HOLDING CELLS ARE 30 FLOORS UNDERGROUND. I HEAR YOU CAN'T USE MAGIC IN THERE.
SCARY
Monday, June 30th Mei Sakura
Eeeek! C-C-Could that be that that legendary
Death No—!? I mean that artifact that reads
WE HAVE NEGI-SENSEI'S LOCATION!
AMAZING. NO CAN HIDE SECRETS FROM BOOKSTORE GIRL!
YOU'RE TRULY DIABOLICAL!
SCARY
AWOOO
DON'T SAY THAT, HARUNA.
HAWOO... WE FAILED IN OUR MISSION.
AND I LET THE CAT OUT OF THE BAG...
!
POOR ONEE-SAMA...
UHUHN うう~ん
UHH うん
UHH うん
SHE'S ALMOST DONE WITH HER TRAINING. SHE WAS LOOKING FORWARD TO WORKING IN THE OUTSIDE WORLD...
......
IT'LL BE OKAY, MEI-CHAN.

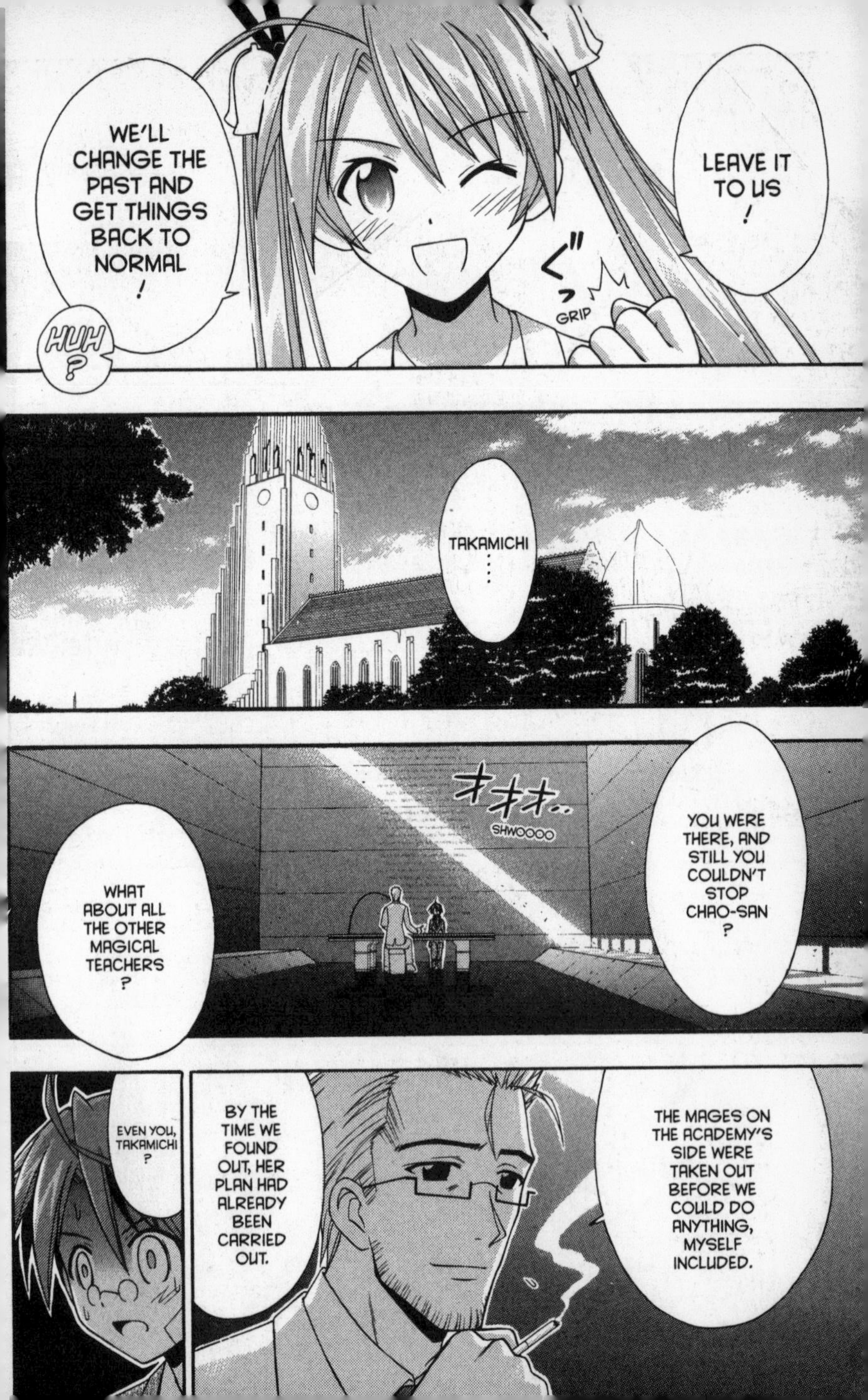
LEAVE IT TO US !
GRIP
WE'LL CHANGE THE PAST AND GET THINGS BACK TO NORMAL !
HUH ?
TAKAMICHI ....
YOU WERE THERE, AND STILL YOU COULDN'T STOP CHAO-SAN ?
SHWOOOO
WHAT ABOUT ALL THE OTHER MAGICAL TEACHERS ?
THE MAGES ON THE ACADEMY'S SIDE WERE TAKEN OUT BEFORE WE COULD DO ANYTHING, MYSELF INCLUDED.
BY THE TIME WE FOUND OUT, HER PLAN HAD ALREADY BEEN CARRIED OUT.
EVEN YOU, TAKAMICHI ?

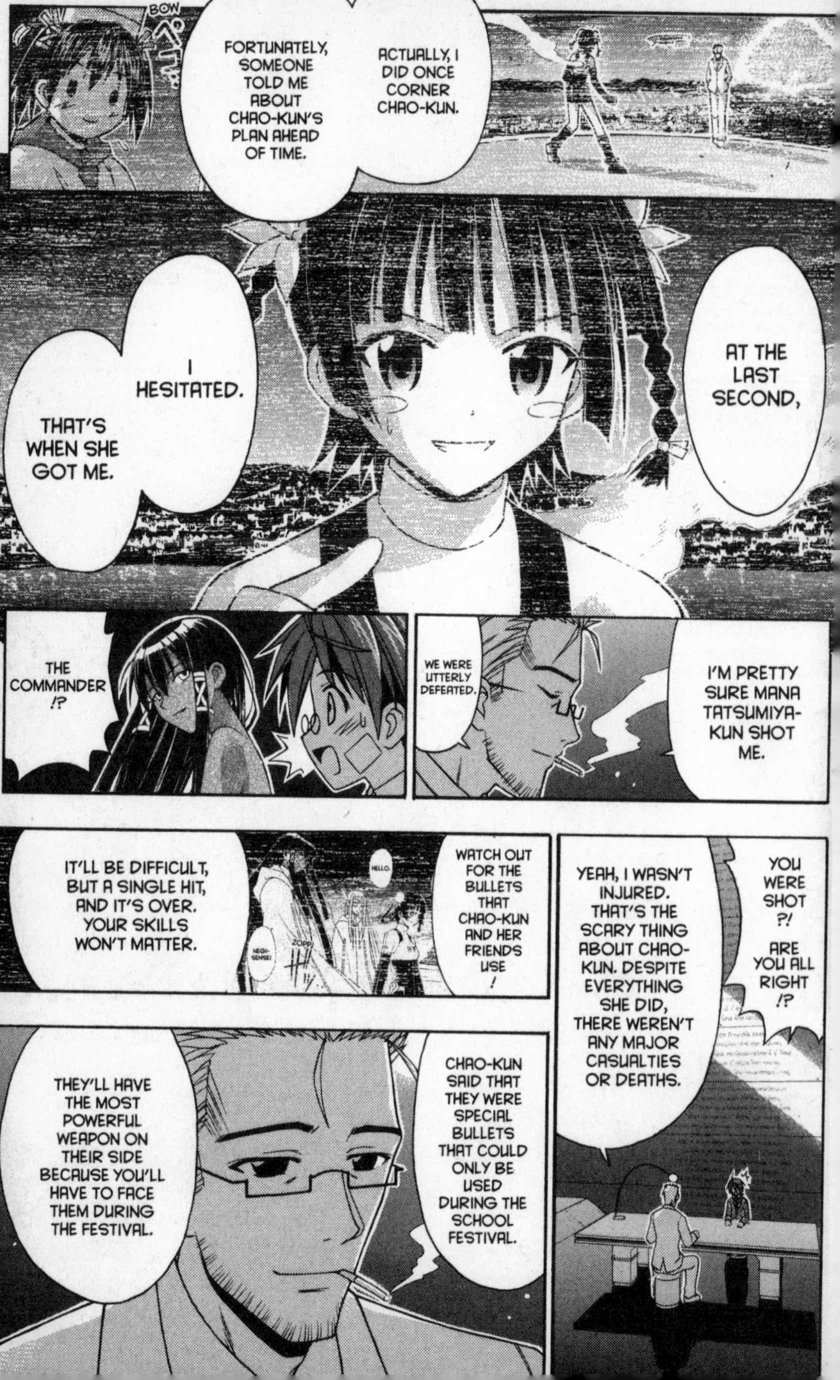
ACTUALLY, I DID ONCE CORNER CHAO-KUN.
FORTUNATELY, SOMEONE TOLD ME ABOUT CHAO-KUN'S PLAN AHEAD OF TIME.
BOW
AT THE LAST SECOND,
I HESITATED.
THAT'S WHEN SHE GOT ME.
I'M PRETTY SURE MANA TATSUMIYA-KUN SHOT ME.
WE WERE UTTERLY DEFEATED.
THE COMMANDER !?
YOU WERE SHOT ?!
ARE YOU ALL RIGHT !?
YEAH, I WASN'T INJURED. THAT'S THE SCARY THING ABOUT CHAO-KUN. DESPITE EVERYTHING SHE DID, THERE WEREN'T ANY MAJOR CASUALTIES OR DEATHS.
WATCH OUT FOR THE BULLETS THAT CHAO-KUN AND HER FRIENDS USE !
HELLO.
ZOPP
NEGI-SENSEI!
IT'LL BE DIFFICULT, BUT A SINGLE HIT, AND IT'S OVER. YOUR SKILLS WON'T MATTER.
CHAO-KUN SAID THAT THEY WERE SPECIAL BULLETS THAT COULD ONLY BE USED DURING THE SCHOOL FESTIVAL.
THEY'LL HAVE THE MOST POWERFUL WEAPON ON THEIR SIDE BECAUSE YOU'LL HAVE TO FACE THEM DURING THE FESTIVAL.

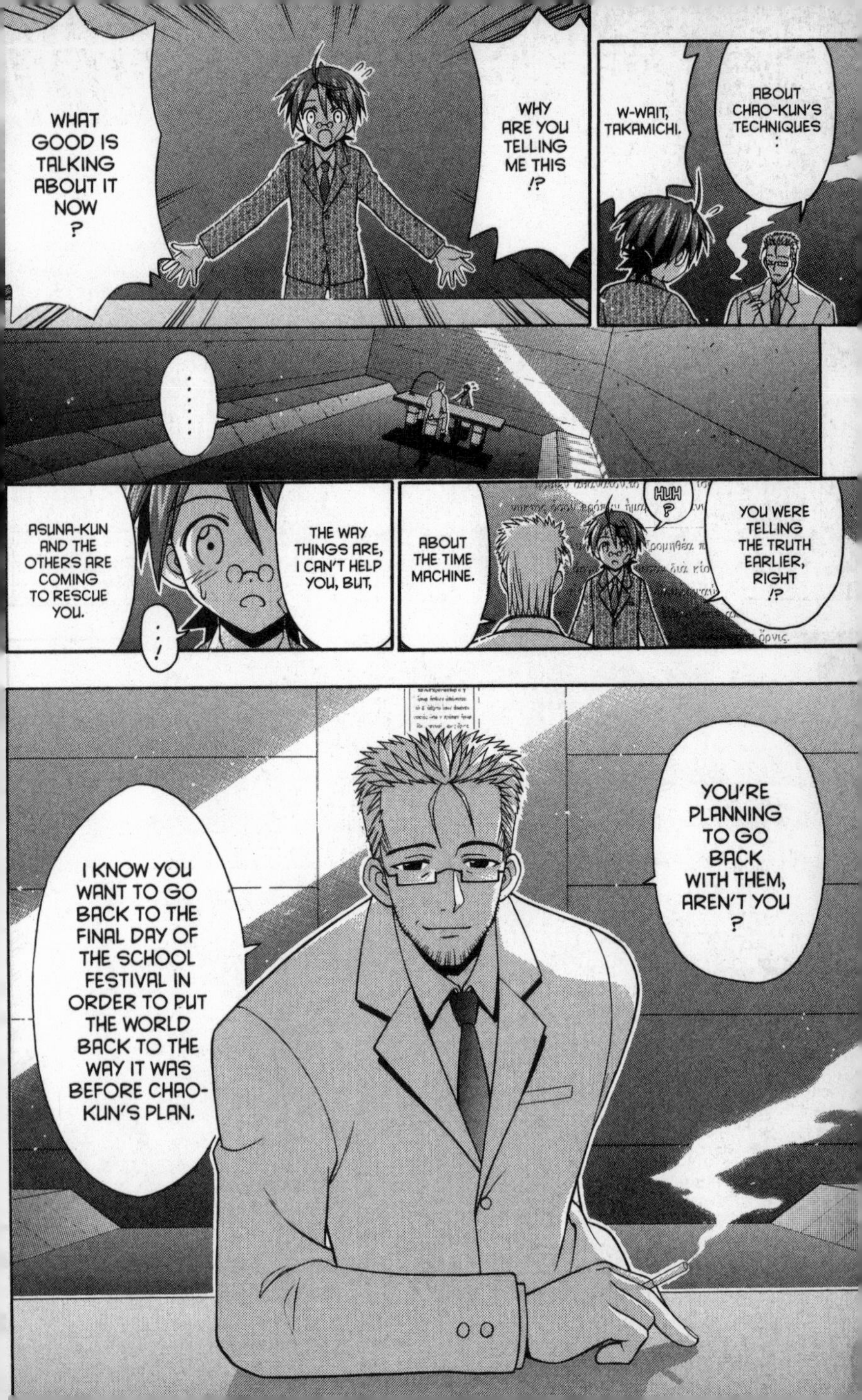
ABOUT CHAO-KUN'S TECHNIQUES :
W-WAIT, TAKAMICHI.
WHY ARE YOU TELLING ME THIS !?
WHAT GOOD IS TALKING ABOUT IT NOW ?
......
YOU WERE TELLING THE TRUTH EARLIER, RIGHT !?
HUH ?
ABOUT THE TIME MACHINE.
THE WAY THINGS ARE, I CAN'T HELP YOU, BUT,
ASUNA-KUN AND THE OTHERS ARE COMING TO RESCUE YOU.
...!
YOU'RE PLANNING TO GO BACK WITH THEM, AREN'T YOU ?
I KNOW YOU WANT TO GO BACK TO THE FINAL DAY OF THE SCHOOL FESTIVAL IN ORDER TO PUT THE WORLD BACK TO THE WAY IT WAS BEFORE CHAO-KUN'S PLAN.

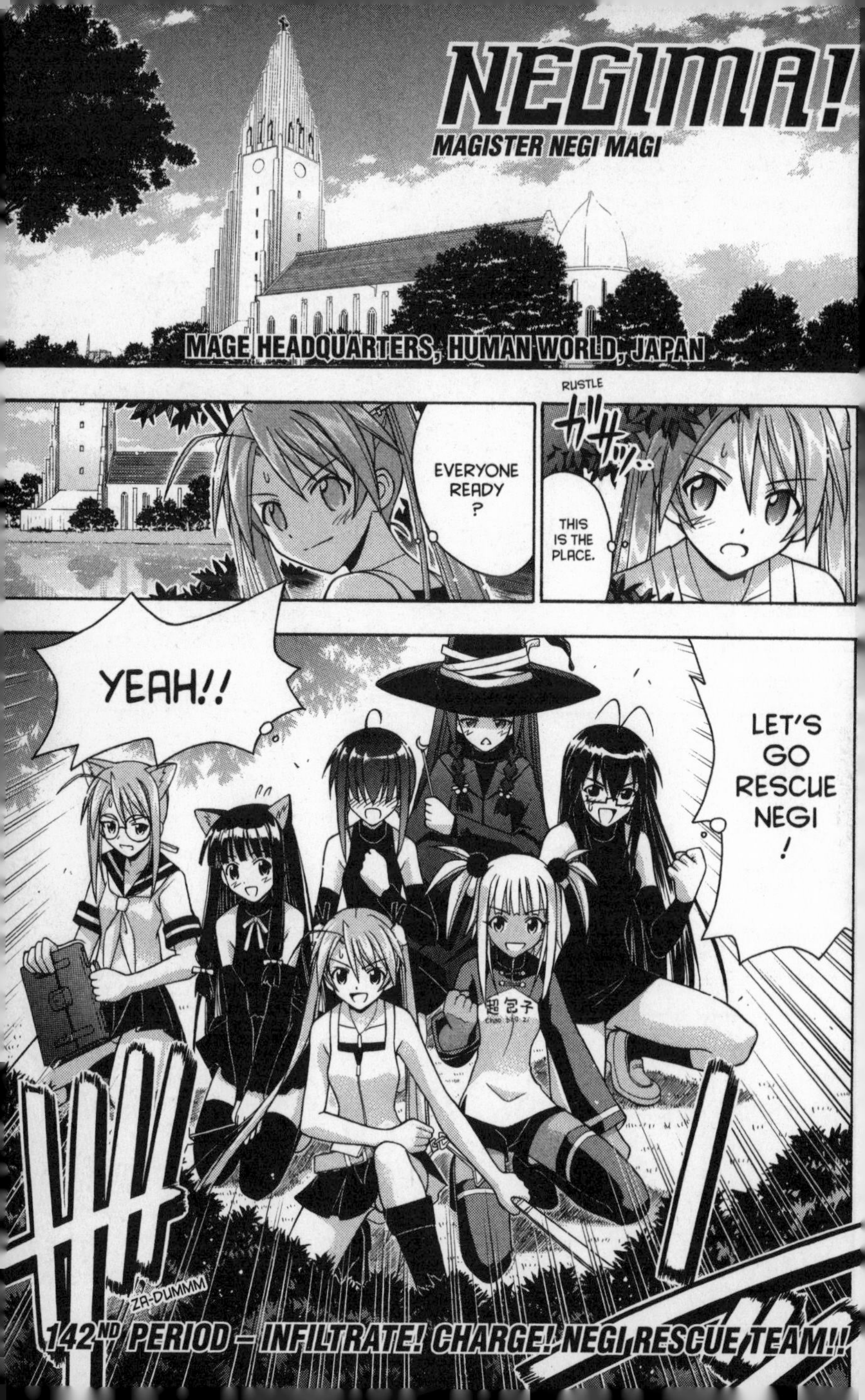
NEGIMA!
MAGISTER NEGI MAGI
MAGE HEADQUARTERS, HUMAN WORLD, JAPAN
RUSTLE
THIS IS THE PLACE.
EVERYONE READY ?
LET'S GO RESCUE NEGI !
YEAH!!
超包子
ZA-DUMMM
142ND PERIOD – INFILTRATE! CHARGE! NEGI RESCUE TEAM!!

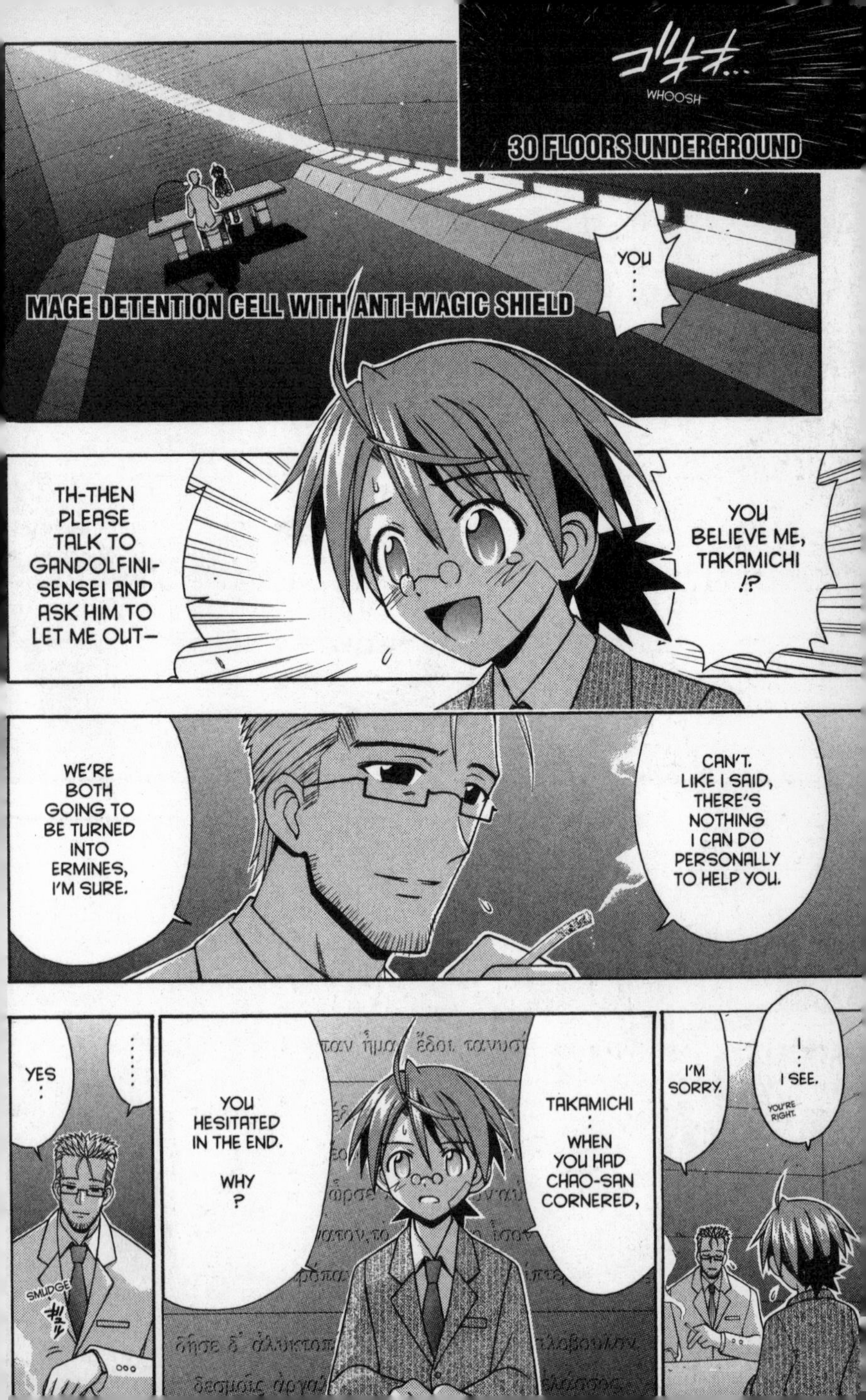
WHOOSH
30 FLOORS UNDERGROUND
YOU......
MAGE DETENTION CELL WITH ANTI-MAGIC SHIELD
YOU BELIEVE ME, TAKAMICHI !?
TH-THEN PLEASE TALK TO GANDOLFINI-SENSEI AND ASK HIM TO LET ME OUT—
CAN'T. LIKE I SAID, THERE'S NOTHING I CAN DO PERSONALLY TO HELP YOU.
WE'RE BOTH GOING TO BE TURNED INTO ERMINES, I'M SURE.
I... I SEE.
YOU'RE RIGHT.
I'M SORRY.
TAKAMICHI: WHEN YOU HAD CHAO-SAN CORNERED,
YOU HESITATED IN THE END. WHY?
......
YES...
SMUDGE

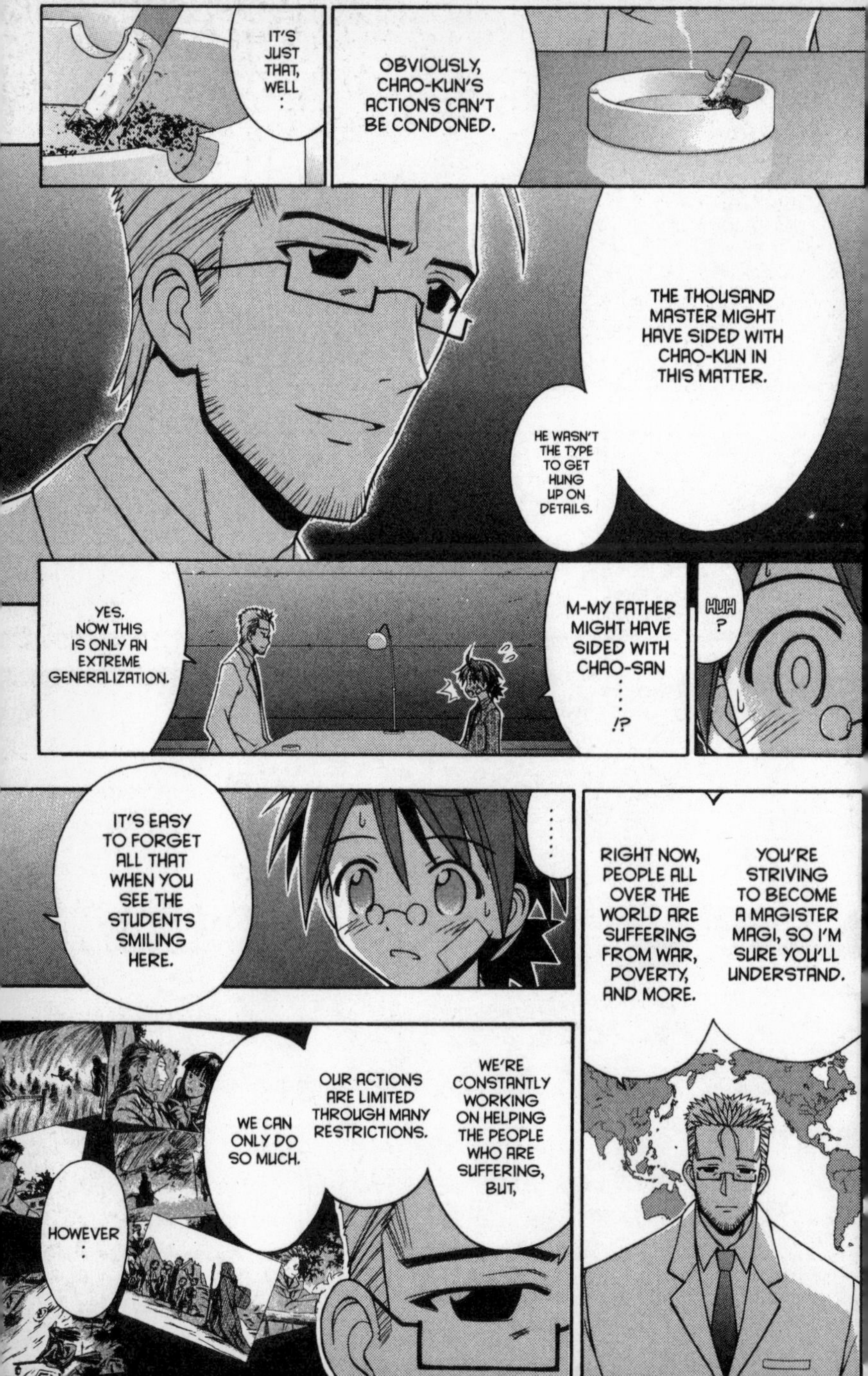
OBVIOUSLY, CHAO-KUN'S ACTIONS CAN'T BE CONDONED.
IT'S JUST THAT, WELL ...
THE THOUSAND MASTER MIGHT HAVE SIDED WITH CHAO-KUN IN THIS MATTER.
HE WASN'T THE TYPE TO GET HUNG UP ON DETAILS.
HUH?
M-MY FATHER MIGHT HAVE SIDED WITH CHAO-SAN .....!?
YES. NOW THIS IS ONLY AN EXTREME GENERALIZATION.
YOU'RE STRIVING TO BECOME A MAGISTER MAGI, SO I'M SURE YOU'LL UNDERSTAND.
RIGHT NOW, PEOPLE ALL OVER THE WORLD ARE SUFFERING FROM WAR, POVERTY, AND MORE.
......
IT'S EASY TO FORGET ALL THAT WHEN YOU SEE THE STUDENTS SMILING HERE.
WE'RE CONSTANTLY WORKING ON HELPING THE PEOPLE WHO ARE SUFFERING, BUT,
OUR ACTIONS ARE LIMITED THROUGH MANY RESTRICTIONS.
WE CAN ONLY DO SO MUCH.
HOWEVER ...

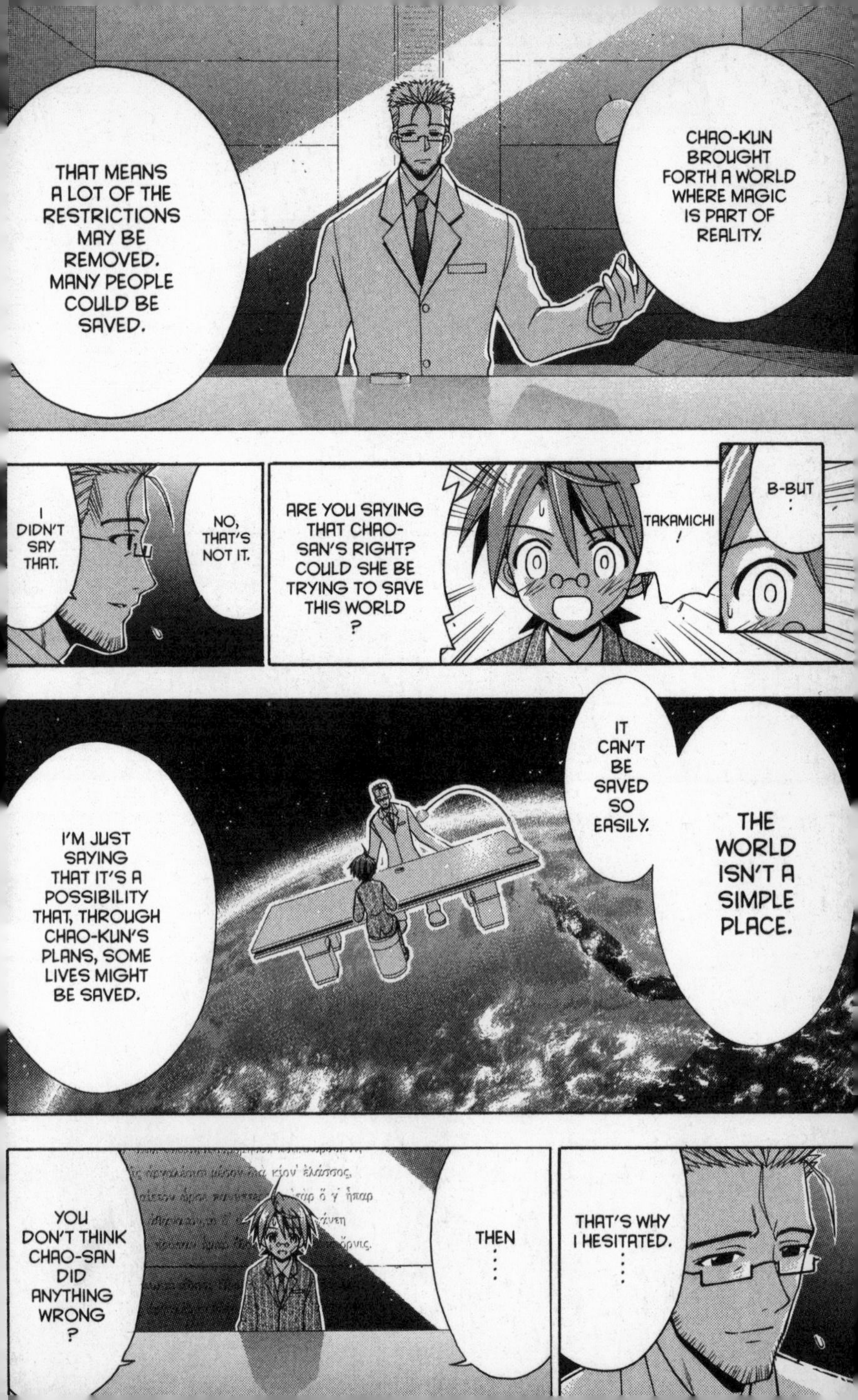
CHAO-KUN BROUGHT FORTH A WORLD WHERE MAGIC IS PART OF REALITY.
THAT MEANS A LOT OF THE RESTRICTIONS MAY BE REMOVED. MANY PEOPLE COULD BE SAVED.
B-BUT :
TAKAMICHI !
ARE YOU SAYING THAT CHAO-SAN'S RIGHT? COULD SHE BE TRYING TO SAVE THIS WORLD ?
NO, THAT'S NOT IT.
I DIDN'T SAY THAT.
IT CAN'T BE SAVED SO EASILY.
THE WORLD ISN'T A SIMPLE PLACE.
I'M JUST SAYING THAT IT'S A POSSIBILITY THAT, THROUGH CHAO-KUN'S PLANS, SOME LIVES MIGHT BE SAVED.
THAT'S WHY I HESITATED. ....
THEN ....
YOU DON'T THINK CHAO-SAN DID ANYTHING WRONG ?

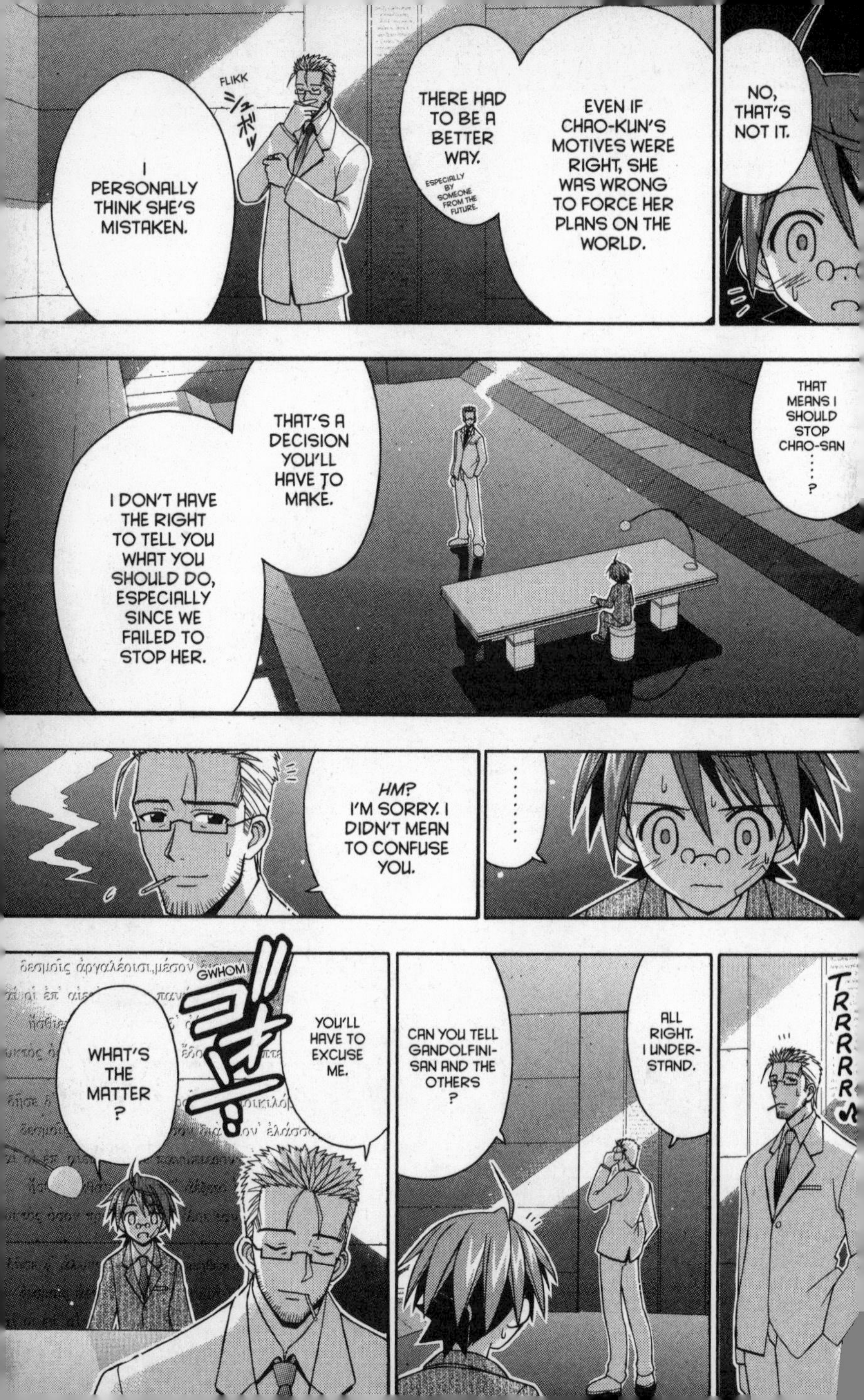
NO, THAT'S NOT IT.
EVEN IF CHAO-KUN'S MOTIVES WERE RIGHT, SHE WAS WRONG TO FORCE HER PLANS ON THE WORLD.
THERE HAD TO BE A BETTER WAY.
ESPECIALLY BY SOMEONE FROM THE FUTURE.
FLIKK
I PERSONALLY THINK SHE'S MISTAKEN.
THAT MEANS I SHOULD STOP CHAO-SAN ....?
THAT'S A DECISION YOU'LL HAVE TO MAKE.
I DON'T HAVE THE RIGHT TO TELL YOU WHAT YOU SHOULD DO, ESPECIALLY SINCE WE FAILED TO STOP HER.
....
HM? I'M SORRY. I DIDN'T MEAN TO CONFUSE YOU.
TRRRR
ALL RIGHT. I UNDERSTAND.
CAN YOU TELL GANDOLFINI-SAN AND THE OTHERS?
GWHOM
YOU'LL HAVE TO EXCUSE ME.
WHAT'S THE MATTER?

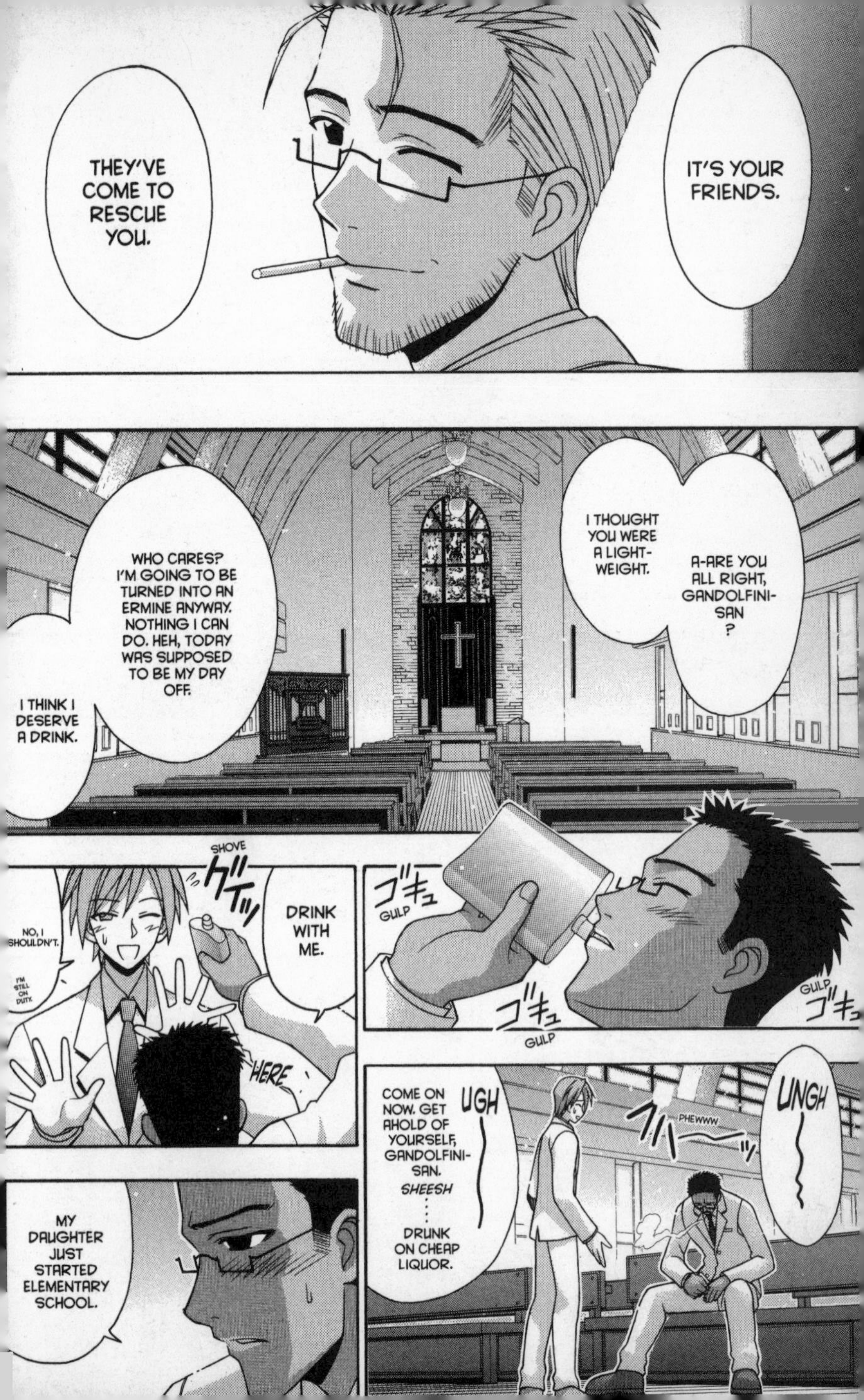

IT'S YOUR FRIENDS.
THEY'VE COME TO RESCUE YOU.
A-ARE YOU ALL RIGHT, GANDOLFINI-SAN ?
I THOUGHT YOU WERE A LIGHT-WEIGHT.
WHO CARES? I'M GOING TO BE TURNED INTO AN ERMINE ANYWAY. NOTHING I CAN DO. HEH, TODAY WAS SUPPOSED TO BE MY DAY OFF.
I THINK I DESERVE A DRINK.
GULP
GULP
GULP
SHOVE
DRINK WITH ME.
NO, I SHOULDN'T.
I'M STILL ON DUTY.
HERE
UNGH
PHEWWW
COME ON NOW. GET AHOLD OF YOURSELF, GANDOLFINI-SAN.
UGH
SHEESH ...
DRUNK ON CHEAP LIQUOR.
MY DAUGHTER JUST STARTED ELEMENTARY SCHOOL.

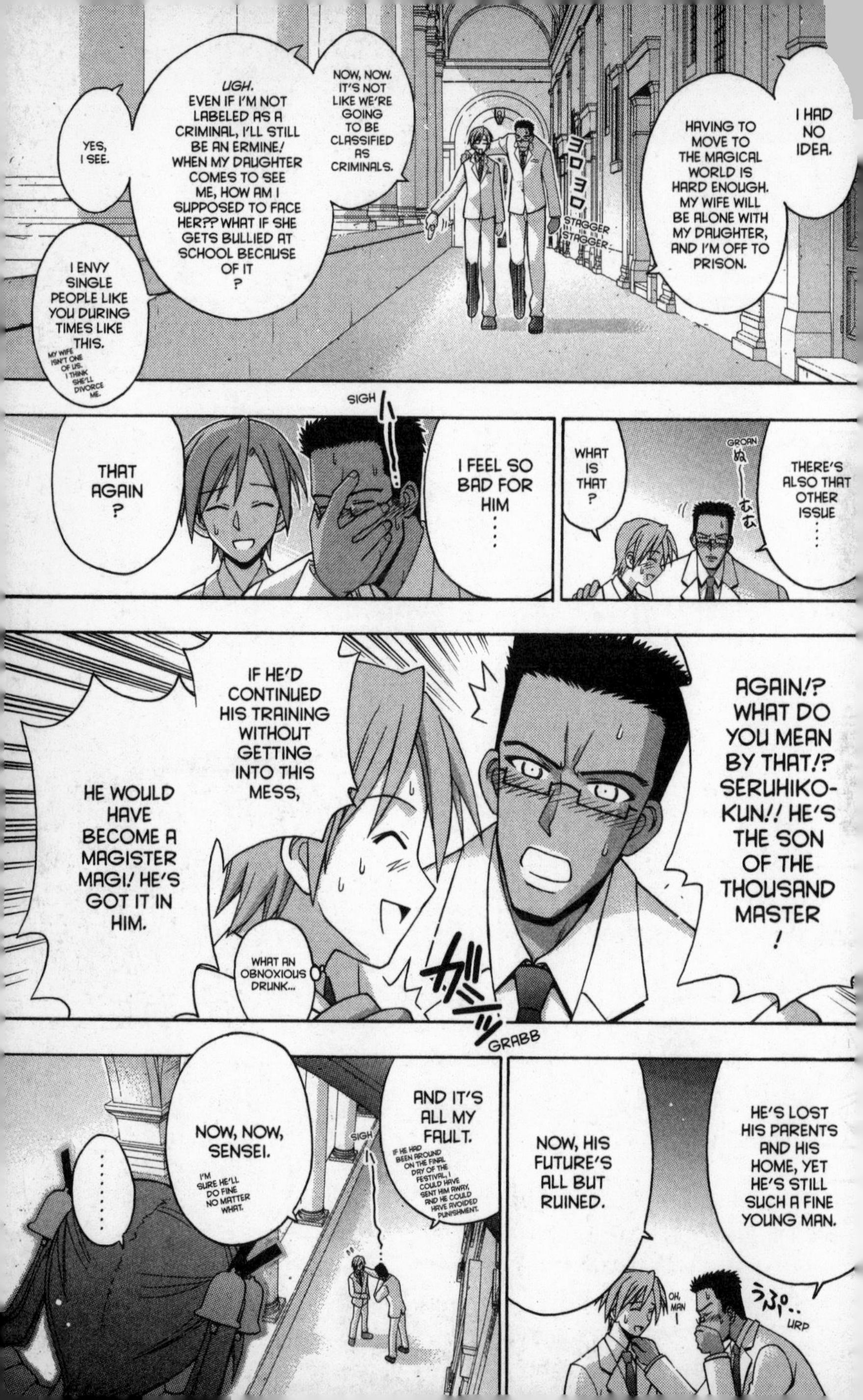
I HAD NO IDEA.
HAVING TO MOVE TO THE MAGICAL WORLD IS HARD ENOUGH. MY WIFE WILL BE ALONE WITH MY DAUGHTER, AND I'M OFF TO PRISON.
STAGGER STAGGER
NOW, NOW. IT'S NOT LIKE WE'RE GOING TO BE CLASSIFIED AS CRIMINALS.
UGH. EVEN IF I'M NOT LABELED AS A CRIMINAL, I'LL STILL BE AN ERMINE! WHEN MY DAUGHTER COMES TO SEE ME, HOW AM I SUPPOSED TO FACE HER?? WHAT IF SHE GETS BULLIED AT SCHOOL BECAUSE OF IT?
YES, I SEE.
I ENVY SINGLE PEOPLE LIKE YOU DURING TIMES LIKE THIS.
MY WIFE ISN'T ONE OF US. I THINK SHE'LL DIVORCE ME.
THERE'S ALSO THAT OTHER ISSUE....
GROAN
WHAT IS THAT?
SIGH
I FEEL SO BAD FOR HIM....
THAT AGAIN?
AGAIN!? WHAT DO YOU MEAN BY THAT!? SERUHIKO-KUN!! HE'S THE SON OF THE THOUSAND MASTER!
IF HE'D CONTINUED HIS TRAINING WITHOUT GETTING INTO THIS MESS,
HE WOULD HAVE BECOME A MAGISTER MAGI! HE'S GOT IT IN HIM.
WHAT AN OBNOXIOUS DRUNK...
GRABB
HE'S LOST HIS PARENTS AND HIS HOME, YET HE'S STILL SUCH A FINE YOUNG MAN.
NOW, HIS FUTURE'S ALL BUT RUINED.
OH, MAN
URP
AND IT'S ALL MY FAULT.
IF HE HAD BEEN AROUND ON THE FINAL DAY OF THE FESTIVAL, I COULD HAVE SENT HIM AWAY, AND HE COULD HAVE AVOIDED PUNISHMENT.
SIGH
NOW, NOW, SENSEI.
I'M SURE HE'LL DO FINE NO MATTER WHAT.
......

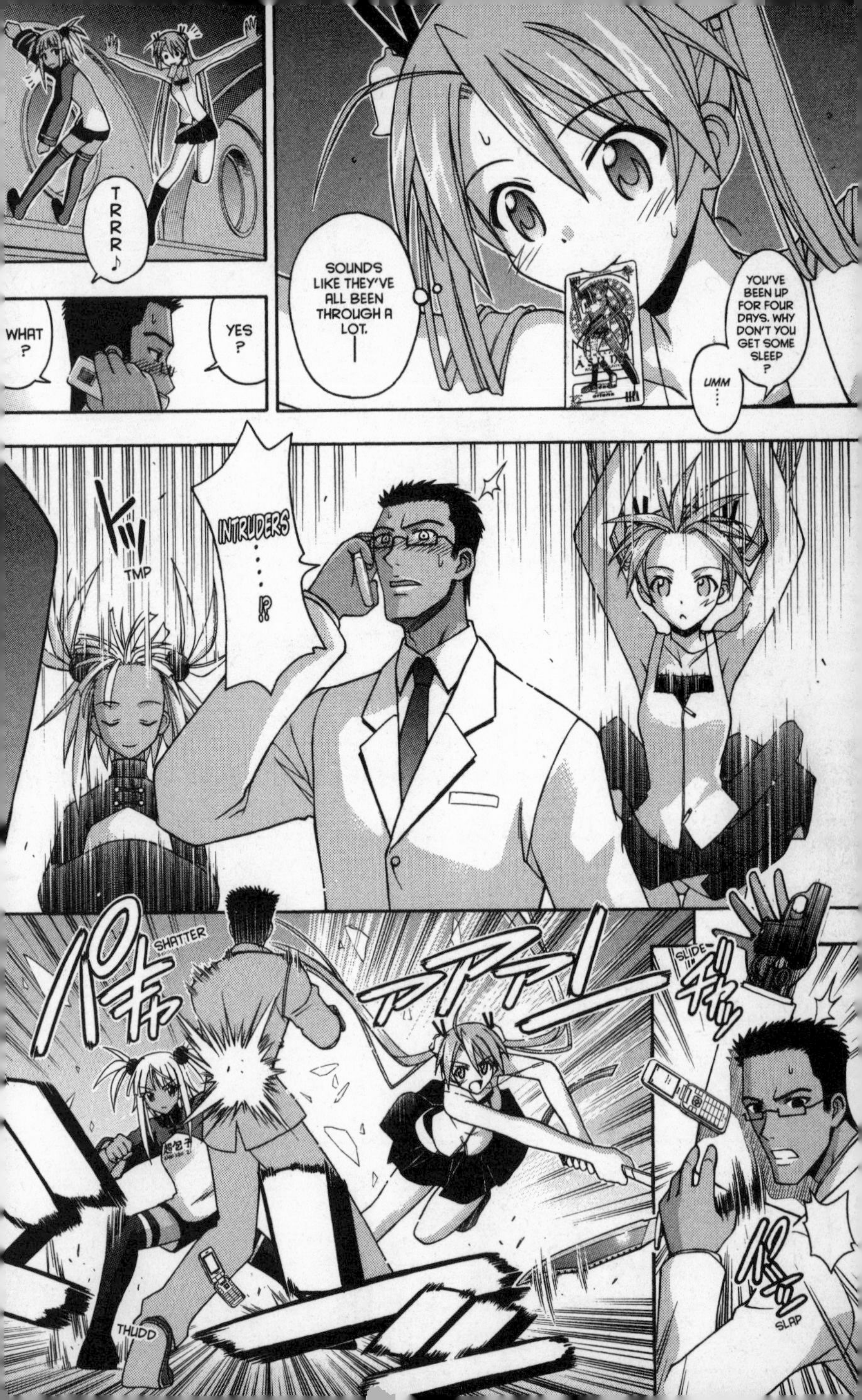
YOU'VE BEEN UP FOR FOUR DAYS. WHY DON'T YOU GET SOME SLEEP?
UMM...
SOUNDS LIKE THEY'VE ALL BEEN THROUGH A LOT.
TRRR♪
YES?
WHAT?
INTRUDERS.....!?
ドッ
TMP
SLIDE
SLAP
SHATTER
THUDD

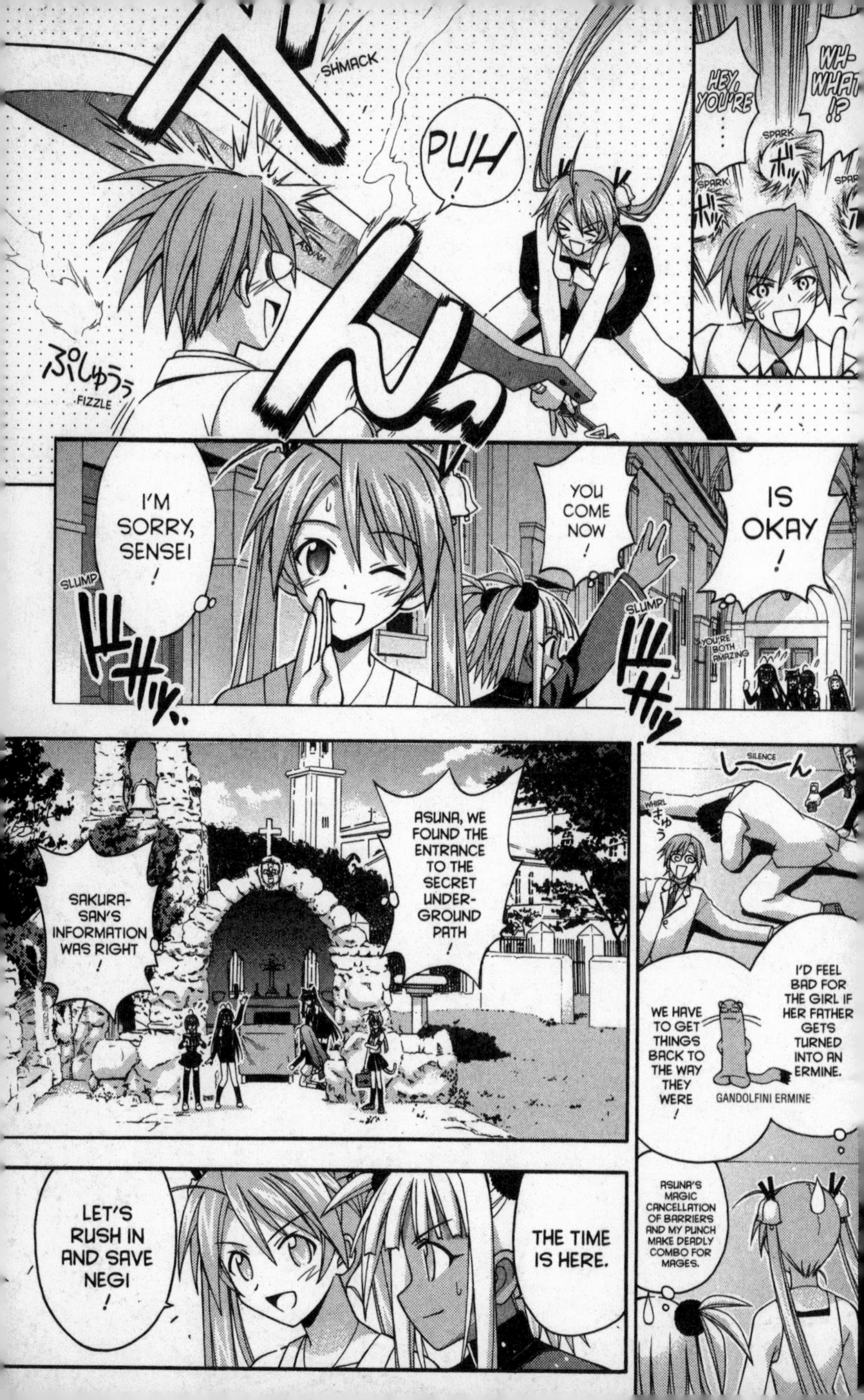

WH-WHAT!?
HEY, YOU'RE...
SPARK
SPARK
SHMACK
PUH!
ASUNA
ぷしゅうう
FIZZLE
IS OKAY!
YOU COME NOW!
YOU'RE BOTH AMAZING!
SLUMP
I'M SORRY, SENSEI!
SLUMP
しーん
SILENCE
WHIRL
きゅう
I'D FEEL BAD FOR THE GIRL IF HER FATHER GETS TURNED INTO AN ERMINE.
WE HAVE TO GET THINGS BACK TO THE WAY THEY WERE!
GANDOLFINI ERMINE
ASUNA'S MAGIC CANCELLATION OF BARRIERS AND MY PUNCH MAKE DEADLY COMBO FOR MAGES.
ASUNA, WE FOUND THE ENTRANCE TO THE SECRET UNDER-GROUND PATH!
SAKURA-SAN'S INFORMATION WAS RIGHT!
THE TIME IS HERE.
LET'S RUSH IN AND SAVE NEGI!

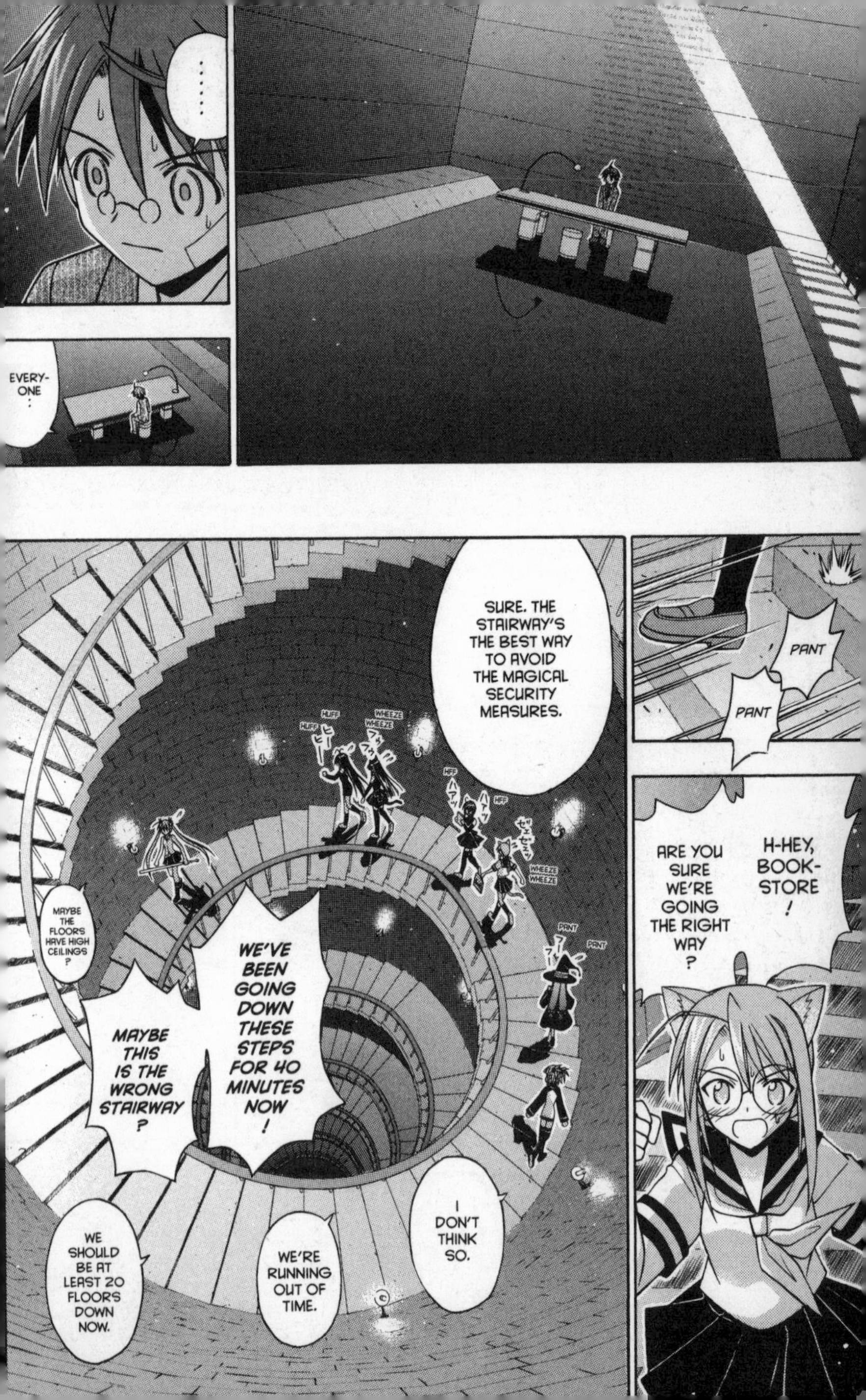
......
EVERY-ONE :
PANT
PANT
H-HEY, BOOK-STORE !
ARE YOU SURE WE'RE GOING THE RIGHT WAY ?
SURE. THE STAIRWAY'S THE BEST WAY TO AVOID THE MAGICAL SECURITY MEASURES.
HUFF HUFF
WHEEZE WHEEZE
HFF HFF
WHEEZE WHEEZE
PANT PANT
WE'VE BEEN GOING DOWN THESE STEPS FOR 40 MINUTES NOW !
MAYBE THIS IS THE WRONG STAIRWAY ?
MAYBE THE FLOORS HAVE HIGH CEILINGS ?
I DON'T THINK SO.
WE'RE RUNNING OUT OF TIME.
WE SHOULD BE AT LEAST 20 FLOORS DOWN NOW.

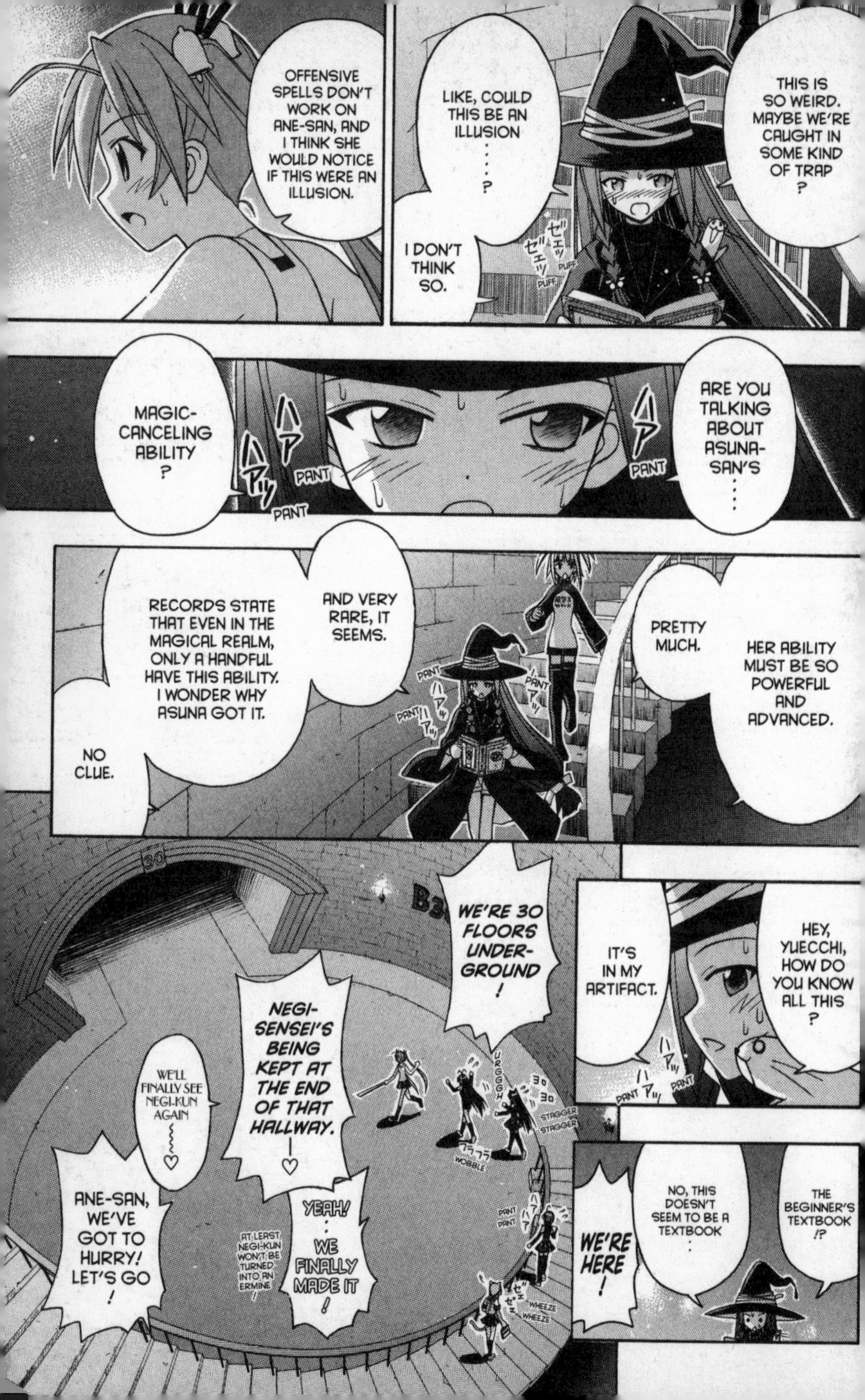
THIS IS SO WEIRD. MAYBE WE'RE CAUGHT IN SOME KIND OF TRAP?
PUFF PUFF
LIKE, COULD THIS BE AN ILLUSION...?
I DON'T THINK SO.
OFFENSIVE SPELLS DON'T WORK ON ANE-SAN, AND I THINK SHE WOULD NOTICE IF THIS WERE AN ILLUSION.
ARE YOU TALKING ABOUT ASUNA-SAN'S...
PANT
PANT
PANT
MAGIC-CANCELING ABILITY?
HER ABILITY MUST BE SO POWERFUL AND ADVANCED.
PRETTY MUCH.
PANT
PANT
PANT
AND VERY RARE, IT SEEMS.
RECORDS STATE THAT EVEN IN THE MAGICAL REALM, ONLY A HANDFUL HAVE THIS ABILITY. I WONDER WHY ASUNA GOT IT.
NO CLUE.
HEY, YUECCHI, HOW DO YOU KNOW ALL THIS?
IT'S IN MY ARTIFACT.
PANT
PANT
THE BEGINNER'S TEXTBOOK!?
NO, THIS DOESN'T SEEM TO BE A TEXTBOOK...
WE'RE HERE!
B30
WE'RE 30 FLOORS UNDERGROUND!
URGGGH
STAGGER STAGGER
WOBBLE
NEGI-SENSEI'S BEING KEPT AT THE END OF THAT HALLWAY. ♡
WE'LL FINALLY SEE NEGI-KUN AGAIN ♡
PANT PANT
YEAH! WE FINALLY MADE IT!
AT LEAST NEGI-KUN WON'T BE TURNED INTO AN ERMINE
WHEEZE WHEEZE
ANE-SAN, WE'VE GOT TO HURRY! LET'S GO!

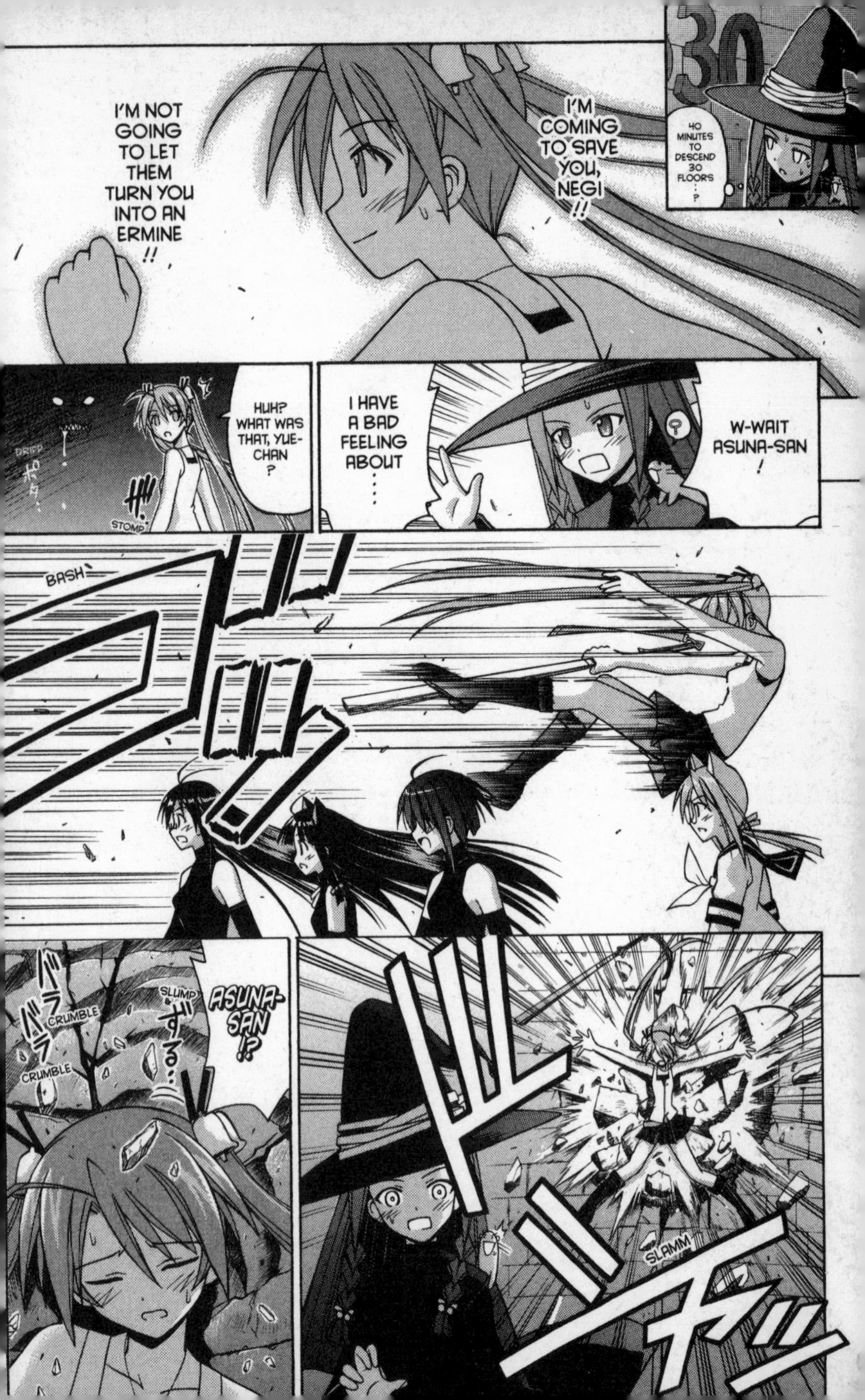

40 MINUTES TO DESCEND 30 FLOORS...?
I'M COMING TO SAVE YOU, NEGI!!
I'M NOT GOING TO LET THEM TURN YOU INTO AN ERMINE!!
W-WAIT ASUNA-SAN!
I HAVE A BAD FEELING ABOUT...
HUH? WHAT WAS THAT, YUE-CHAN?
DRIP
STOMP
BASH
SLAMM
ASUNA-SAN!?
SLUMP
CRUMBLE
CRUMBLE

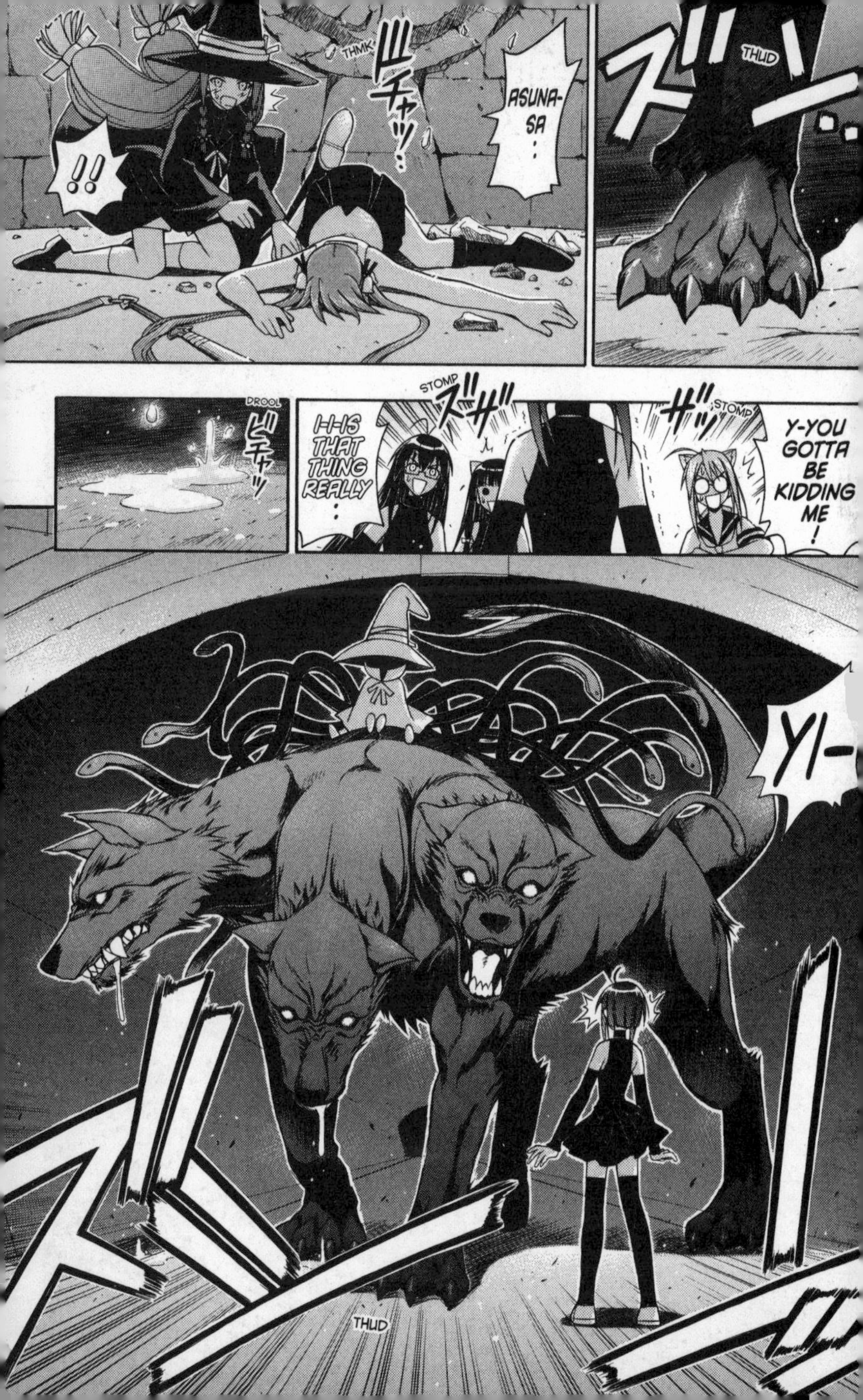

ズン
THUD
ASUNA-SA...
ドチャッ
THMK
!!
Y-YOU GOTTA BE KIDDING ME!
ザッ
STOMP
ズザ
STOMP
I-I-IS THAT THING REALLY...
ビチャッ
DROOL
YI-
ズン
THUD

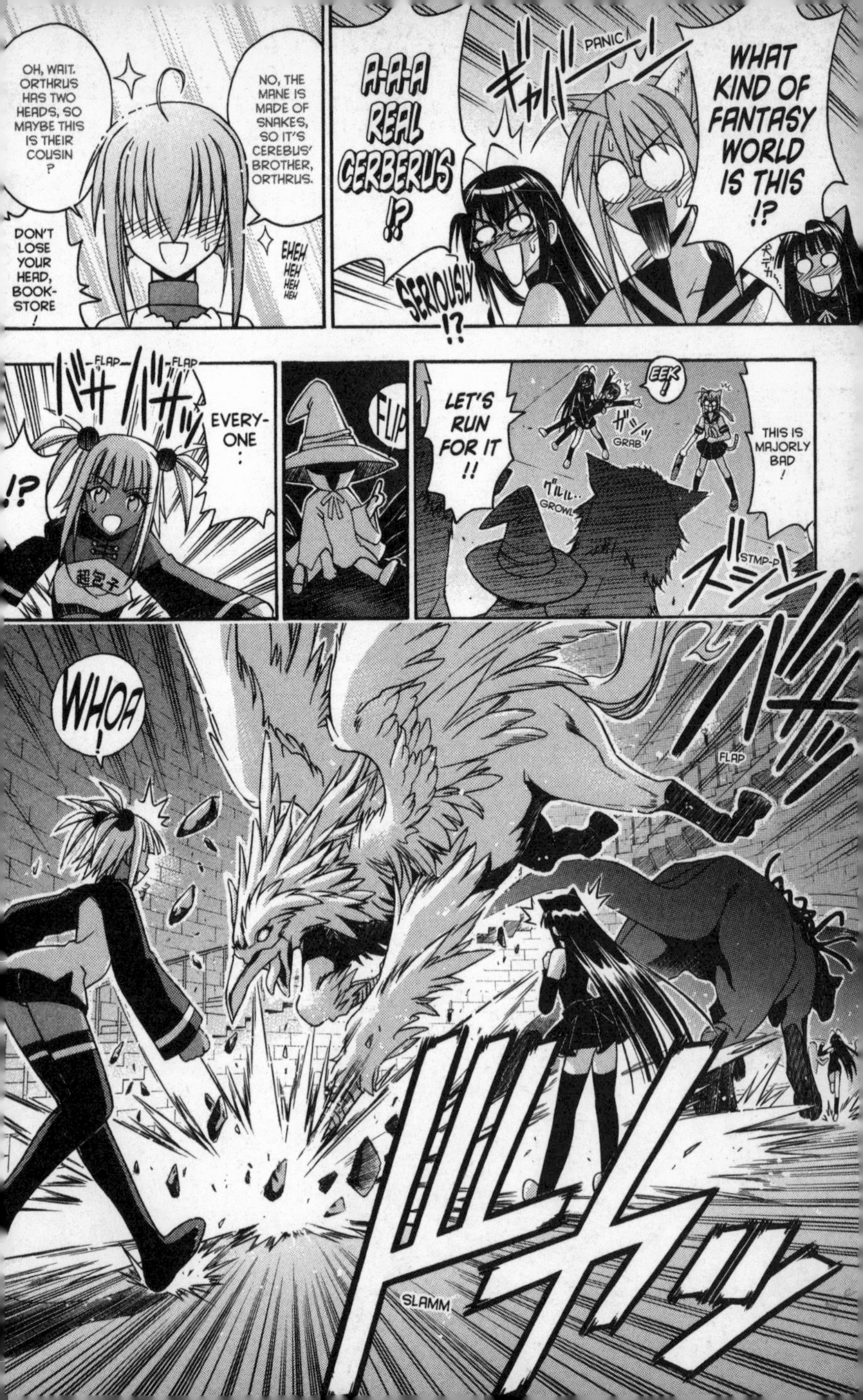
WHAT KIND OF FANTASY WORLD IS THIS !?
PANIC
A-A-A REAL CERBERUS !?
SERIOUSLY !?
NO, THE MANE IS MADE OF SNAKES, SO IT'S CEREBUS' BROTHER, ORTHRUS.
EHEH HEH HEH HEH
OH, WAIT. ORTHRUS HAS TWO HEADS, SO MAYBE THIS IS THEIR COUSIN ?
DON'T LOSE YOUR HEAD, BOOK-STORE !
EEK !
GRAB
THIS IS MAJORLY BAD !
LET'S RUN FOR IT !!
GROWL
STMP-P
FLIP
FLAP
FLAP
EVERY-ONE :
!?
FLAP
WHOA !
SLAMM

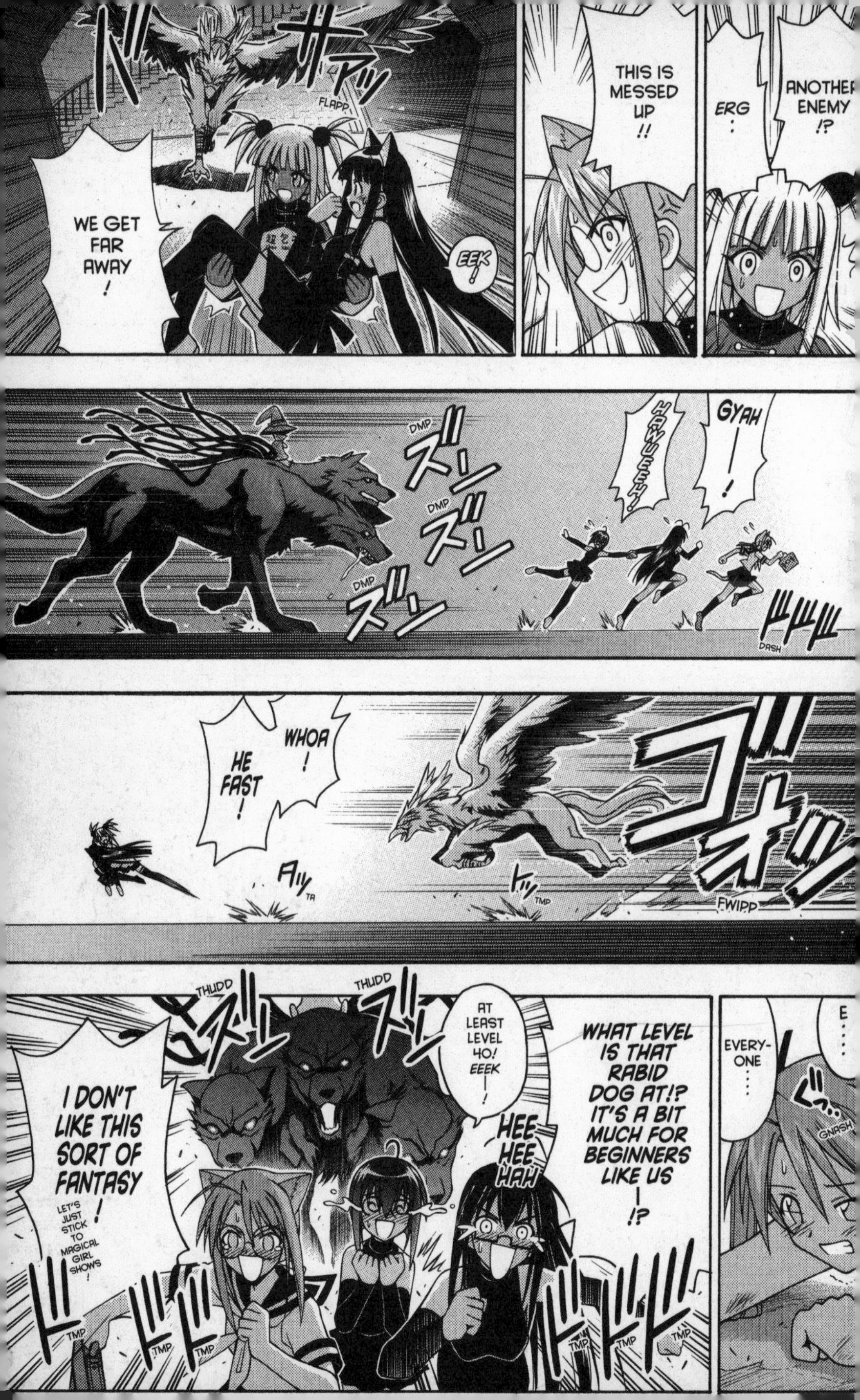
ANOTHER ENEMY !?
ERG :
THIS IS MESSED UP !!
FLAPP
WE GET FAR AWAY !
EEK !
GYAH — !
HAWUEEH!
DMP
DMP
DMP
DASH
FWIPP
TMP
WHOA !
HE FAST !
TA
E.....
EVERY-ONE.....
GNASH
WHAT LEVEL IS THAT RABID DOG AT!? IT'S A BIT MUCH FOR BEGINNERS LIKE US —!?
AT LEAST LEVEL 40! EEEK —!
HEE HEE HAH
THUDD
THUDD
I DON'T LIKE THIS SORT OF FANTASY !
LET'S JUST STICK TO MAGICAL GIRL SHOWS !
TMP TMP TMP TMP TMP TMP

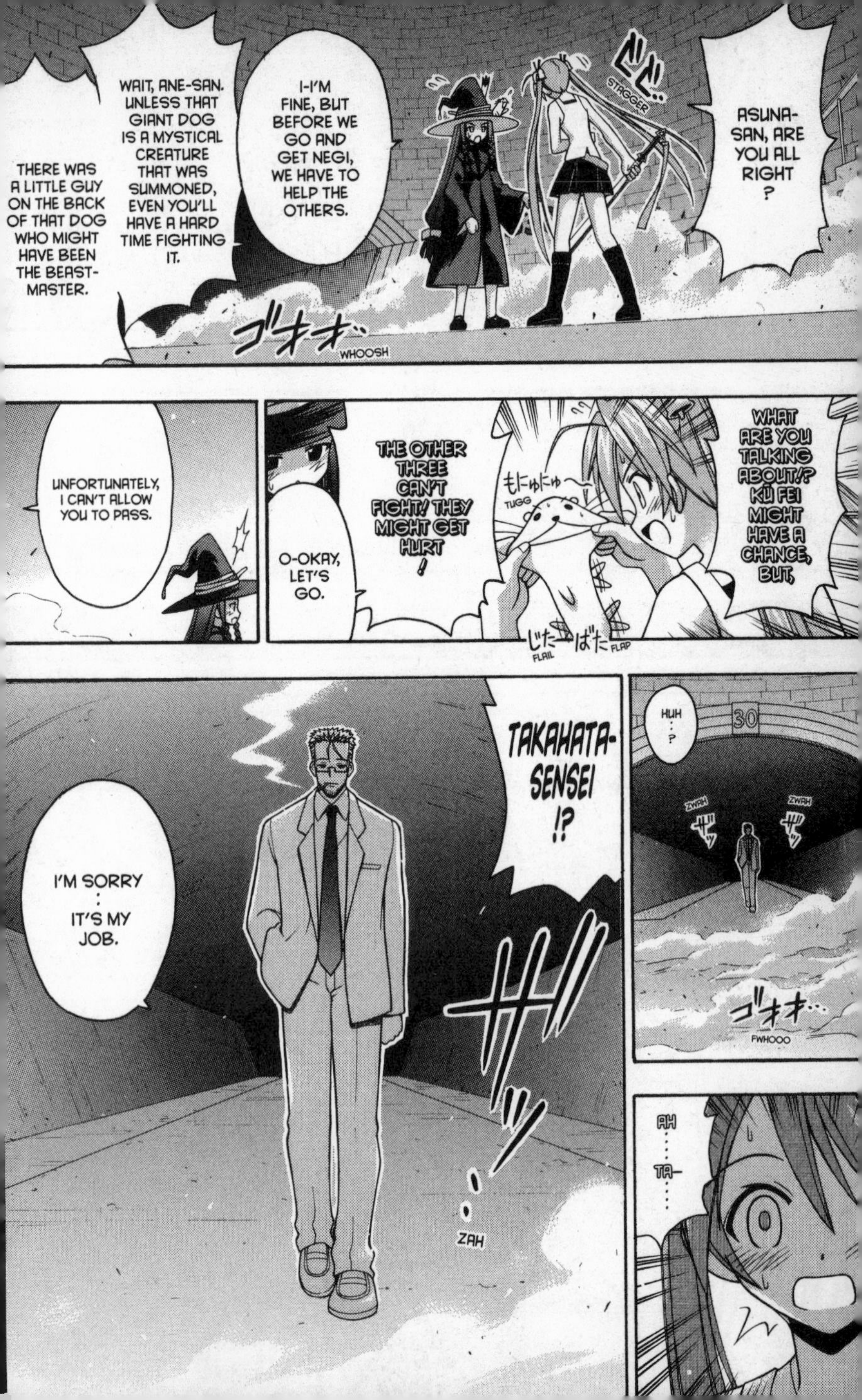

ASUNA-SAN, ARE YOU ALL RIGHT?
STAGGER
I-I'M FINE, BUT BEFORE WE GO AND GET NEGI, WE HAVE TO HELP THE OTHERS.
WAIT, ANE-SAN. UNLESS THAT GIANT DOG IS A MYSTICAL CREATURE THAT WAS SUMMONED, EVEN YOU'LL HAVE A HARD TIME FIGHTING IT.
THERE WAS A LITTLE GUY ON THE BACK OF THAT DOG WHO MIGHT HAVE BEEN THE BEAST-MASTER.
ゴオオ
WHOOSH
WHAT ARE YOU TALKING ABOUT!? KU FEI MIGHT HAVE A CHANCE, BUT,
TUGG
THE OTHER THREE CAN'T FIGHT! THEY MIGHT GET HURT!
O-OKAY, LET'S GO.
FLAIL
FLAP
UNFORTUNATELY, I CAN'T ALLOW YOU TO PASS.
HUH...?
30
ZWAH
ZWAH
FWHOOO
AH... TA-...
TAKAHATA-SENSEI!?
ZAH
I'M SORRY: IT'S MY JOB.

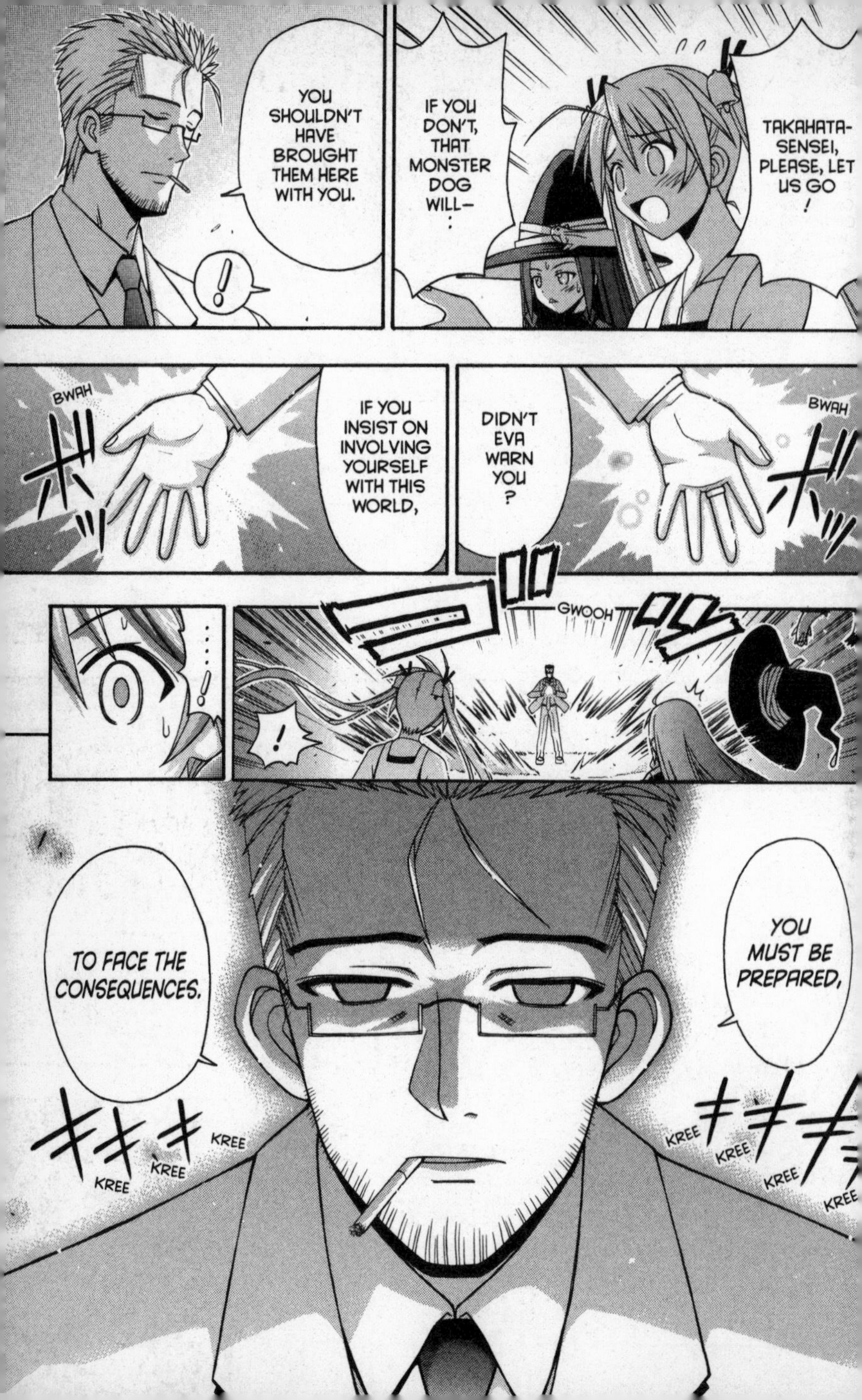
TAKAHATA-SENSEI, PLEASE, LET US GO!
IF YOU DON'T, THAT MONSTER DOG WILL—:
YOU SHOULDN'T HAVE BROUGHT THEM HERE WITH YOU.
!
BWAH
DIDN'T EVA WARN YOU?
IF YOU INSIST ON INVOLVING YOURSELF WITH THIS WORLD,
BWAH
GWOOH
!
...!
YOU MUST BE PREPARED,
TO FACE THE CONSEQUENCES.
KREE
KREE
KREE
KREE
KREE
KREE
KREE

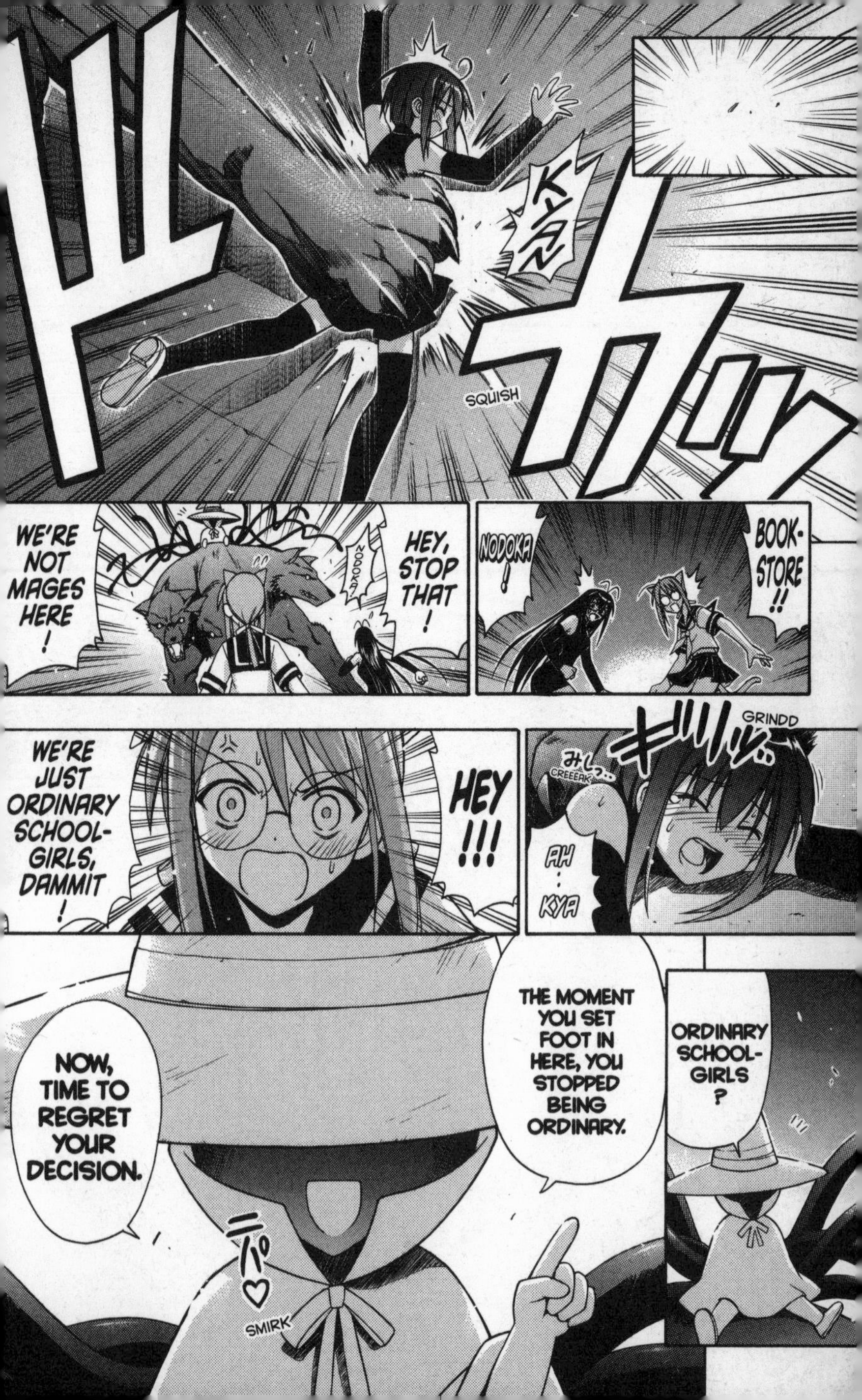
KYAN
SQUISH
BOOK-STORE!!
NODOKA!
HEY, STOP THAT!
NODOKA!
WE'RE NOT MAGES HERE!
GRINDD
みしっ..
CREEEAK
AH.. KYA
HEY!!!
WE'RE JUST ORDINARY SCHOOL-GIRLS, DAMMIT!
ORDINARY SCHOOL-GIRLS?
THE MOMENT YOU SET FOOT IN HERE, YOU STOPPED BEING ORDINARY.
NOW, TIME TO REGRET YOUR DECISION.
SMIRK

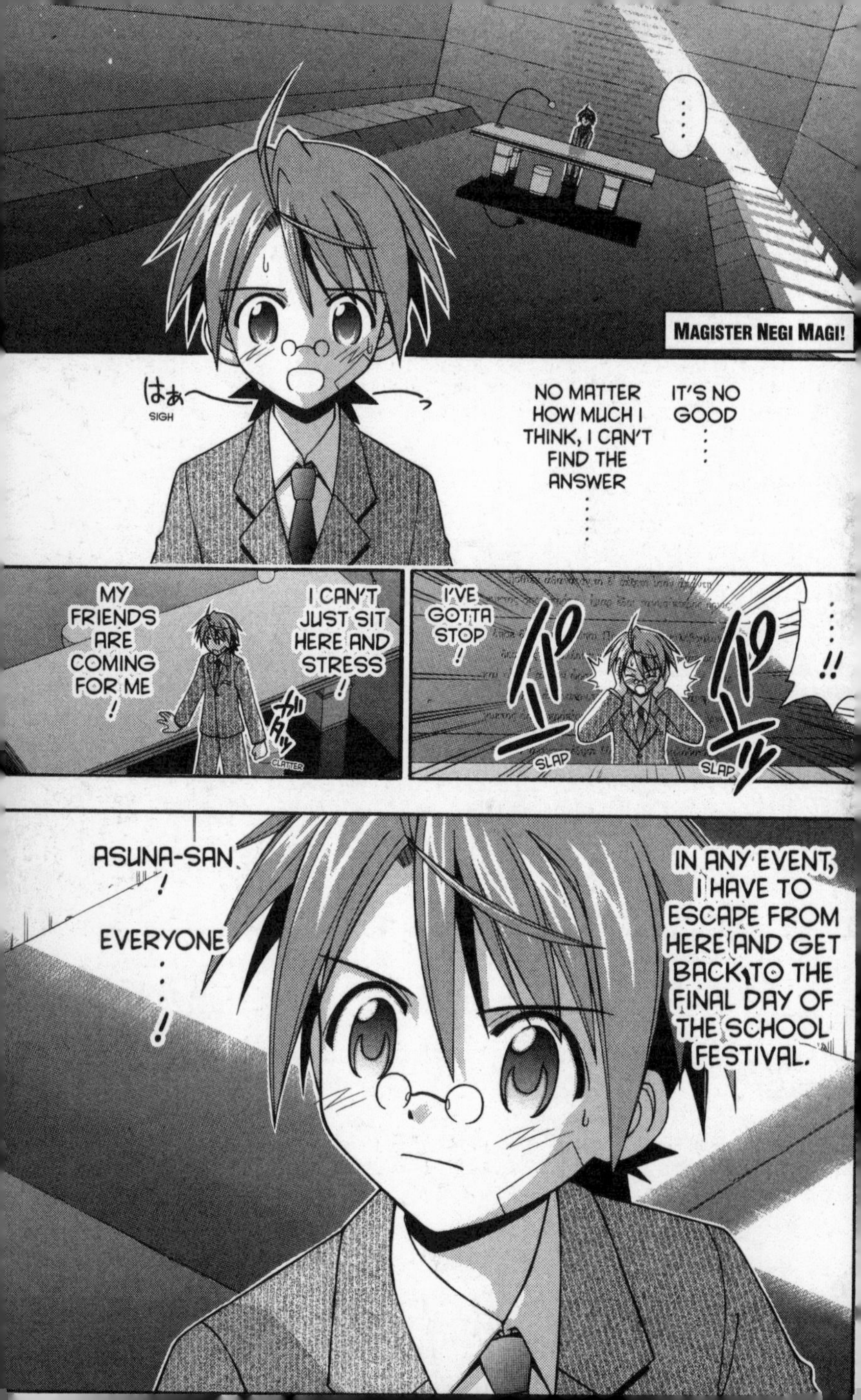

. . .
MAGISTER NEGI MAGI!
IT'S NO GOOD . . .
NO MATTER HOW MUCH I THINK, I CAN'T FIND THE ANSWER . . .
はぁ~
SIGH
. . . !!
I'VE GOTTA STOP!
パン
SLAP
パンッ
SLAP
I CAN'T JUST SIT HERE AND STRESS!
MY FRIENDS ARE COMING FOR ME!
ガタッ
CLATTER
IN ANY EVENT, I HAVE TO ESCAPE FROM HERE AND GET BACK TO THE FINAL DAY OF THE SCHOOL FESTIVAL.
ASUNA-SAN!
EVERYONE . . . !

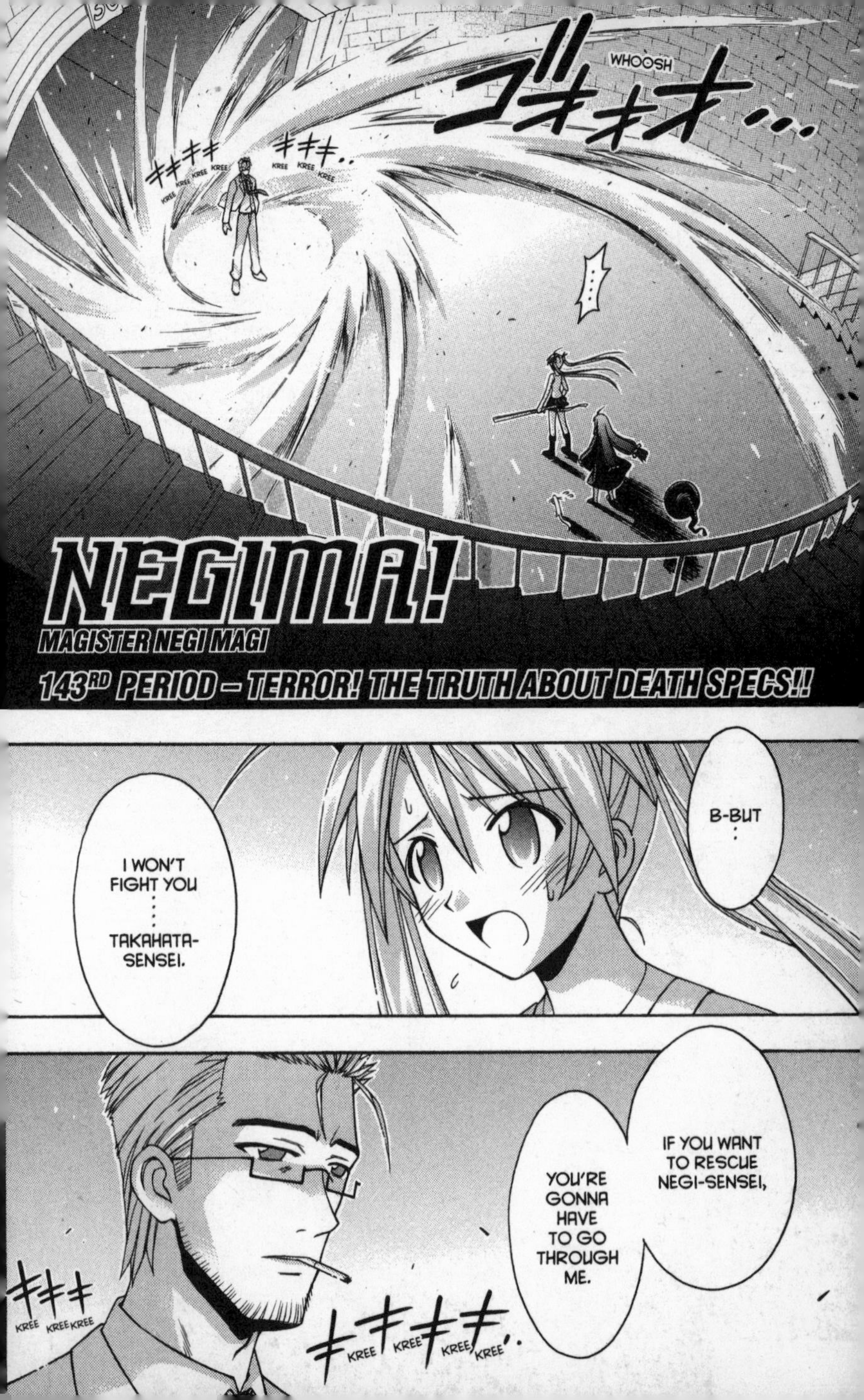
WHOOSH
KREE KREE KREE KREE
KREE KREE KREE
!...
NEGIMA!
MAGISTER NEGI MAGI
143RD PERIOD – TERROR! THE TRUTH ABOUT DEATH SPECS!!
B-BUT...
I WON'T FIGHT YOU... TAKAHATA-SENSEI.
IF YOU WANT TO RESCUE NEGI-SENSEI,
YOU'RE GONNA HAVE TO GO THROUGH ME.
KREE KREE KREE
KREE KREE KREE KREE

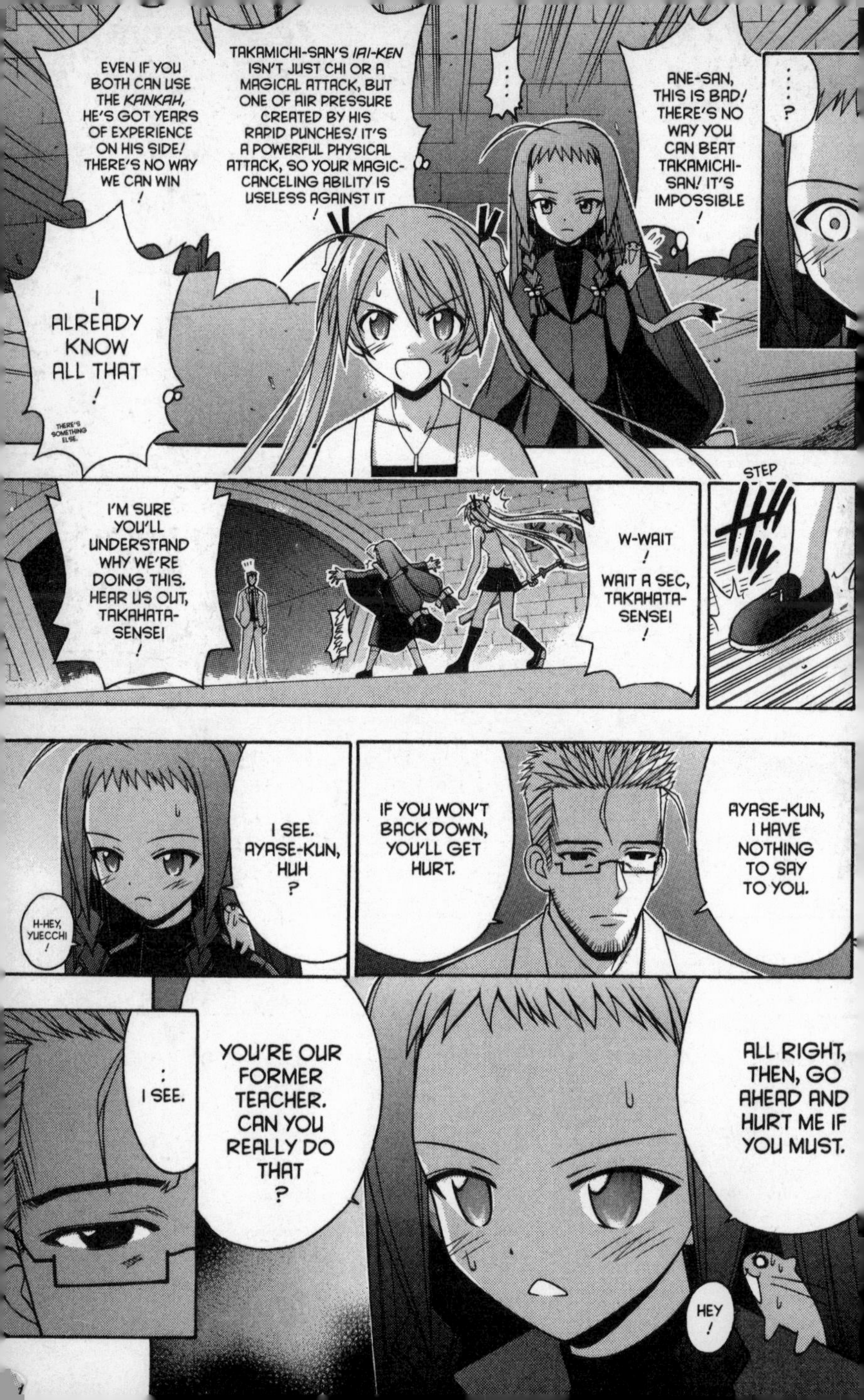
...?
ANE-SAN, THIS IS BAD! THERE'S NO WAY YOU CAN BEAT TAKAMICHI-SAN! IT'S IMPOSSIBLE!
...
TAKAMICHI-SAN'S *IAI-KEN* ISN'T JUST CHI OR A MAGICAL ATTACK, BUT ONE OF AIR PRESSURE CREATED BY HIS RAPID PUNCHES! IT'S A POWERFUL PHYSICAL ATTACK, SO YOUR MAGIC-CANCELING ABILITY IS USELESS AGAINST IT!
EVEN IF YOU BOTH CAN USE THE *KANKAH*, HE'S GOT YEARS OF EXPERIENCE ON HIS SIDE! THERE'S NO WAY WE CAN WIN!
I ALREADY KNOW ALL THAT!
THERE'S SOMETHING ELSE.
STEP
W-WAIT! WAIT A SEC, TAKAHATA-SENSEI!
I'M SURE YOU'LL UNDERSTAND WHY WE'RE DOING THIS. HEAR US OUT, TAKAHATA-SENSEI!
AYASE-KUN, I HAVE NOTHING TO SAY TO YOU.
IF YOU WON'T BACK DOWN, YOU'LL GET HURT.
I SEE. AYASE-KUN, HUH?
H-HEY, YUECCHI!
ALL RIGHT, THEN, GO AHEAD AND HURT ME IF YOU MUST.
HEY!
YOU'RE OUR FORMER TEACHER. CAN YOU REALLY DO THAT?
: I SEE.

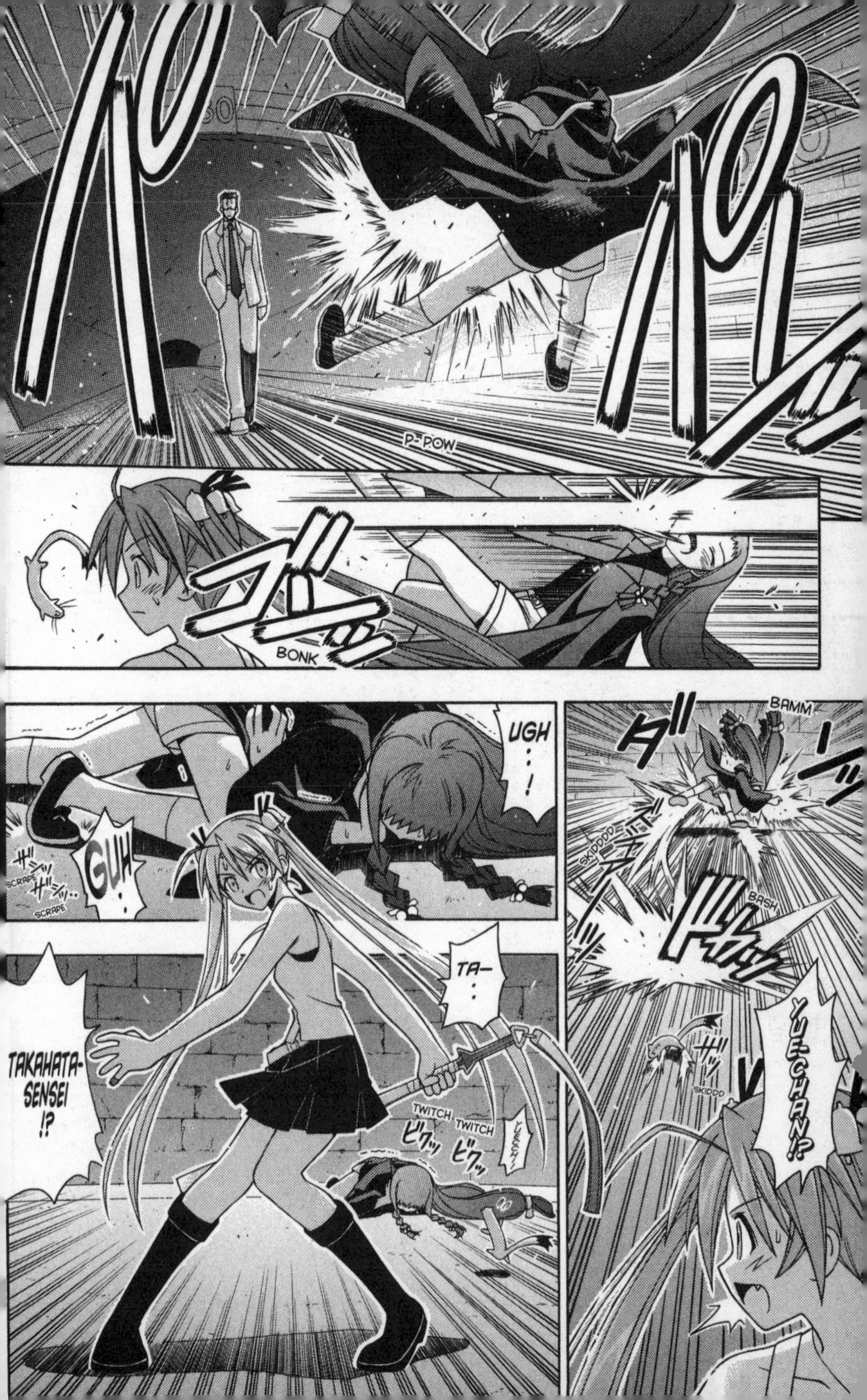

P-POW
BONK
BAMM
SKIDDDD
BASH
YUE-CHAN!?
SKIDDD
UGH...!
GUH...
SCRAPE
SCRAPE
TA-...
TAKAHATA-SENSEI!?
TWITCH
TWITCH

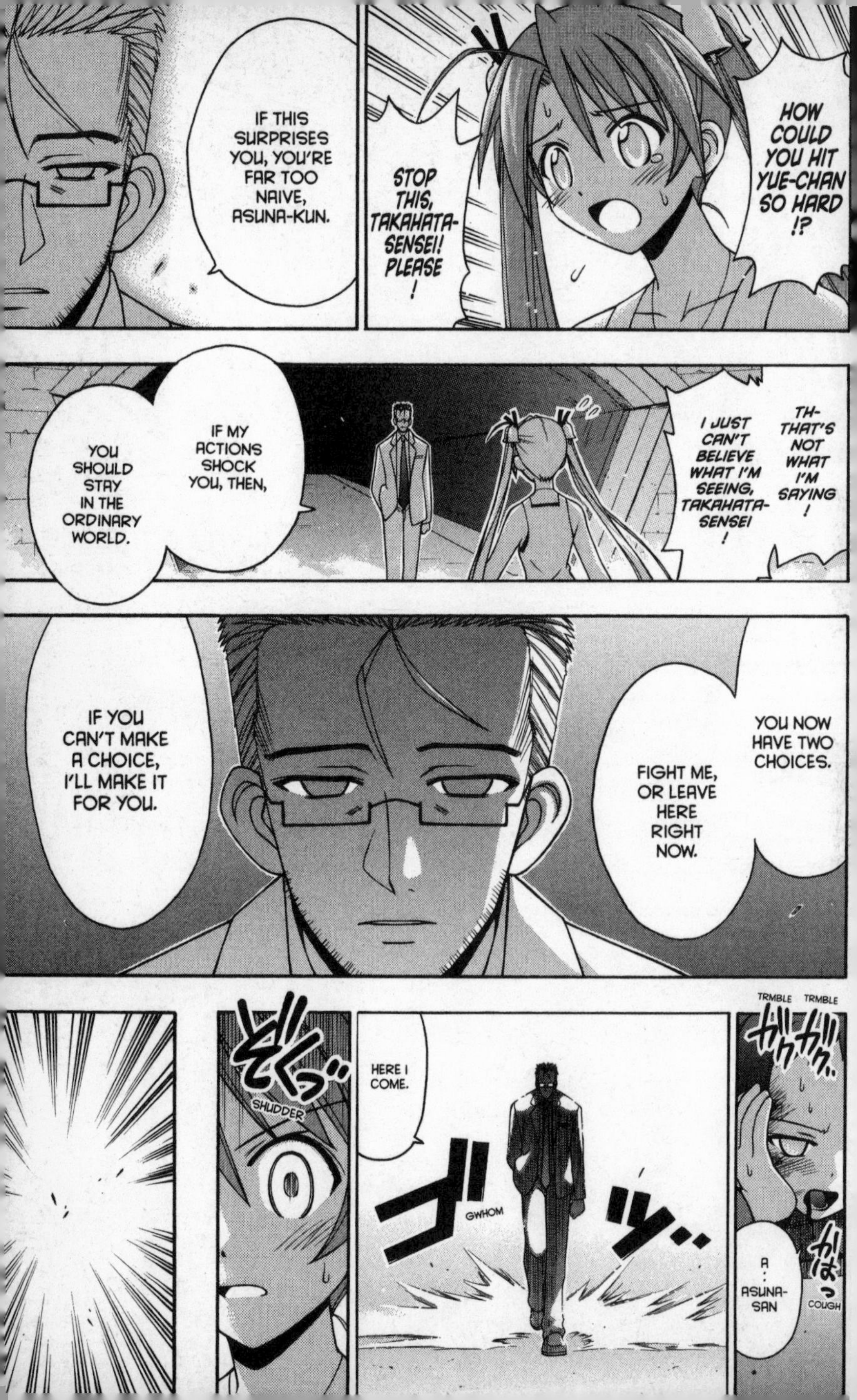
HOW COULD YOU HIT YUE-CHAN SO HARD !?
STOP THIS, TAKAHATA-SENSEI! PLEASE !
IF THIS SURPRISES YOU, YOU'RE FAR TOO NAIVE, ASUNA-KUN.
TH-THAT'S NOT WHAT I'M SAYING !
I JUST CAN'T BELIEVE WHAT I'M SEEING, TAKAHATA-SENSEI !
IF MY ACTIONS SHOCK YOU, THEN,
YOU SHOULD STAY IN THE ORDINARY WORLD.
YOU NOW HAVE TWO CHOICES.
FIGHT ME, OR LEAVE HERE RIGHT NOW.
IF YOU CAN'T MAKE A CHOICE, I'LL MAKE IT FOR YOU.
TRMBLE TRMBLE
A... ASUNA-SAN
COUGH
HERE I COME.
GWHOM
SHUDDER

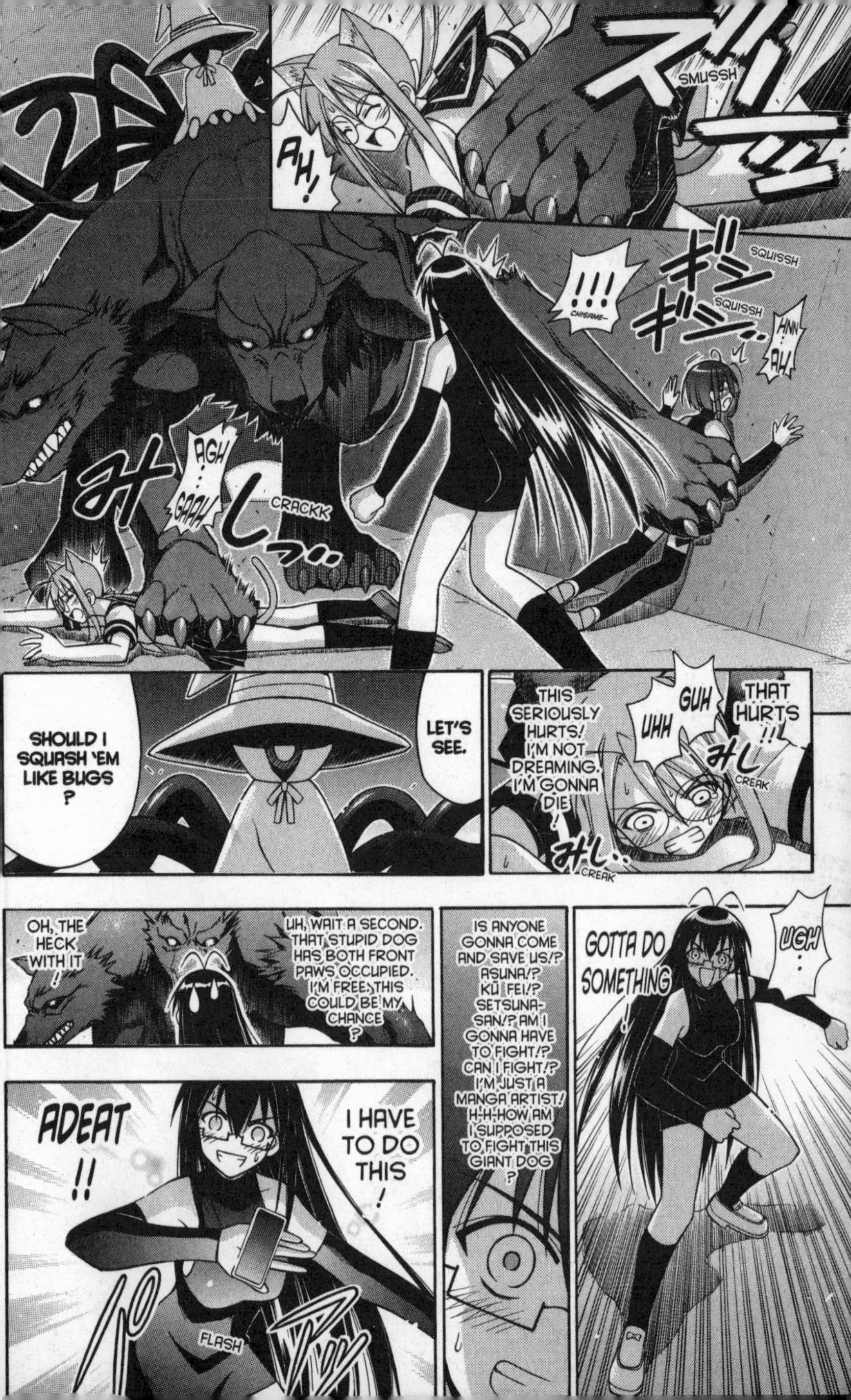
SMUSSH
AH!
SQUISSH
SQUISSH
!!!
CHISAME—
HNN... AH
AGH... GAAH
CRACKK
THAT HURTS!!
GUH
UHH
THIS SERIOUSLY HURTS! I'M NOT DREAMING. I'M GONNA DIE!
みし
CREAK
みし..
CREAK
LET'S SEE.
SHOULD I SQUASH 'EM LIKE BUGS?
UGH...
GOTTA DO SOMETHING!
IS ANYONE GONNA COME AND SAVE US!? ASUNA!? KŪ FEI!? SETSUNA-SAN!? AM I GONNA HAVE TO FIGHT!? CAN I FIGHT!? I'M JUST A MANGA ARTIST! H-H-HOW AM I SUPPOSED TO FIGHT THIS GIANT DOG?
UH, WAIT A SECOND. THAT STUPID DOG HAS BOTH FRONT PAWS OCCUPIED. I'M FREE. THIS COULD BE MY CHANCE?
OH, THE HECK WITH IT!
I HAVE TO DO THIS!
ADEAT!!
FLASH

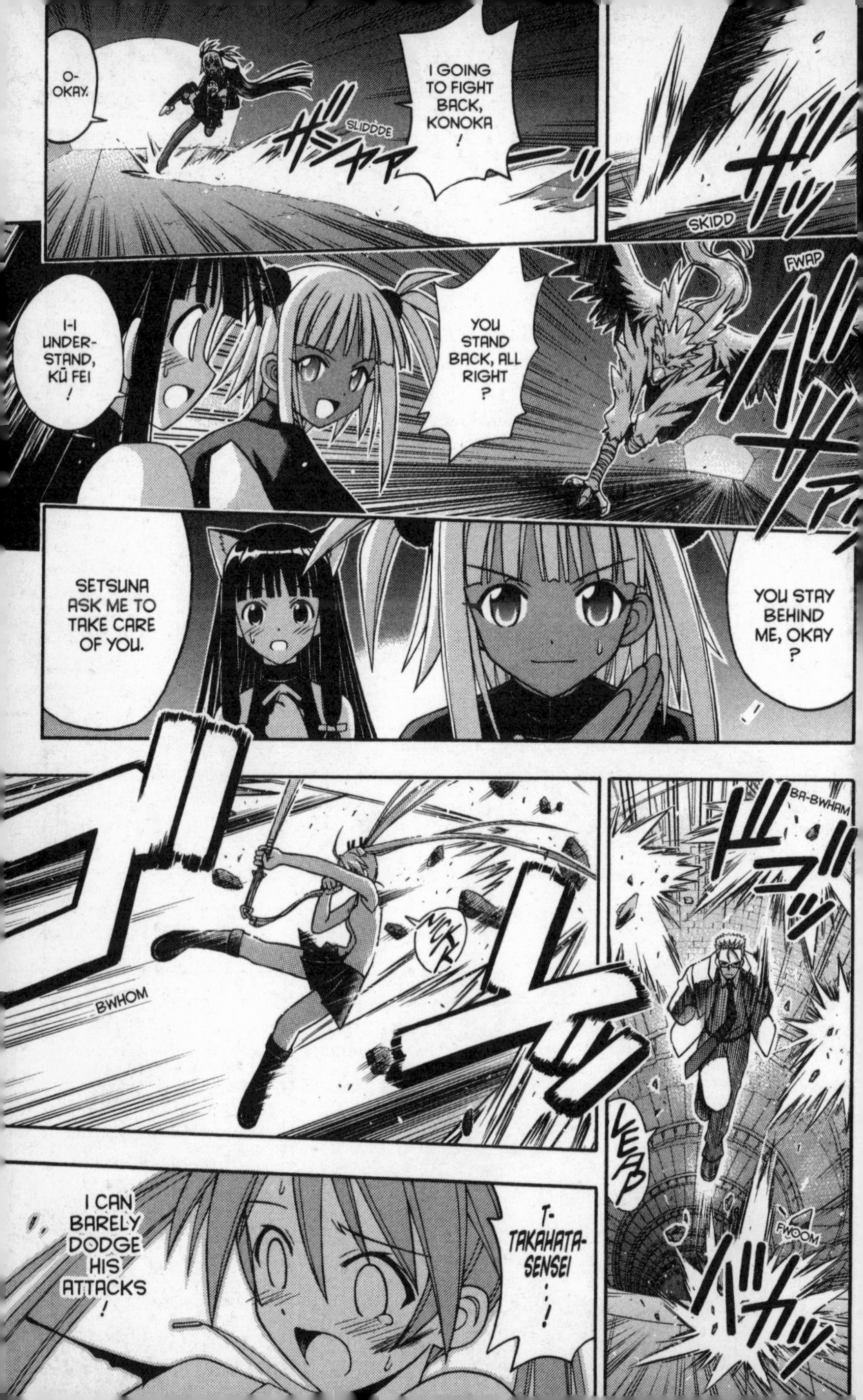
SKIDD
I GOING TO FIGHT BACK, KONOKA!
O-OKAY.
SLIDDDE
FWAP
YOU STAND BACK, ALL RIGHT?
I-I UNDERSTAND, KŪ FEI!
YOU STAY BEHIND ME, OKAY?
SETSUNA ASK ME TO TAKE CARE OF YOU.
BA-BWHAM
LEAP
FWOOM
BWHOM
T-TAKAHATA-SENSEI...!
I CAN BARELY DODGE HIS ATTACKS!

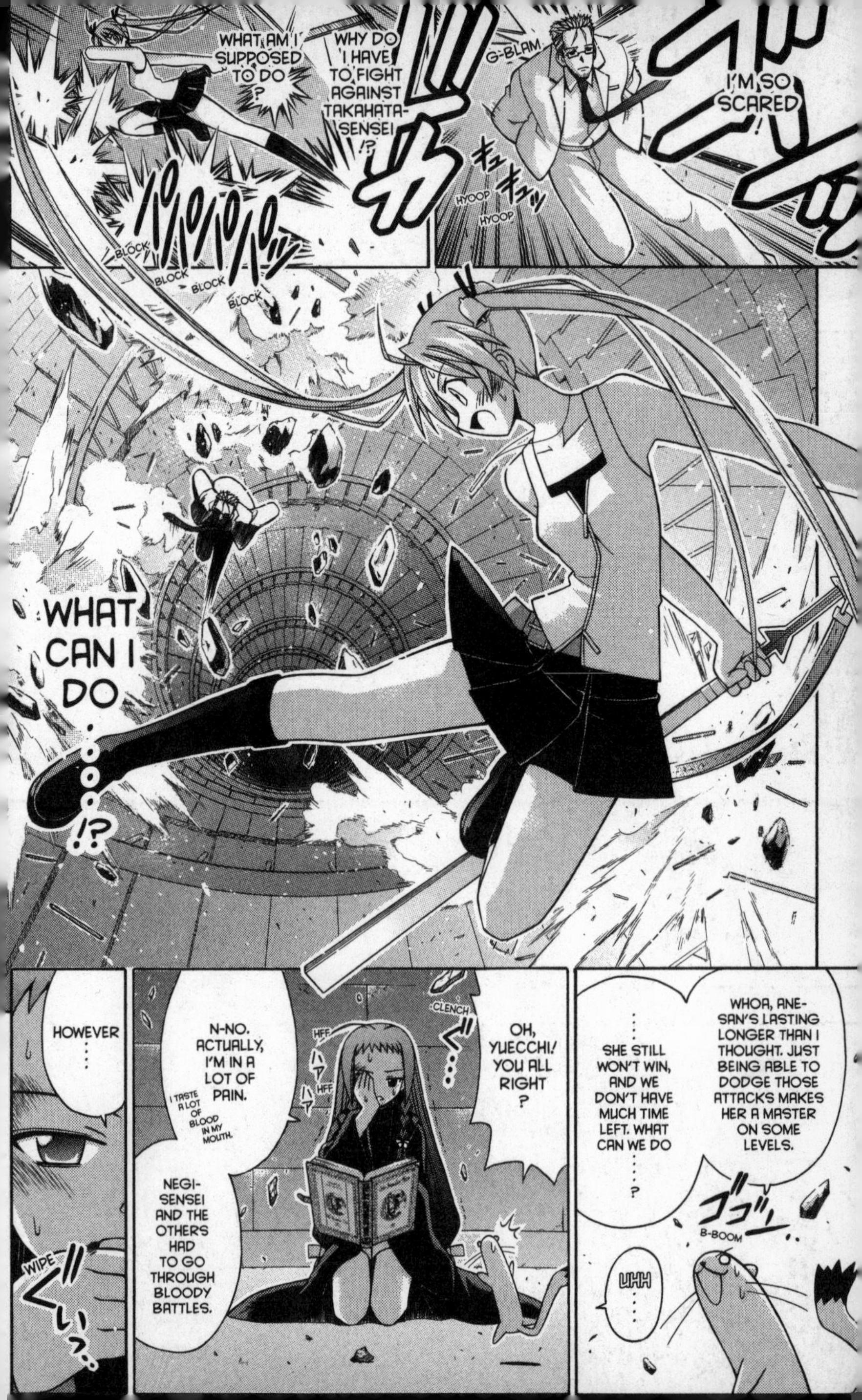
G-BLAM
I'M SO SCARED!
HYOOP
HYOOP
WHY DO I HAVE TO FIGHT AGAINST TAKAHATA-SENSEI!?
WHAT AM I SUPPOSED TO DO?
BLOCK
BLOCK
BLOCK
BLOCK
WHAT CAN I DO......!?
WHOA, ANE-SAN'S LASTING LONGER THAN I THOUGHT. JUST BEING ABLE TO DODGE THOSE ATTACKS MAKES HER A MASTER ON SOME LEVELS.
......SHE STILL WON'T WIN, AND WE DON'T HAVE MUCH TIME LEFT. WHAT CAN WE DO......?
B-BOOM
UHH......
OH, YUECCHI! YOU ALL RIGHT?
CLENCH
HFF
HFF
N-NO. ACTUALLY, I'M IN A LOT OF PAIN.
I TASTE A LOT OF BLOOD IN MY MOUTH.
NEGI-SENSEI AND THE OTHERS HAD TO GO THROUGH BLOODY BATTLES.
HOWEVER......
WIPE

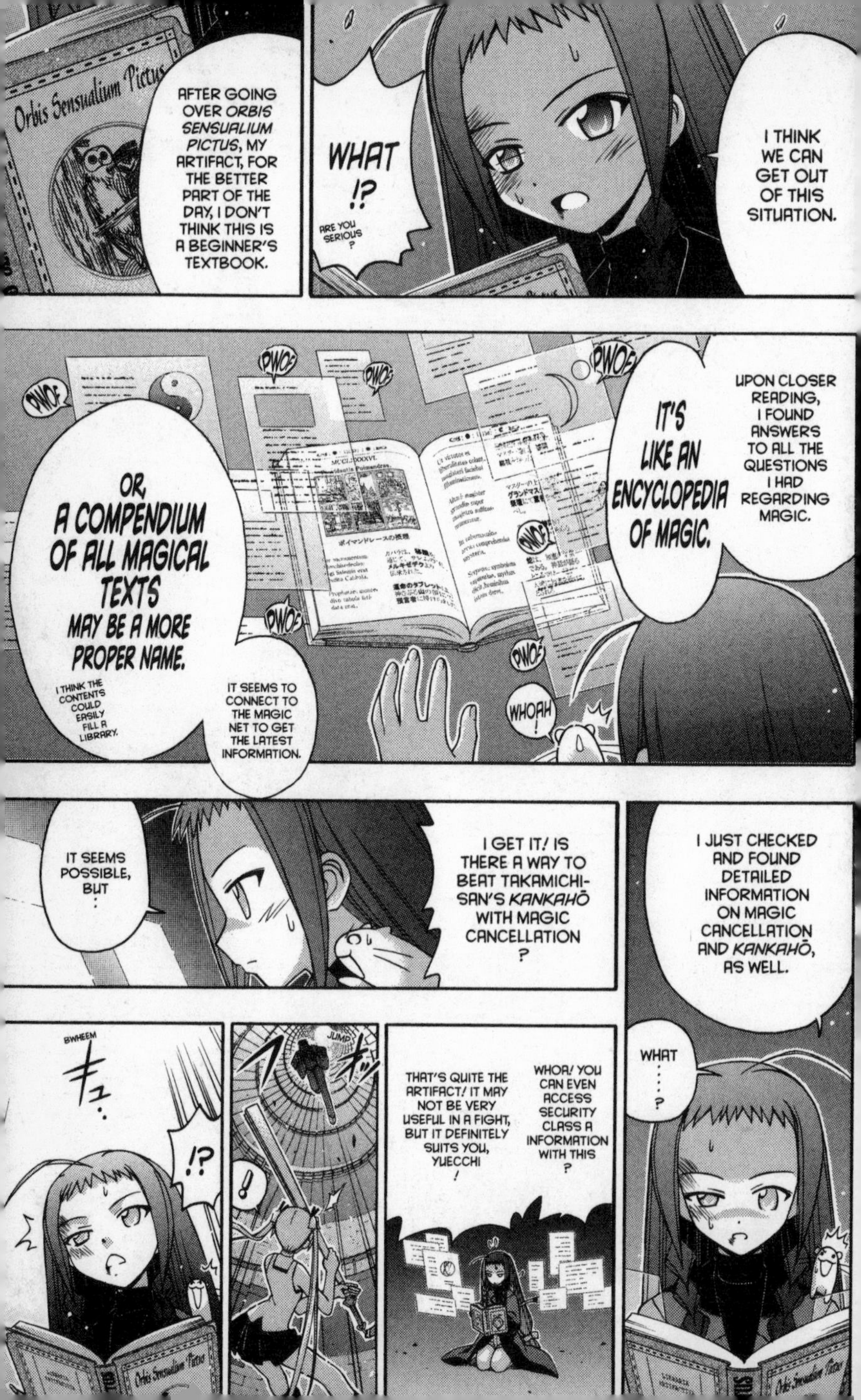
I THINK WE CAN GET OUT OF THIS SITUATION.
WHAT !?
ARE YOU SERIOUS ?
AFTER GOING OVER *ORBIS SENSUALIUM PICTUS*, MY ARTIFACT, FOR THE BETTER PART OF THE DAY, I DON'T THINK THIS IS A BEGINNER'S TEXTBOOK.
Orbis Sensualium Pictus
UPON CLOSER READING, I FOUND ANSWERS TO ALL THE QUESTIONS I HAD REGARDING MAGIC.
IT'S LIKE AN ENCYCLOPEDIA OF MAGIC.
PWOF
PWOF
PWOF
PWOF
OR, A COMPENDIUM OF ALL MAGICAL TEXTS MAY BE A MORE PROPER NAME.
I THINK THE CONTENTS COULD EASILY FILL A LIBRARY.
IT SEEMS TO CONNECT TO THE MAGIC NET TO GET THE LATEST INFORMATION.
PWOF
PWOF
PWOF
WHOAH !
I JUST CHECKED AND FOUND DETAILED INFORMATION ON MAGIC CANCELLATION AND *KANKAHŌ*, AS WELL.
I GET IT! IS THERE A WAY TO BEAT TAKAMICHI-SAN'S *KANKAHŌ* WITH MAGIC CANCELLATION ?
IT SEEMS POSSIBLE, BUT . . .
WHAT . . . . ?
WHOA! YOU CAN EVEN ACCESS SECURITY CLASS A INFORMATION WITH THIS ?
THAT'S QUITE THE ARTIFACT! IT MAY NOT BE VERY USEFUL IN A FIGHT, BUT IT DEFINITELY SUITS YOU, YUECCHI !
JUMP
!
BWHEEM
!?
Orbis Sensualium Pictus

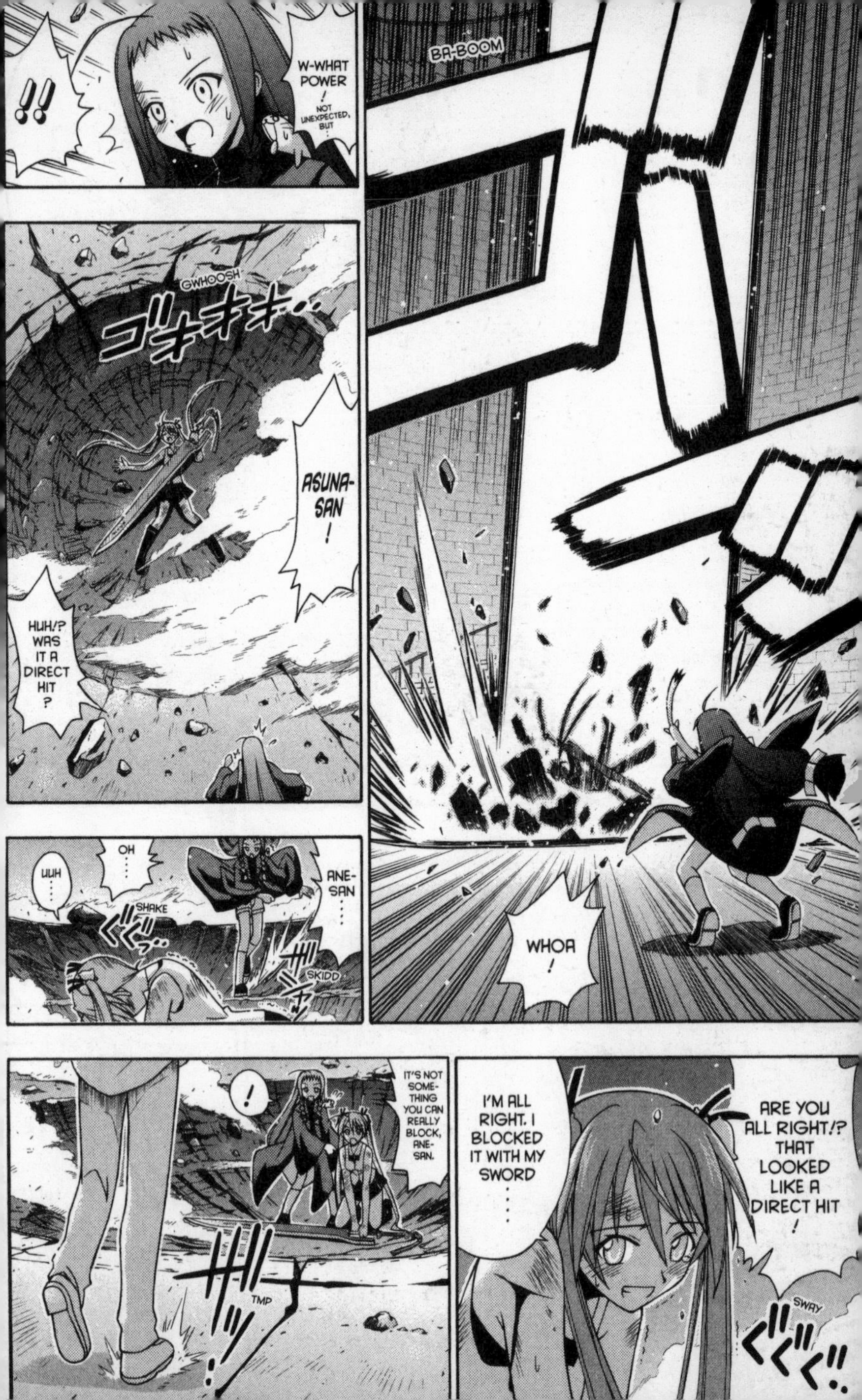

BA-BOOM
WHOA!
W-WHAT POWER!
NOT UNEXPECTED, BUT...
!!
GWHOOSH
ASUNA-SAN!
HUH!? WAS IT A DIRECT HIT?
ANE-SAN...
OH...
UUH...
SHAKE
SKIDD
ARE YOU ALL RIGHT!? THAT LOOKED LIKE A DIRECT HIT!
I'M ALL RIGHT. I BLOCKED IT WITH MY SWORD...
SWAY
IT'S NOT SOMETHING YOU CAN REALLY BLOCK, ANE-SAN.
!
TMP

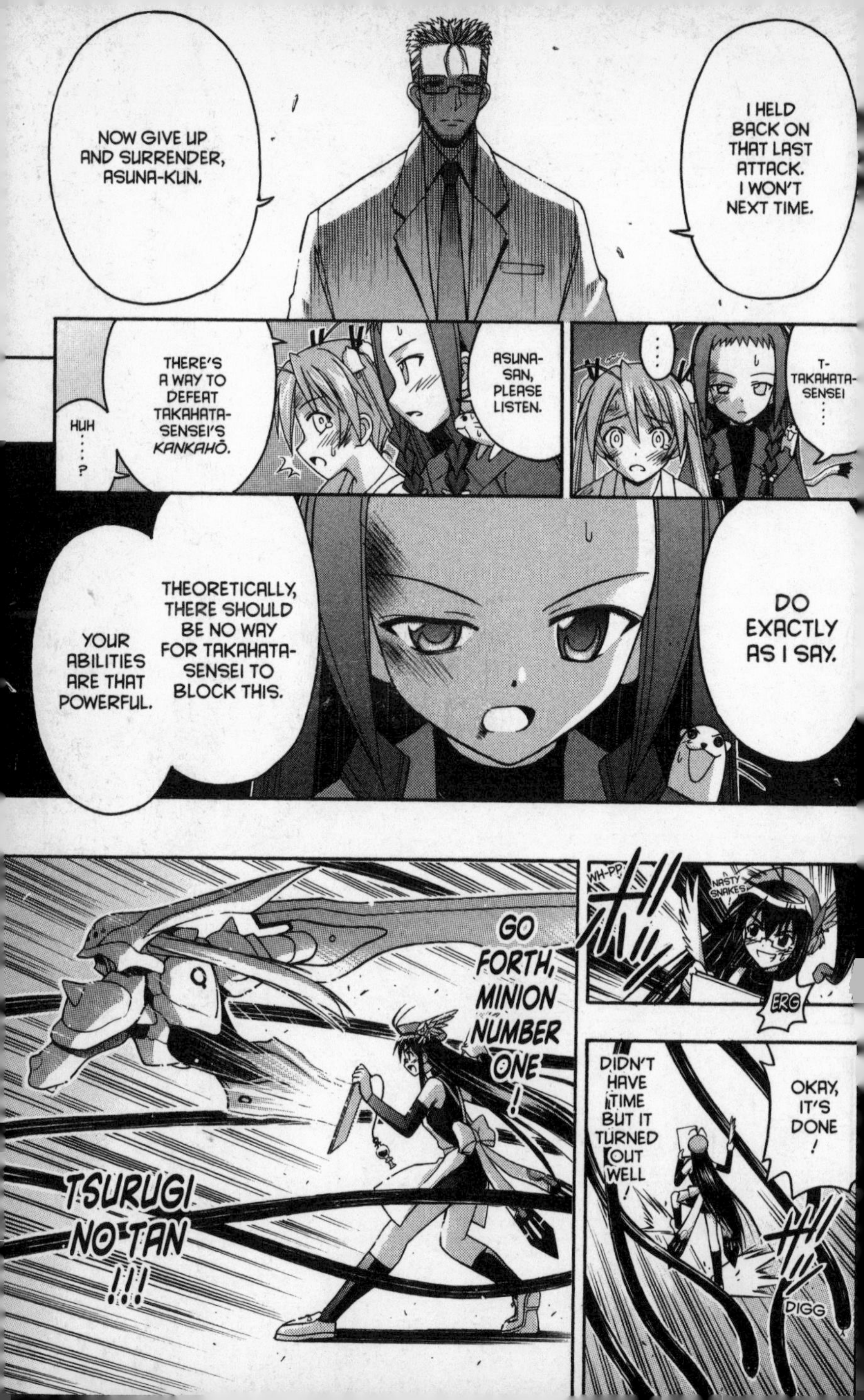
I HELD BACK ON THAT LAST ATTACK. I WON'T NEXT TIME.
NOW GIVE UP AND SURRENDER, ASUNA-KUN.
T-TAKAHATA-SENSEI ....
....
ASUNA-SAN, PLEASE LISTEN.
THERE'S A WAY TO DEFEAT TAKAHATA-SENSEI'S *KANKAHŌ*.
HUH ....?
DO EXACTLY AS I SAY.
THEORETICALLY, THERE SHOULD BE NO WAY FOR TAKAHATA-SENSEI TO BLOCK THIS.
YOUR ABILITIES ARE THAT POWERFUL.
WH-PP
NASTY SNAKES
ERG
OKAY, IT'S DONE!
DIDN'T HAVE TIME BUT IT TURNED OUT WELL!
DIGG
GO FORTH, MINION NUMBER ONE!
TSURUGI NO TAN!!!

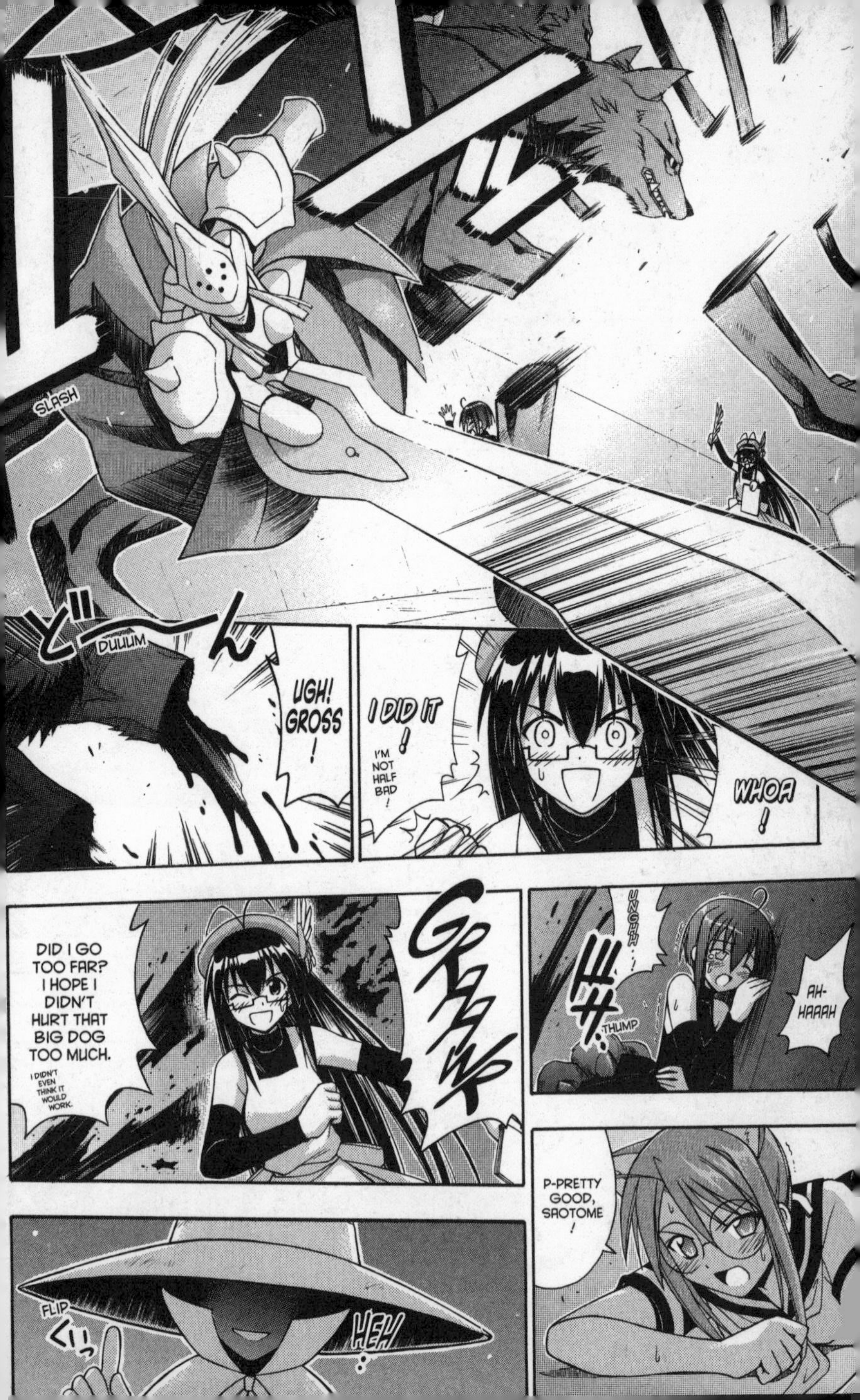
SLASH
WHOA!
I DID IT!
I'M NOT HALF BAD!
UGH! GROSS!
DUUUM
UNGHH...!
THUMP
AH-HAAAH
DID I GO TOO FAR? I HOPE I DIDN'T HURT THAT BIG DOG TOO MUCH.
I DIDN'T EVEN THINK IT WOULD WORK.
P-PRETTY GOOD, SAOTOME!
FLIP
HEH

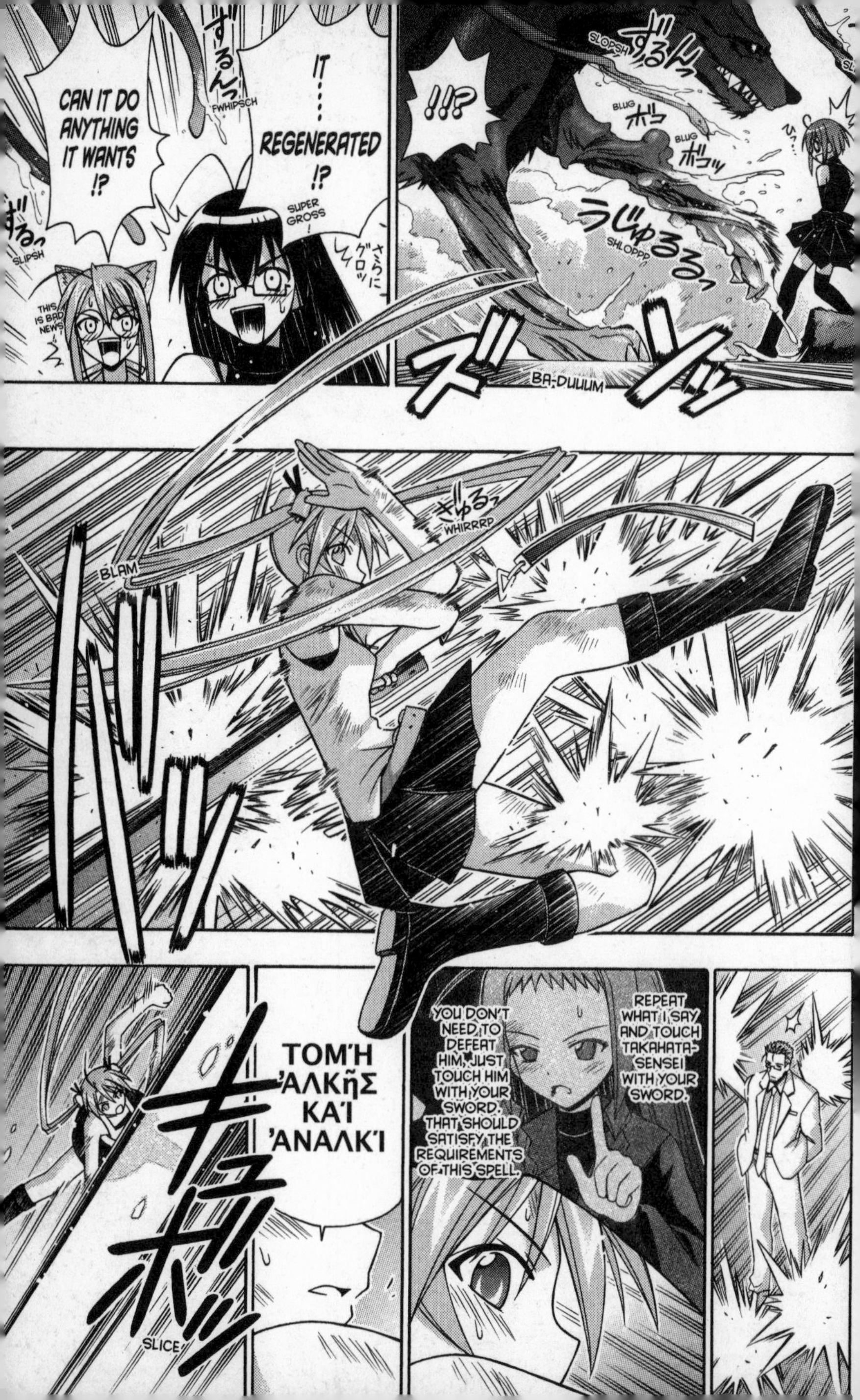
!!?
SLOPSH ずるんっ
BLUG ボコ
BLUG ボコッ
うじゅるるっ
SHLOPPP
BA-DUUUM
IT... REGENERATED!?
SUPER GROSS!
さらにグロッ
ずるんっ
FWHIPSCH
CAN IT DO ANYTHING IT WANTS!?
ずるっ
SLIPSH
THIS IS BAD NEWS
ぎゅるっ
WHIRRRP
BLAM
REPEAT WHAT I SAY AND TOUCH TAKAHATA-SENSEI WITH YOUR SWORD.
YOU DON'T NEED TO DEFEAT HIM, JUST TOUCH HIM WITH YOUR SWORD. THAT SHOULD SATISFY THE REQUIREMENTS OF THIS SPELL.
ΤΟΜ'Η 'ΑΛΚῆΣ ΚΑ'Ι 'ΑΝΑΛΚ'Ι
SLICE

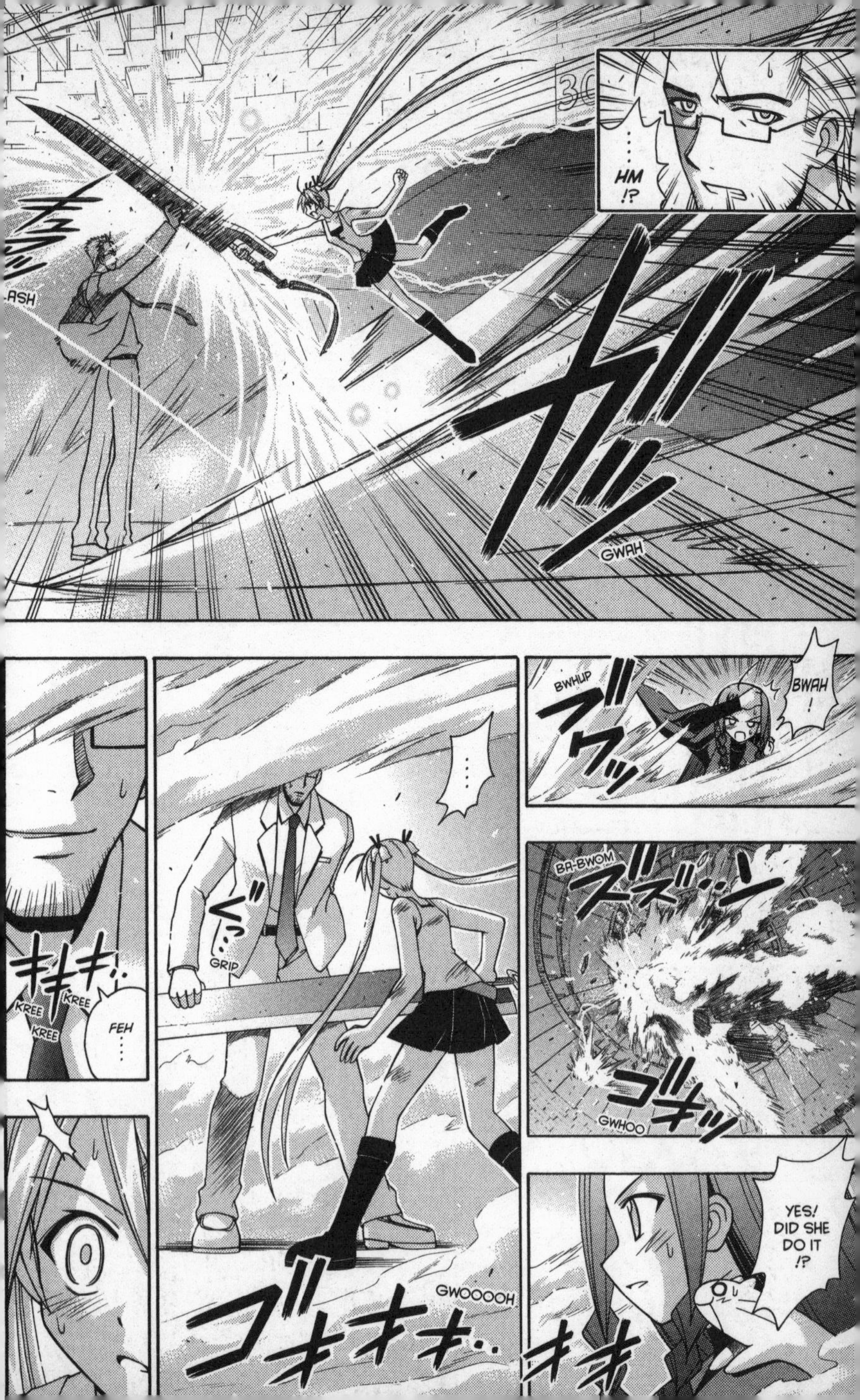

......
HM !?
ASH
GWAH
BWHUP
BWAH !
BA-BWOM
GWHOO
YES! DID SHE DO IT !?
......
GRIP
GWOOOOH
KREE
KREE
KREE
FEH ......

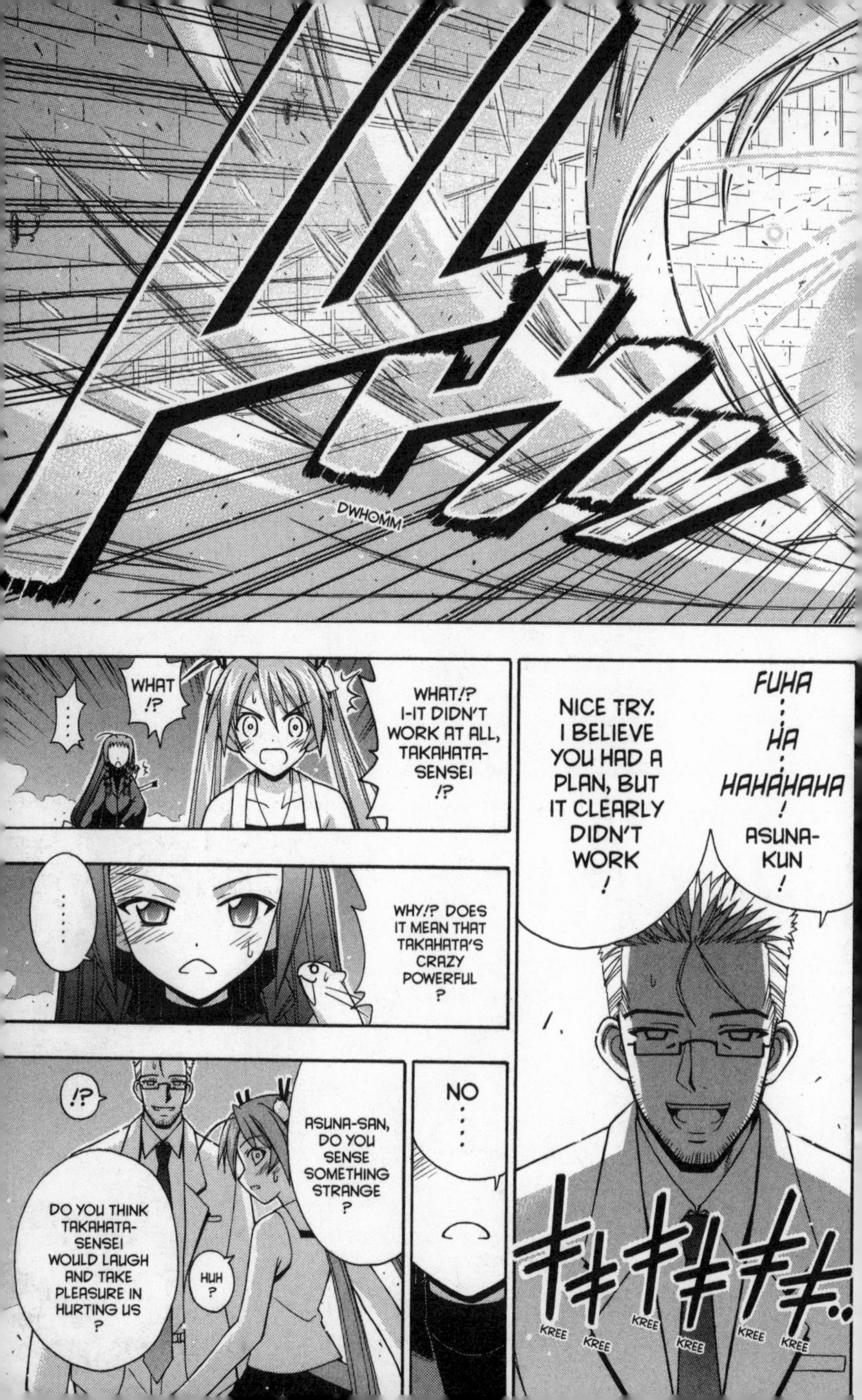
DWHOMM
FUHA... HA... HAHAHAHA! ASUNA-KUN!
NICE TRY. I BELIEVE YOU HAD A PLAN, BUT IT CLEARLY DIDN'T WORK!
KREE KREE KREE KREE KREE KREE
WHAT!? I-IT DIDN'T WORK AT ALL, TAKAHATA-SENSEI!?
WHAT!?
...
WHY!? DOES IT MEAN THAT TAKAHATA'S CRAZY POWERFUL?
......
NO...
ASUNA-SAN, DO YOU SENSE SOMETHING STRANGE?
!?
HUH?
DO YOU THINK TAKAHATA-SENSEI WOULD LAUGH AND TAKE PLEASURE IN HURTING US?

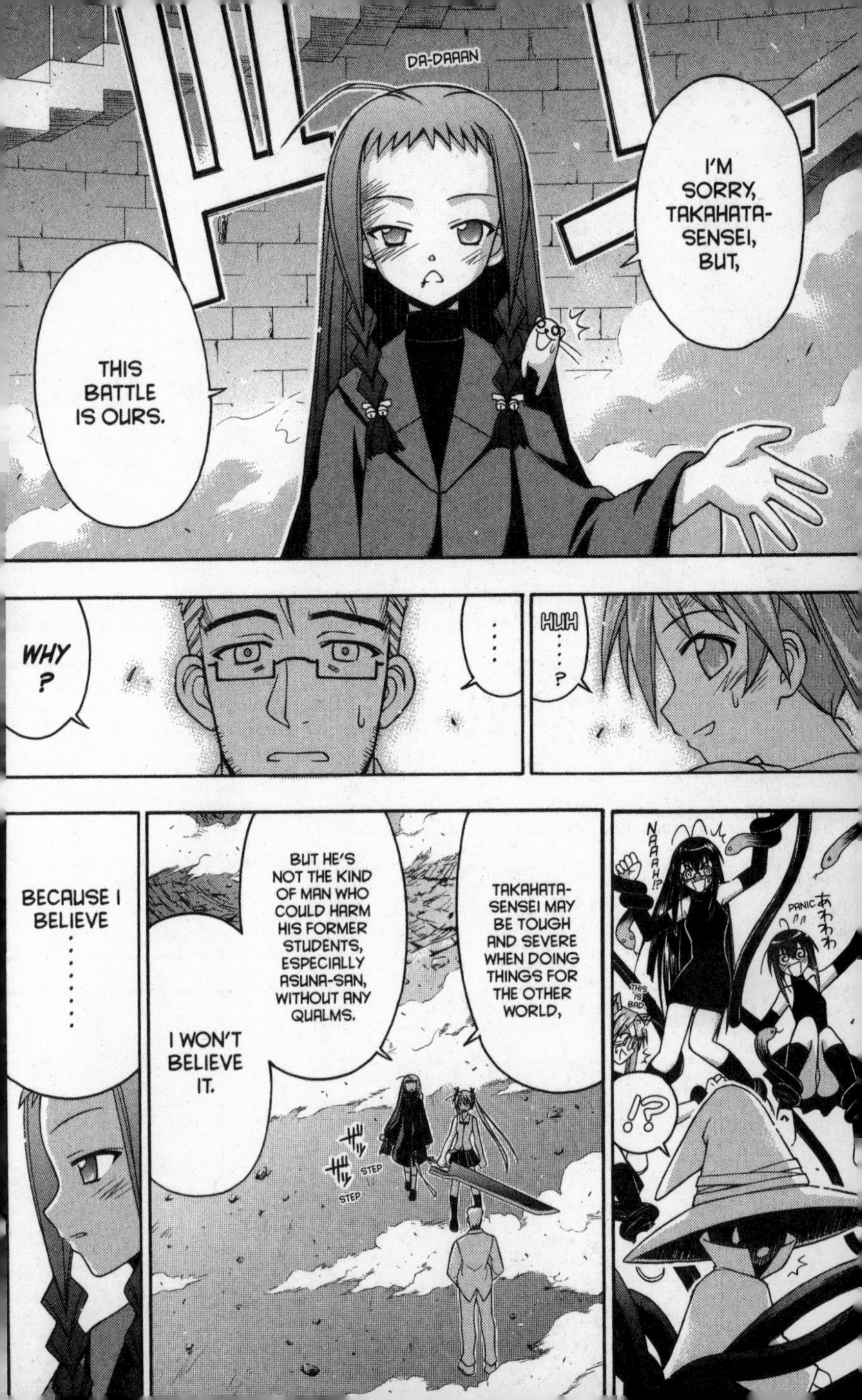
DA-DAAAN
I'M SORRY, TAKAHATA-SENSEI, BUT,
THIS BATTLE IS OURS.
HUH....?
....
WHY?
NAAAAH!?
PANIC あわわわ
THIS IS BAD.
!?
TAKAHATA-SENSEI MAY BE TOUGH AND SEVERE WHEN DOING THINGS FOR THE OTHER WORLD,
BUT HE'S NOT THE KIND OF MAN WHO COULD HARM HIS FORMER STUDENTS, ESPECIALLY ASUNA-SAN, WITHOUT ANY QUALMS.
I WON'T BELIEVE IT.
STEP
STEP
BECAUSE I BELIEVE........

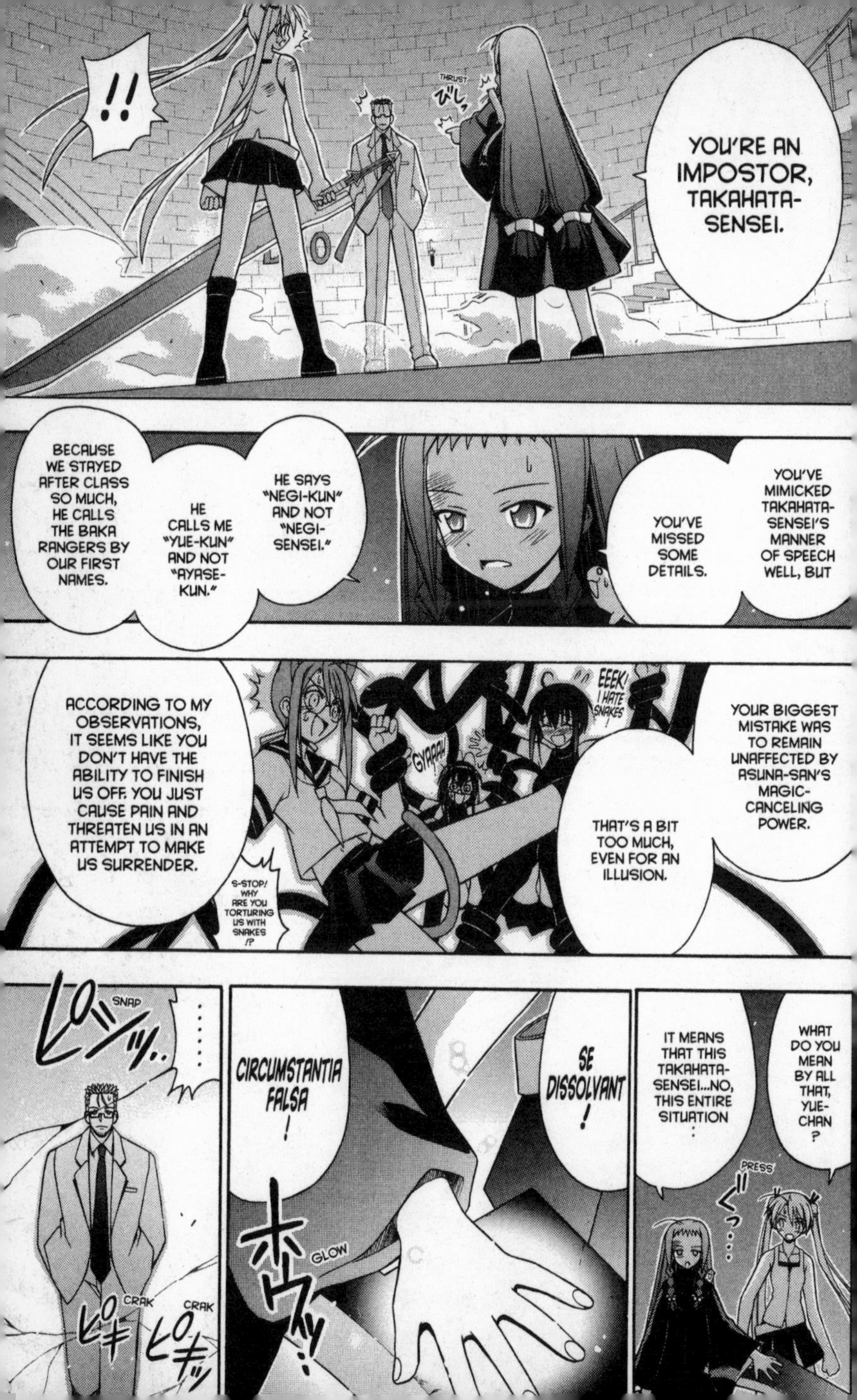
YOU'RE AN IMPOSTOR, TAKAHATA-SENSEI.
THRUST
!!
YOU'VE MIMICKED TAKAHATA-SENSEI'S MANNER OF SPEECH WELL, BUT
YOU'VE MISSED SOME DETAILS.
HE SAYS "NEGI-KUN" AND NOT "NEGI-SENSEI."
HE CALLS ME "YUE-KUN" AND NOT "AYASE-KUN."
BECAUSE WE STAYED AFTER CLASS SO MUCH, HE CALLS THE BAKA RANGERS BY OUR FIRST NAMES.
YOUR BIGGEST MISTAKE WAS TO REMAIN UNAFFECTED BY ASUNA-SAN'S MAGIC-CANCELING POWER.
EEEK! I HATE SNAKES!
THAT'S A BIT TOO MUCH, EVEN FOR AN ILLUSION.
GYAAAH
ACCORDING TO MY OBSERVATIONS, IT SEEMS LIKE YOU DON'T HAVE THE ABILITY TO FINISH US OFF. YOU JUST CAUSE PAIN AND THREATEN US IN AN ATTEMPT TO MAKE US SURRENDER.
S-STOP! WHY ARE YOU TORTURING US WITH SNAKES!?
WHAT DO YOU MEAN BY ALL THAT, YUE-CHAN?
IT MEANS THAT THIS TAKAHATA-SENSEI...NO, THIS ENTIRE SITUATION
PRESS
SE DISSOLVANT!
CIRCUMSTANTIA FALSA!
GLOW
SNAP
......
CRAK
CRAK

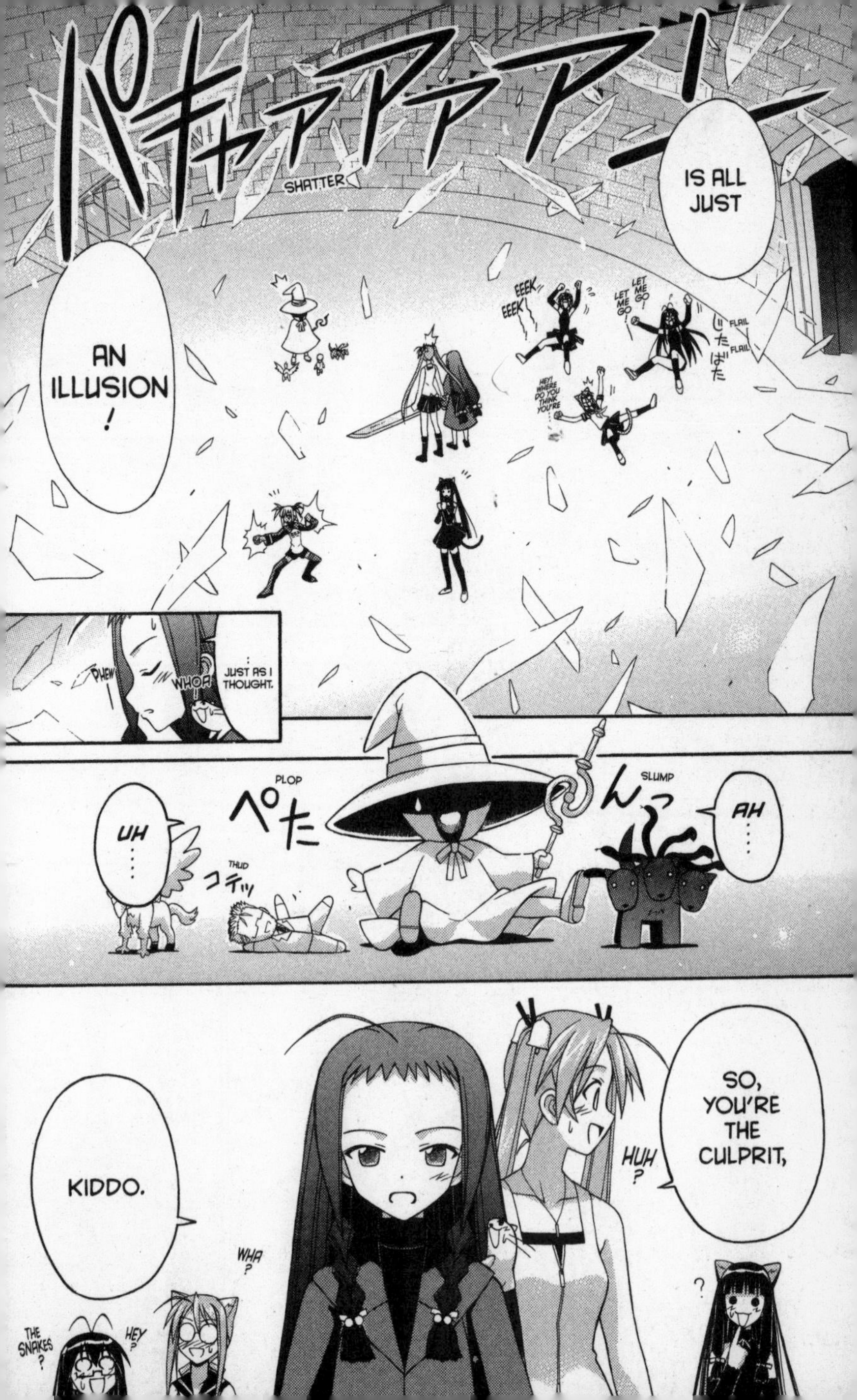
パキャアアアー
SHATTER
IS ALL JUST
AN ILLUSION!
LET ME GO LET ME GO
EEEK EEEK
じたばた
FLAIL FLAIL
HEY! WHERE DO YOU THINK YOU'RE...
...JUST AS I THOUGHT.
WHOA
PHEW
AH...
んっ
SLUMP
ぺた
PLOP
コテッ
THUD
UH...
SO, YOU'RE THE CULPRIT,
HUH?
KIDDO.
?
WHA?
HEY?
THE SNAKES?

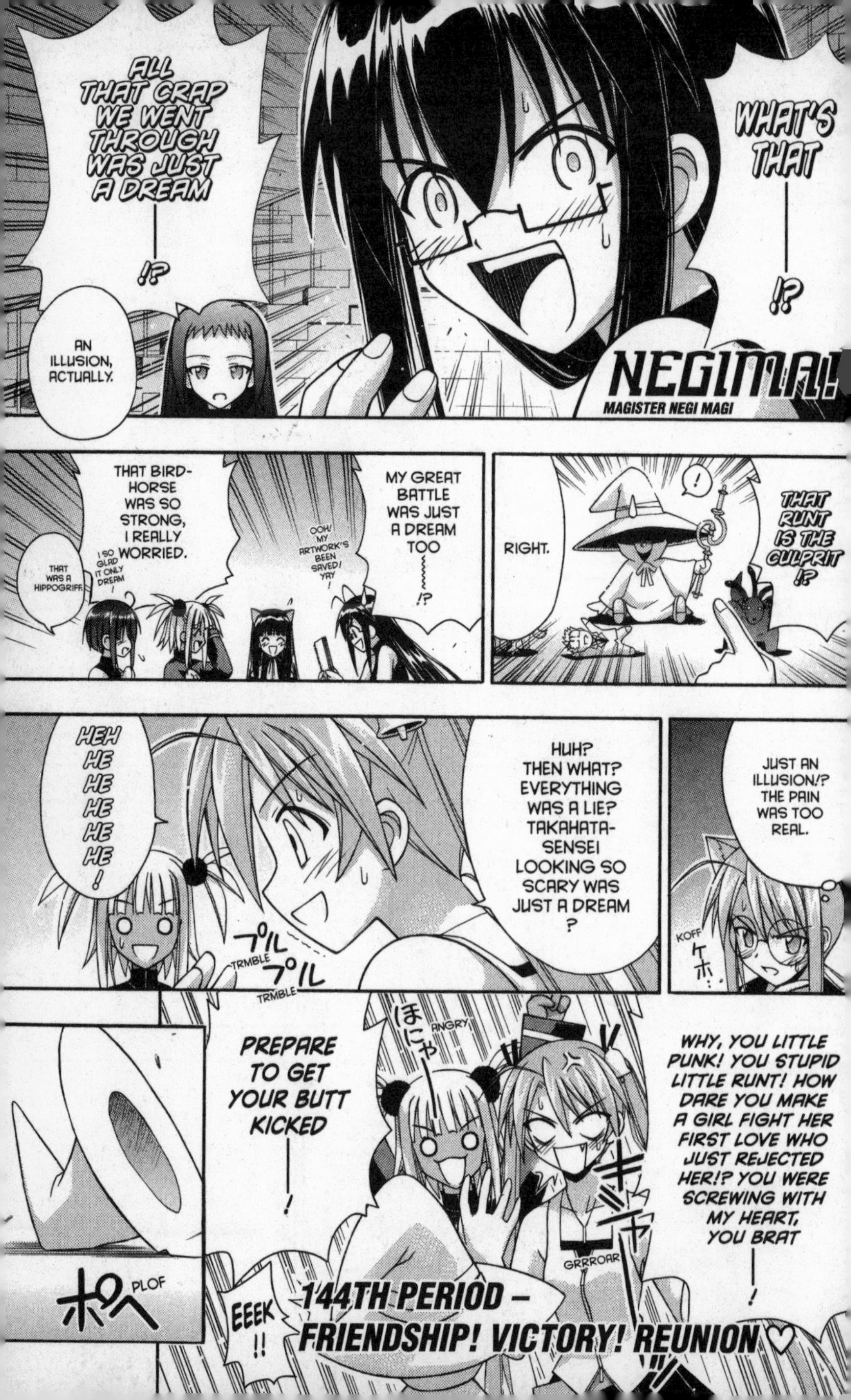
WHAT'S THAT —!?
ALL THAT CRAP WE WENT THROUGH WAS JUST A DREAM —!?
AN ILLUSION, ACTUALLY.
NEGIMA!
MAGISTER NEGI MAGI
THAT RUNT IS THE CULPRIT!?
!
RIGHT.
MY GREAT BATTLE WAS JUST A DREAM TOO ~~~!?
OOH! MY ARTWORK'S BEEN SAVED! YAY!
THAT BIRD-HORSE WAS SO STRONG, I REALLY WORRIED.
I SO GLAD IT ONLY DREAM!
THAT WAS A HIPPOGRIFF.
JUST AN ILLUSION!? THE PAIN WAS TOO REAL.
ケホ… KOFF
HUH? THEN WHAT? EVERYTHING WAS A LIE? TAKAHATA-SENSEI LOOKING SO SCARY WAS JUST A DREAM?
プル TRMBLE プル TRMBLE
HEH HE HE HE HE HE!
WHY, YOU LITTLE PUNK! YOU STUPID LITTLE RUNT! HOW DARE YOU MAKE A GIRL FIGHT HER FIRST LOVE WHO JUST REJECTED HER!? YOU WERE SCREWING WITH MY HEART, YOU BRAT —!
ギャ— GRRROAR
ほにゃ ANGRY
PREPARE TO GET YOUR BUTT KICKED —!
EEEK!!
144TH PERIOD – FRIENDSHIP! VICTORY! REUNION ♡
ポへ PLOF

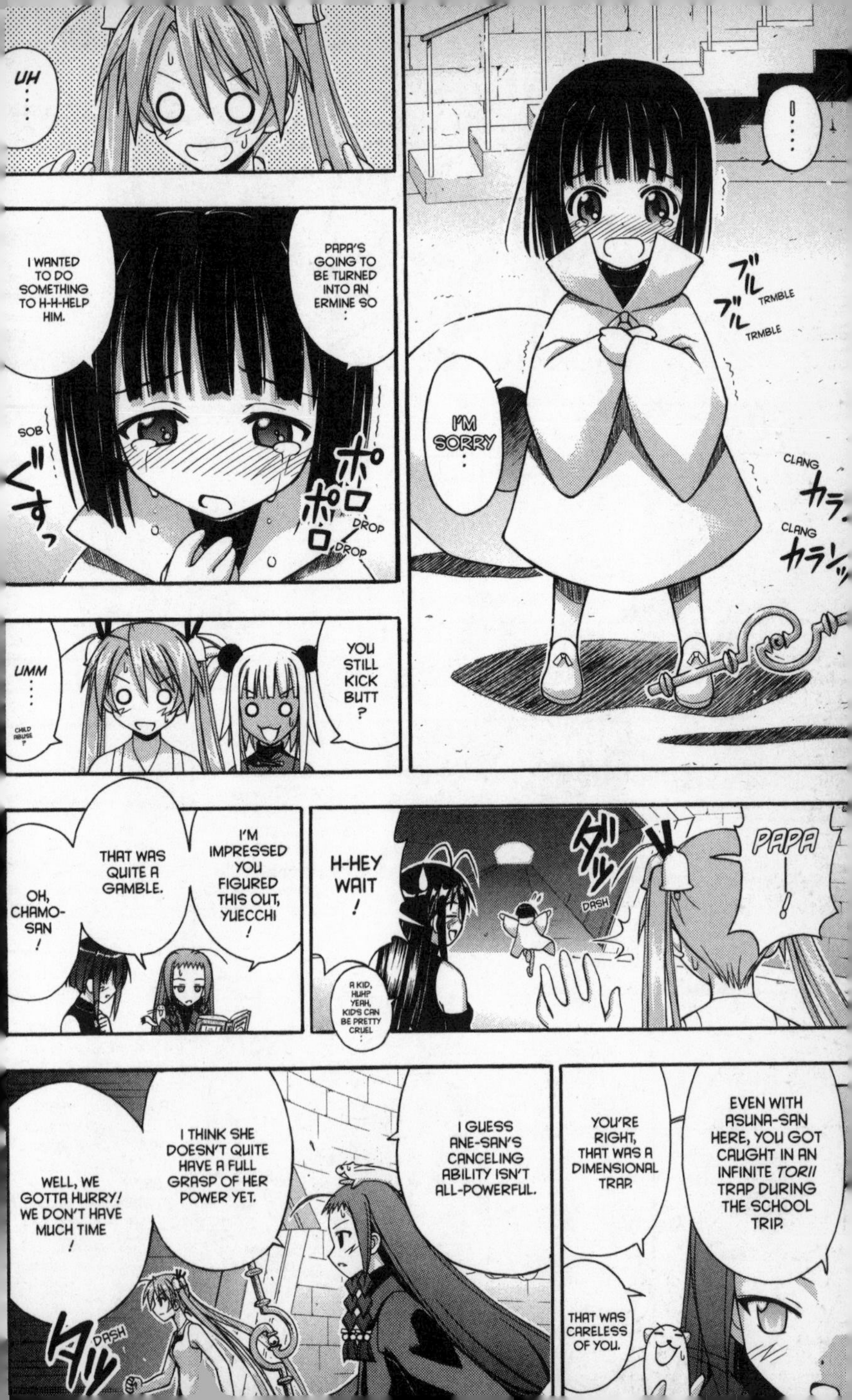
0.....
ブル
TRMBLE
ブル
TRMBLE
I'M SORRY...
CLANG
カラ
CLANG
カランッ
UH.....
PAPA'S GOING TO BE TURNED INTO AN ERMINE SO...
I WANTED TO DO SOMETHING TO H-H-HELP HIM.
SOB
ぐすっ
ポロ
DROP
ポロ
DROP
YOU STILL KICK BUTT?
UMM.....
CHILD ABUSE?
PAPA...!
ダッ
DASH
H-HEY WAIT!
A KID, HUH? YEAH, KID'S CAN BE PRETTY CRUEL...
I'M IMPRESSED YOU FIGURED THIS OUT, YUECCHI!
THAT WAS QUITE A GAMBLE.
OH, CHAMO-SAN!
EVEN WITH ASUNA-SAN HERE, YOU GOT CAUGHT IN AN INFINITE *TORII* TRAP DURING THE SCHOOL TRIP.
YOU'RE RIGHT, THAT WAS A DIMENSIONAL TRAP.
THAT WAS CARELESS OF YOU.
I GUESS ANE-SAN'S CANCELING ABILITY ISN'T ALL-POWERFUL.
I THINK SHE DOESN'T QUITE HAVE A FULL GRASP OF HER POWER YET.
WELL, WE GOTTA HURRY! WE DON'T HAVE MUCH TIME!
ダッ
DASH

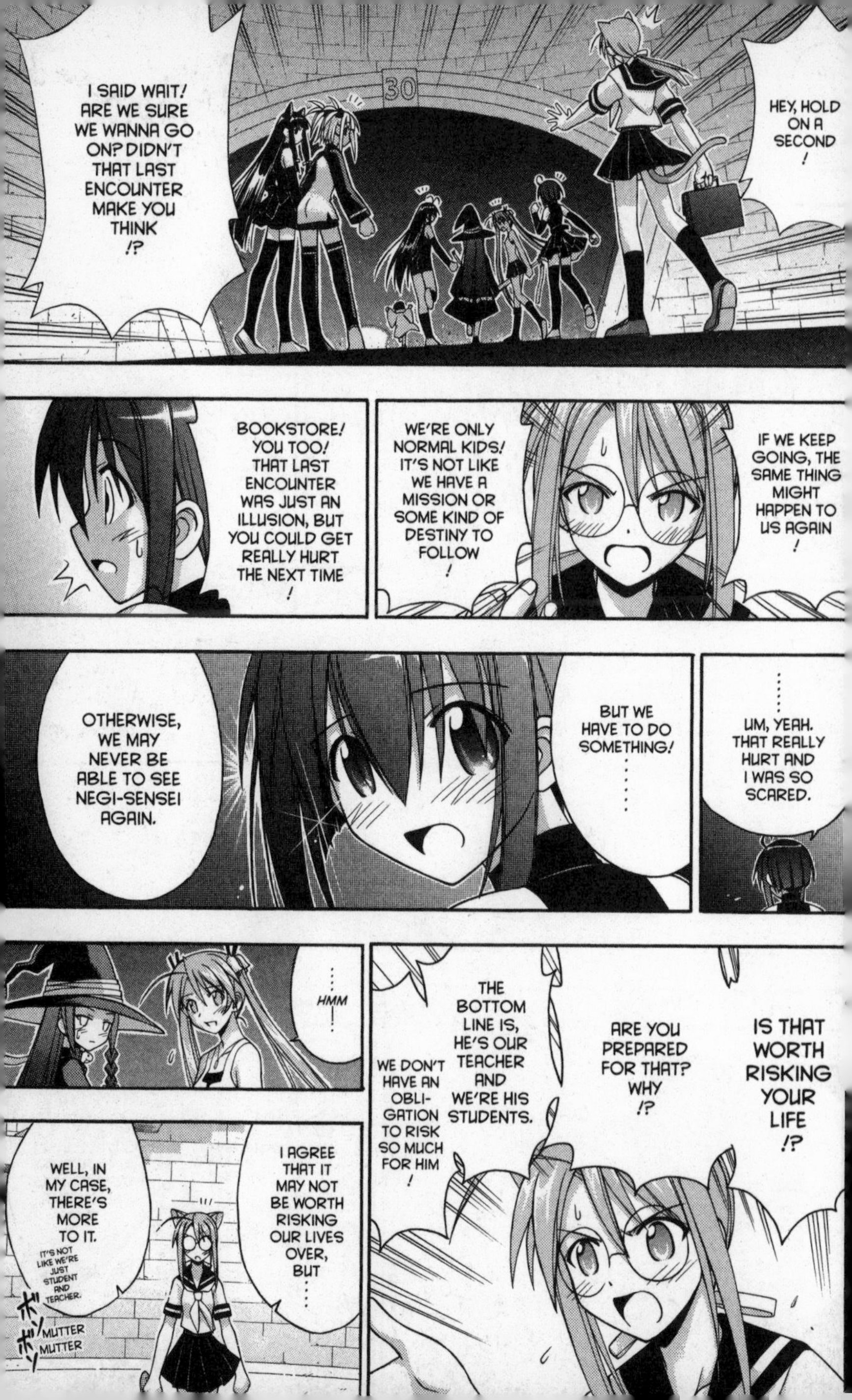
30
HEY, HOLD ON A SECOND!
I SAID WAIT! ARE WE SURE WE WANNA GO ON? DIDN'T THAT LAST ENCOUNTER MAKE YOU THINK!?
IF WE KEEP GOING, THE SAME THING MIGHT HAPPEN TO US AGAIN!
WE'RE ONLY NORMAL KIDS! IT'S NOT LIKE WE HAVE A MISSION OR SOME KIND OF DESTINY TO FOLLOW!
BOOKSTORE! YOU TOO! THAT LAST ENCOUNTER WAS JUST AN ILLUSION, BUT YOU COULD GET REALLY HURT THE NEXT TIME!
...... UM, YEAH. THAT REALLY HURT AND I WAS SO SCARED.
BUT WE HAVE TO DO SOMETHING! ......
OTHERWISE, WE MAY NEVER BE ABLE TO SEE NEGI-SENSEI AGAIN.
IS THAT WORTH RISKING YOUR LIFE!?
ARE YOU PREPARED FOR THAT? WHY!?
THE BOTTOM LINE IS, HE'S OUR TEACHER AND WE'RE HIS STUDENTS.
WE DON'T HAVE AN OBLIGATION TO RISK SO MUCH FOR HIM!
...HMM!
I AGREE THAT IT MAY NOT BE WORTH RISKING OUR LIVES OVER, BUT....
WELL, IN MY CASE, THERE'S MORE TO IT.
IT'S NOT LIKE WE'RE JUST STUDENT AND TEACHER.
ボソ MUTTER
ボソ MUTTER

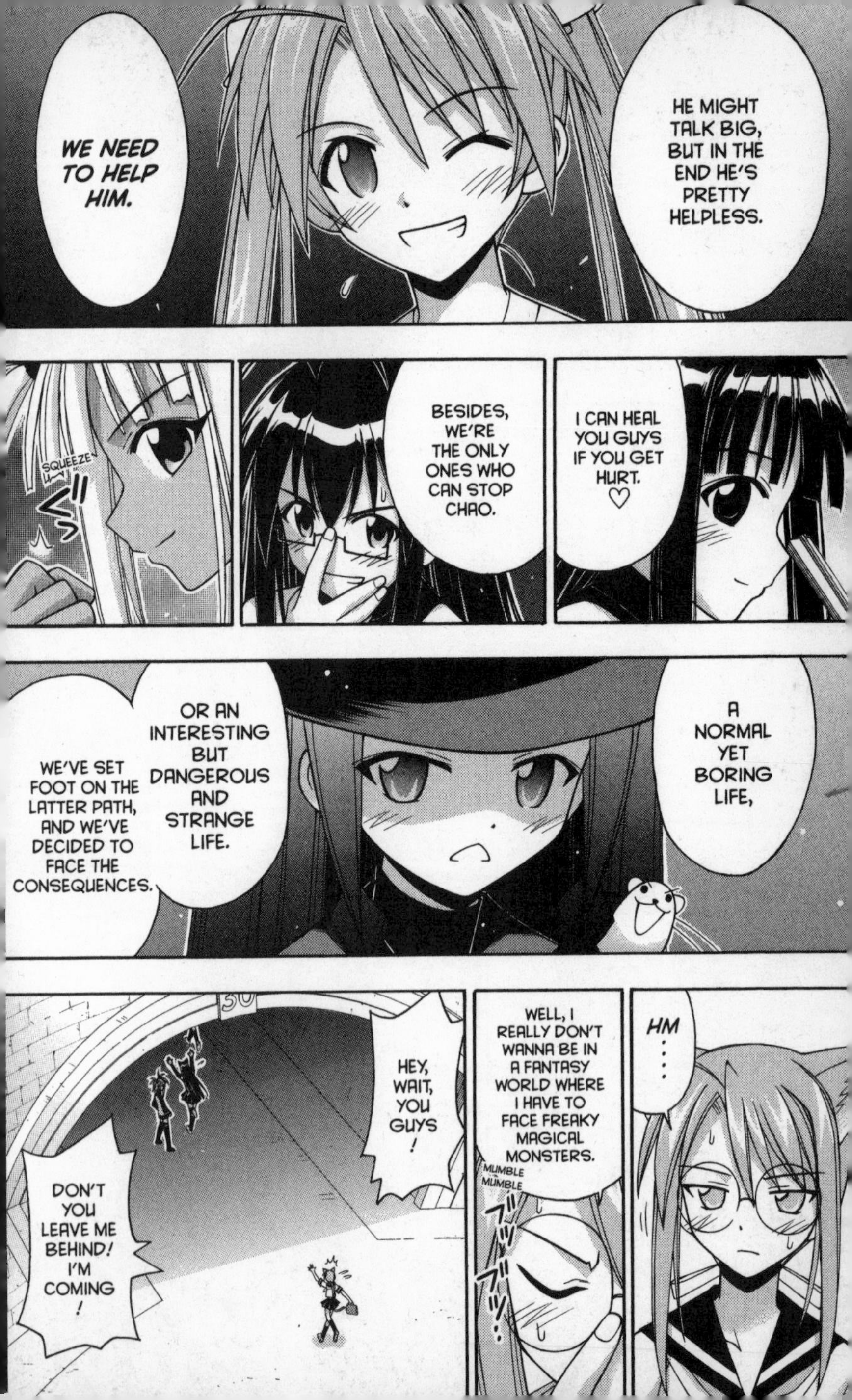
HE MIGHT TALK BIG, BUT IN THE END HE'S PRETTY HELPLESS.
WE NEED TO HELP HIM.
I CAN HEAL YOU GUYS IF YOU GET HURT. ♡
BESIDES, WE'RE THE ONLY ONES WHO CAN STOP CHAO.
SQUEEZE
A NORMAL YET BORING LIFE,
OR AN INTERESTING BUT DANGEROUS AND STRANGE LIFE.
WE'VE SET FOOT ON THE LATTER PATH, AND WE'VE DECIDED TO FACE THE CONSEQUENCES.
HM ....
WELL, I REALLY DON'T WANNA BE IN A FANTASY WORLD WHERE I HAVE TO FACE FREAKY MAGICAL MONSTERS.
MUMBLE MUMBLE
30
HEY, WAIT, YOU GUYS!
DON'T YOU LEAVE ME BEHIND! I'M COMING!

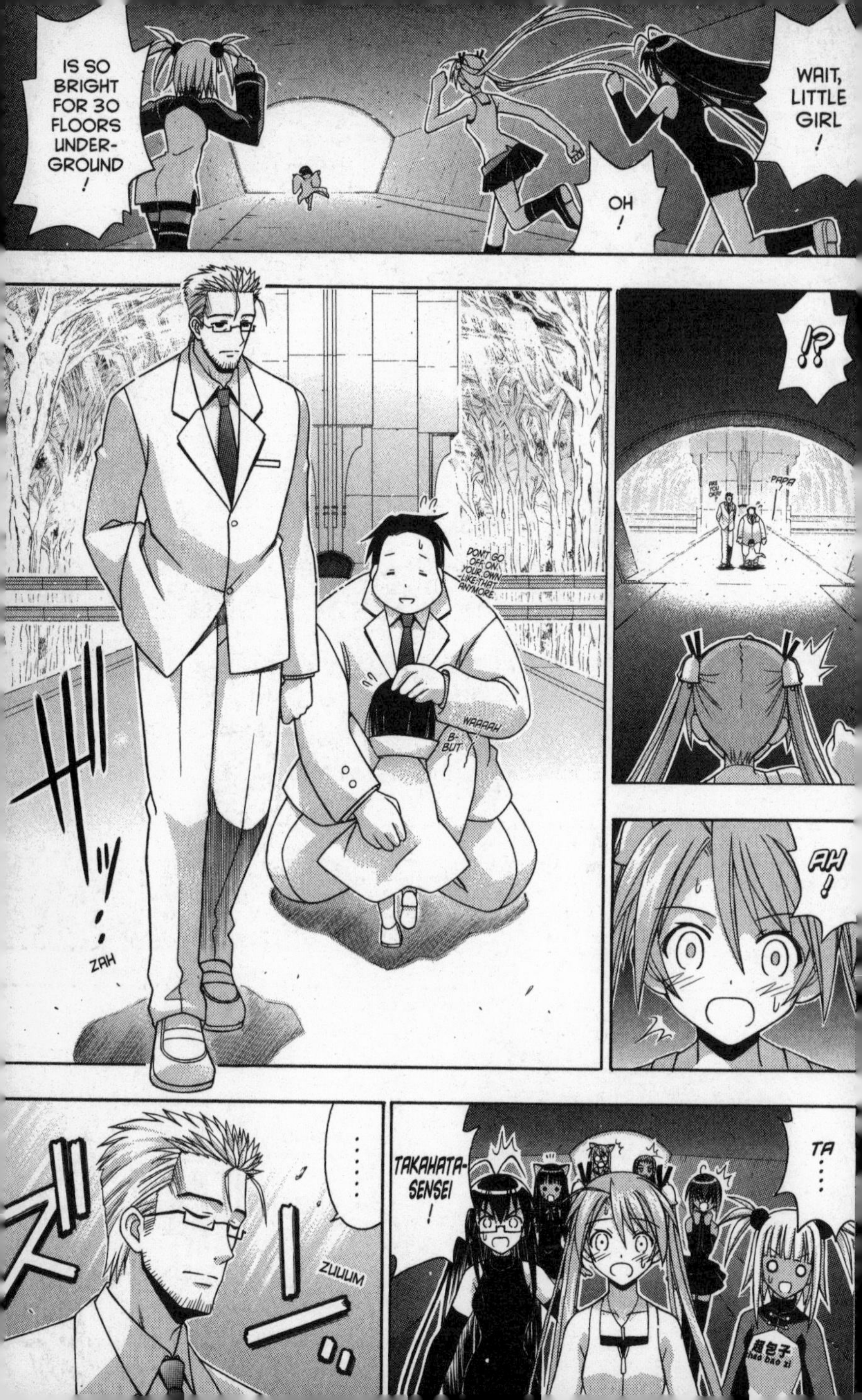
WAIT, LITTLE GIRL!
OH!
IS SO BRIGHT FOR 30 FLOORS UNDER-GROUND!
!?
PAPA!
ARE YOU OKAY?
AH!
DON'T GO OFF ON YOUR OWN LIKE THAT ANYMORE.
WAAAAH
B-BUT
ZAH
TA.....
TAKAHATA-SENSEI!
......
ZUUUM

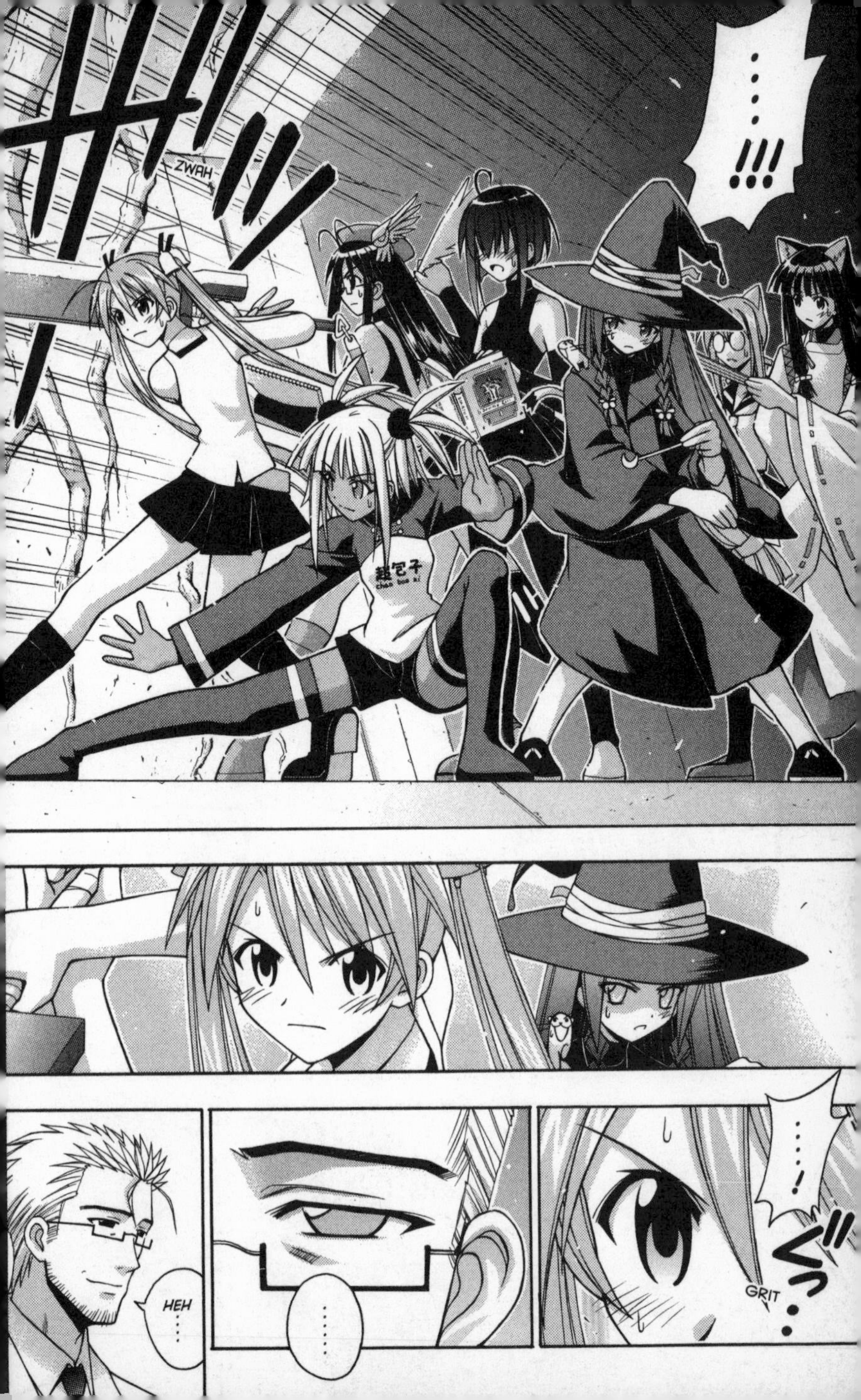

...!!!
ZWAH
超包子
chao bao zi
...!
GRIT
......
HEH...

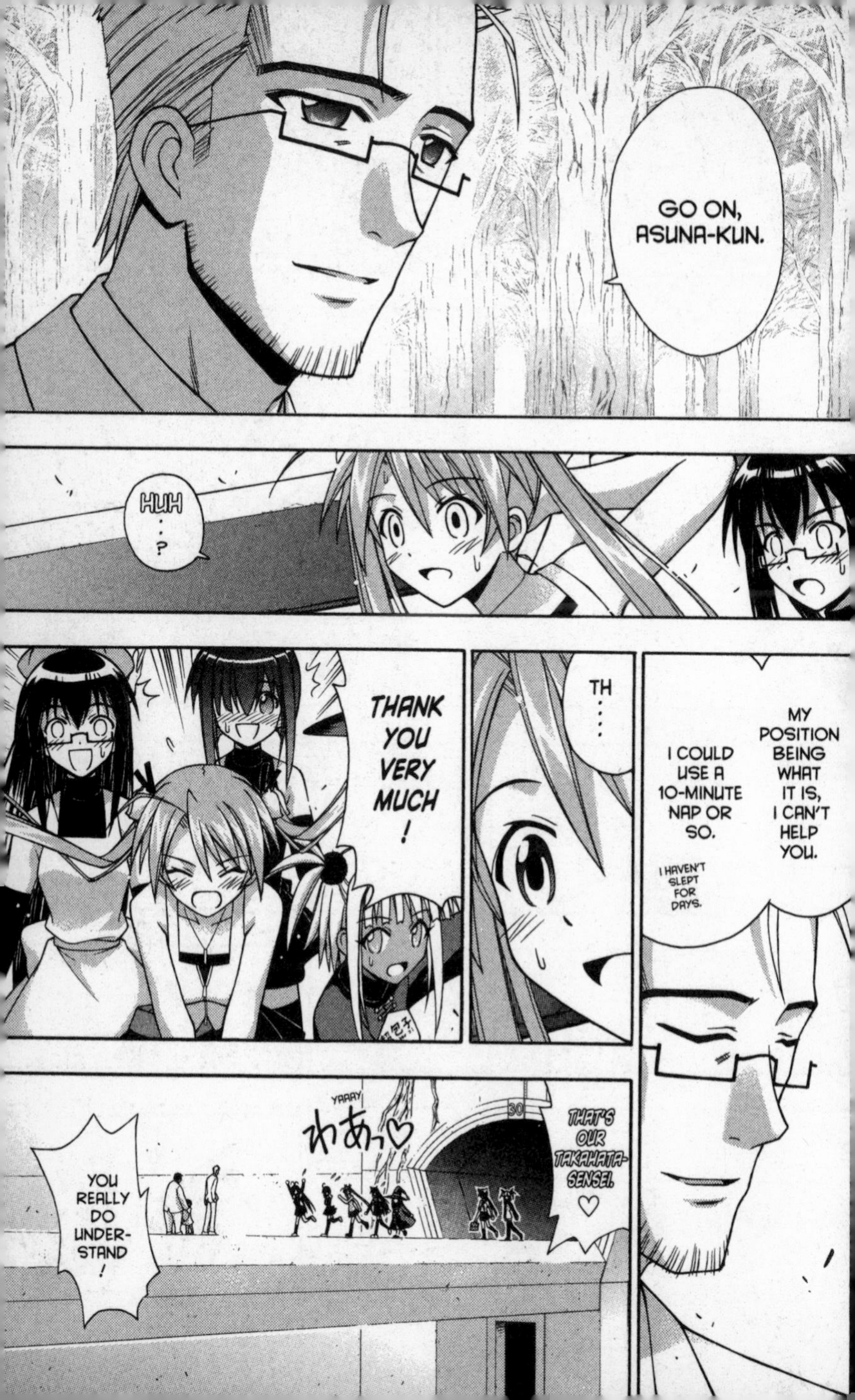
GO ON, ASUNA-KUN.
HUH...?
MY POSITION BEING WHAT IT IS, I CAN'T HELP YOU.
I COULD USE A 10-MINUTE NAP OR SO.
I HAVEN'T SLEPT FOR DAYS.
TH...
THANK YOU VERY MUCH!
THAT'S OUR TAKAHATA-SENSEI. ♡
30
YAAAY
わあっ♡
YOU REALLY DO UNDER-STAND!

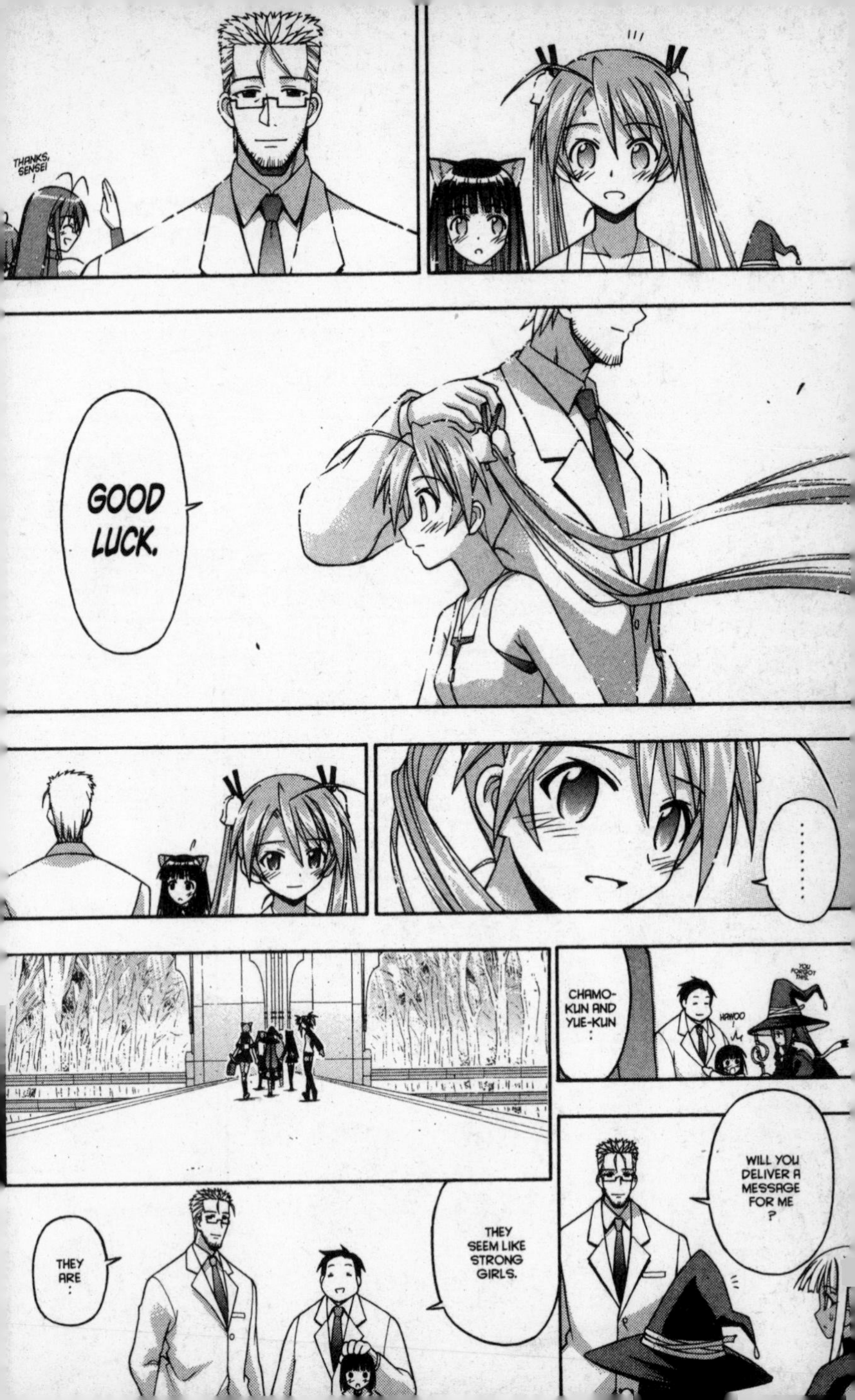
THANKS, SENSEI!
GOOD LUCK.
....
CHAMO-KUN AND YUE-KUN...
YOU FORGOT THIS.
HAWOO!
WILL YOU DELIVER A MESSAGE FOR ME?
THEY SEEM LIKE STRONG GIRLS.
THEY ARE...

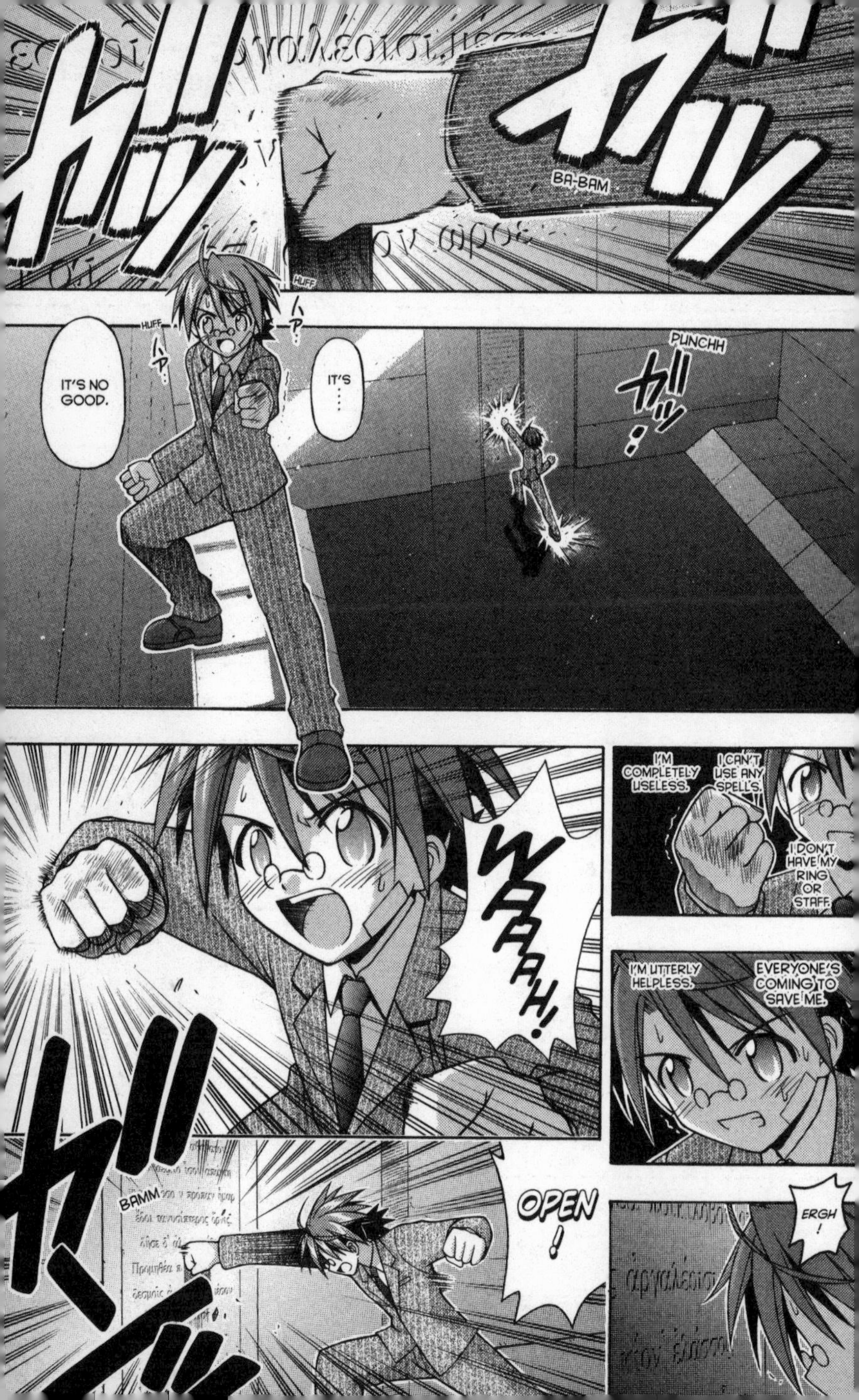
BA-BAM
HUFF
PUNCHH
IT'S ....
HUFF
IT'S NO GOOD.
I CAN'T USE ANY SPELLS.
I'M COMPLETELY USELESS.
I DON'T HAVE MY RING OR STAFF.
EVERYONE'S COMING TO SAVE ME.
I'M UTTERLY HELPLESS.
WAAAH!
ERGH!
OPEN!
BAMM

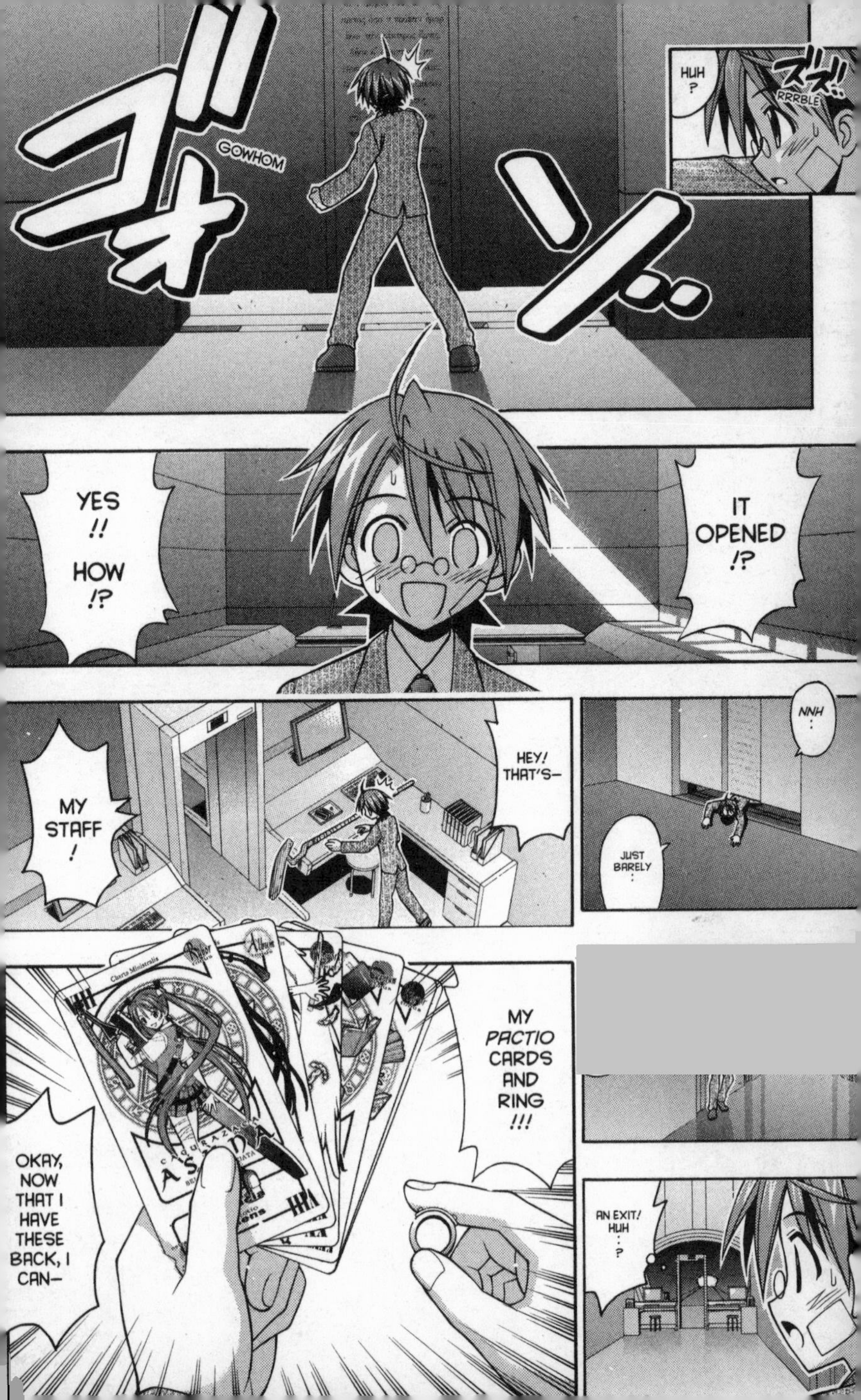
HUH ?
ズズ!!
RRRBLE
ゴォン‥
GOWHOM
IT OPENED !?
YES !! HOW !?
NNH . .
JUST BARELY . .
HEY! THAT'S—
MY STAFF !
AN EXIT! HUH . . ?
MY PACTIO CARDS AND RING !!!
OKAY, NOW THAT I HAVE THESE BACK, I CAN—

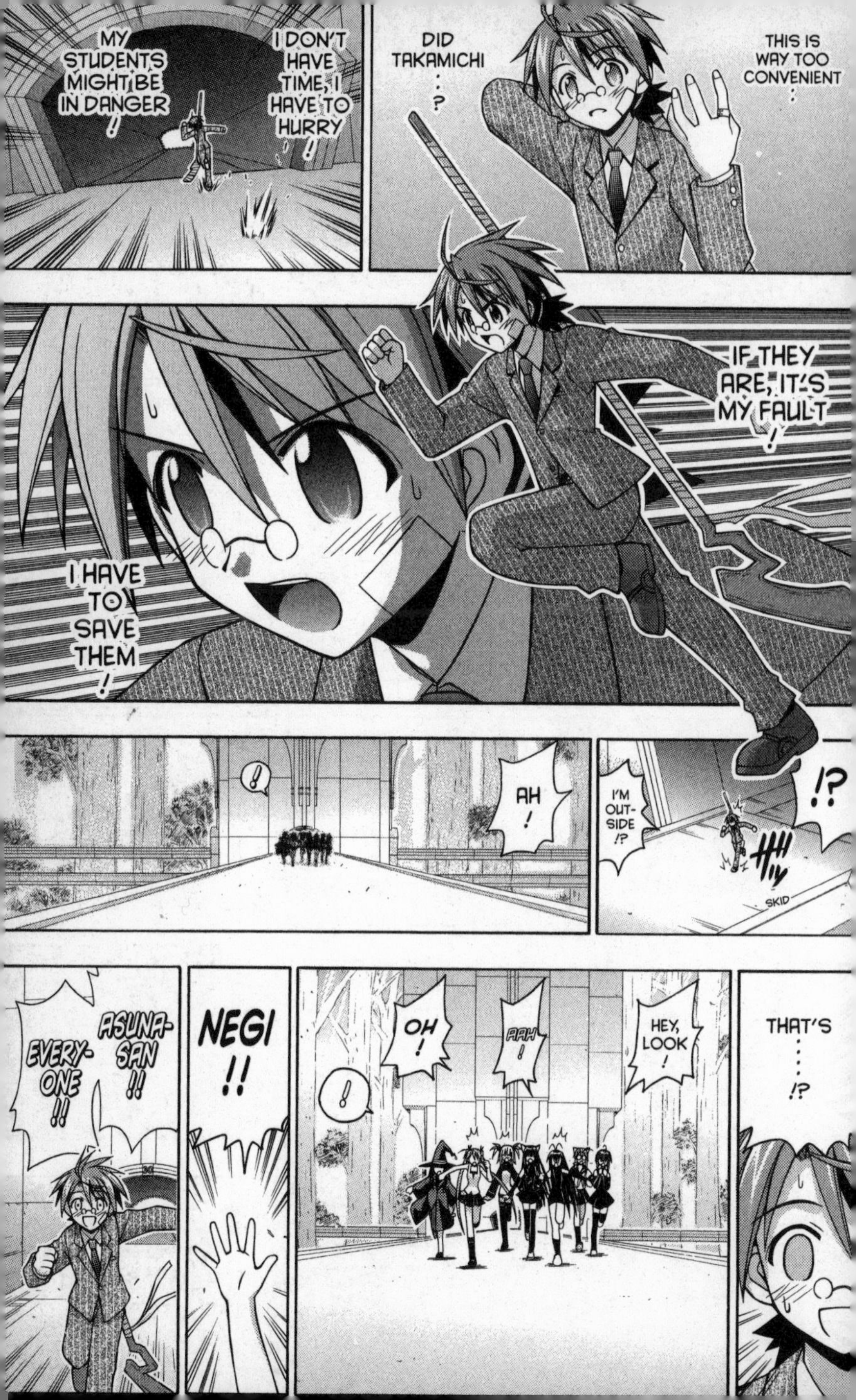
THIS IS WAY TOO CONVENIENT...
DID TAKAMICHI...?
I DON'T HAVE TIME, I HAVE TO HURRY!
MY STUDENTS MIGHT BE IN DANGER!
IF THEY ARE, IT'S MY FAULT!
I HAVE TO SAVE THEM!
!?
I'M OUT-SIDE!?
SKID
AH!
!
THAT'S.....!?
HEY, LOOK!
AAH!
OH!
!
NEGI!!
ASUNA-SAN!!
EVERY-ONE!!

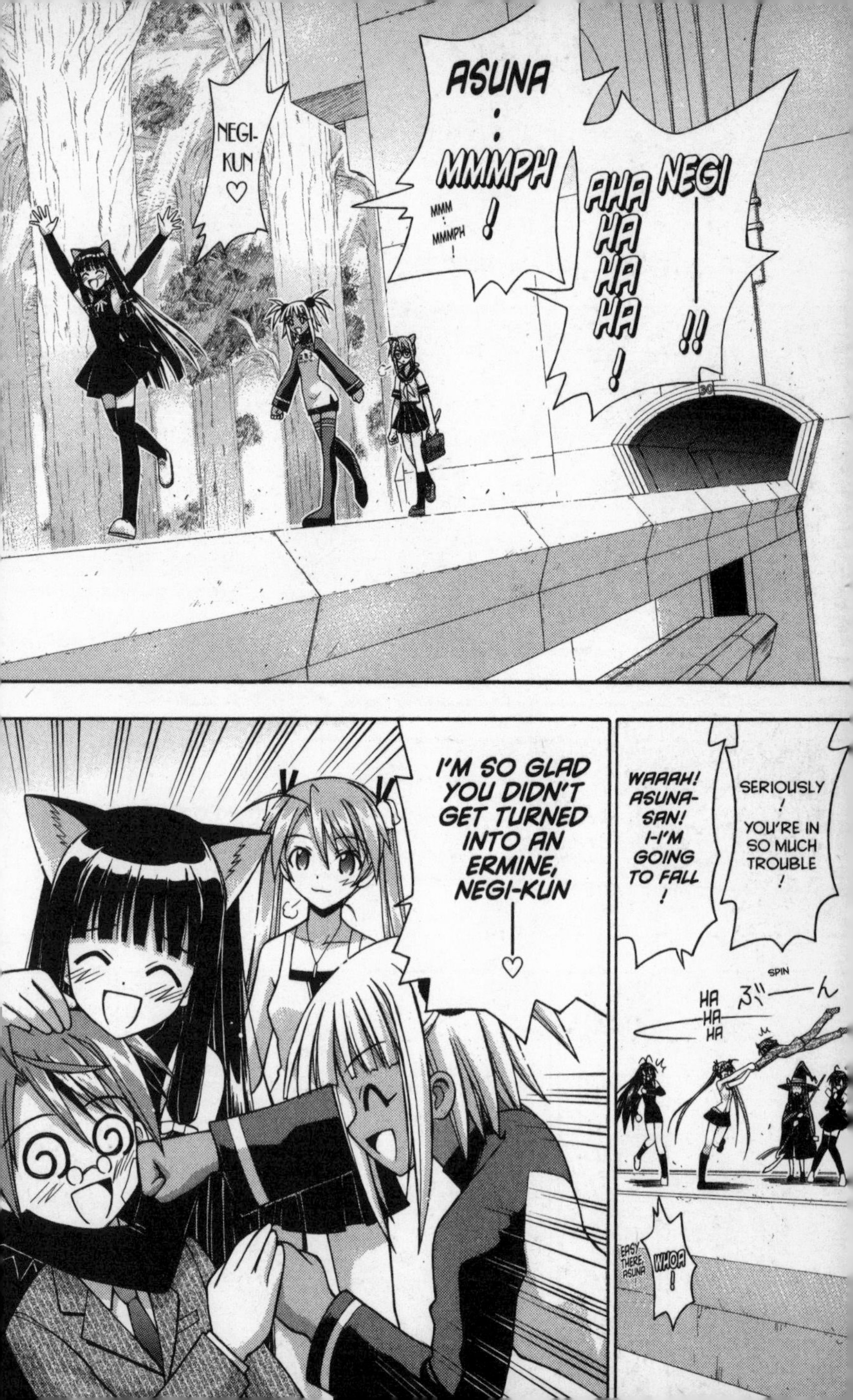
NEGI—!!
AHAHAHAHA!
ASUNA : : MMMPH!
MMM : MMMPH!
NEGI-KUN ♡
SERIOUSLY! YOU'RE IN SO MUCH TROUBLE!
WAAAH! ASUNA-SAN! I-I'M GOING TO FALL!
SPIN ぶーーん
HA HA HA
WHOA!
EASY THERE, ASUNA
I'M SO GLAD YOU DIDN'T GET TURNED INTO AN ERMINE, NEGI-KUN—♡

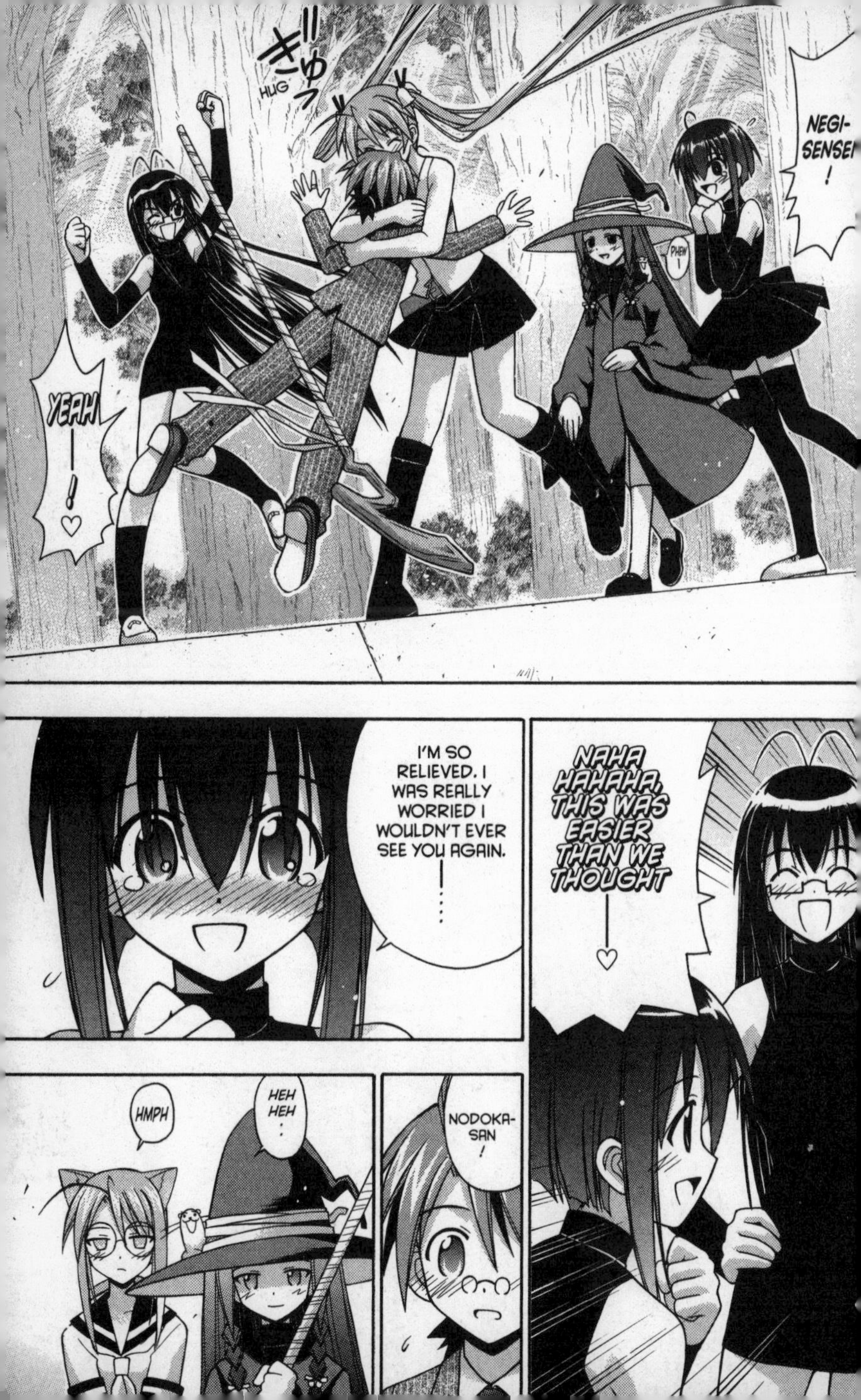
NEGI-SENSEI!
PHEW
きゅっ
HUG
YEAH—!♡
NAHA HAHAHA, THIS WAS EASIER THAN WE THOUGHT—♡
I'M SO RELIEVED. I WAS REALLY WORRIED I WOULDN'T EVER SEE YOU AGAIN.—…
NODOKA-SAN!
HEH HEH…
HMPH

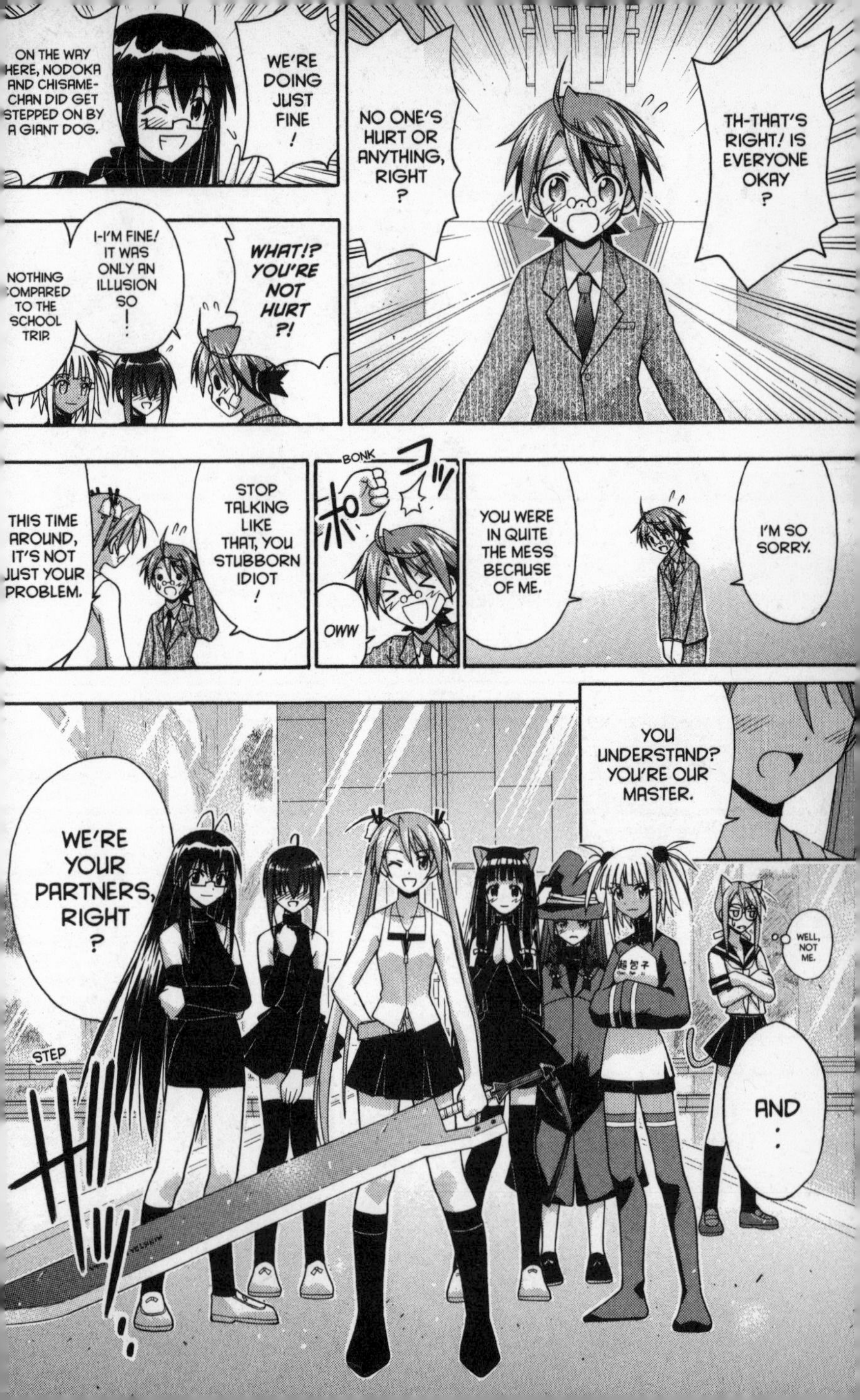
TH-THAT'S RIGHT! IS EVERYONE OKAY?
NO ONE'S HURT OR ANYTHING, RIGHT?
WE'RE DOING JUST FINE!
ON THE WAY HERE, NODOKA AND CHISAME-CHAN DID GET STEPPED ON BY A GIANT DOG.
WHAT!? YOU'RE NOT HURT?!
I-I'M FINE! IT WAS ONLY AN ILLUSION SO!
NOTHING COMPARED TO THE SCHOOL TRIP.
I'M SO SORRY.
YOU WERE IN QUITE THE MESS BECAUSE OF ME.
BONK
OWW
STOP TALKING LIKE THAT, YOU STUBBORN IDIOT!
THIS TIME AROUND, IT'S NOT JUST YOUR PROBLEM.
YOU UNDERSTAND? YOU'RE OUR MASTER.
WE'RE YOUR PARTNERS, RIGHT?
WELL, NOT ME.
AND:
STEP

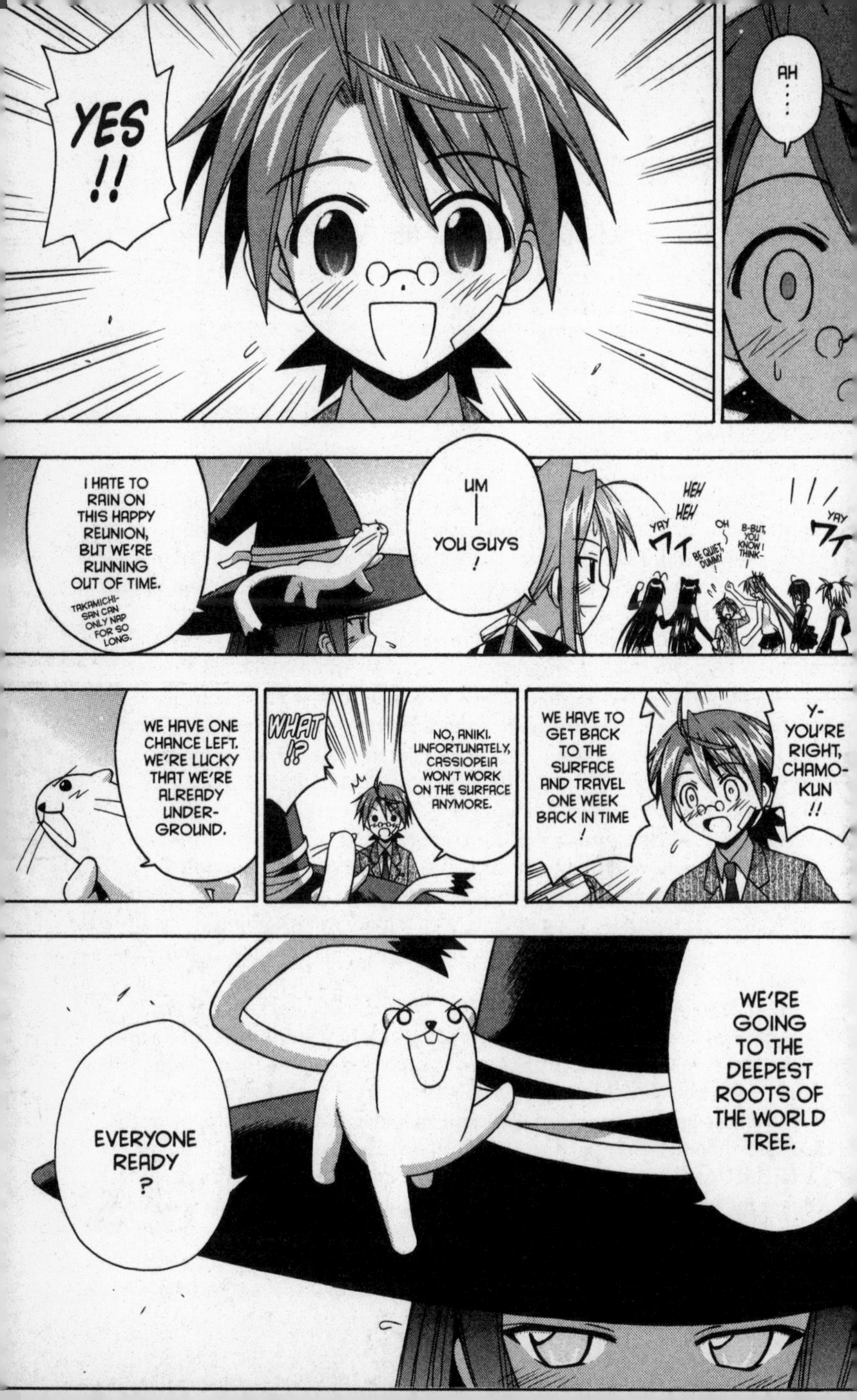
AH ......
YES !!
YAY
B-BUT, YOU KNOW! THINK-
OH BE QUIET, DUMMY!
HEH HEH
YAY
UM — YOU GUYS!
I HATE TO RAIN ON THIS HAPPY REUNION, BUT WE'RE RUNNING OUT OF TIME.
TAKAMICHI-SAN CAN ONLY NAP FOR SO LONG.
Y-YOU'RE RIGHT, CHAMO-KUN!!
WE HAVE TO GET BACK TO THE SURFACE AND TRAVEL ONE WEEK BACK IN TIME!
NO, ANIKI. UNFORTUNATELY, CASSIOPEIA WON'T WORK ON THE SURFACE ANYMORE.
WHAT!?
WE HAVE ONE CHANCE LEFT. WE'RE LUCKY THAT WE'RE ALREADY UNDER-GROUND.
WE'RE GOING TO THE DEEPEST ROOTS OF THE WORLD TREE.
EVERYONE READY?

LEXICON MAGICUM NEGIMARIUM

■世界図絵

オルビス・センスアリウム・ピクトゥス

ORBIS SENSUALIUM PICTUS

By the power of the Pactio with Negi, Yue Ayase is awarded this artifact. She also receives a flying broom and a mage's robe and pointed hat.

As shown in the story, this artifact is primarily an encyclopedia of magic. As one reads on, the user is able to follow related links in order to find more and more detailed information, but in order to understand the entries, the reader must already have a basic grasp of the material. So, even before reading, the user must be well versed in magical study in order to properly make use of it.

Although the encyclopedia is a very powerful tool, it has one major flaw. The book is connected to Mage-Net and is therefore constantly being updated, so that old data is always being overwritten by new information. Up-to-date information is indeed a powerful tool, yet something important may be lost in the process. For example, old and yet still significant information about ancient magic (such as rituals performed in the days of yore) might accidentally be deleted to make room for new data. This counters the methodology of nineteenth-century philology of ancient texts. The *Orbis Sensualium Pictus* was not created to emphasize ancient texts with a modern viewpoint but as a book of dynamic writings based on the feudalistic system of the ancient cultures of words.

John Amos Comenius (1592–1670), a Czech educator, created the *Orbis Sensualium Pictus,* a children's textbook, with a guide to some Latin words. It is unknown if the artifact was created first or not. *Orbis Sensualium Pictus,* translated simply, means, "The Visible World in Pictures." The book explains basic pronunciation of the Latin alphabet and lists a series of words over 150 chapters, starting with DEUS (God) and ending with JUDICIUM EXTREMUM (Final Judgment). At the end, an entry reads, "You have now studied the basic Latin vocabulary" and concludes with "now take your leave," encouraging the reader to be independent. As a side note, Comenius was said to have strong connections with the secret societies of Renaissance Magic (Rose) and the Christian Counterreformation (Cross). It is not known whether these were societies of mages.

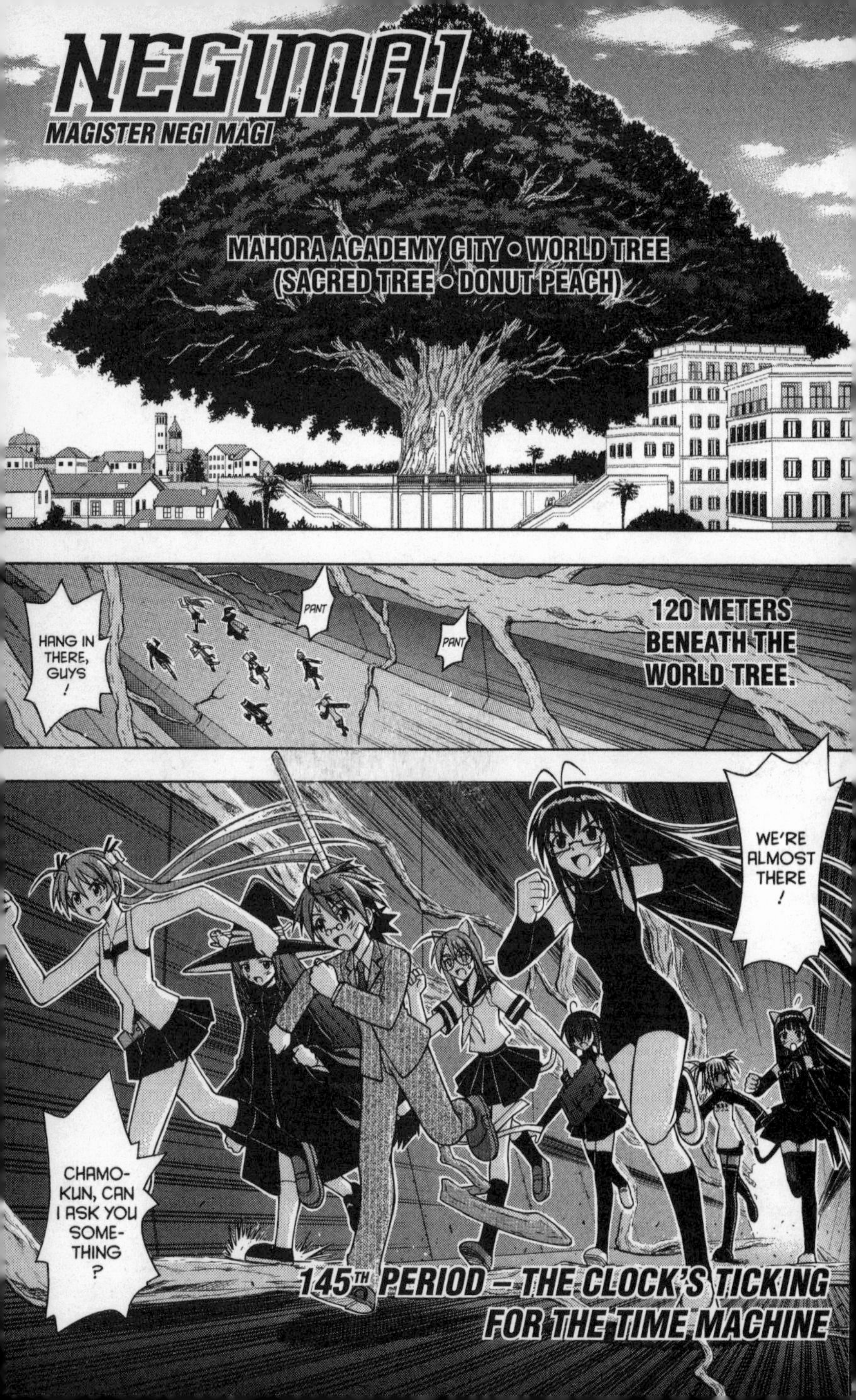
NEGIMA!
MAGISTER NEGI MAGI
MAHORA ACADEMY CITY • WORLD TREE (SACRED TREE • DONUT PEACH)
120 METERS BENEATH THE WORLD TREE.
PANT
PANT
HANG IN THERE, GUYS!
WE'RE ALMOST THERE!
CHAMO-KUN, CAN I ASK YOU SOMETHING?
145TH PERIOD – THE CLOCK'S TICKING FOR THE TIME MACHINE

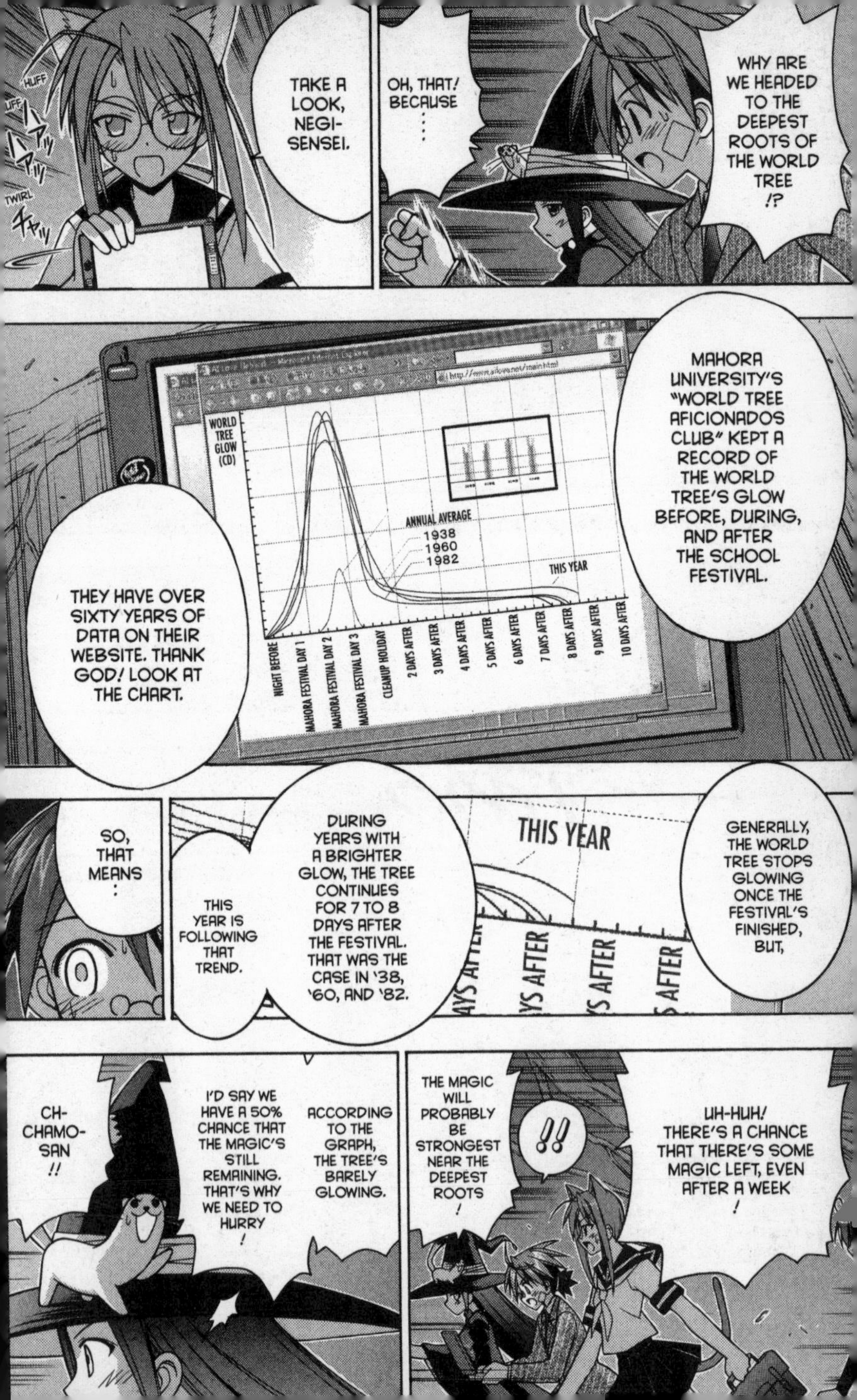
WHY ARE WE HEADED TO THE DEEPEST ROOTS OF THE WORLD TREE !?
OH, THAT! BECAUSE ...
TAKE A LOOK, NEGI-SENSEI.
HUFF
HUFF
ハァッ ハァッ
TWIRL
チャッ
MAHORA UNIVERSITY'S "WORLD TREE AFICIONADOS CLUB" KEPT A RECORD OF THE WORLD TREE'S GLOW BEFORE, DURING, AND AFTER THE SCHOOL FESTIVAL.
WORLD TREE GLOW (CD)
ANNUAL AVERAGE
1938
1960
1982
THIS YEAR
NIGHT BEFORE
MAHORA FESTIVAL DAY 1
MAHORA FESTIVAL DAY 2
MAHORA FESTIVAL DAY 3
CLEANUP HOLIDAY
2 DAYS AFTER
3 DAYS AFTER
4 DAYS AFTER
5 DAYS AFTER
6 DAYS AFTER
7 DAYS AFTER
8 DAYS AFTER
9 DAYS AFTER
10 DAYS AFTER
THEY HAVE OVER SIXTY YEARS OF DATA ON THEIR WEBSITE. THANK GOD! LOOK AT THE CHART.
GENERALLY, THE WORLD TREE STOPS GLOWING ONCE THE FESTIVAL'S FINISHED, BUT,
THIS YEAR
DURING YEARS WITH A BRIGHTER GLOW, THE TREE CONTINUES FOR 7 TO 8 DAYS AFTER THE FESTIVAL. THAT WAS THE CASE IN '38, '60, AND '82.
THIS YEAR IS FOLLOWING THAT TREND.
SO, THAT MEANS :
UH-HUH! THERE'S A CHANCE THAT THERE'S SOME MAGIC LEFT, EVEN AFTER A WEEK !
!!
THE MAGIC WILL PROBABLY BE STRONGEST NEAR THE DEEPEST ROOTS !
ACCORDING TO THE GRAPH, THE TREE'S BARELY GLOWING.
I'D SAY WE HAVE A 50% CHANCE THAT THE MAGIC'S STILL REMAINING. THAT'S WHY WE NEED TO HURRY !
CH-CHAMO-SAN !!

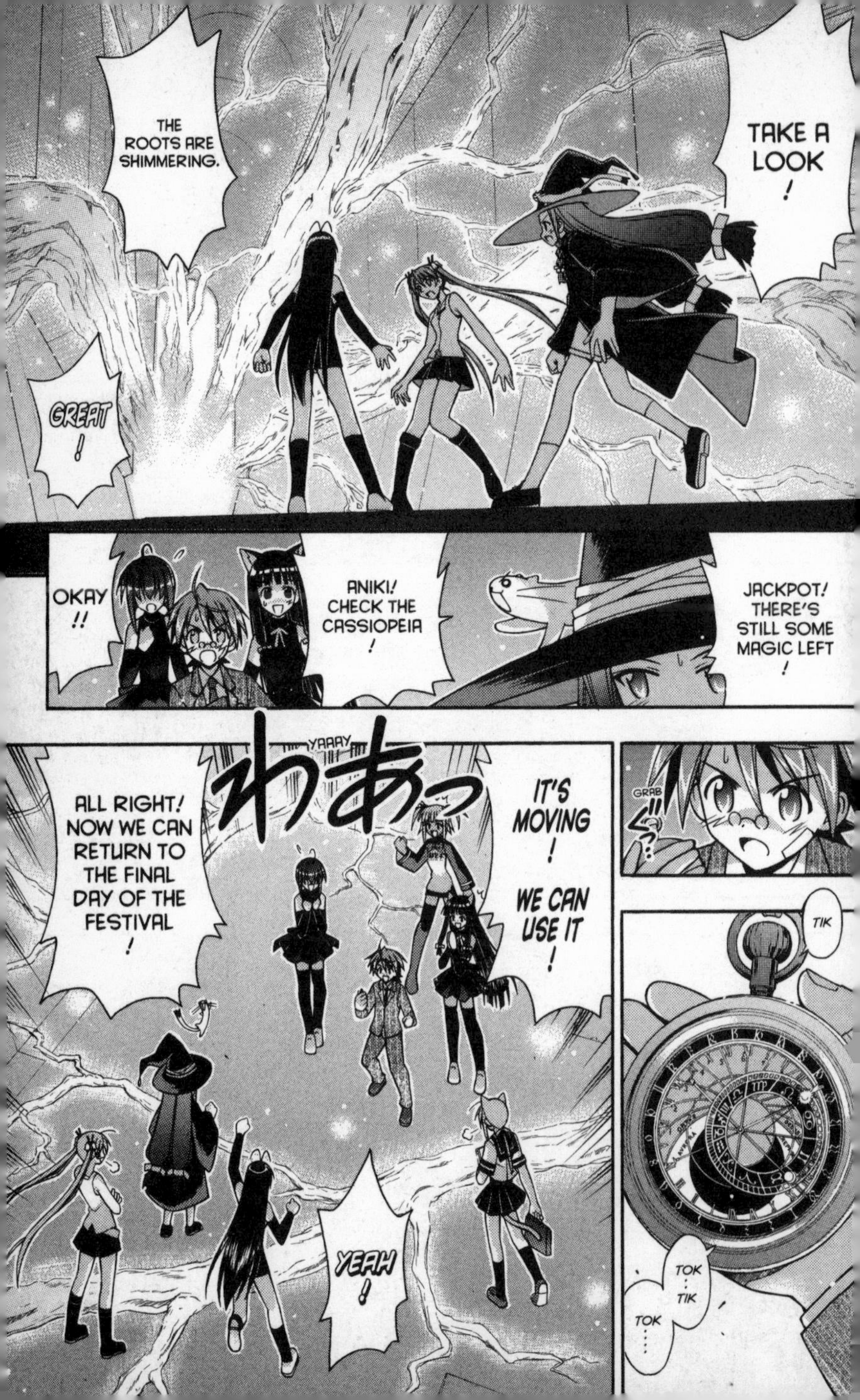
TAKE A LOOK!
THE ROOTS ARE SHIMMERING.
GREAT!
JACKPOT! THERE'S STILL SOME MAGIC LEFT!
ANIKI! CHECK THE CASSIOPEIA!
OKAY!!
GRAB
TIK
TOK
TIK
TOK.....
IT'S MOVING!
WE CAN USE IT!
わあっ
YAAAY
ALL RIGHT! NOW WE CAN RETURN TO THE FINAL DAY OF THE FESTIVAL!
YEAH!

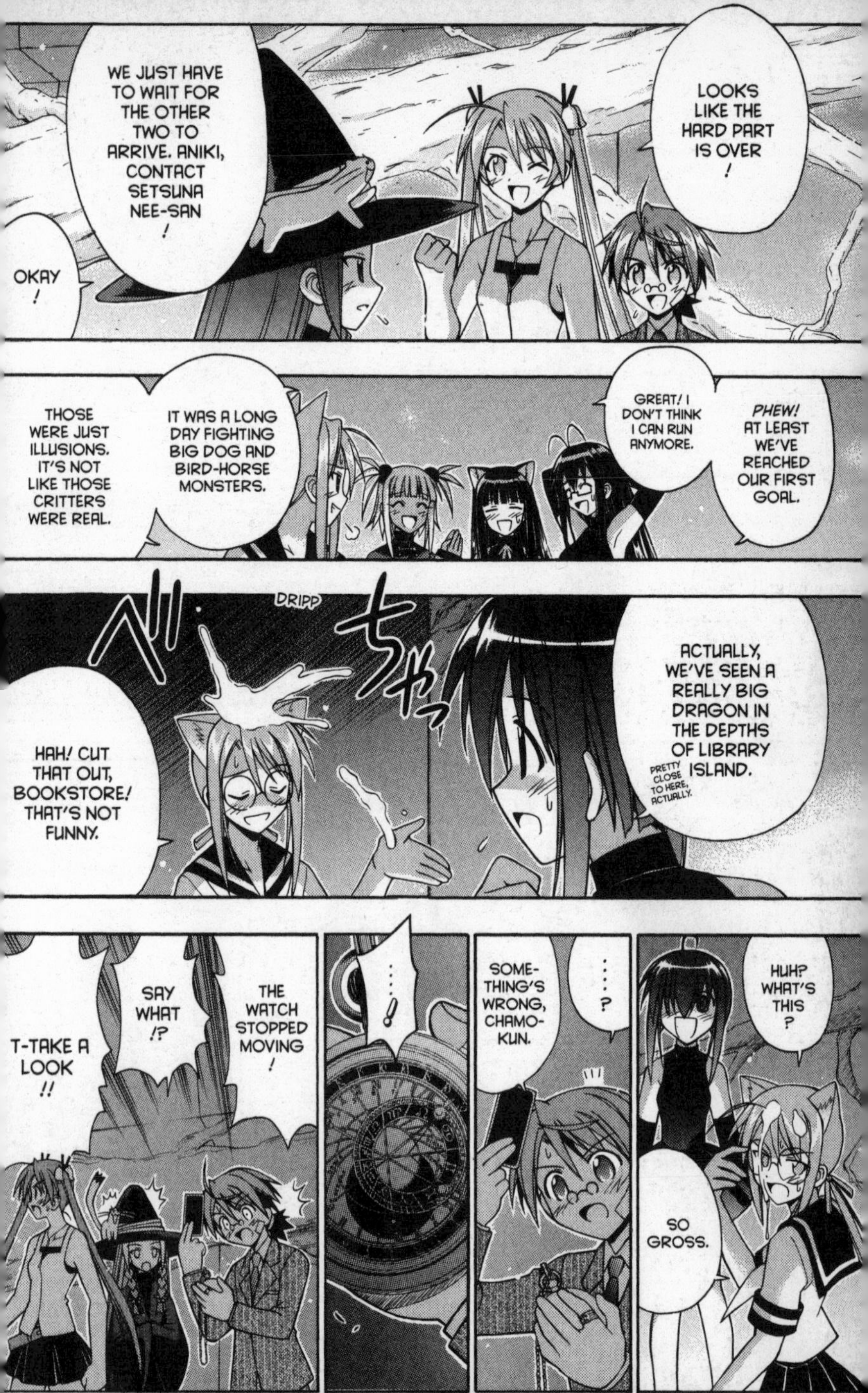
LOOKS LIKE THE HARD PART IS OVER !
WE JUST HAVE TO WAIT FOR THE OTHER TWO TO ARRIVE. ANIKI, CONTACT SETSUNA NEE-SAN !
OKAY !
PHEW! AT LEAST WE'VE REACHED OUR FIRST GOAL.
GREAT! I DON'T THINK I CAN RUN ANYMORE.
IT WAS A LONG DAY FIGHTING BIG DOG AND BIRD-HORSE MONSTERS.
THOSE WERE JUST ILLUSIONS. IT'S NOT LIKE THOSE CRITTERS WERE REAL.
ACTUALLY, WE'VE SEEN A REALLY BIG DRAGON IN THE DEPTHS OF LIBRARY ISLAND.
PRETTY CLOSE TO HERE, ACTUALLY.
ちゃっ
DRIPP
HAH! CUT THAT OUT, BOOKSTORE! THAT'S NOT FUNNY.
HUH? WHAT'S THIS ?
SO GROSS.
...?
SOME-THING'S WRONG, CHAMO-KUN.
...!
THE WATCH STOPPED MOVING !
SAY WHAT !?
T-TAKE A LOOK !!

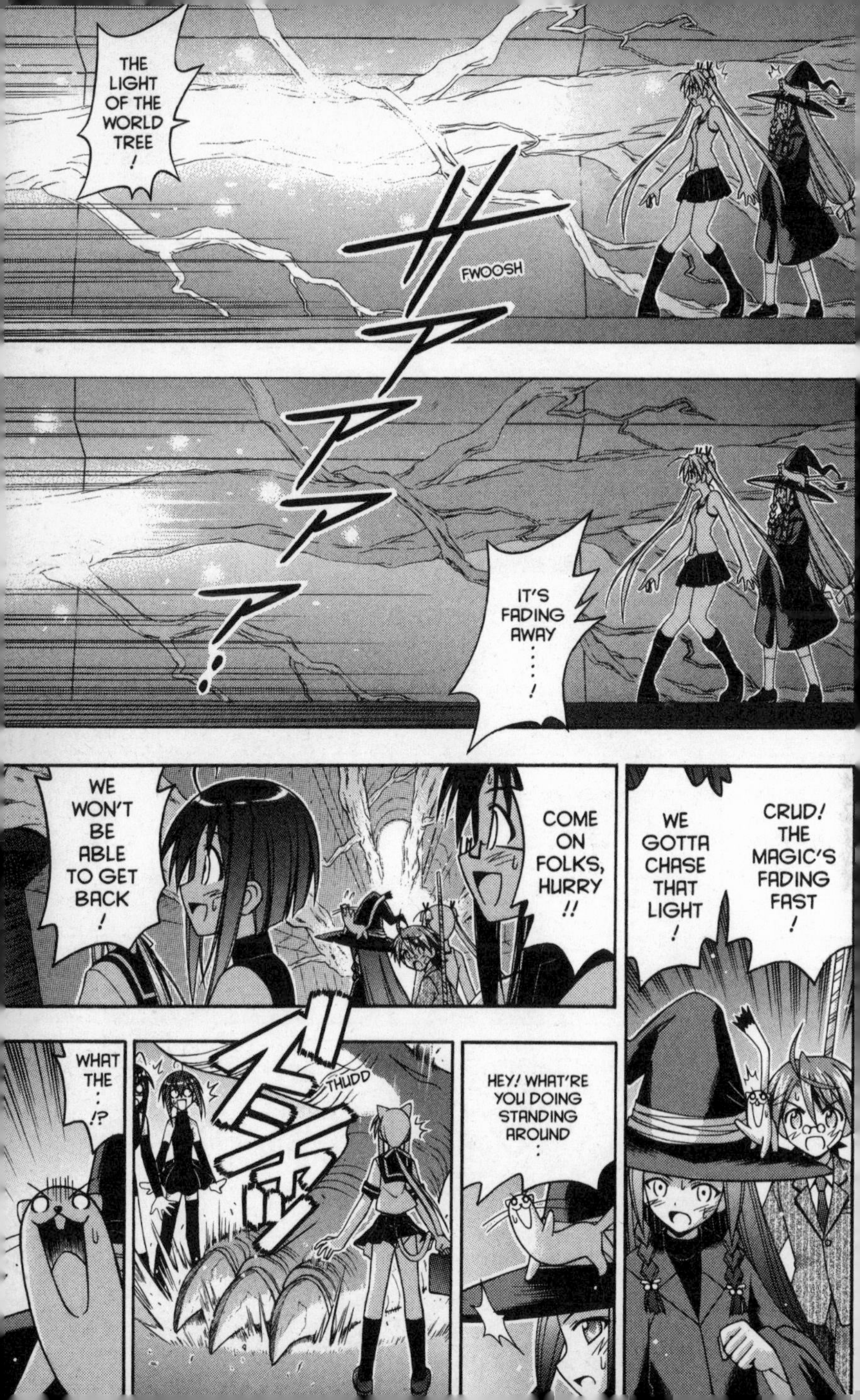
THE LIGHT OF THE WORLD TREE!
FWOOSH
IT'S FADING AWAY.....!
CRUD! THE MAGIC'S FADING FAST!
WE GOTTA CHASE THAT LIGHT!
COME ON FOLKS, HURRY!!
WE WON'T BE ABLE TO GET BACK!
HEY! WHAT'RE YOU DOING STANDING AROUND...
THUDD
WHAT THE...!?

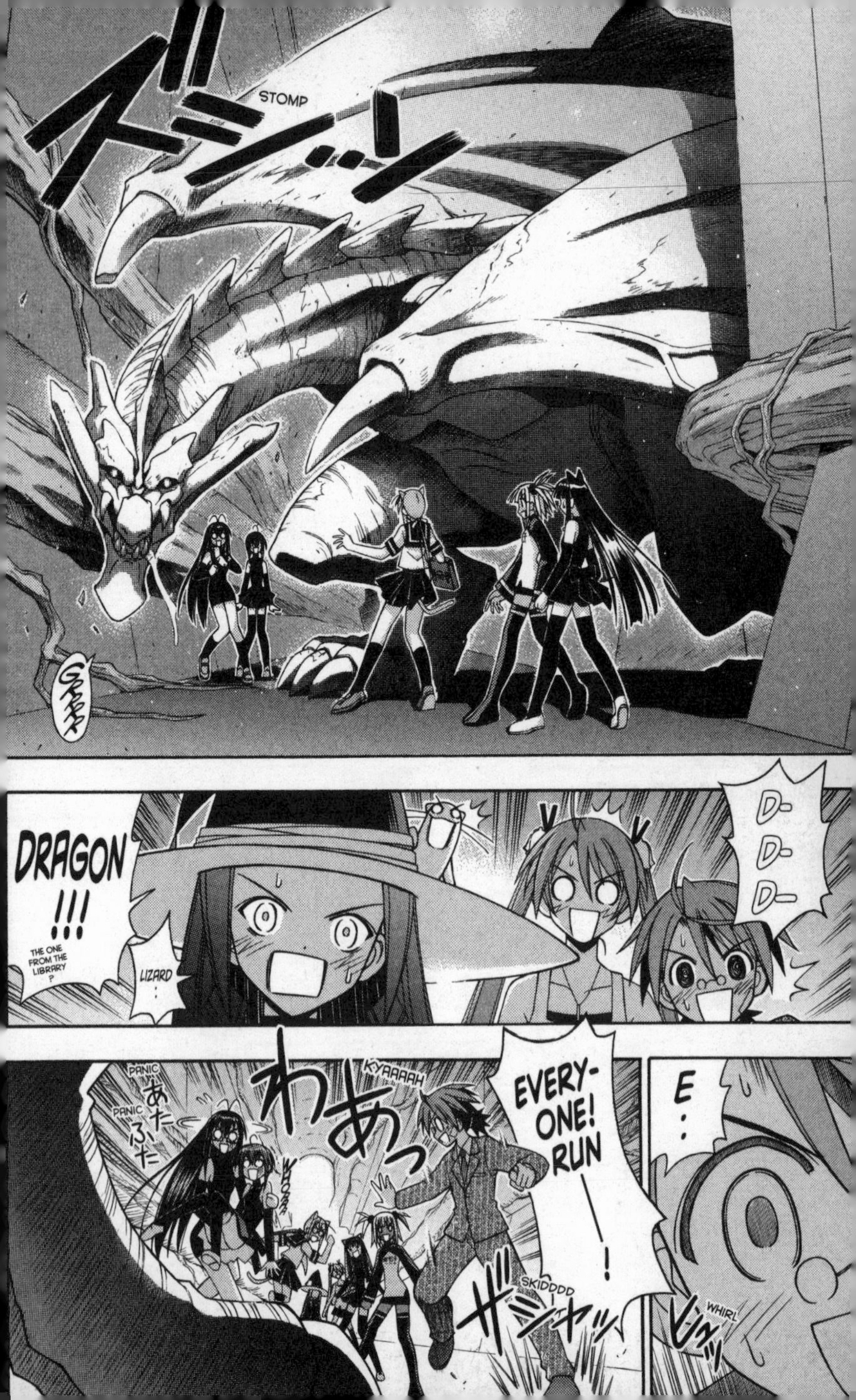
STOMP
GRRRR
D- D- D-
DRAGON !!!
LIZARD ...
THE ONE FROM THE LIBRARY ?
E ...
WHIRL
EVERY-ONE! RUN —!
SKIDDDD
わあっ
KYAAAAH
あたふた
PANIC
PANIC
WHOAAA

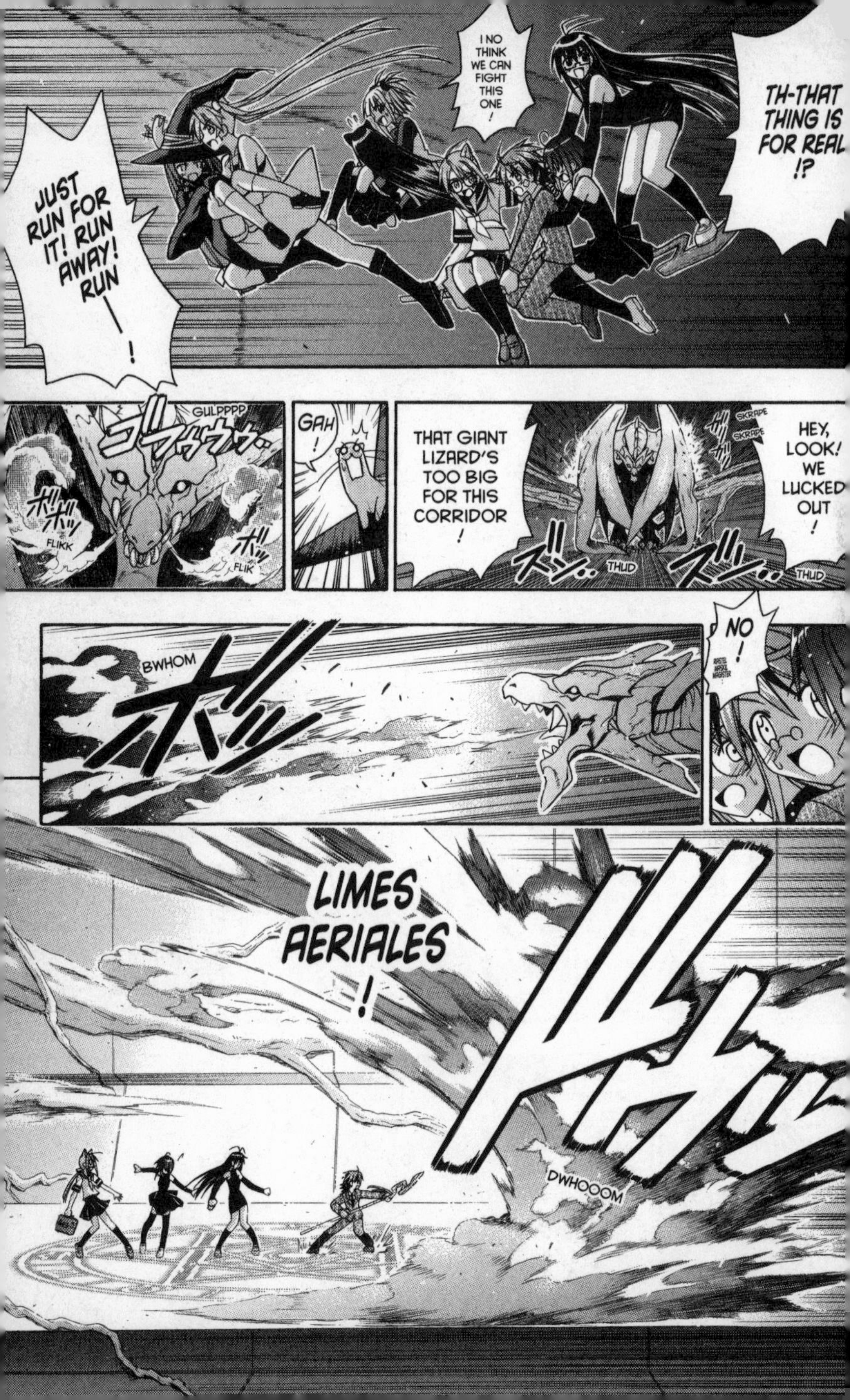
TH-THAT THING IS FOR REAL !?
I NO THINK WE CAN FIGHT THIS ONE !
JUST RUN FOR IT! RUN AWAY! RUN — !
HEY, LOOK! WE LUCKED OUT !
SKRAPE SKRAPE
THAT GIANT LIZARD'S TOO BIG FOR THIS CORRIDOR !
THUD
THUD
GAH !
GULPPPP
FLIKK
FLIK
NO !
BWHOM
LIMES AERIALES !
DWHOOOM

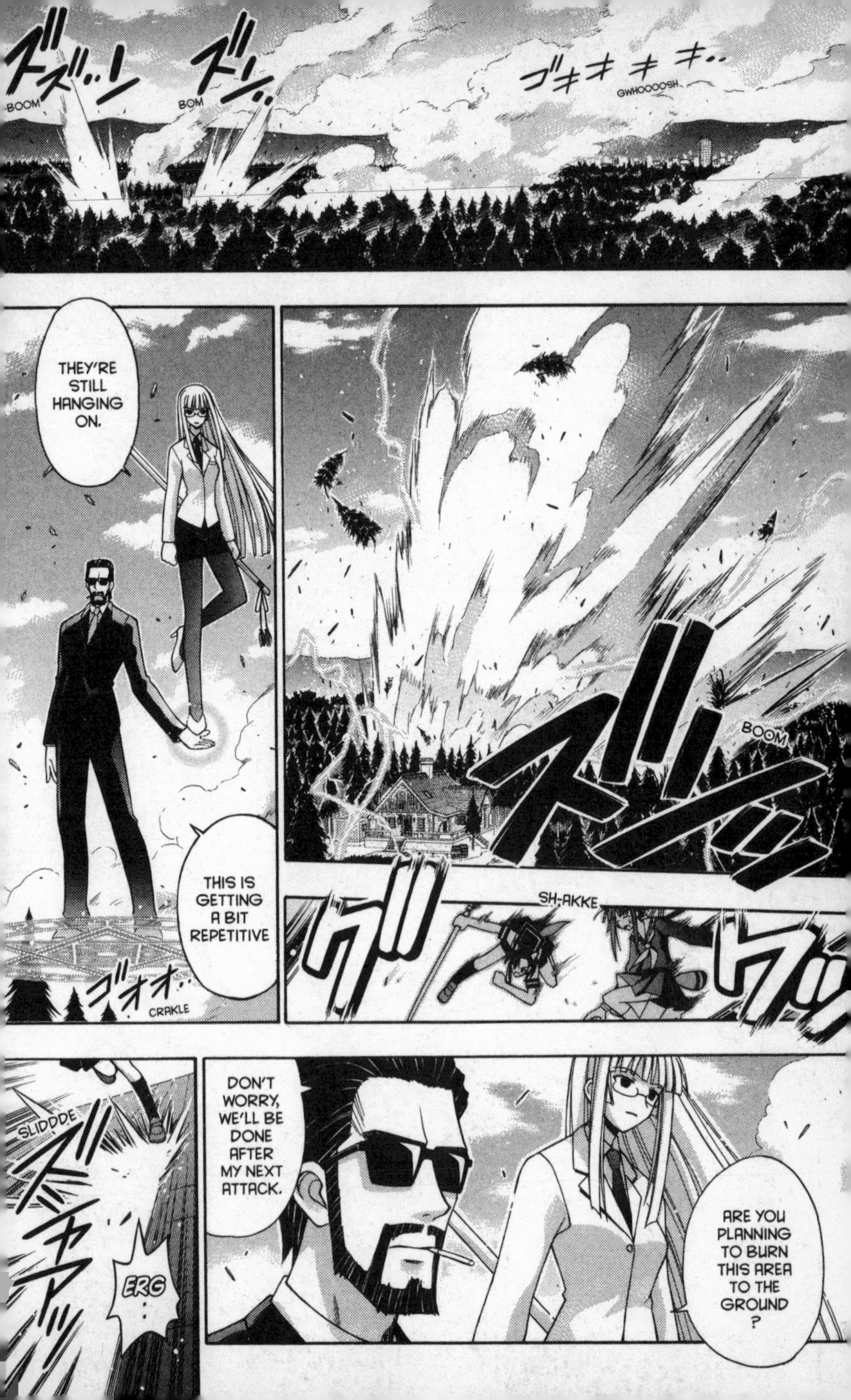
GWHOOOOSH
BOM
BOOM
BOOM
SH-AKKE
THEY'RE STILL HANGING ON.
THIS IS GETTING A BIT REPETITIVE
CRAKLE
ARE YOU PLANNING TO BURN THIS AREA TO THE GROUND?
DON'T WORRY, WE'LL BE DONE AFTER MY NEXT ATTACK.
SLIDDDE
ERG

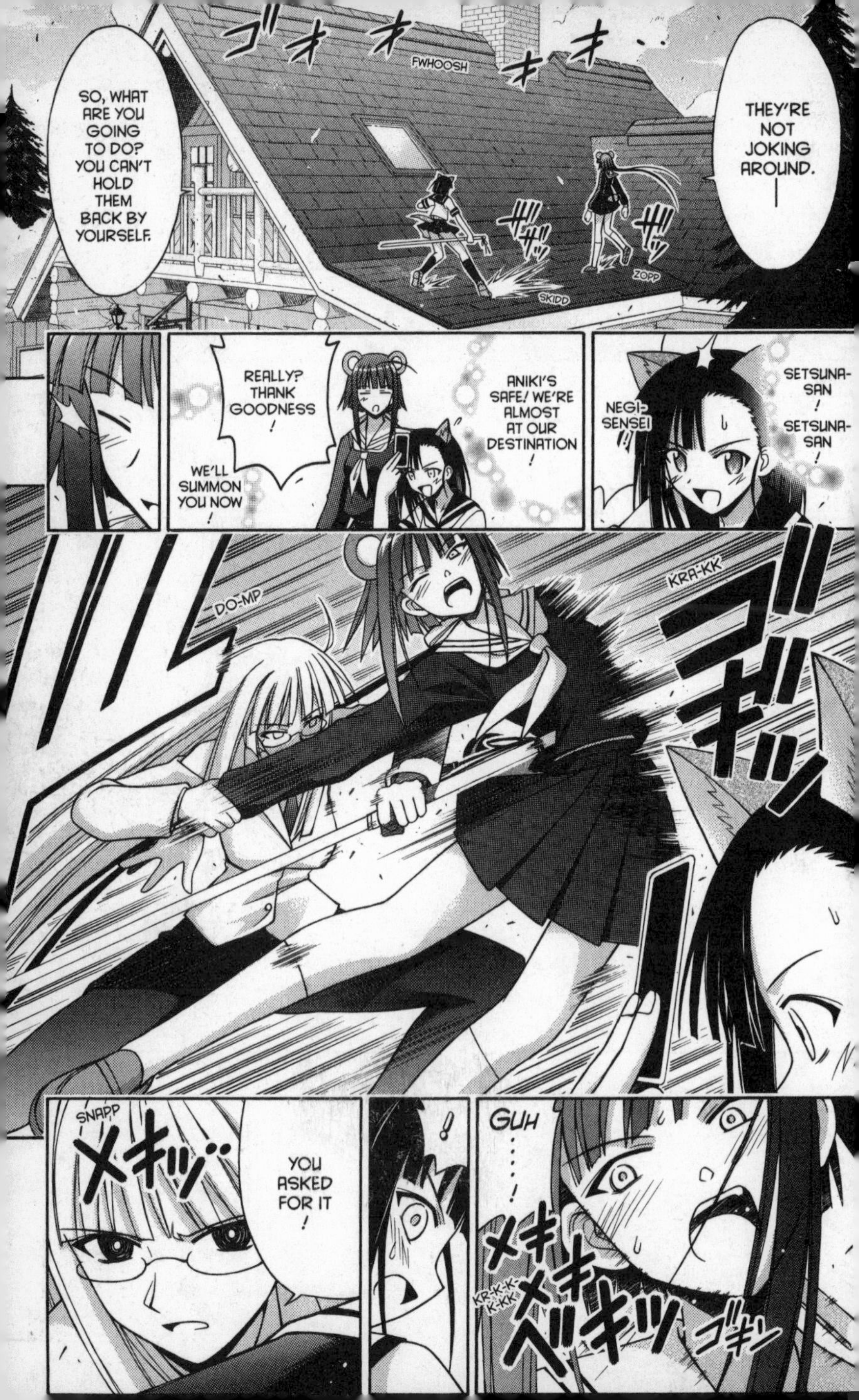
THEY'RE NOT JOKING AROUND. —
FWHOOSH
ZOPP
SKIDD
SO, WHAT ARE YOU GOING TO DO? YOU CAN'T HOLD THEM BACK BY YOURSELF.
SETSUNA-SAN! SETSUNA-SAN!
NEGI-SENSEI!!
ANIKI'S SAFE! WE'RE ALMOST AT OUR DESTINATION!
REALLY? THANK GOODNESS!
WE'LL SUMMON YOU NOW!
KRA-KK
DO-MP
GUH.....!
KR-K-K-K-KK
!
SNAPP
YOU ASKED FOR IT!

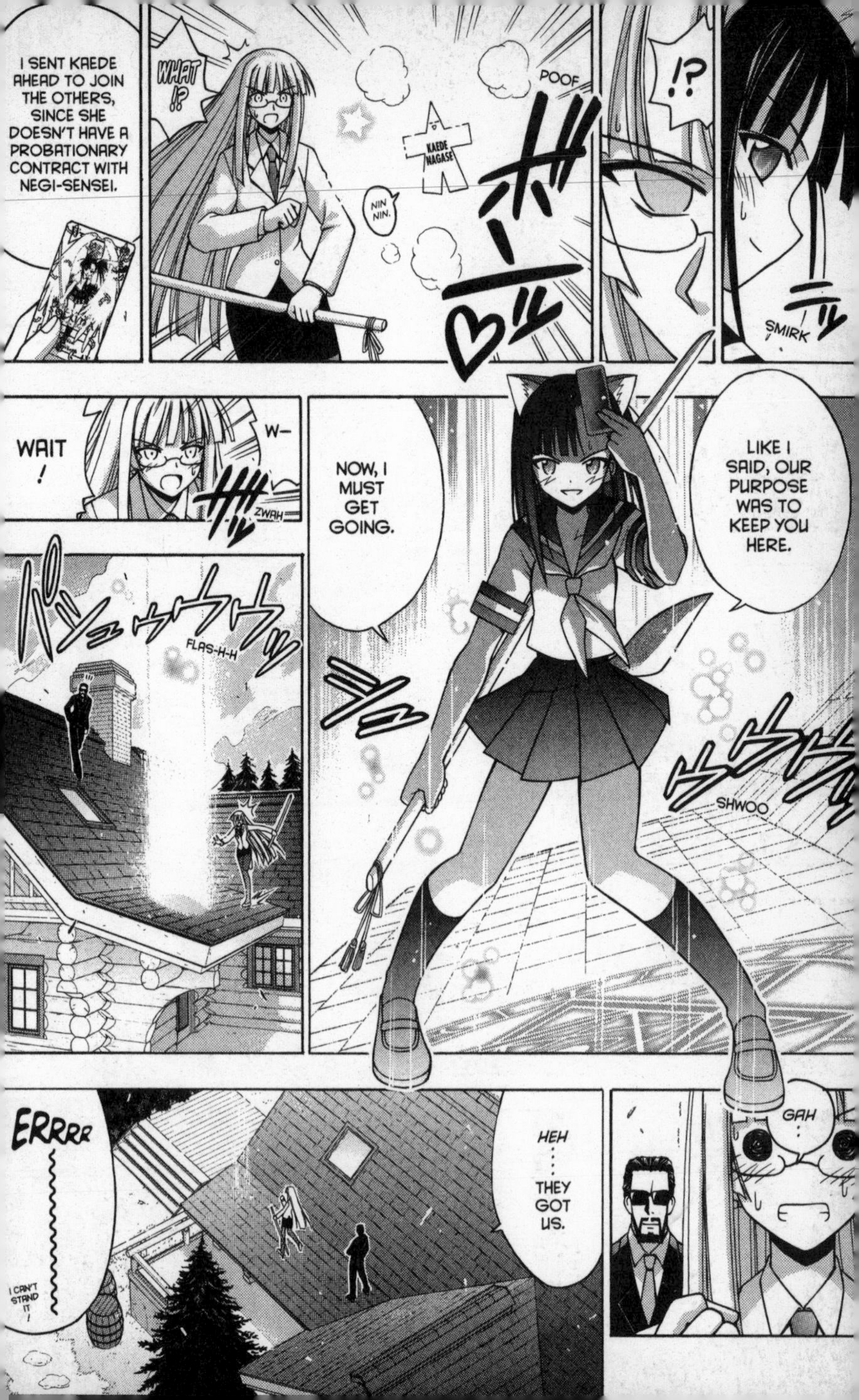

!?
SMIRK
POOF
KAEDE NAGASE
NIN NIN.
WHAT !?
I SENT KAEDE AHEAD TO JOIN THE OTHERS, SINCE SHE DOESN'T HAVE A PROBATIONARY CONTRACT WITH NEGI-SENSEI.
LIKE I SAID, OUR PURPOSE WAS TO KEEP YOU HERE.
NOW, I MUST GET GOING.
SHWOO
W— WAIT !
ZWAH
FLAS-H-H
GAH
HEH... THEY GOT US.
ERRRR
I CAN'T STAND IT !

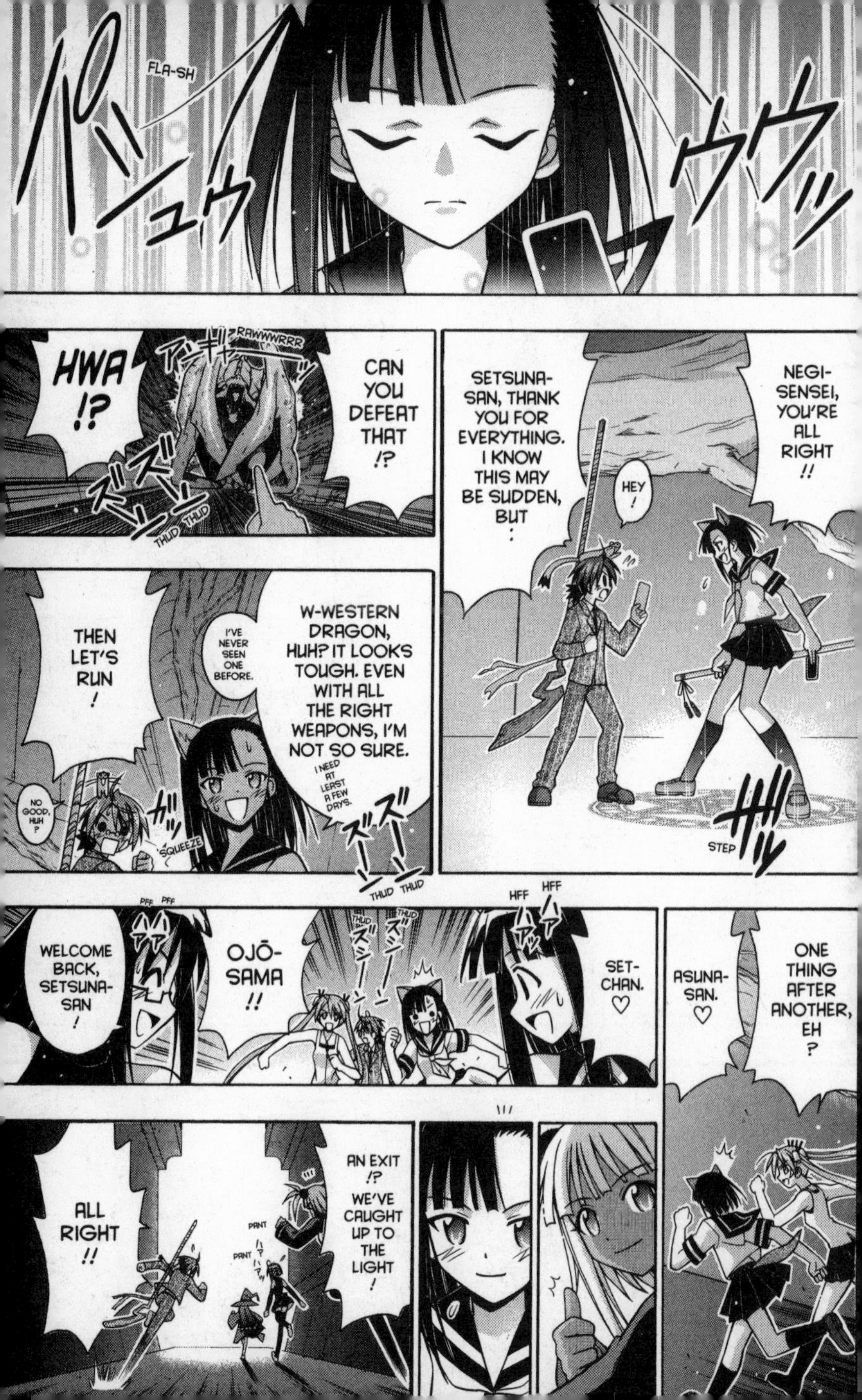

FLA-SH
NEGI-SENSEI, YOU'RE ALL RIGHT!!
SETSUNA-SAN, THANK YOU FOR EVERYTHING. I KNOW THIS MAY BE SUDDEN, BUT:
HEY!
STEP
CAN YOU DEFEAT THAT!?
HWA!?
RAWWWRRR
THUD THUD
W-WESTERN DRAGON, HUH? IT LOOKS TOUGH. EVEN WITH ALL THE RIGHT WEAPONS, I'M NOT SO SURE.
I'VE NEVER SEEN ONE BEFORE.
I NEED AT LEAST A FEW DAYS.
THEN LET'S RUN!
NO GOOD, HUH?
SQUEEZE
THUD THUD
ONE THING AFTER ANOTHER, EH?
ASUNA-SAN. ♡
SET-CHAN. ♡
HFF HFF
THUD THUD
OJŌ-SAMA!!
WELCOME BACK, SETSUNA-SAN!
PFF PFF
AN EXIT!? WE'VE CAUGHT UP TO THE LIGHT!
PANT PANT
ALL RIGHT!!

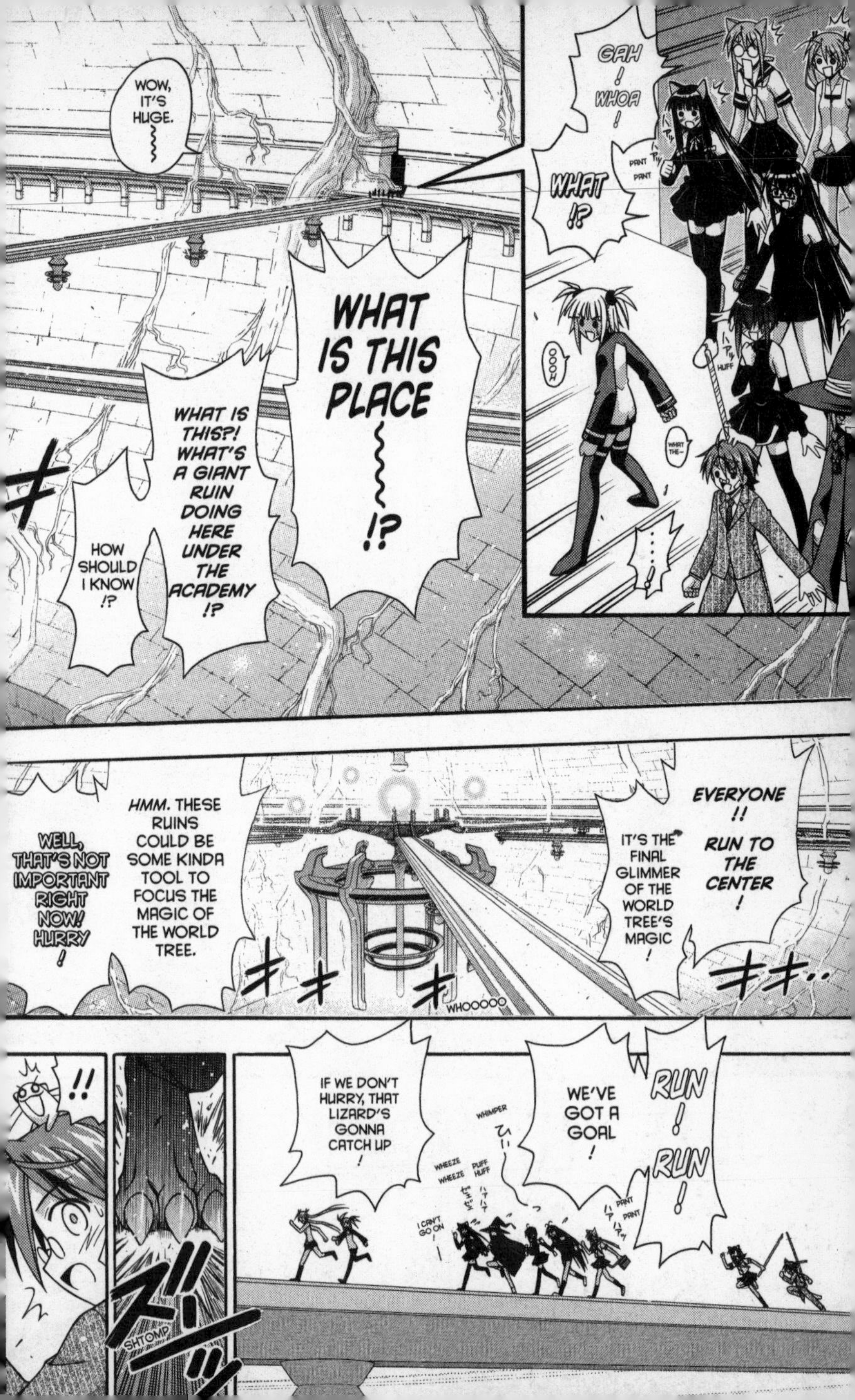
GAH! WHOA!
PANT PANT
WHAT !?
OOOH
WHAT THE—
...!
WOW, IT'S HUGE.
WHAT IS THIS PLACE !?
WHAT IS THIS?! WHAT'S A GIANT RUIN DOING HERE UNDER THE ACADEMY !?
HOW SHOULD I KNOW !?
EVERYONE !! RUN TO THE CENTER !
IT'S THE FINAL GLIMMER OF THE WORLD TREE'S MAGIC !
HMM. THESE RUINS COULD BE SOME KINDA TOOL TO FOCUS THE MAGIC OF THE WORLD TREE.
WELL, THAT'S NOT IMPORTANT RIGHT NOW! HURRY !
WHOOOOO
RUN ! RUN !
WE'VE GOT A GOAL !
PANT PANT
WHIMPER
IF WE DON'T HURRY, THAT LIZARD'S GONNA CATCH UP !
PUFF HUFF
WHEEZE WHEEZE
I CAN'T GO ON !
SHTOMP
!!

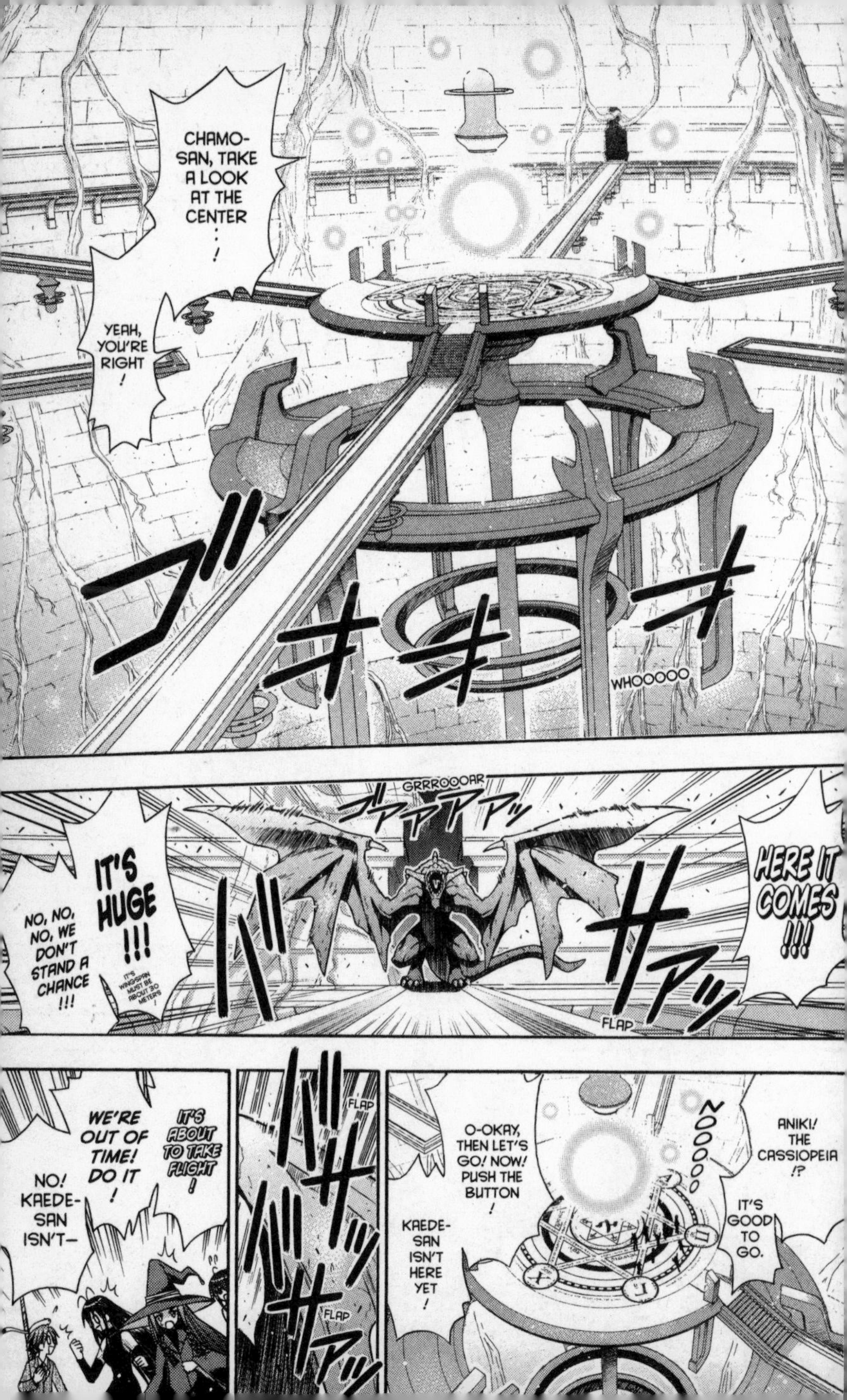
CHAMO-SAN, TAKE A LOOK AT THE CENTER...!
YEAH, YOU'RE RIGHT!
WHOOOOO
GRRROOOAR
HERE IT COMES!!!
FLAP
IT'S HUGE!!!
IT'S WINGSPAN MUST BE ABOUT 30 METERS!
NO, NO, NO, WE DON'T STAND A CHANCE!!!
ANIKI! THE CASSIOPEIA!?
IT'S GOOD TO GO.
NOOOOOO
O-OKAY, THEN LET'S GO! NOW! PUSH THE BUTTON!
KAEDE-SAN ISN'T HERE YET!
FLAP
FLAP
IT'S ABOUT TO TAKE FLIGHT!
WE'RE OUT OF TIME! DO IT!
NO! KAEDE-SAN ISN'T—

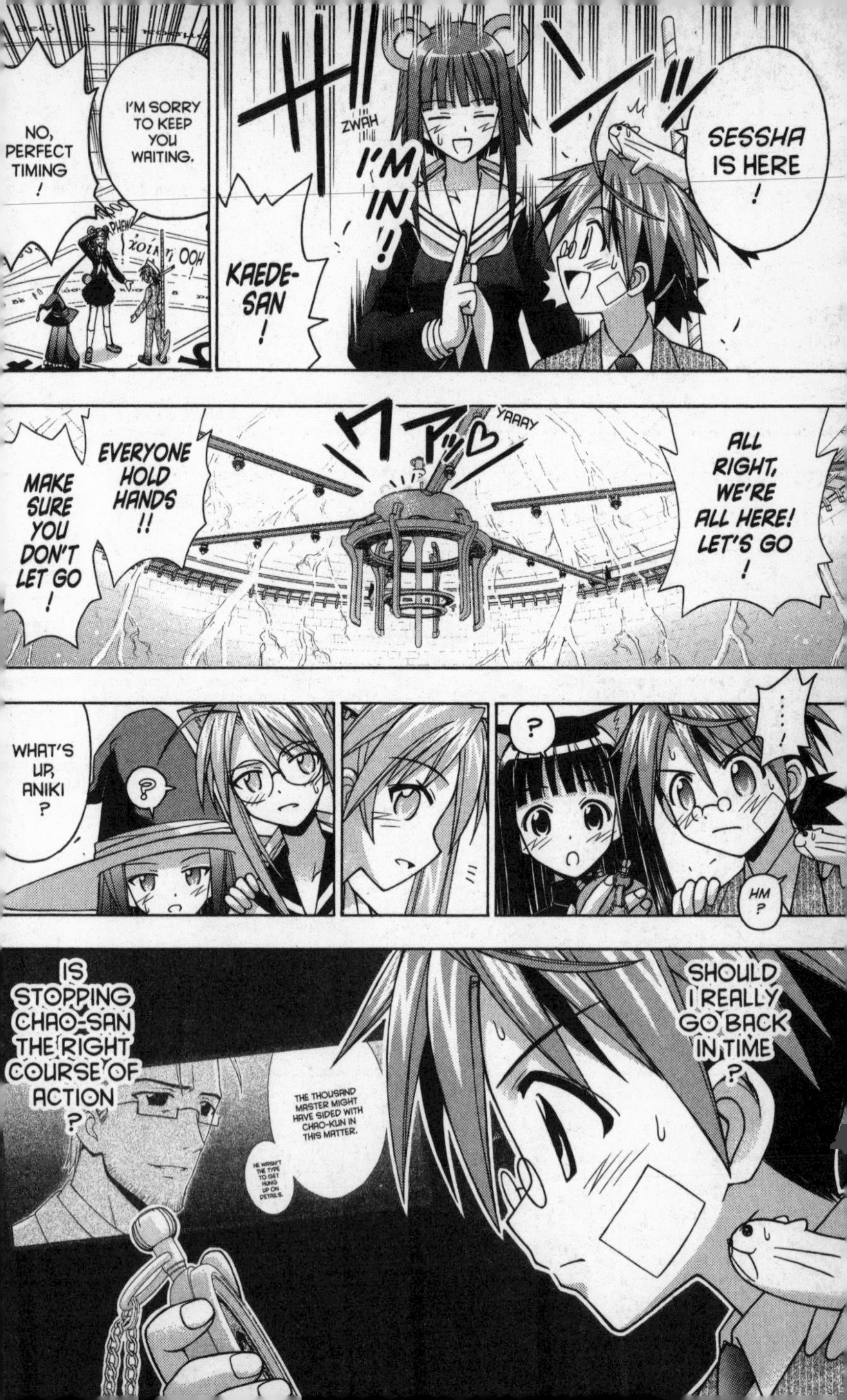
SESSHA IS HERE!
ZWAH
I'M IN!!
KAEDE-SAN!
I'M SORRY TO KEEP YOU WAITING.
NO, PERFECT TIMING!
OOH
ALL RIGHT, WE'RE ALL HERE! LET'S GO!
YAAAY
EVERYONE HOLD HANDS!!
MAKE SURE YOU DON'T LET GO!
...!
?
HM?
?
WHAT'S UP, ANIKI?
SHOULD I REALLY GO BACK IN TIME?
THE THOUSAND MASTER MIGHT HAVE SIDED WITH CHAO-KUN IN THIS MATTER.
HE WASN'T THE TYPE TO GET HUNG UP ON DETAILS.
IS STOPPING CHAO-SAN THE RIGHT COURSE OF ACTION?

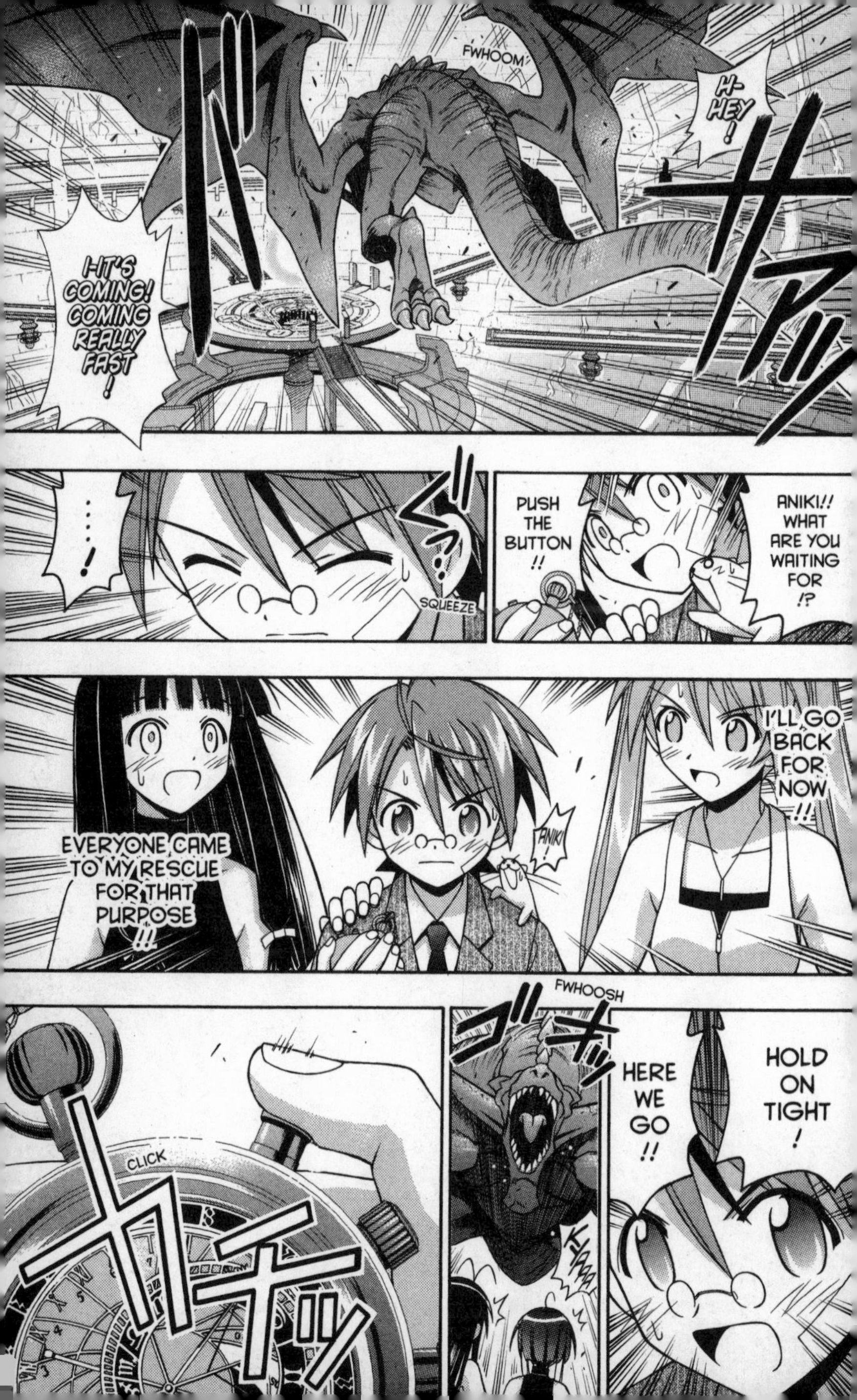

FWHOOM
H-HEY!
I-IT'S COMING! COMING REALLY FAST!
ANIKI!! WHAT ARE YOU WAITING FOR!?
PUSH THE BUTTON!!
SQUEEZE
...!
I'LL GO BACK FOR NOW!!
ANIKI!
EVERYONE CAME TO MY RESCUE FOR THAT PURPOSE!!
HOLD ON TIGHT!
HERE WE GO!!
FWHOOSH
CLICK

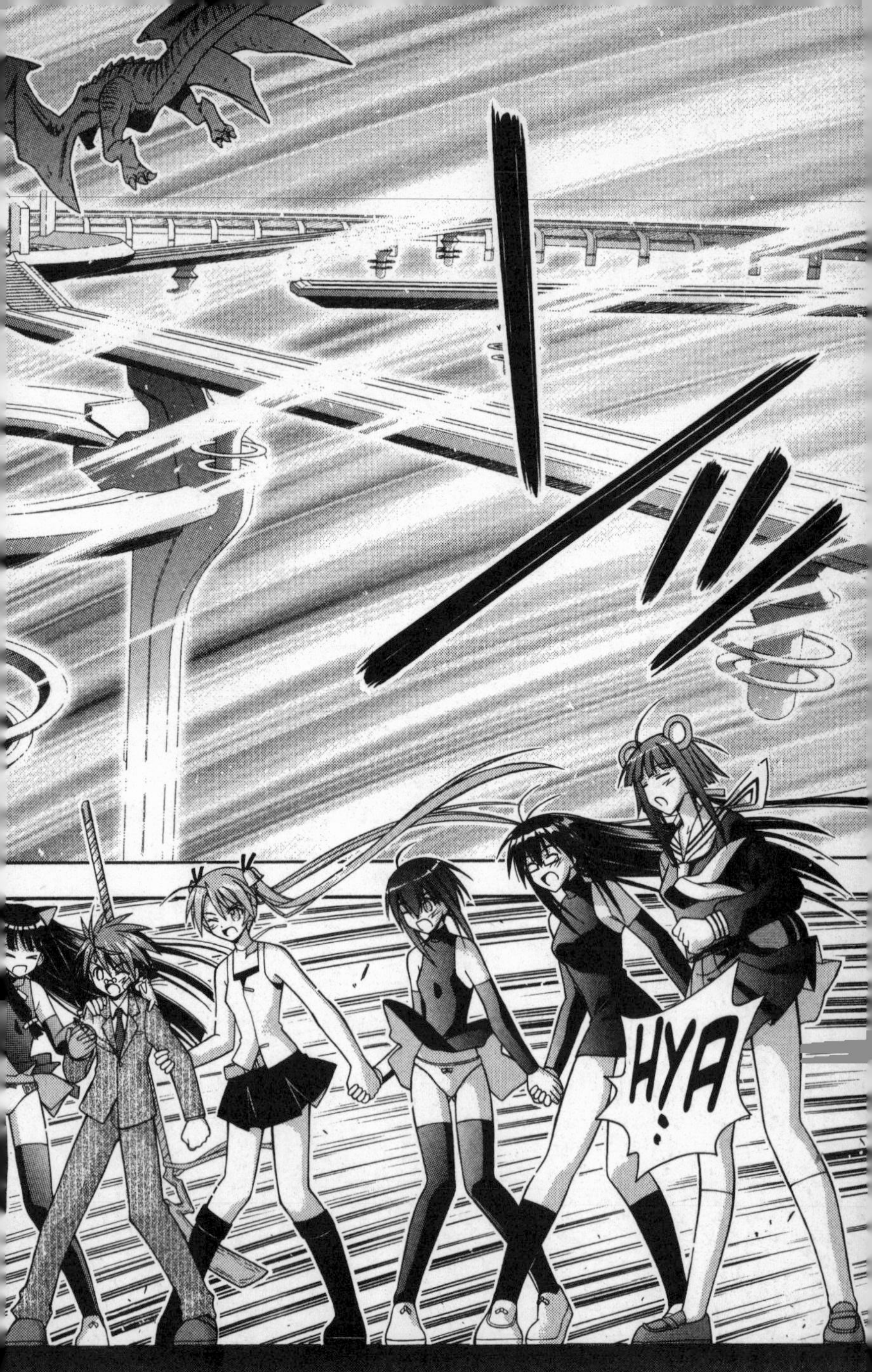
HYA!

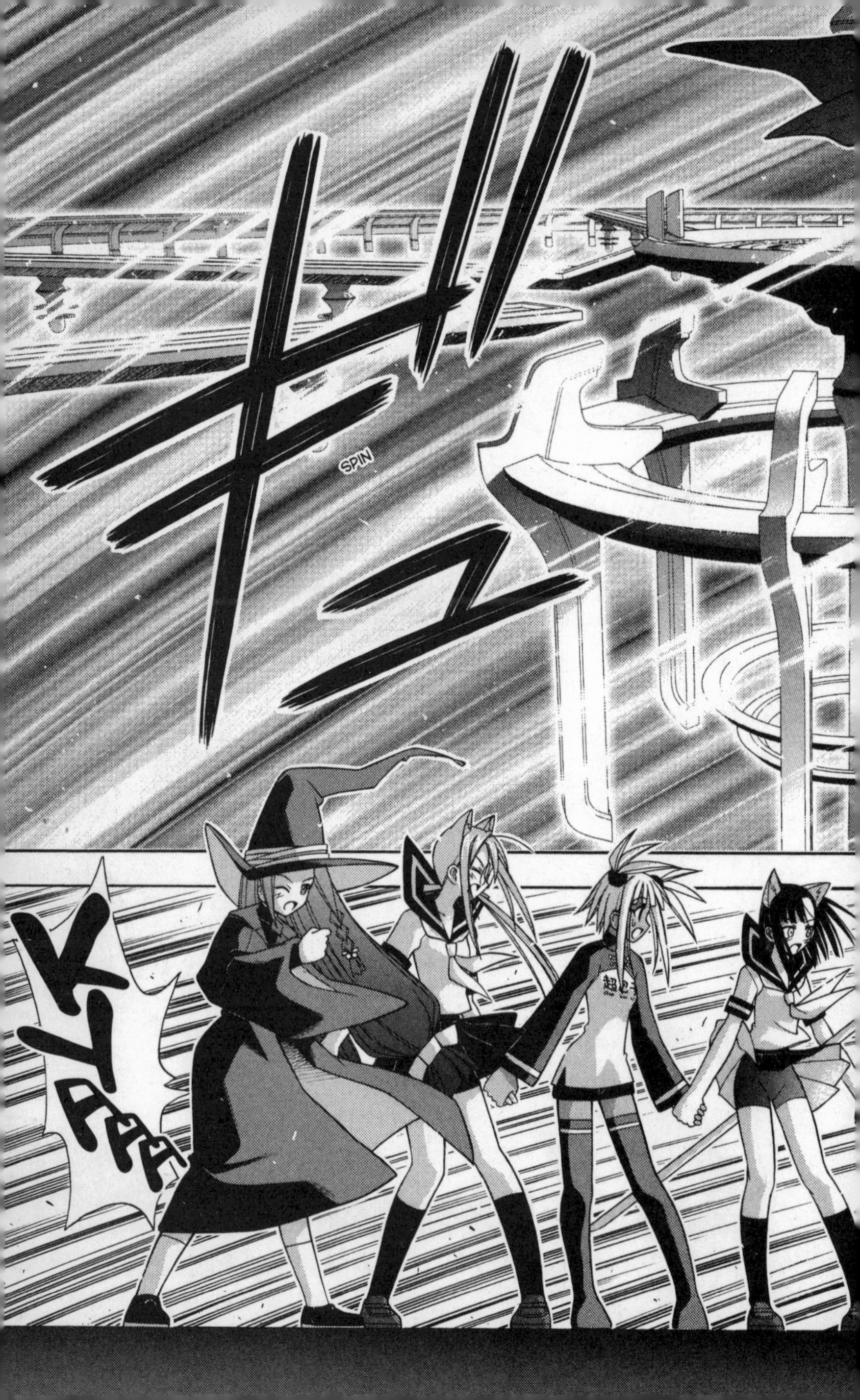
SPIN
KYAAAA

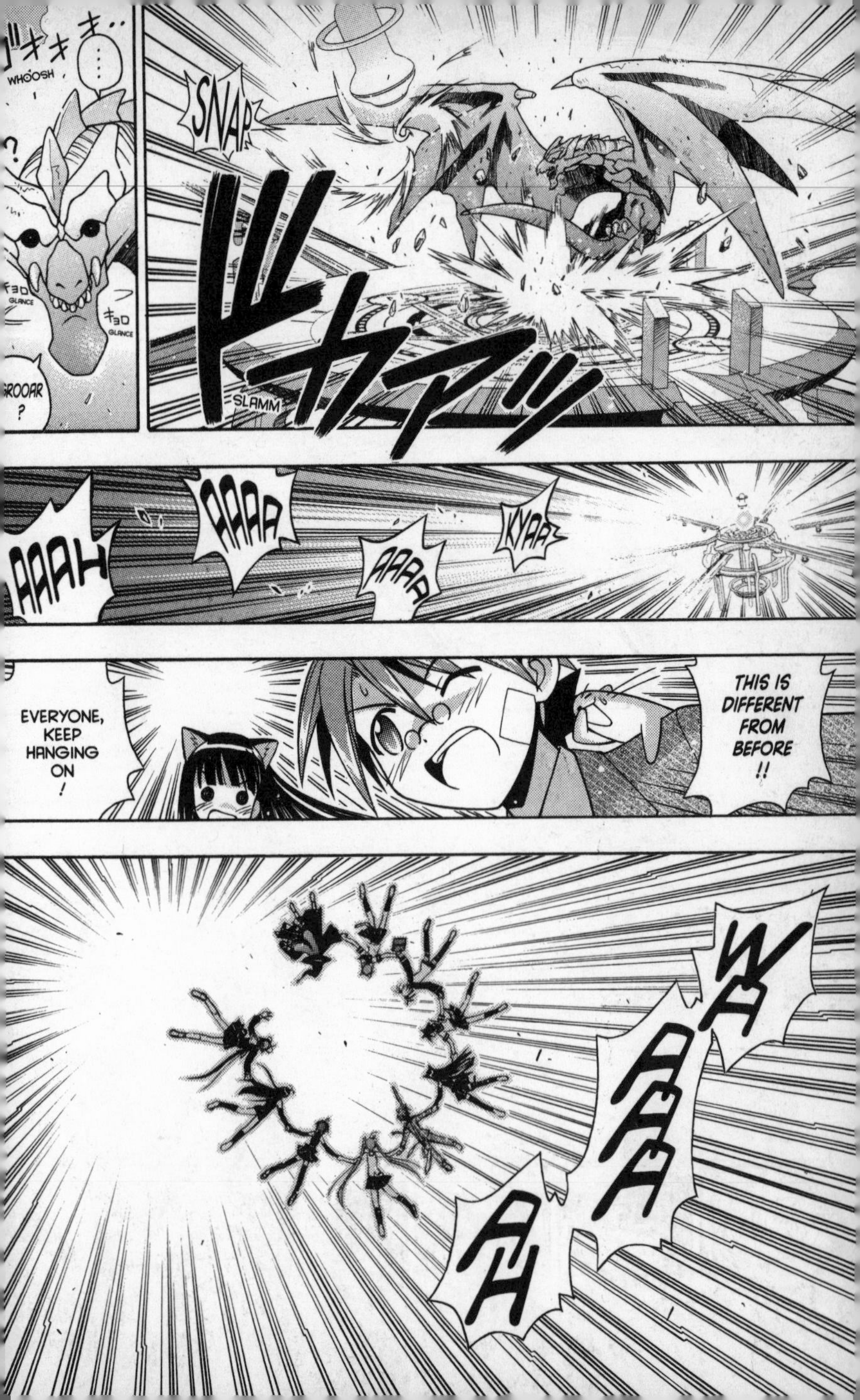
SNAP
SLAMM
...
WHOOSH
?
キョロ
GLANCE
キョロ
GLANCE
GROOAR ?
KYAA
AAAA
AAAA
AAAH
THIS IS DIFFERENT FROM BEFORE !!
EVERYONE, KEEP HANGING ON!
WAAAAAAH

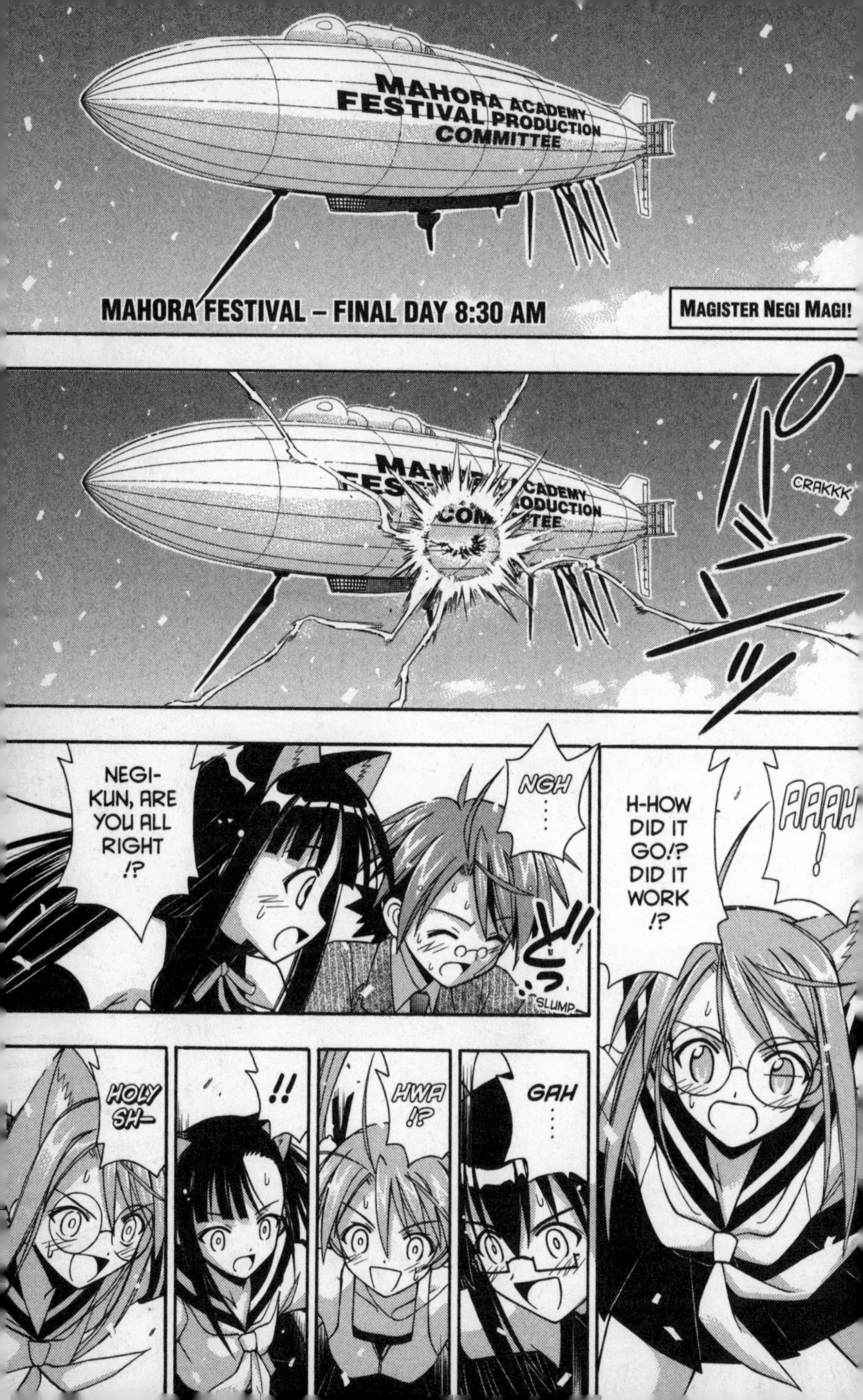
MAHORA ACADEMY FESTIVAL PRODUCTION COMMITTEE
MAGISTER NEGI MAGI!
MAHORA FESTIVAL – FINAL DAY 8:30 AM
CRAKKK
AAAH!
H-HOW DID IT GO!? DID IT WORK!?
NGH....
NEGI-KUN, ARE YOU ALL RIGHT!?
SLUMP
GAH....
HWA!?
!!
HOLY SH–

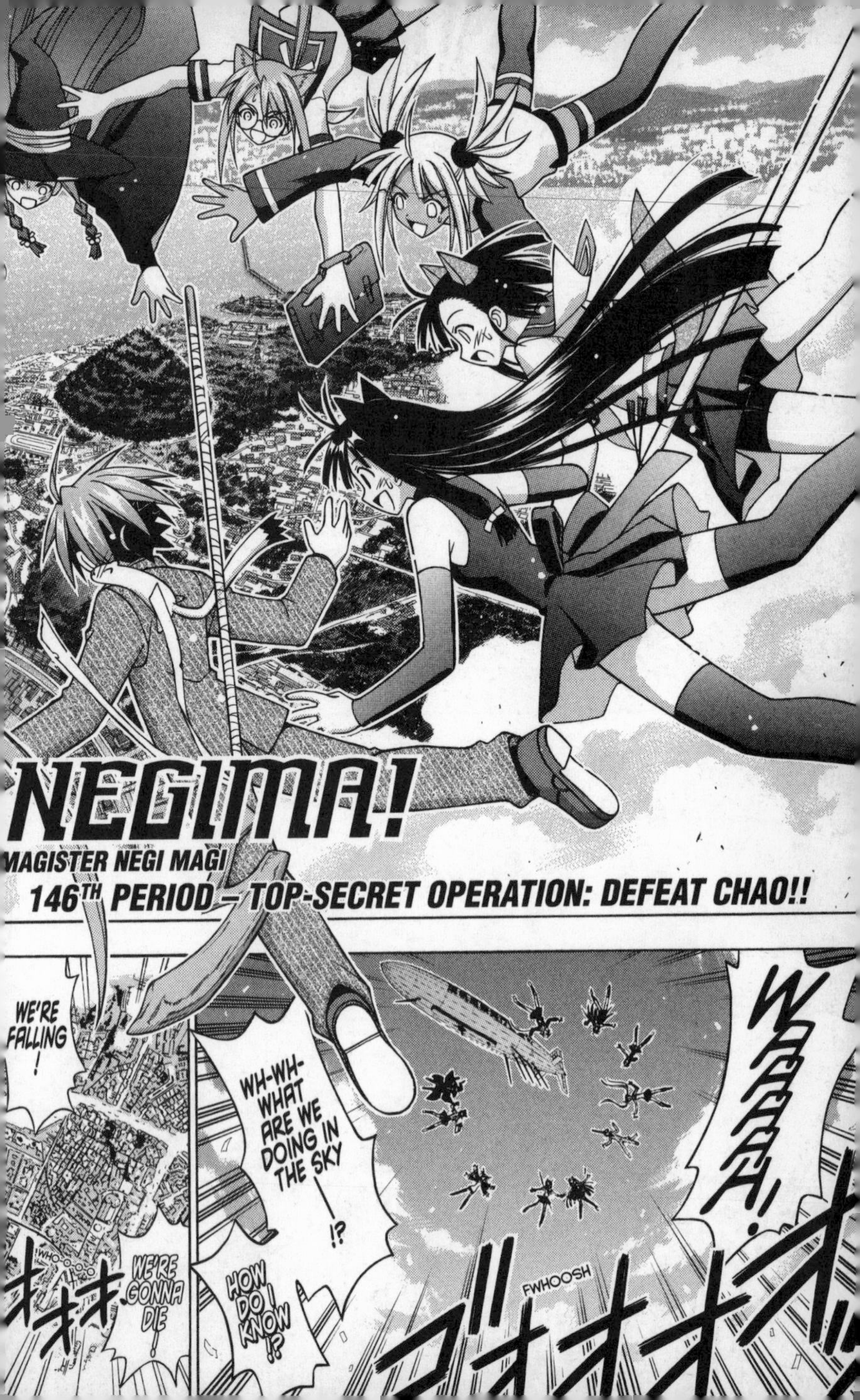
NEGIMA!
MAGISTER NEGI MAGI
146TH PERIOD – TOP-SECRET OPERATION: DEFEAT CHAO!!
WH-WH-WHAT ARE WE DOING IN THE SKY—!?
HOW DO I KNOW!?
FWHOOSH
WE'RE FALLING!
WE'RE GONNA DIE!

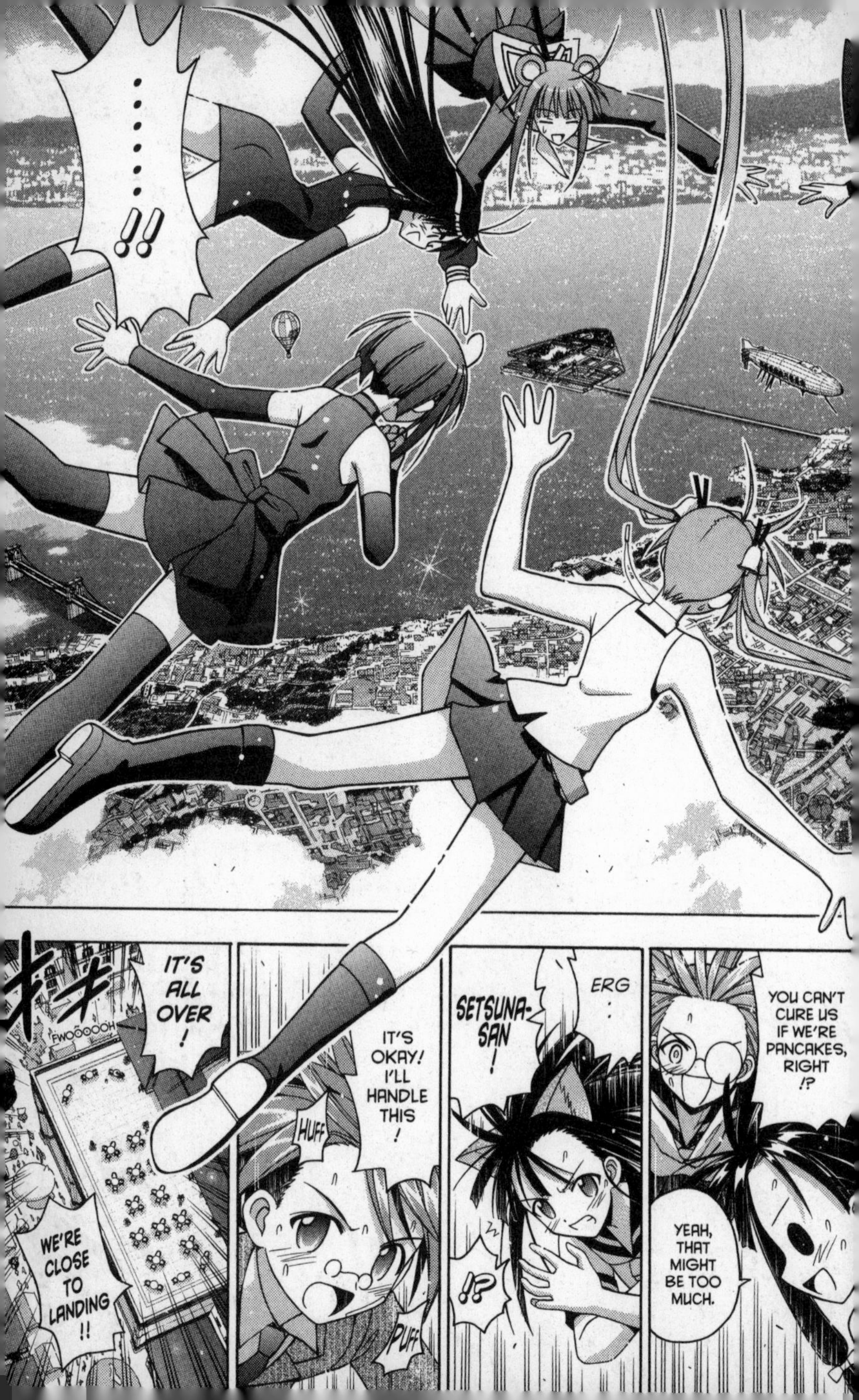
......!!
YOU CAN'T CURE US IF WE'RE PANCAKES, RIGHT!?
YEAH, THAT MIGHT BE TOO MUCH.
ERG
SETSUNA-SAN!
!?
IT'S OKAY! I'LL HANDLE THIS!
HUFF
PUFF
IT'S ALL OVER!
FWOOOOOH
WE'RE CLOSE TO LANDING!!

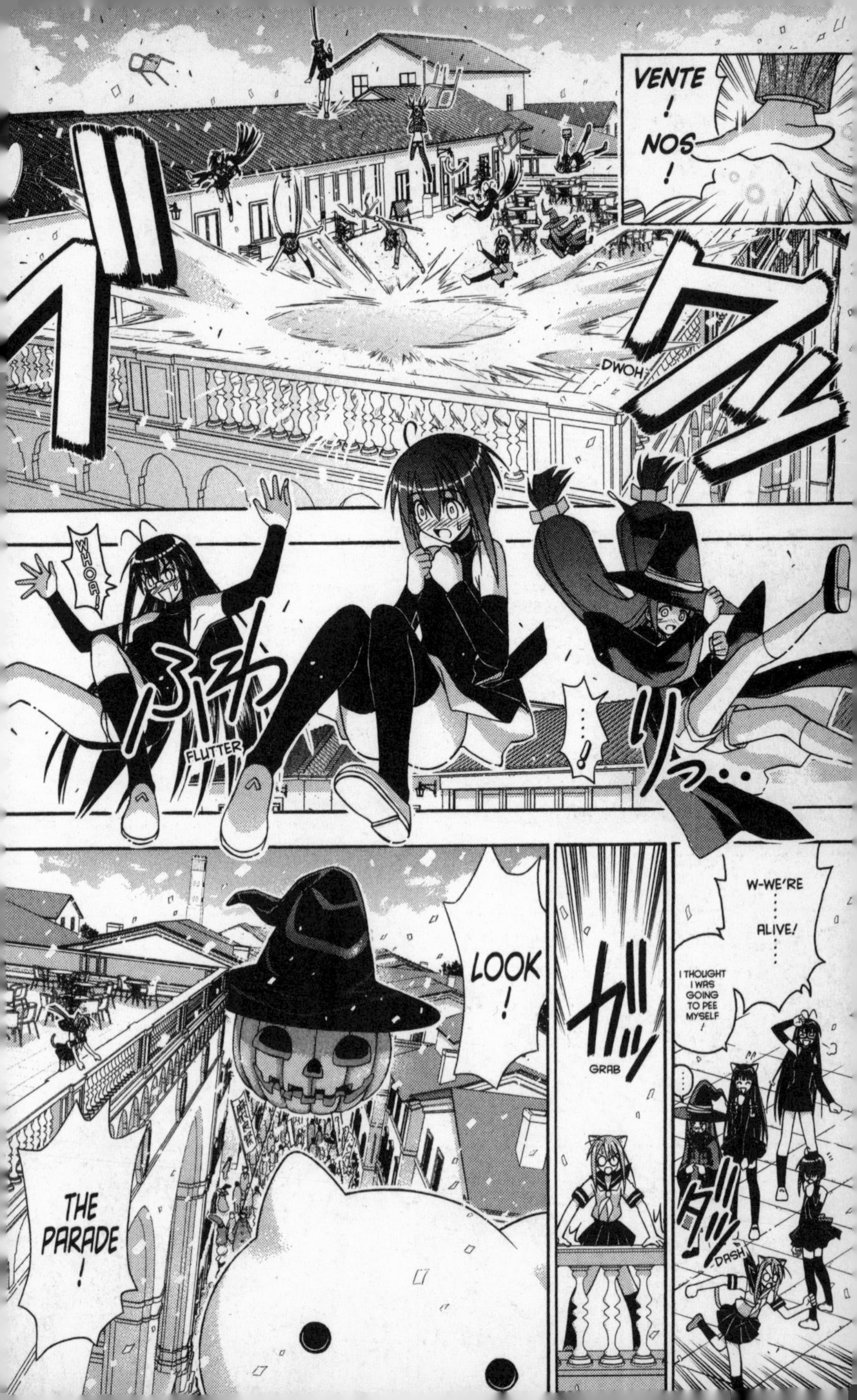
VENTE! NOS!
DWOH
...!
FLUTTER
WHOA!
W-WE'RE...... ALIVE!......
I THOUGHT I WAS GOING TO PEE MYSELF!
DASH
GRAB
LOOK!
THE PARADE!

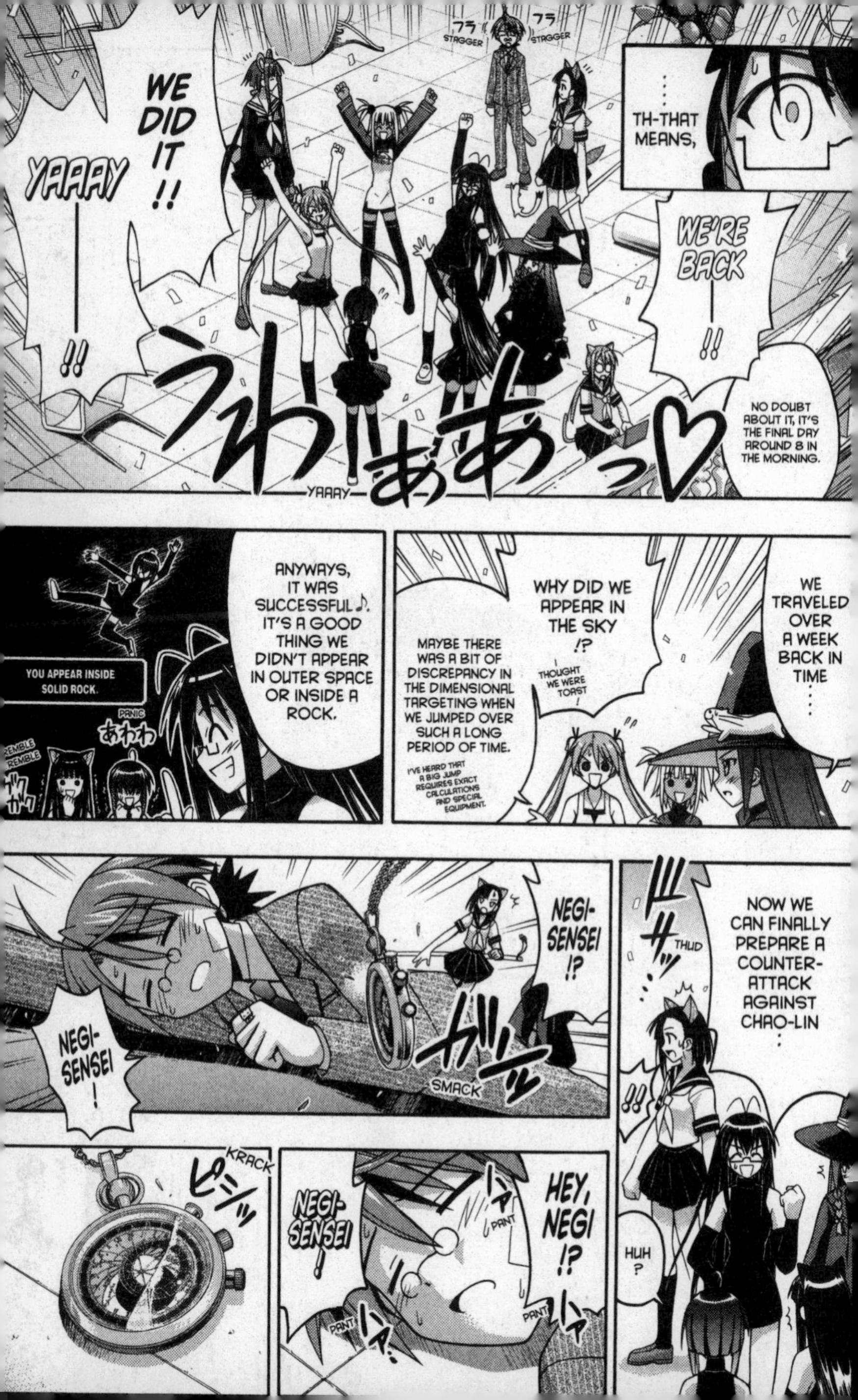

...
TH-THAT MEANS,
WE'RE BACK —!!
NO DOUBT ABOUT IT, IT'S THE FINAL DAY AROUND 8 IN THE MORNING.
フラ STAGGER
フラ STAGGER
WE DID IT!!
YAAAY —!!
YAAAY
WE TRAVELED OVER A WEEK BACK IN TIME...
WHY DID WE APPEAR IN THE SKY!?
I THOUGHT WE WERE TOAST!
MAYBE THERE WAS A BIT OF DISCREPANCY IN THE DIMENSIONAL TARGETING WHEN WE JUMPED OVER SUCH A LONG PERIOD OF TIME.
I'VE HEARD THAT A BIG JUMP REQUIRES EXACT CALCULATIONS AND SPECIAL EQUIPMENT.
ANYWAYS, IT WAS SUCCESSFUL♪. IT'S A GOOD THING WE DIDN'T APPEAR IN OUTER SPACE OR INSIDE A ROCK.
YOU APPEAR INSIDE SOLID ROCK.
PANIC あわわ
TREMBLE TREMBLE
NOW WE CAN FINALLY PREPARE A COUNTER-ATTACK AGAINST CHAO-LIN...
THUD
!!
HUH?
NEGI-SENSEI!?
SMACK
NEGI-SENSEI!
HEY, NEGI!?
ハァ PANT
ハァ PANT
ハァ PANT
NEGI-SENSEI!
KRACK

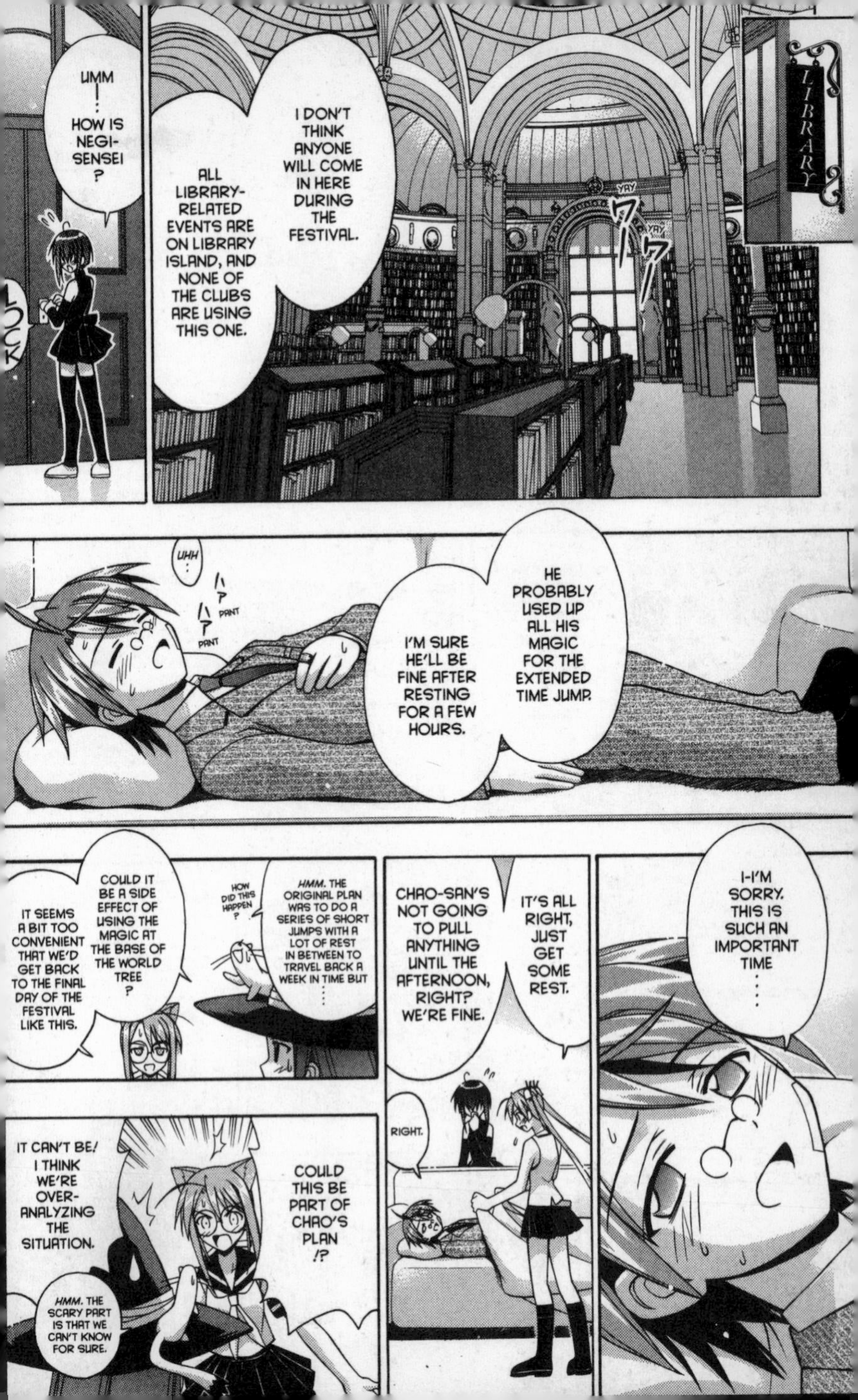
LIBRARY
YAY
YAY
I DON'T THINK ANYONE WILL COME IN HERE DURING THE FESTIVAL.
ALL LIBRARY-RELATED EVENTS ARE ON LIBRARY ISLAND, AND NONE OF THE CLUBS ARE USING THIS ONE.
UMM... HOW IS NEGI-SENSEI?
LOCK
HE PROBABLY USED UP ALL HIS MAGIC FOR THE EXTENDED TIME JUMP.
I'M SURE HE'LL BE FINE AFTER RESTING FOR A FEW HOURS.
UHH...
PANT
PANT
I-I'M SORRY. THIS IS SUCH AN IMPORTANT TIME...
IT'S ALL RIGHT, JUST GET SOME REST.
CHAO-SAN'S NOT GOING TO PULL ANYTHING UNTIL THE AFTERNOON, RIGHT? WE'RE FINE.
RIGHT.
HMM. THE ORIGINAL PLAN WAS TO DO A SERIES OF SHORT JUMPS WITH A LOT OF REST IN BETWEEN TO TRAVEL BACK A WEEK IN TIME BUT...
HOW DID THIS HAPPEN?
COULD IT BE A SIDE EFFECT OF USING THE MAGIC AT THE BASE OF THE WORLD TREE?
IT SEEMS A BIT TOO CONVENIENT THAT WE'D GET BACK TO THE FINAL DAY OF THE FESTIVAL LIKE THIS.
COULD THIS BE PART OF CHAO'S PLAN!?
IT CAN'T BE! I THINK WE'RE OVER-ANALYZING THE SITUATION.
HMM. THE SCARY PART IS THAT WE CAN'T KNOW FOR SURE.

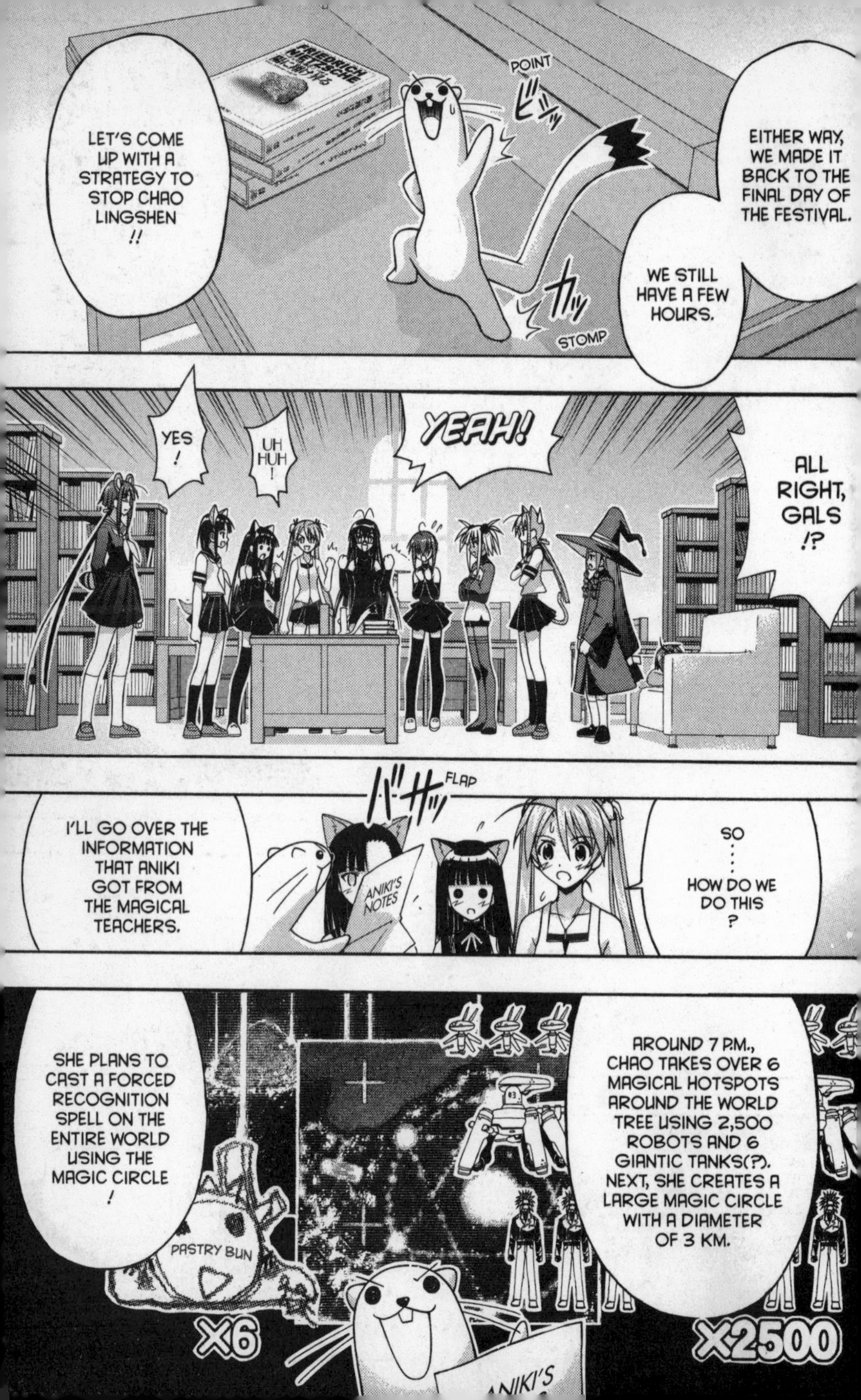
EITHER WAY, WE MADE IT BACK TO THE FINAL DAY OF THE FESTIVAL.
WE STILL HAVE A FEW HOURS.
POINT
STOMP
LET'S COME UP WITH A STRATEGY TO STOP CHAO LINGSHEN !!
FRIEDRICH NIETZSCHE
ALL RIGHT, GALS !?
YEAH!
UH HUH !
YES !
FLAP
SO ... HOW DO WE DO THIS ?
I'LL GO OVER THE INFORMATION THAT ANIKI GOT FROM THE MAGICAL TEACHERS.
ANIKI'S NOTES
AROUND 7 P.M., CHAO TAKES OVER 6 MAGICAL HOTSPOTS AROUND THE WORLD TREE USING 2,500 ROBOTS AND 6 GIANTIC TANKS(?). NEXT, SHE CREATES A LARGE MAGIC CIRCLE WITH A DIAMETER OF 3 KM.
X2500
SHE PLANS TO CAST A FORCED RECOGNITION SPELL ON THE ENTIRE WORLD USING THE MAGIC CIRCLE !
PASTRY BUN
X6
ANIKI'S

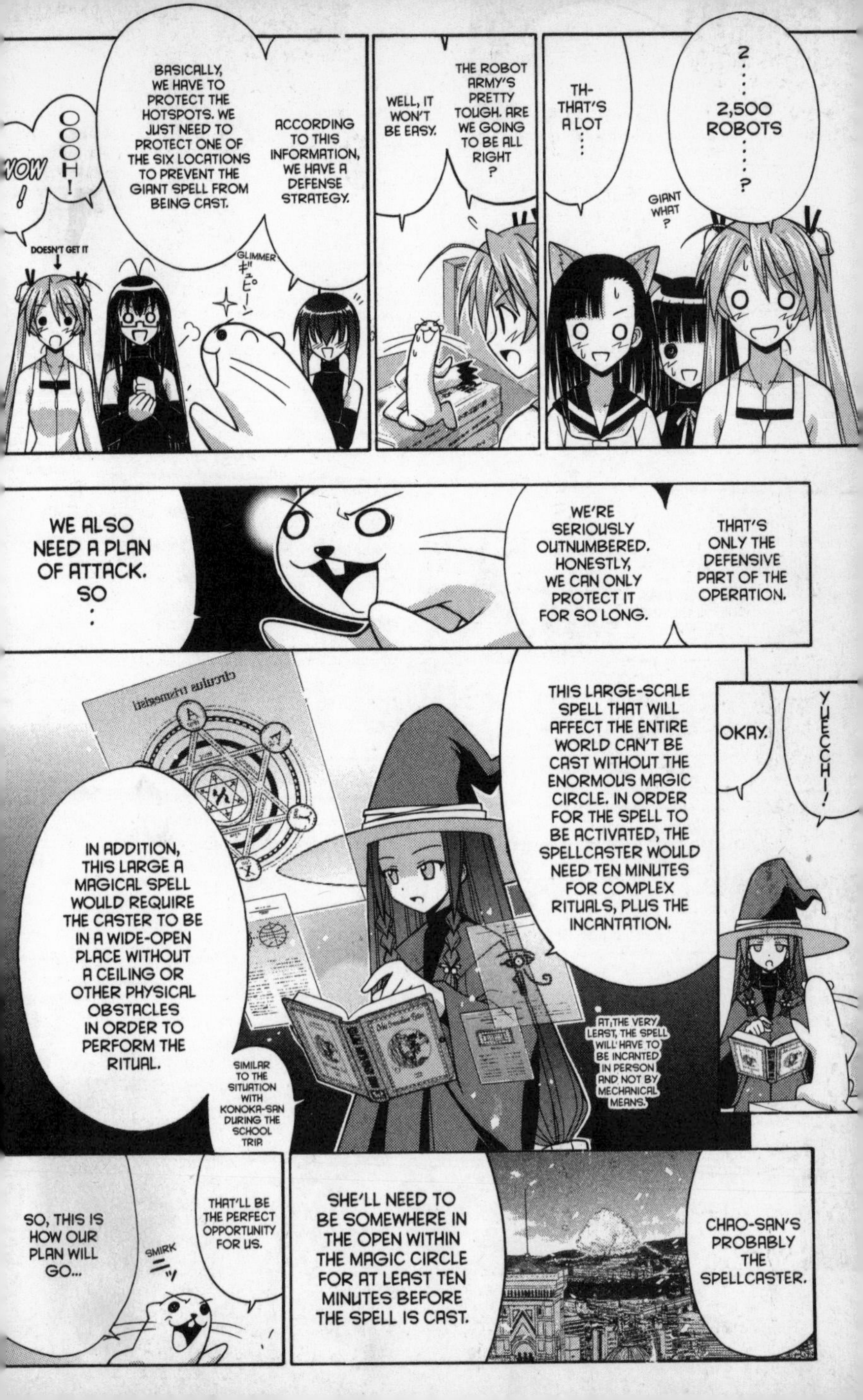
2... 2,500 ROBOTS...?
GIANT WHAT?
TH-THAT'S A LOT...
THE ROBOT ARMY'S PRETTY TOUGH. ARE WE GOING TO BE ALL RIGHT?
WELL, IT WON'T BE EASY.
ACCORDING TO THIS INFORMATION, WE HAVE A DEFENSE STRATEGY.
GLIMMER
BASICALLY, WE HAVE TO PROTECT THE HOTSPOTS. WE JUST NEED TO PROTECT ONE OF THE SIX LOCATIONS TO PREVENT THE GIANT SPELL FROM BEING CAST.
OOOH!
WOW!
DOESN'T GET IT
THAT'S ONLY THE DEFENSIVE PART OF THE OPERATION.
WE'RE SERIOUSLY OUTNUMBERED. HONESTLY, WE CAN ONLY PROTECT IT FOR SO LONG.
WE ALSO NEED A PLAN OF ATTACK. SO...
YUECCHI!
OKAY.
THIS LARGE-SCALE SPELL THAT WILL AFFECT THE ENTIRE WORLD CAN'T BE CAST WITHOUT THE ENORMOUS MAGIC CIRCLE. IN ORDER FOR THE SPELL TO BE ACTIVATED, THE SPELLCASTER WOULD NEED TEN MINUTES FOR COMPLEX RITUALS, PLUS THE INCANTATION.
AT THE VERY LEAST, THE SPELL WILL HAVE TO BE INCANTED IN PERSON AND NOT BY MECHANICAL MEANS.
IN ADDITION, THIS LARGE A MAGICAL SPELL WOULD REQUIRE THE CASTER TO BE IN A WIDE-OPEN PLACE WITHOUT A CEILING OR OTHER PHYSICAL OBSTACLES IN ORDER TO PERFORM THE RITUAL.
SIMILAR TO THE SITUATION WITH KONOKA-SAN DURING THE SCHOOL TRIP.
CHAO-SAN'S PROBABLY THE SPELLCASTER.
SHE'LL NEED TO BE SOMEWHERE IN THE OPEN WITHIN THE MAGIC CIRCLE FOR AT LEAST TEN MINUTES BEFORE THE SPELL IS CAST.
THAT'LL BE THE PERFECT OPPORTUNITY FOR US.
SMIRK
SO, THIS IS HOW OUR PLAN WILL GO...

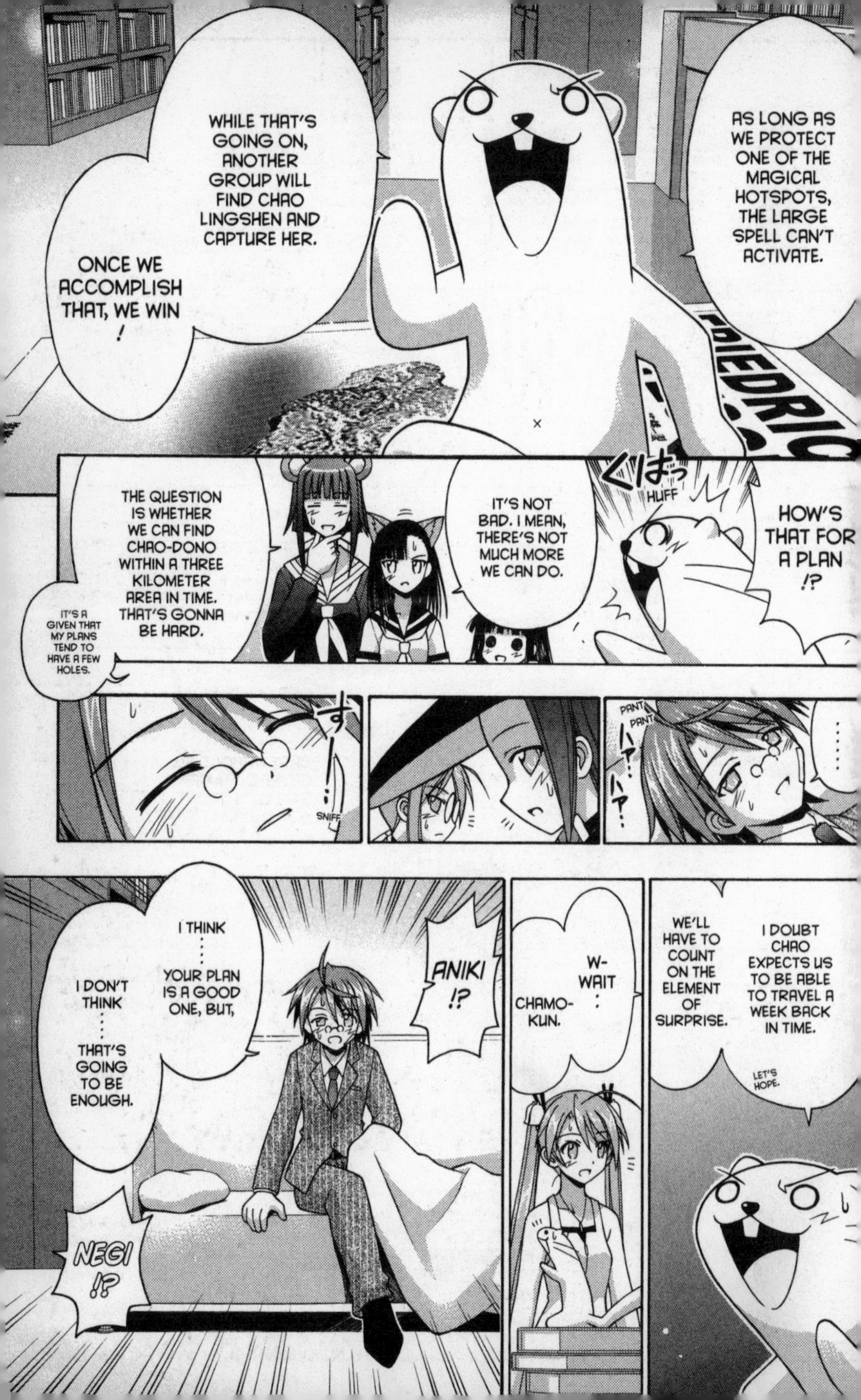
AS LONG AS WE PROTECT ONE OF THE MAGICAL HOTSPOTS, THE LARGE SPELL CAN'T ACTIVATE.
WHILE THAT'S GOING ON, ANOTHER GROUP WILL FIND CHAO LINGSHEN AND CAPTURE HER.
ONCE WE ACCOMPLISH THAT, WE WIN!
くはっ
HUFF
HOW'S THAT FOR A PLAN!?
IT'S NOT BAD. I MEAN, THERE'S NOT MUCH MORE WE CAN DO.
THE QUESTION IS WHETHER WE CAN FIND CHAO-DONO WITHIN A THREE KILOMETER AREA IN TIME. THAT'S GONNA BE HARD.
IT'S A GIVEN THAT MY PLANS TEND TO HAVE A FEW HOLES.
PANT PANT
ハァ… ハァ…
......
す
SNIFF
I DOUBT CHAO EXPECTS US TO BE ABLE TO TRAVEL A WEEK BACK IN TIME.
WE'LL HAVE TO COUNT ON THE ELEMENT OF SURPRISE.
LET'S HOPE.
W-WAIT...
CHAMO-KUN.
ANIKI!?
I THINK... YOUR PLAN IS A GOOD ONE, BUT,
I DON'T THINK... THAT'S GOING TO BE ENOUGH.
NEGI!?

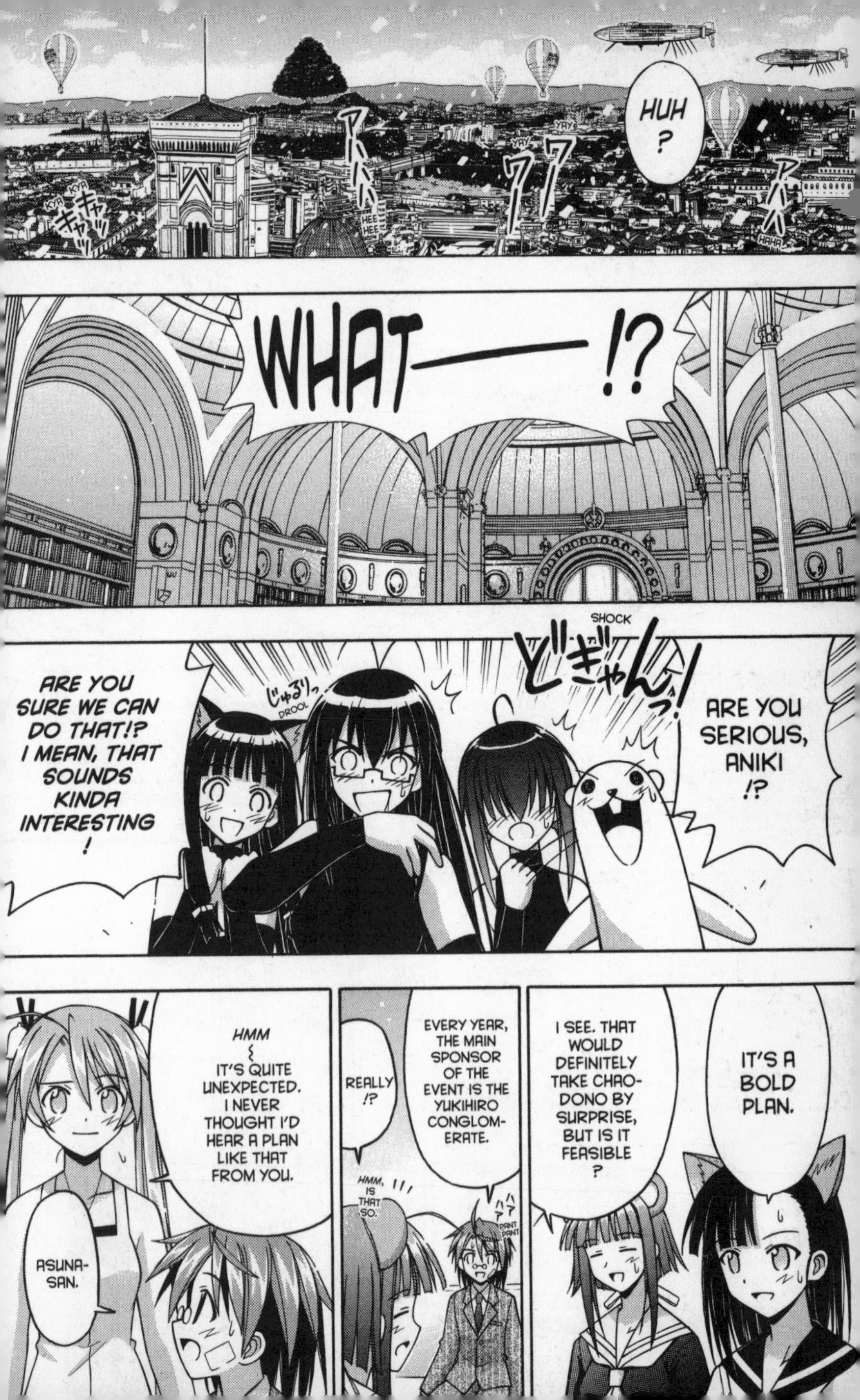
HUH?
HAHA
YAY
YAY
HEE HEE
KYA KYA
WHAT——!?
ARE YOU SERIOUS, ANIKI!?
SHOCK
DROOL
ARE YOU SURE WE CAN DO THAT!? I MEAN, THAT SOUNDS KINDA INTERESTING!
IT'S A BOLD PLAN.
I SEE. THAT WOULD DEFINITELY TAKE CHAO-DONO BY SURPRISE, BUT IS IT FEASIBLE?
EVERY YEAR, THE MAIN SPONSOR OF THE EVENT IS THE YUKIHIRO CONGLOMERATE.
PANT PANT
REALLY!?
HMM, IS THAT SO.
HMM~ IT'S QUITE UNEXPECTED. I NEVER THOUGHT I'D HEAR A PLAN LIKE THAT FROM YOU.
ASUNA-SAN.

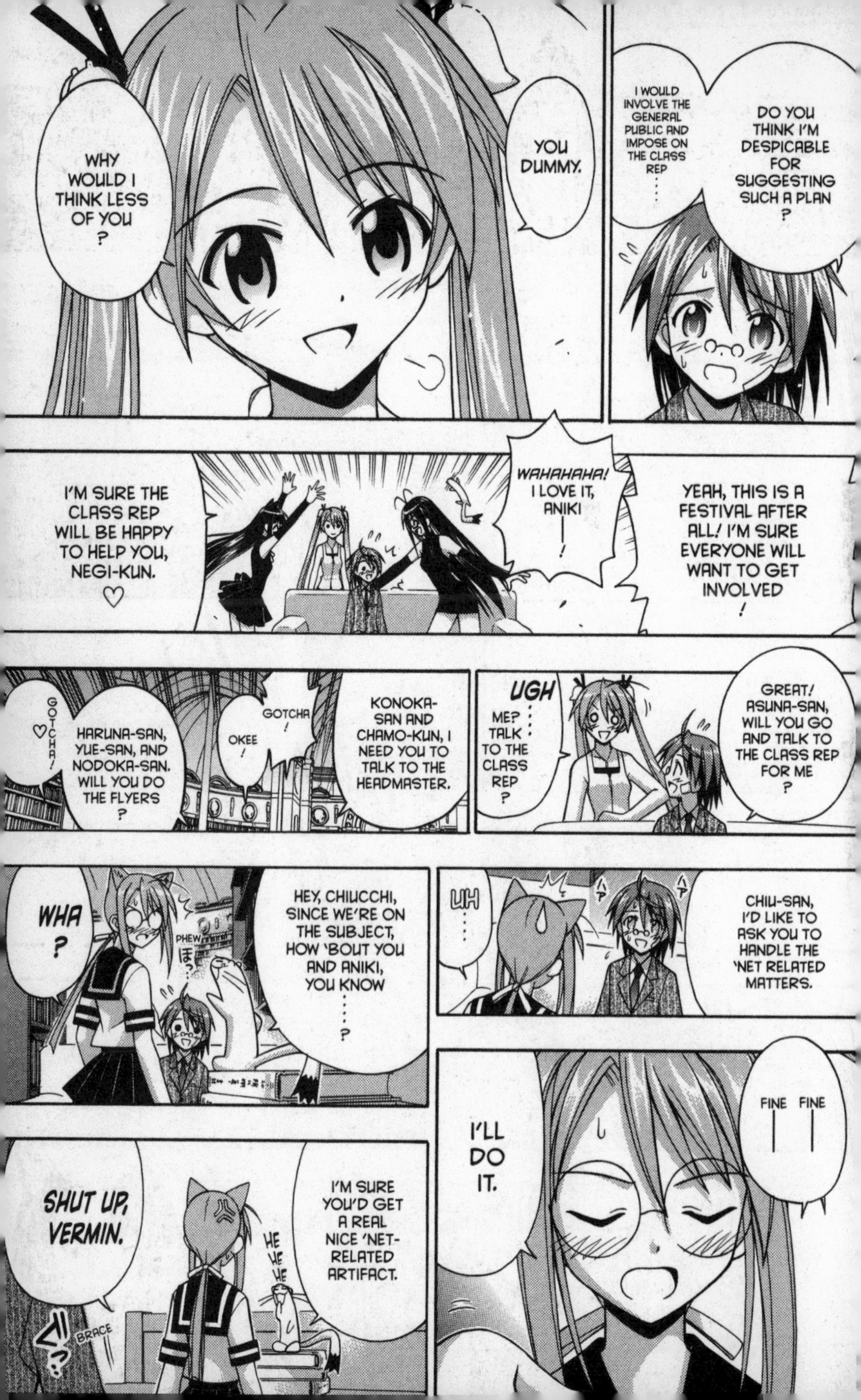

DO YOU THINK I'M DESPICABLE FOR SUGGESTING SUCH A PLAN?
I WOULD INVOLVE THE GENERAL PUBLIC AND IMPOSE ON THE CLASS REP...
YOU DUMMY.
WHY WOULD I THINK LESS OF YOU?
YEAH, THIS IS A FESTIVAL AFTER ALL! I'M SURE EVERYONE WILL WANT TO GET INVOLVED!
WAHAHAHA! I LOVE IT, ANIKI!
I'M SURE THE CLASS REP WILL BE HAPPY TO HELP YOU, NEGI-KUN. ♡
GREAT! ASUNA-SAN, WILL YOU GO AND TALK TO THE CLASS REP FOR ME?
UGH
ME? TALK TO THE CLASS REP?
KONOKA-SAN AND CHAMO-KUN, I NEED YOU TO TALK TO THE HEADMASTER.
GOTCHA!
OKEE!
HARUNA-SAN, YUE-SAN, AND NODOKA-SAN. WILL YOU DO THE FLYERS?
GOTCHA! ♡
CHIU-SAN, I'D LIKE TO ASK YOU TO HANDLE THE 'NET RELATED MATTERS.
UH...
HEY, CHIUCCHI, SINCE WE'RE ON THE SUBJECT, HOW 'BOUT YOU AND ANIKI, YOU KNOW...?
PHEW
WHA?
FINE FINE
I'LL DO IT.
I'M SURE YOU'D GET A REAL NICE 'NET-RELATED ARTIFACT.
HE HE HE
SHUT UP, VERMIN.
BRACE

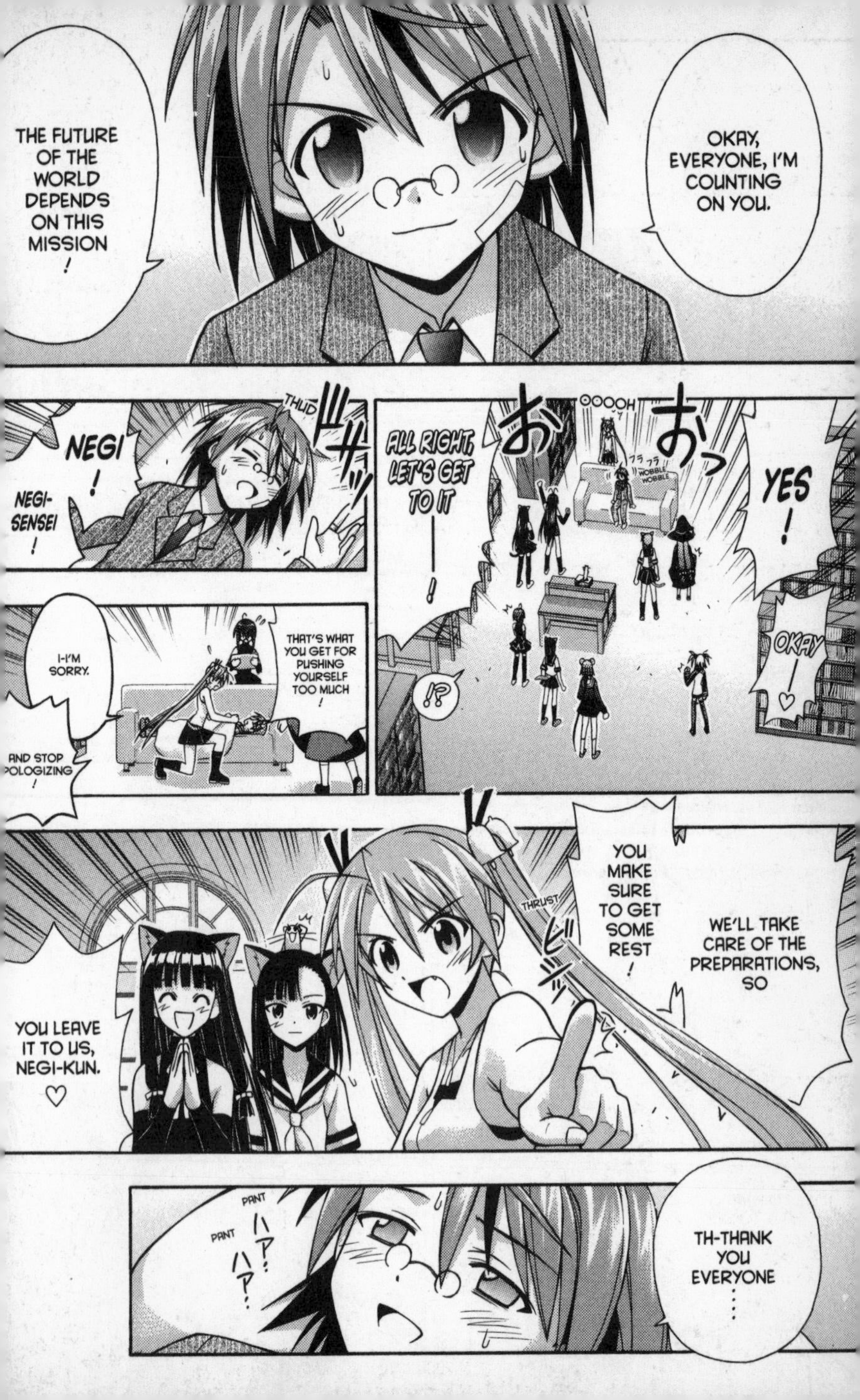

OKAY, EVERYONE, I'M COUNTING ON YOU.
THE FUTURE OF THE WORLD DEPENDS ON THIS MISSION!
YES!
OOOOH
WOBBLE WOBBLE
ALL RIGHT, LET'S GET TO IT—!
OKAY! ♡
!?
THUD
NEGI!
NEGI-SENSEI!
THAT'S WHAT YOU GET FOR PUSHING YOURSELF TOO MUCH!
I-I'M SORRY.
AND STOP POLOGIZING!
WE'LL TAKE CARE OF THE PREPARATIONS, SO
YOU MAKE SURE TO GET SOME REST!
THRUST
YOU LEAVE IT TO US, NEGI-KUN. ♡
TH-THANK YOU EVERYONE…
PANT
PANT

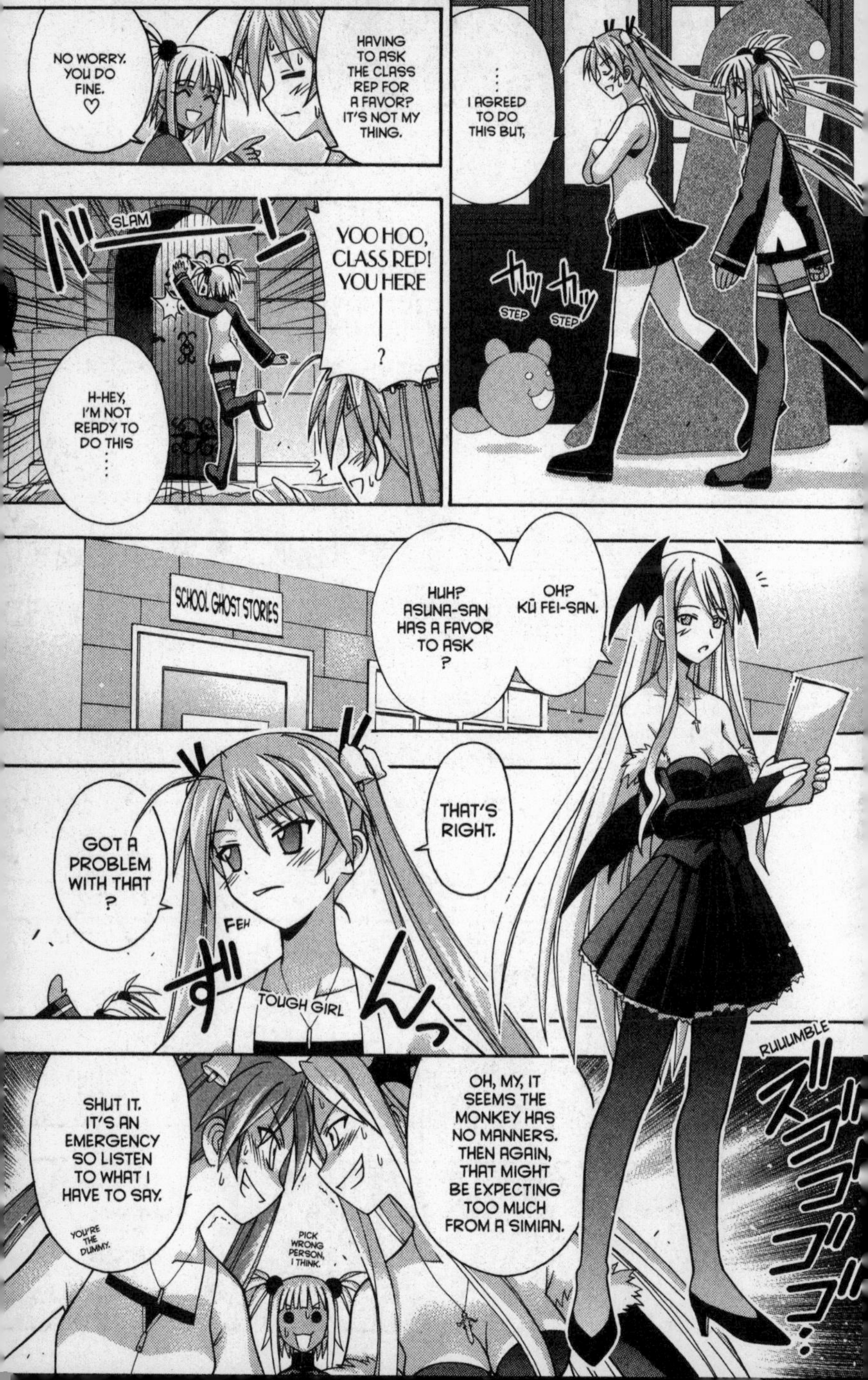

... I AGREED TO DO THIS BUT,
STEP STEP
HAVING TO ASK THE CLASS REP FOR A FAVOR? IT'S NOT MY THING.
NO WORRY. YOU DO FINE. ♡
YOO HOO, CLASS REP! YOU HERE —?
SLAM
H-HEY, I'M NOT READY TO DO THIS ....
OH? KŪ FEI-SAN.
HUH? ASUNA-SAN HAS A FAVOR TO ASK?
SCHOOL GHOST STORIES
THAT'S RIGHT.
GOT A PROBLEM WITH THAT?
FEH
TOUGH GIRL
RUUUMBLE
OH, MY, IT SEEMS THE MONKEY HAS NO MANNERS. THEN AGAIN, THAT MIGHT BE EXPECTING TOO MUCH FROM A SIMIAN.
SHUT IT. IT'S AN EMERGENCY SO LISTEN TO WHAT I HAVE TO SAY.
PICK WRONG PERSON, I THINK.
YOU'RE THE DUMMY.

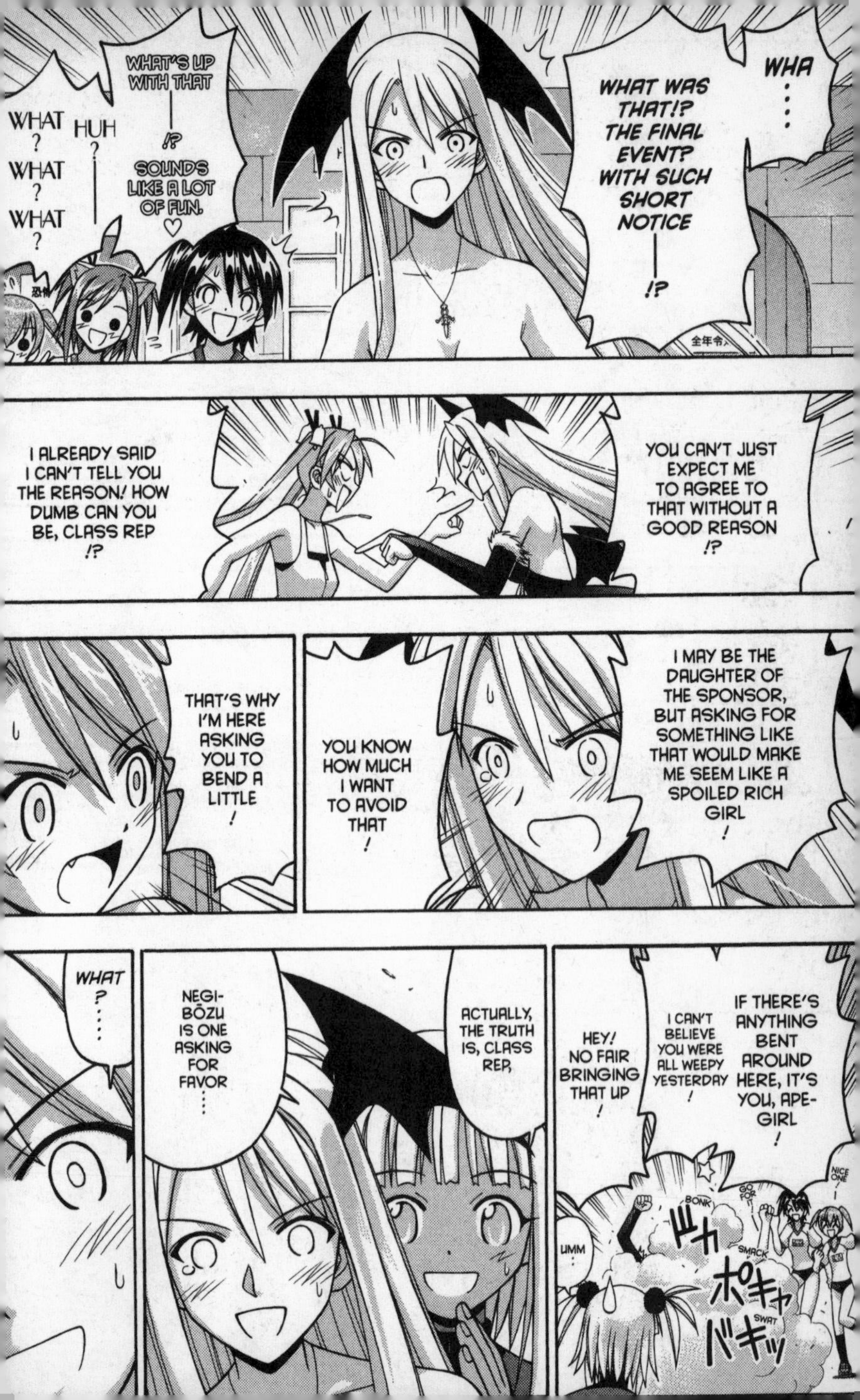
WHA....
WHAT WAS THAT!? THE FINAL EVENT? WITH SUCH SHORT NOTICE—!?
WHAT'S UP WITH THAT—!?
SOUNDS LIKE A LOT OF FUN. ♡
HUH?
WHAT? WHAT? WHAT?
YOU CAN'T JUST EXPECT ME TO AGREE TO THAT WITHOUT A GOOD REASON!?
I ALREADY SAID I CAN'T TELL YOU THE REASON! HOW DUMB CAN YOU BE, CLASS REP!?
I MAY BE THE DAUGHTER OF THE SPONSOR, BUT ASKING FOR SOMETHING LIKE THAT WOULD MAKE ME SEEM LIKE A SPOILED RICH GIRL!
YOU KNOW HOW MUCH I WANT TO AVOID THAT!
THAT'S WHY I'M HERE ASKING YOU TO BEND A LITTLE!
IF THERE'S ANYTHING BENT AROUND HERE, IT'S YOU, APE-GIRL!
I CAN'T BELIEVE YOU WERE ALL WEEPY YESTERDAY!
HEY! NO FAIR BRINGING THAT UP!
NICE ONE!
GO FOR IT!
ドカ
BONK
ポキャ
SMACK
バギッ
SWAT
UMM...
ACTUALLY, THE TRUTH IS, CLASS REP,
NEGI-BŌZU IS ONE ASKING FOR FAVOR....
WHAT?.....

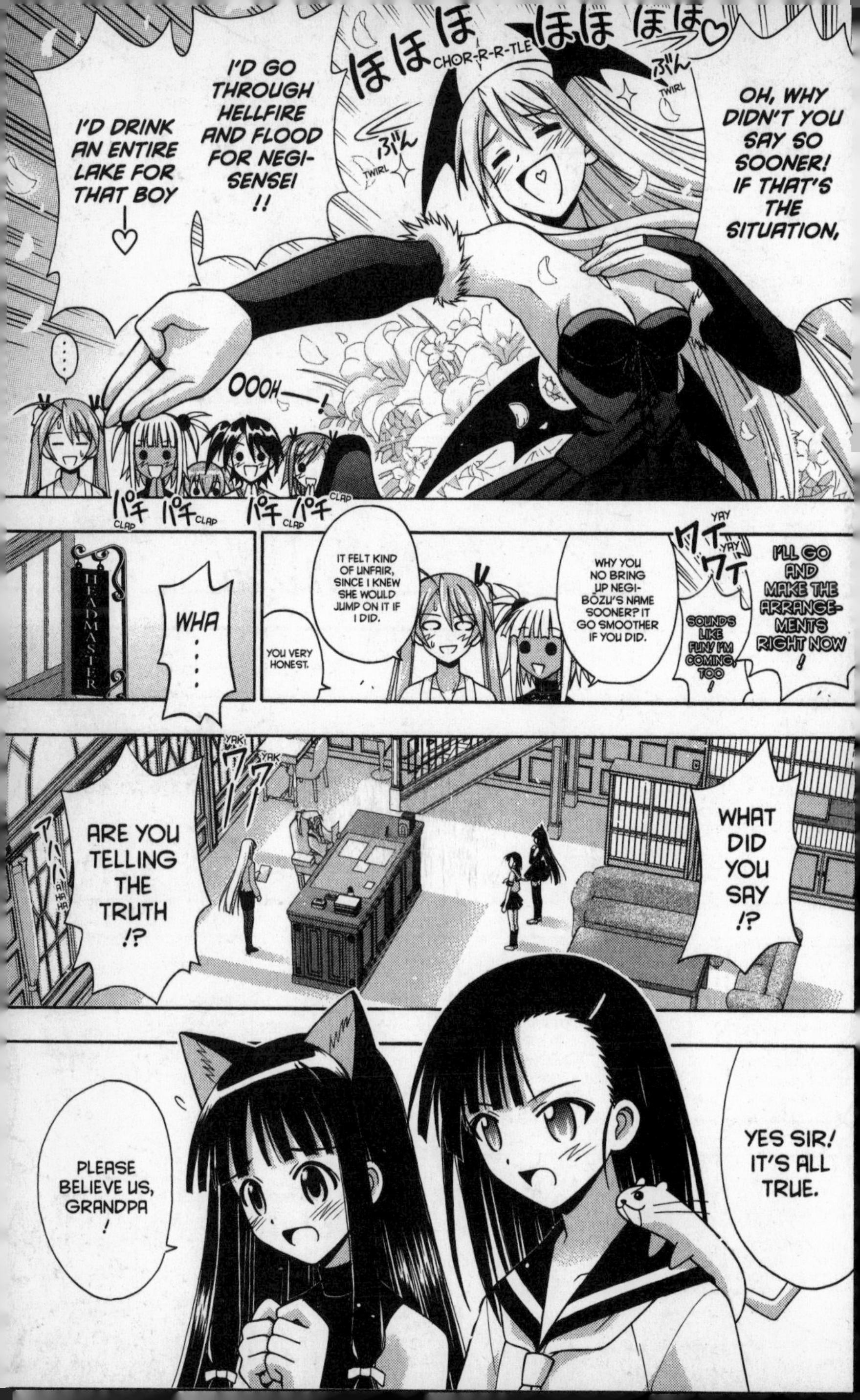
OH, WHY DIDN'T YOU SAY SO SOONER! IF THAT'S THE SITUATION,
ほほほ CHOR-R-R-TLE ほほ ほほ♡
ぶん TWIRL
ぶん TWIRL
I'D GO THROUGH HELLFIRE AND FLOOD FOR NEGI-SENSEI !!
I'D DRINK AN ENTIRE LAKE FOR THAT BOY ♡
...
OOOH—!
パチ CLAP パチ CLAP パチ CLAP パチ CLAP
I'LL GO AND MAKE THE ARRANGEMENTS RIGHT NOW!
ワイ YAY ワイ YAY
SOUNDS LIKE FUN! I'M COMING, TOO!
WHY YOU NO BRING UP NEGI-BŌZU'S NAME SOONER? IT GO SMOOTHER IF YOU DID.
IT FELT KIND OF UNFAIR, SINCE I KNEW SHE WOULD JUMP ON IT IF I DID.
YOU VERY HONEST.
HEADMASTER
WHA...
WHAT DID YOU SAY !?
ワ YAK ワ YAK
ARE YOU TELLING THE TRUTH !?
アハハ AHAHA
YES SIR! IT'S ALL TRUE.
PLEASE BELIEVE US, GRANDPA!

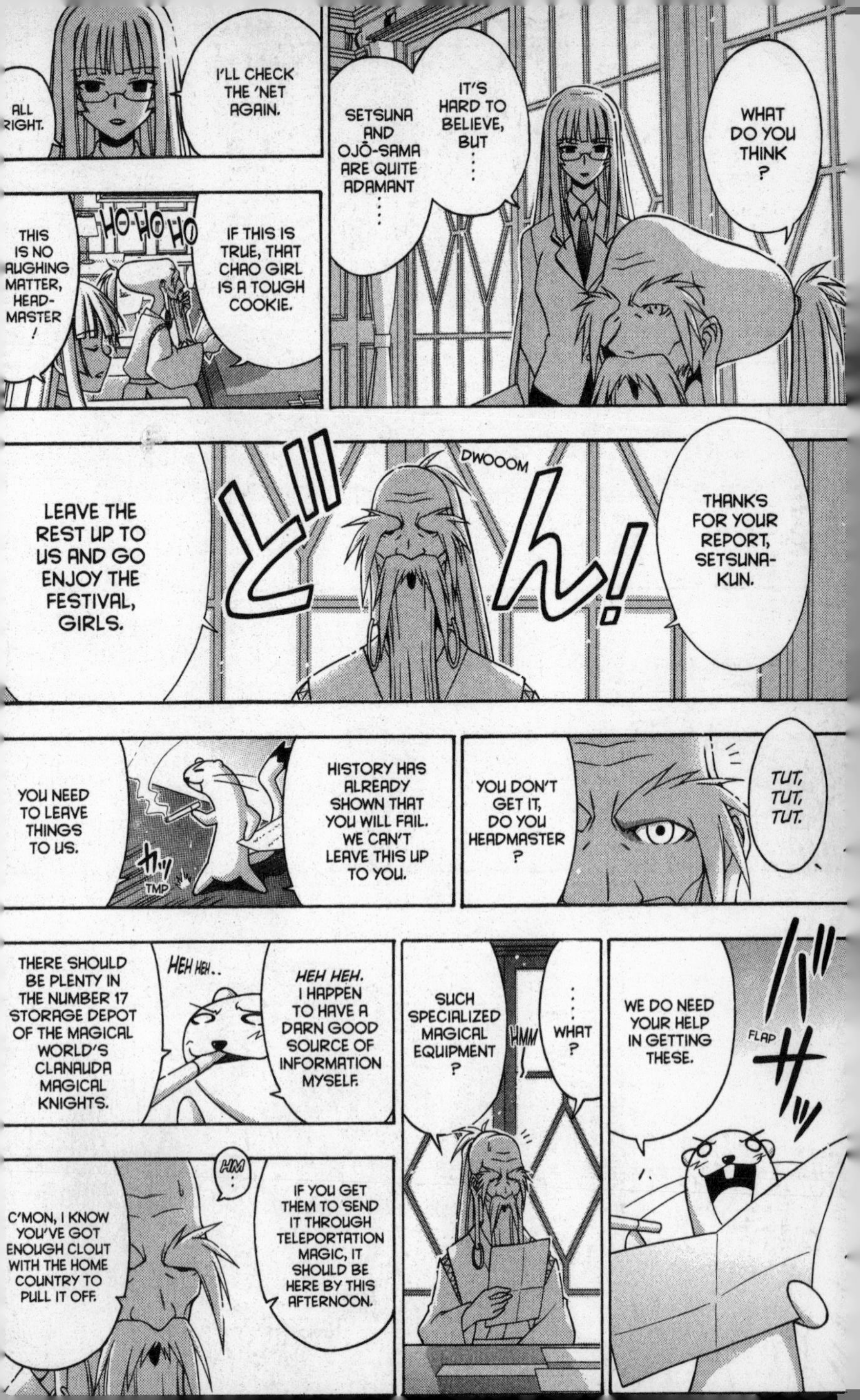
WHAT DO YOU THINK?
IT'S HARD TO BELIEVE, BUT...
SETSUNA AND OJŌ-SAMA ARE QUITE ADAMANT...
I'LL CHECK THE 'NET AGAIN.
ALL RIGHT.
HO HO HO
IF THIS IS TRUE, THAT CHAO GIRL IS A TOUGH COOKIE.
THIS IS NO AUGHING MATTER, HEAD-MASTER!
THANKS FOR YOUR REPORT, SETSUNA-KUN.
DWOOOM
どん!
LEAVE THE REST UP TO US AND GO ENJOY THE FESTIVAL, GIRLS.
TUT, TUT, TUT.
YOU DON'T GET IT, DO YOU HEADMASTER?
HISTORY HAS ALREADY SHOWN THAT YOU WILL FAIL. WE CAN'T LEAVE THIS UP TO YOU.
カッ
TMP
YOU NEED TO LEAVE THINGS TO US.
バサッ
FLAP
WE DO NEED YOUR HELP IN GETTING THESE.
...WHAT?
HMM
SUCH SPECIALIZED MAGICAL EQUIPMENT?
HEH HEH. I HAPPEN TO HAVE A DARN GOOD SOURCE OF INFORMATION MYSELF.
HEH HEH..
THERE SHOULD BE PLENTY IN THE NUMBER 17 STORAGE DEPOT OF THE MAGICAL WORLD'S CLANAUDA MAGICAL KNIGHTS.
IF YOU GET THEM TO SEND IT THROUGH TELEPORTATION MAGIC, IT SHOULD BE HERE BY THIS AFTERNOON.
HM...
C'MON, I KNOW YOU'VE GOT ENOUGH CLOUT WITH THE HOME COUNTRY TO PULL IT OFF.

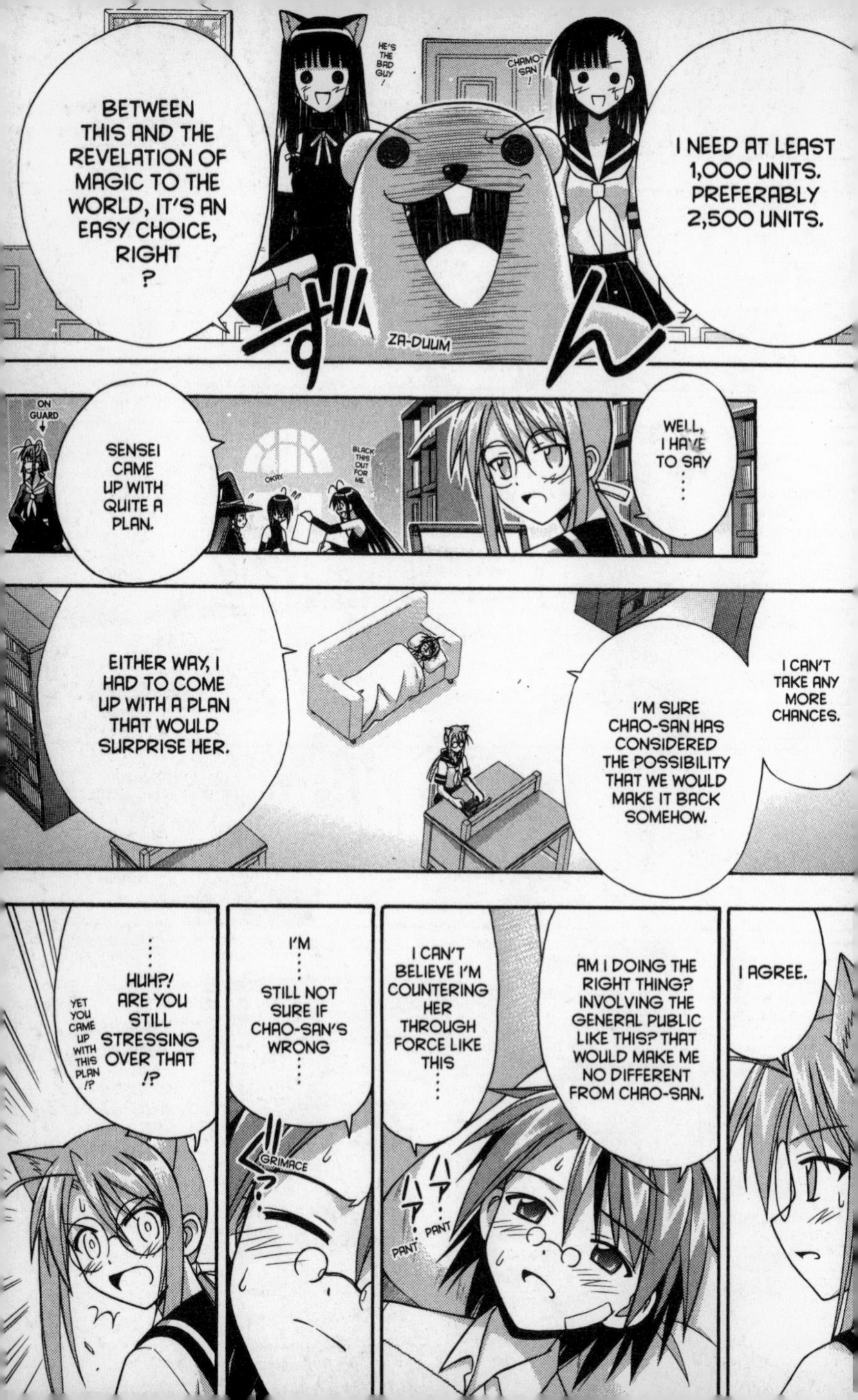
I NEED AT LEAST 1,000 UNITS. PREFERABLY 2,500 UNITS.
CHAMO-SAN!
HE'S THE BAD GUY!
BETWEEN THIS AND THE REVELATION OF MAGIC TO THE WORLD, IT'S AN EASY CHOICE, RIGHT?
ZA-DUUM
WELL, I HAVE TO SAY......
BLACK THIS OUT FOR ME.
OKAY.
SENSEI CAME UP WITH QUITE A PLAN.
ON GUARD
I'M SURE CHAO-SAN HAS CONSIDERED THE POSSIBILITY THAT WE WOULD MAKE IT BACK SOMEHOW.
I CAN'T TAKE ANY MORE CHANCES.
EITHER WAY, I HAD TO COME UP WITH A PLAN THAT WOULD SURPRISE HER.
I AGREE.
AM I DOING THE RIGHT THING? INVOLVING THE GENERAL PUBLIC LIKE THIS? THAT WOULD MAKE ME NO DIFFERENT FROM CHAO-SAN.
PANT
PANT
I CAN'T BELIEVE I'M COUNTERING HER THROUGH FORCE LIKE THIS......
I'M... STILL NOT SURE IF CHAO-SAN'S WRONG...
GRIMACE
...HUH?! ARE YOU STILL STRESSING OVER THAT!?
YET YOU CAME UP WITH THIS PLAN!?

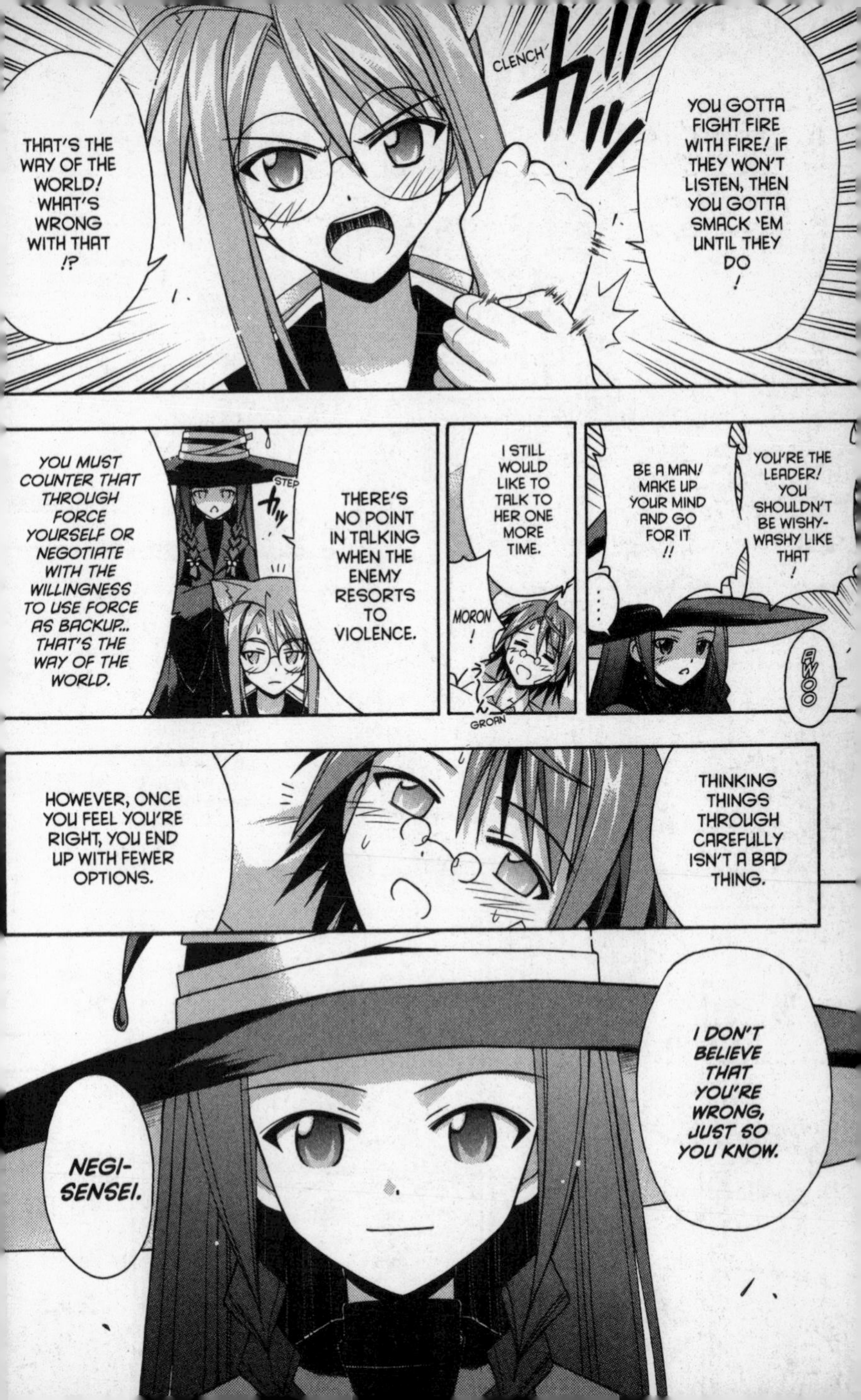
CLENCH
YOU GOTTA FIGHT FIRE WITH FIRE! IF THEY WON'T LISTEN, THEN YOU GOTTA SMACK 'EM UNTIL THEY DO!
THAT'S THE WAY OF THE WORLD! WHAT'S WRONG WITH THAT!?
YOU'RE THE LEADER! YOU SHOULDN'T BE WISHY-WASHY LIKE THAT!
BE A MAN! MAKE UP YOUR MIND AND GO FOR IT!!
AWOO
...
I STILL WOULD LIKE TO TALK TO HER ONE MORE TIME.
MORON!
GROAN
THERE'S NO POINT IN TALKING WHEN THE ENEMY RESORTS TO VIOLENCE.
STEP
YOU MUST COUNTER THAT THROUGH FORCE YOURSELF OR NEGOTIATE WITH THE WILLINGNESS TO USE FORCE AS BACKUP... THAT'S THE WAY OF THE WORLD.
THINKING THINGS THROUGH CAREFULLY ISN'T A BAD THING.
HOWEVER, ONCE YOU FEEL YOU'RE RIGHT, YOU END UP WITH FEWER OPTIONS.
I DON'T BELIEVE THAT YOU'RE WRONG, JUST SO YOU KNOW.
NEGI-SENSEI.

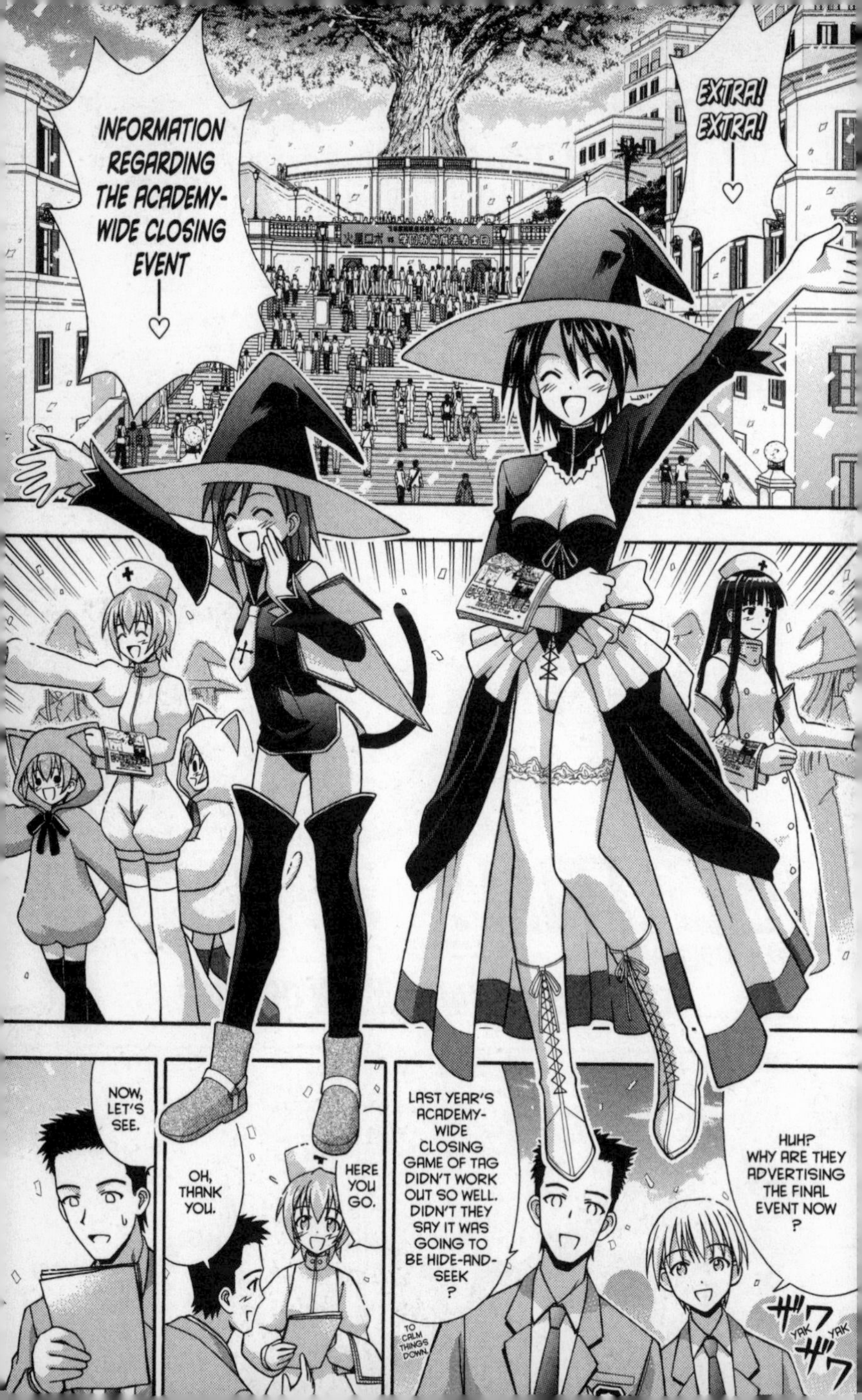
EXTRA! EXTRA! ♥
INFORMATION REGARDING THE ACADEMY-WIDE CLOSING EVENT ♥
HUH? WHY ARE THEY ADVERTISING THE FINAL EVENT NOW?
LAST YEAR'S ACADEMY-WIDE CLOSING GAME OF TAG DIDN'T WORK OUT SO WELL. DIDN'T THEY SAY IT WAS GOING TO BE HIDE-AND-SEEK?
YAK YAK
TO CALM THINGS DOWN.
HERE YOU GO.
OH, THANK YOU.
NOW, LET'S SEE.

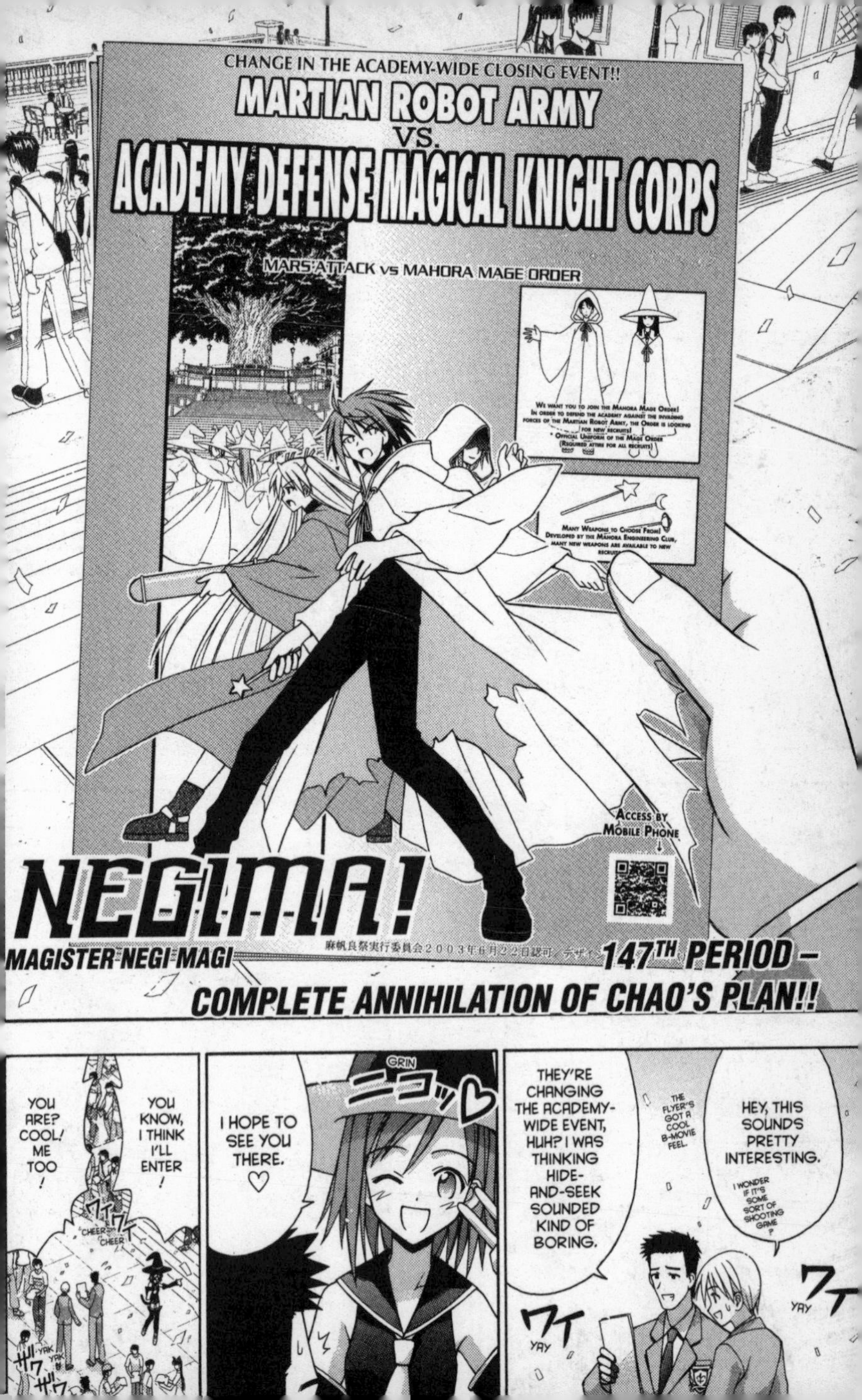

CHANGE IN THE ACADEMY-WIDE CLOSING EVENT!!
MARTIAN ROBOT ARMY
VS.
ACADEMY DEFENSE MAGICAL KNIGHT CORPS
MARS ATTACK vs MAHORA MAGE ORDER
We want you to join the Mahora Mage Order! In order to defend the academy against the invading forces of the Martian Robot Army, the Order is looking for new recruits!
* Official Uniform of the Mage Order (Required attire for all recruits)
Many Weapons to Choose From! Developed by the Mahora Engineering Club, many new weapons are available to new
Access by Mobile Phone
NEGIMA!
MAGISTER NEGI MAGI
麻帆良祭実行委員会２００３年６月２２日認可／デザイン
147TH PERIOD – COMPLETE ANNIHILATION OF CHAO'S PLAN!!
HEY, THIS SOUNDS PRETTY INTERESTING.
I WONDER IF IT'S SOME SORT OF SHOOTING GAME?
THE FLYER'S GOT A COOL B-MOVIE FEEL.
THEY'RE CHANGING THE ACADEMY-WIDE EVENT, HUH? I WAS THINKING HIDE-AND-SEEK SOUNDED KIND OF BORING.
YAY
YAY
GRIN
I HOPE TO SEE YOU THERE. ♡
YOU KNOW, I THINK I'LL ENTER!
YOU ARE? COOL! ME TOO!
CHEER CHEER
YAK YAK

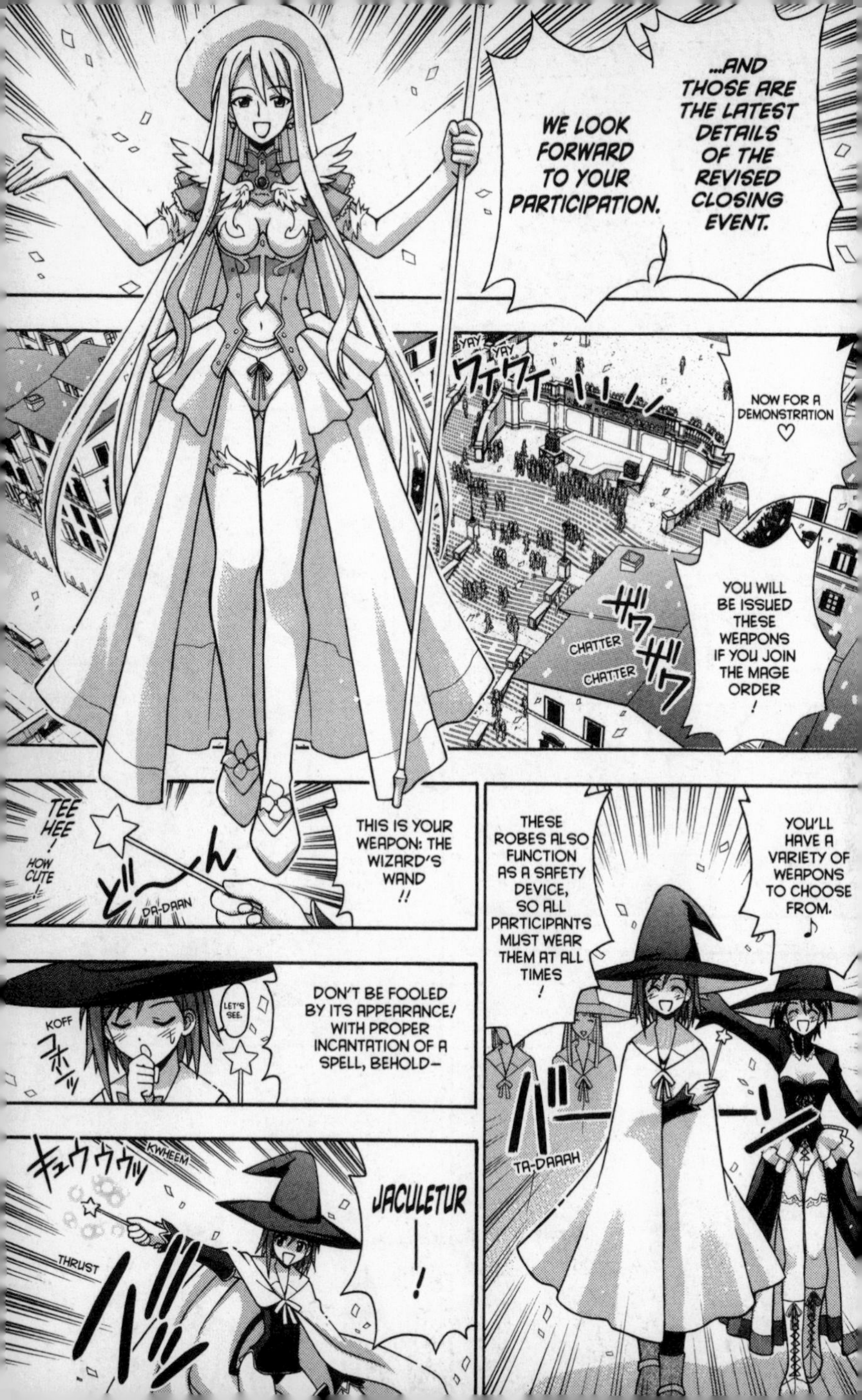
...AND THOSE ARE THE LATEST DETAILS OF THE REVISED CLOSING EVENT.
WE LOOK FORWARD TO YOUR PARTICIPATION.
YAY YAY
ワイワイ
NOW FOR A DEMONSTRATION ♡
YOU WILL BE ISSUED THESE WEAPONS IF YOU JOIN THE MAGE ORDER!
ザワザワ
CHATTER CHATTER
YOU'LL HAVE A VARIETY OF WEAPONS TO CHOOSE FROM. ♪
THESE ROBES ALSO FUNCTION AS A SAFETY DEVICE, SO ALL PARTICIPANTS MUST WEAR THEM AT ALL TIMES!
TA-DAAAH
THIS IS YOUR WEAPON: THE WIZARD'S WAND!!
TEE HEE!
HOW CUTE!
DA-DAAN
DON'T BE FOOLED BY ITS APPEARANCE! WITH PROPER INCANTATION OF A SPELL, BEHOLD—
LET'S SEE.
KOFF
JACULETUR—!
KWHEEM
THRUST

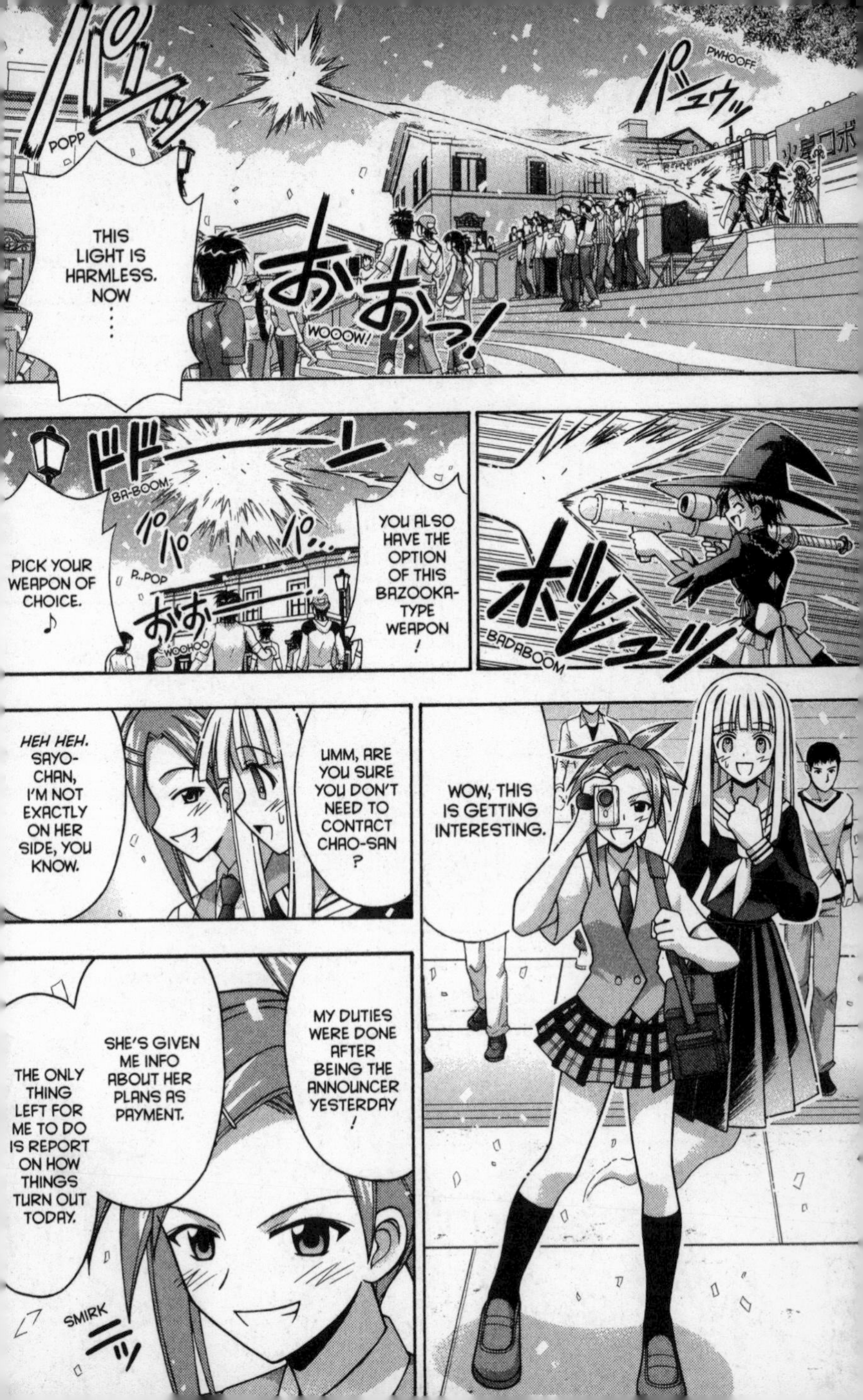
PWHOOFF
POPP
THIS LIGHT IS HARMLESS. NOW ......
WOOOW!
BADABOOM
YOU ALSO HAVE THE OPTION OF THIS BAZOOKA-TYPE WEAPON!
BA-BOOM
P...POP
PICK YOUR WEAPON OF CHOICE. ♪
WOOHOO
WOW, THIS IS GETTING INTERESTING.
UMM, ARE YOU SURE YOU DON'T NEED TO CONTACT CHAO-SAN?
HEH HEH. SAYO-CHAN, I'M NOT EXACTLY ON HER SIDE, YOU KNOW.
MY DUTIES WERE DONE AFTER BEING THE ANNOUNCER YESTERDAY!
SHE'S GIVEN ME INFO ABOUT HER PLANS AS PAYMENT.
THE ONLY THING LEFT FOR ME TO DO IS REPORT ON HOW THINGS TURN OUT TODAY.
SMIRK

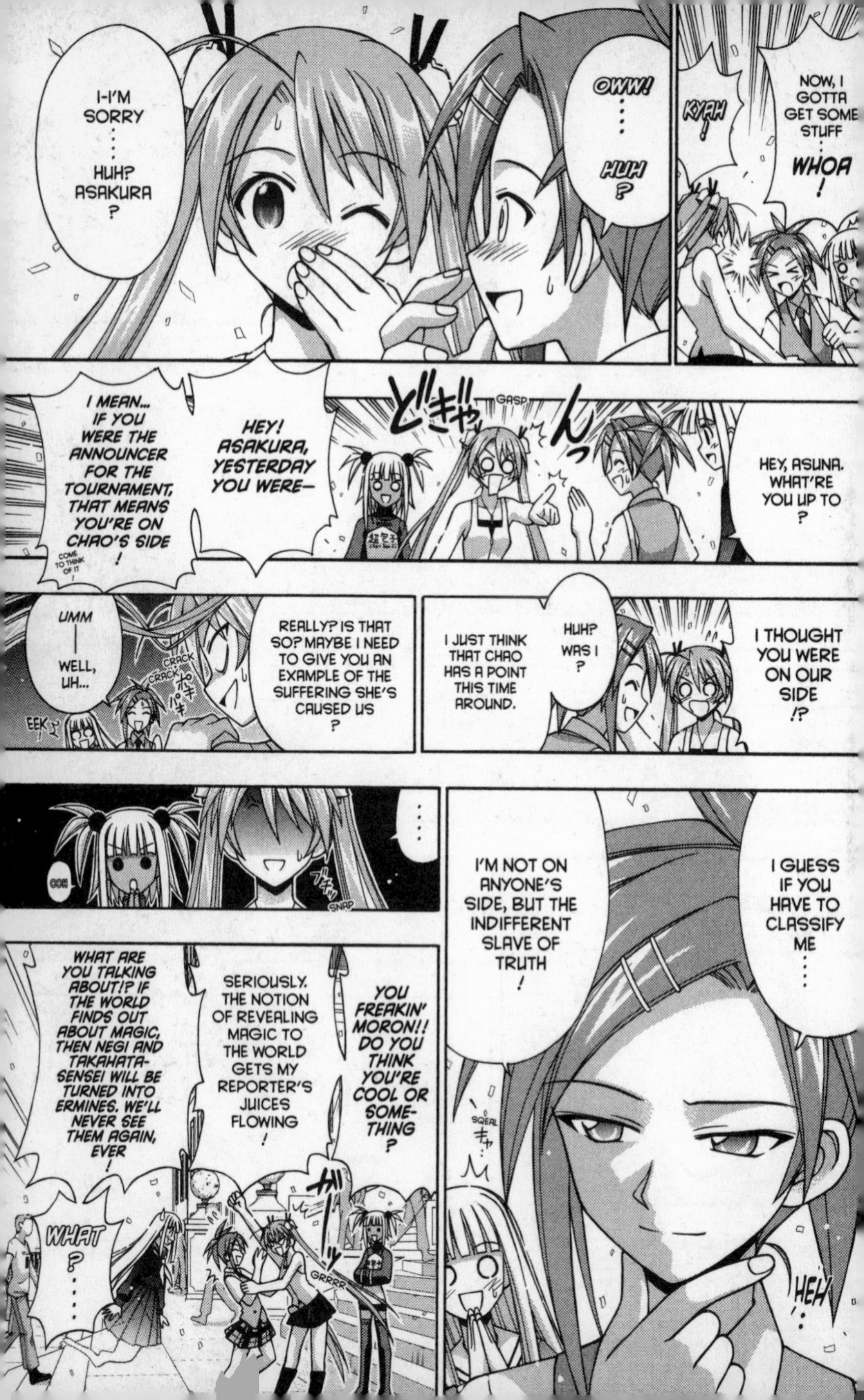
NOW, I GOTTA GET SOME STUFF... WHOA!
KYAH!
OWW!... HUH?
I-I'M SORRY... HUH? ASAKURA?
HEY, ASUNA. WHAT'RE YOU UP TO?
GASP
HEY! ASAKURA, YESTERDAY YOU WERE—
I MEAN... IF YOU WERE THE ANNOUNCER FOR THE TOURNAMENT, THAT MEANS YOU'RE ON CHAO'S SIDE!
COME TO THINK OF IT!
I THOUGHT YOU WERE ON OUR SIDE!?
HUH? WAS I?
I JUST THINK THAT CHAO HAS A POINT THIS TIME AROUND.
REALLY? IS THAT SO? MAYBE I NEED TO GIVE YOU AN EXAMPLE OF THE SUFFERING SHE'S CAUSED US?
CRACK CRACK
UMM — WELL, UH...
EEK
I GUESS IF YOU HAVE TO CLASSIFY ME...
I'M NOT ON ANYONE'S SIDE, BUT THE INDIFFERENT SLAVE OF TRUTH!
SQEAL
HEH
...
SNAP
OOH
YOU FREAKIN' MORON!! DO YOU THINK YOU'RE COOL OR SOMETHING?
SERIOUSLY. THE NOTION OF REVEALING MAGIC TO THE WORLD GETS MY REPORTER'S JUICES FLOWING!
WHAT ARE YOU TALKING ABOUT!? IF THE WORLD FINDS OUT ABOUT MAGIC, THEN NEGI AND TAKAHATA-SENSEI WILL BE TURNED INTO ERMINES. WE'LL NEVER SEE THEM AGAIN, EVER!
GRRRR
WHAT?...

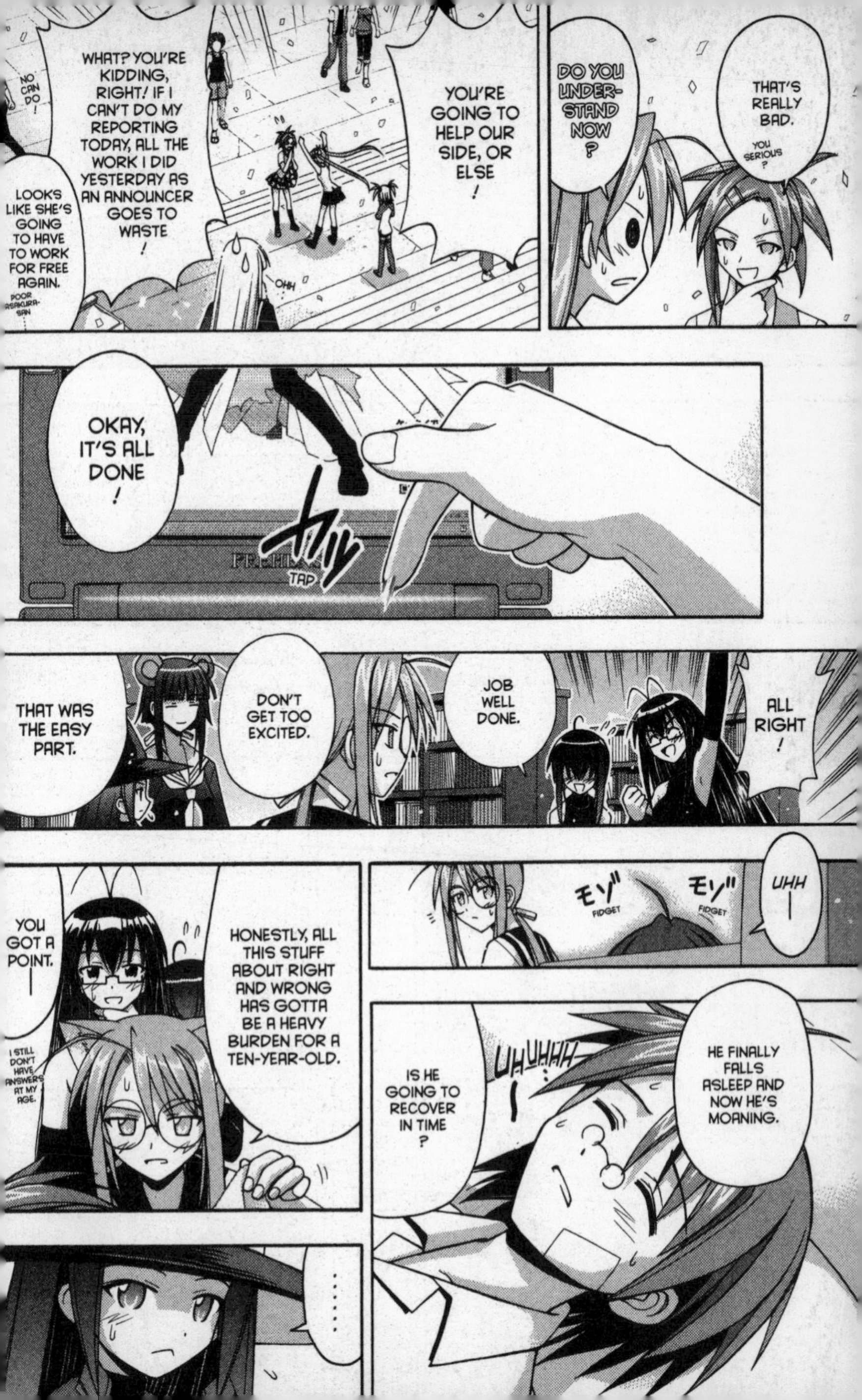
THAT'S REALLY BAD.
YOU SERIOUS?
DO YOU UNDER-STAND NOW?
YOU'RE GOING TO HELP OUR SIDE, OR ELSE!
WHAT? YOU'RE KIDDING, RIGHT! IF I CAN'T DO MY REPORTING TODAY, ALL THE WORK I DID YESTERDAY AS AN ANNOUNCER GOES TO WASTE!
NO CAN DO!
OHH
LOOKS LIKE SHE'S GOING TO HAVE TO WORK FOR FREE AGAIN.
POOR ASAKURA-SAN...
TAP
OKAY, IT'S ALL DONE!
ALL RIGHT!
JOB WELL DONE.
DON'T GET TOO EXCITED.
THAT WAS THE EASY PART.
UHH—
FIDGET
FIDGET
HE FINALLY FALLS ASLEEP AND NOW HE'S MORNING.
UHUHHH...
IS HE GOING TO RECOVER IN TIME?
HONESTLY, ALL THIS STUFF ABOUT RIGHT AND WRONG HAS GOTTA BE A HEAVY BURDEN FOR A TEN-YEAR-OLD.
YOU GOT A POINT—
I STILL DON'T HAVE ANSWERS AT MY AGE.
......

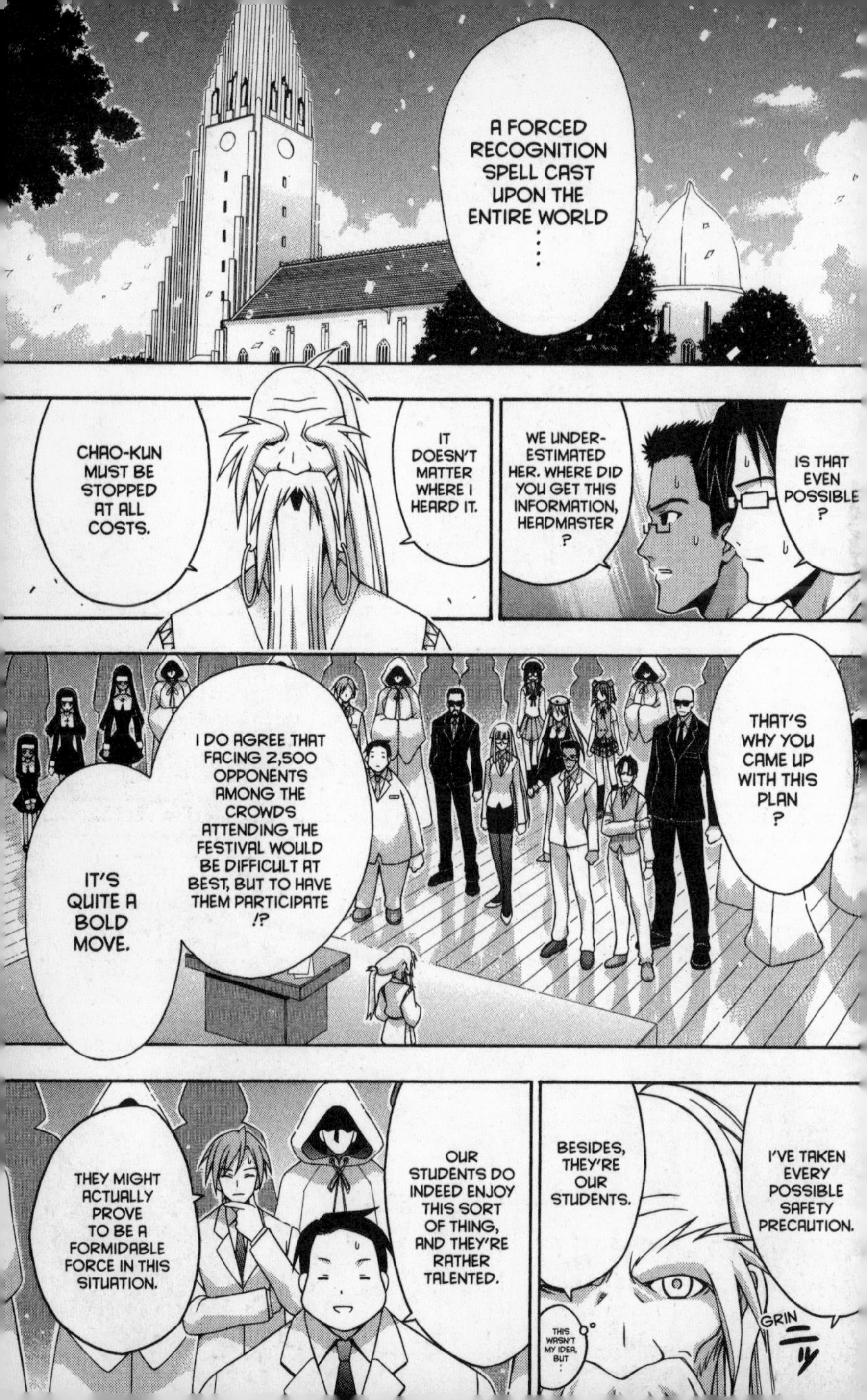
A FORCED RECOGNITION SPELL CAST UPON THE ENTIRE WORLD ......
IS THAT EVEN POSSIBLE?
WE UNDER-ESTIMATED HER. WHERE DID YOU GET THIS INFORMATION, HEADMASTER?
IT DOESN'T MATTER WHERE I HEARD IT.
CHAO-KUN MUST BE STOPPED AT ALL COSTS.
THAT'S WHY YOU CAME UP WITH THIS PLAN?
I DO AGREE THAT FACING 2,500 OPPONENTS AMONG THE CROWDS ATTENDING THE FESTIVAL WOULD BE DIFFICULT AT BEST, BUT TO HAVE THEM PARTICIPATE!?
IT'S QUITE A BOLD MOVE.
I'VE TAKEN EVERY POSSIBLE SAFETY PRECAUTION.
BESIDES, THEY'RE OUR STUDENTS.
THIS WASN'T MY IDEA, BUT...
GRIN
OUR STUDENTS DO INDEED ENJOY THIS SORT OF THING, AND THEY'RE RATHER TALENTED.
THEY MIGHT ACTUALLY PROVE TO BE A FORMIDABLE FORCE IN THIS SITUATION.

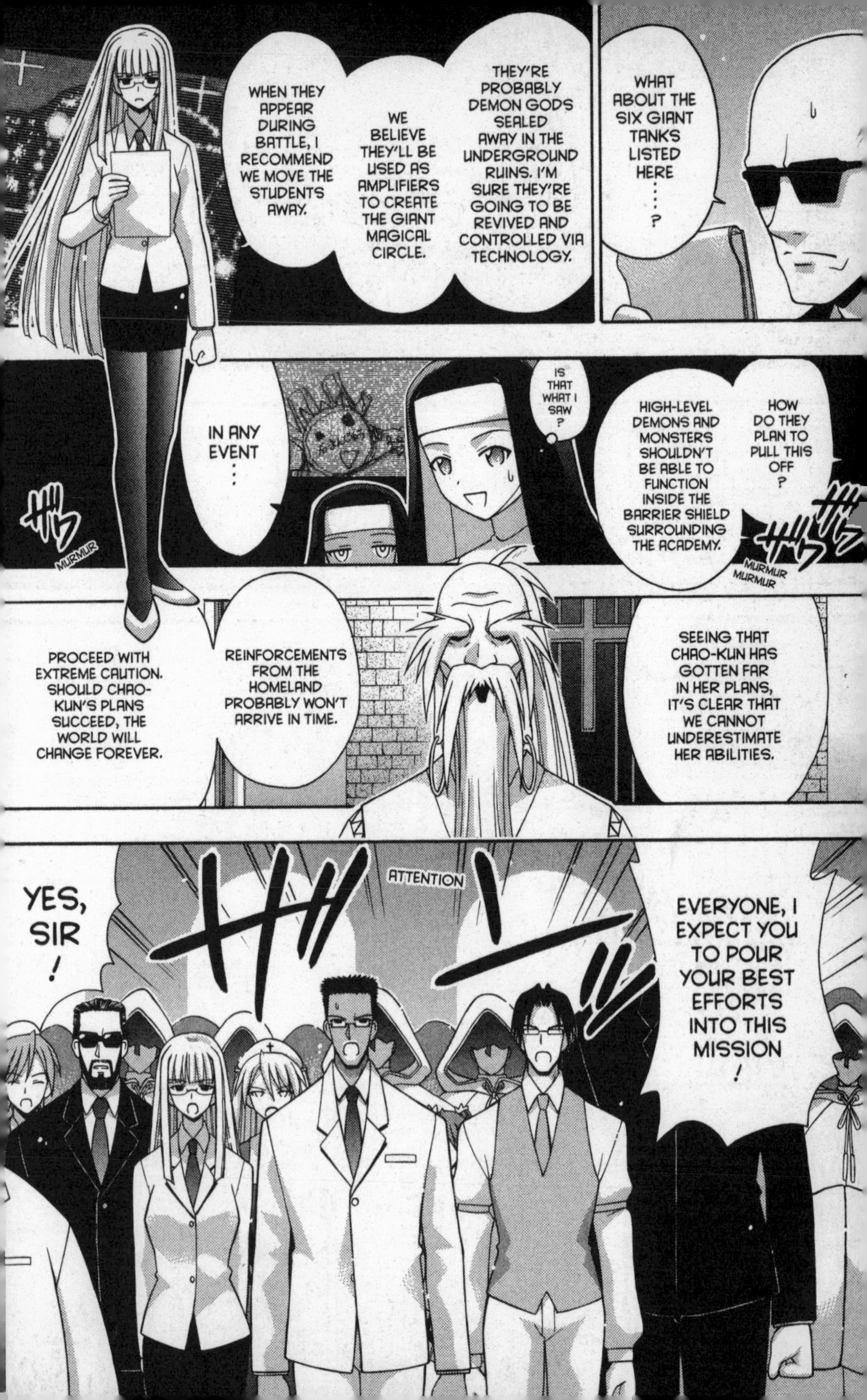
WHAT ABOUT THE SIX GIANT TANKS LISTED HERE ...?
THEY'RE PROBABLY DEMON GODS SEALED AWAY IN THE UNDERGROUND RUINS. I'M SURE THEY'RE GOING TO BE REVIVED AND CONTROLLED VIA TECHNOLOGY.
WE BELIEVE THEY'LL BE USED AS AMPLIFIERS TO CREATE THE GIANT MAGICAL CIRCLE.
WHEN THEY APPEAR DURING BATTLE, I RECOMMEND WE MOVE THE STUDENTS AWAY.
HOW DO THEY PLAN TO PULL THIS OFF?
HIGH-LEVEL DEMONS AND MONSTERS SHOULDN'T BE ABLE TO FUNCTION INSIDE THE BARRIER SHIELD SURROUNDING THE ACADEMY.
MURMUR MURMUR
IS THAT WHAT I SAW?
IN ANY EVENT ...
MURMUR
SEEING THAT CHAO-KUN HAS GOTTEN FAR IN HER PLANS, IT'S CLEAR THAT WE CANNOT UNDERESTIMATE HER ABILITIES.
REINFORCEMENTS FROM THE HOMELAND PROBABLY WON'T ARRIVE IN TIME.
PROCEED WITH EXTREME CAUTION. SHOULD CHAO-KUN'S PLANS SUCCEED, THE WORLD WILL CHANGE FOREVER.
EVERYONE, I EXPECT YOU TO POUR YOUR BEST EFFORTS INTO THIS MISSION!
ATTENTION
YES, SIR!

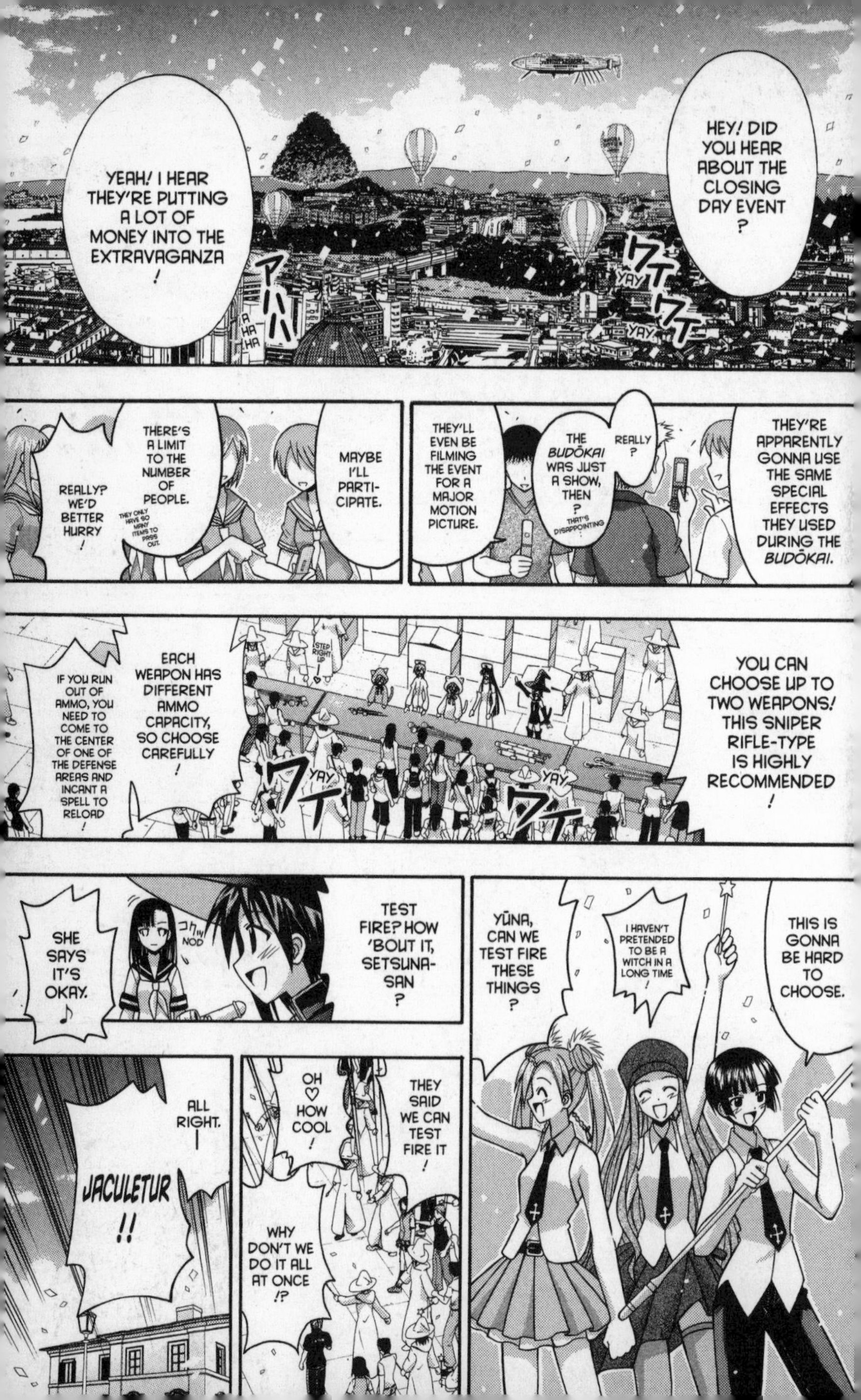
HEY! DID YOU HEAR ABOUT THE CLOSING DAY EVENT?
ワイワイ YAY YAY
YEAH! I HEAR THEY'RE PUTTING A LOT OF MONEY INTO THE EXTRAVAGANZA!
アハハ AHAHA
THEY'RE APPARENTLY GONNA USE THE SAME SPECIAL EFFECTS THEY USED DURING THE *BUDŌKAI*.
REALLY?
THE *BUDŌKAI* WAS JUST A SHOW, THEN?
THAT'S DISAPPOINTING
THEY'LL EVEN BE FILMING THE EVENT FOR A MAJOR MOTION PICTURE.
MAYBE I'LL PARTI-CIPATE.
THERE'S A LIMIT TO THE NUMBER OF PEOPLE.
THEY ONLY HAVE SO MANY ITEMS TO PASS OUT.
REALLY? WE'D BETTER HURRY!
YOU CAN CHOOSE UP TO TWO WEAPONS! THIS SNIPER RIFLE-TYPE IS HIGHLY RECOMMENDED!
STEP RIGHT UP ♡
EACH WEAPON HAS DIFFERENT AMMO CAPACITY, SO CHOOSE CAREFULLY!
IF YOU RUN OUT OF AMMO, YOU NEED TO COME TO THE CENTER OF ONE OF THE DEFENSE AREAS AND INCANT A SPELL TO RELOAD!
ワイ YAY
ワイ YAY
THIS IS GONNA BE HARD TO CHOOSE.
I HAVEN'T PRETENDED TO BE A WITCH IN A LONG TIME!
YŪNA, CAN WE TEST FIRE THESE THINGS?
TEST FIRE? HOW 'BOUT IT, SETSUNA-SAN?
コクッ NOD
SHE SAYS IT'S OKAY. ♪
THEY SAID WE CAN TEST FIRE IT!
OH ♡ HOW COOL!
WHY DON'T WE DO IT ALL AT ONCE!?
ALL RIGHT.
JACULETUR!!

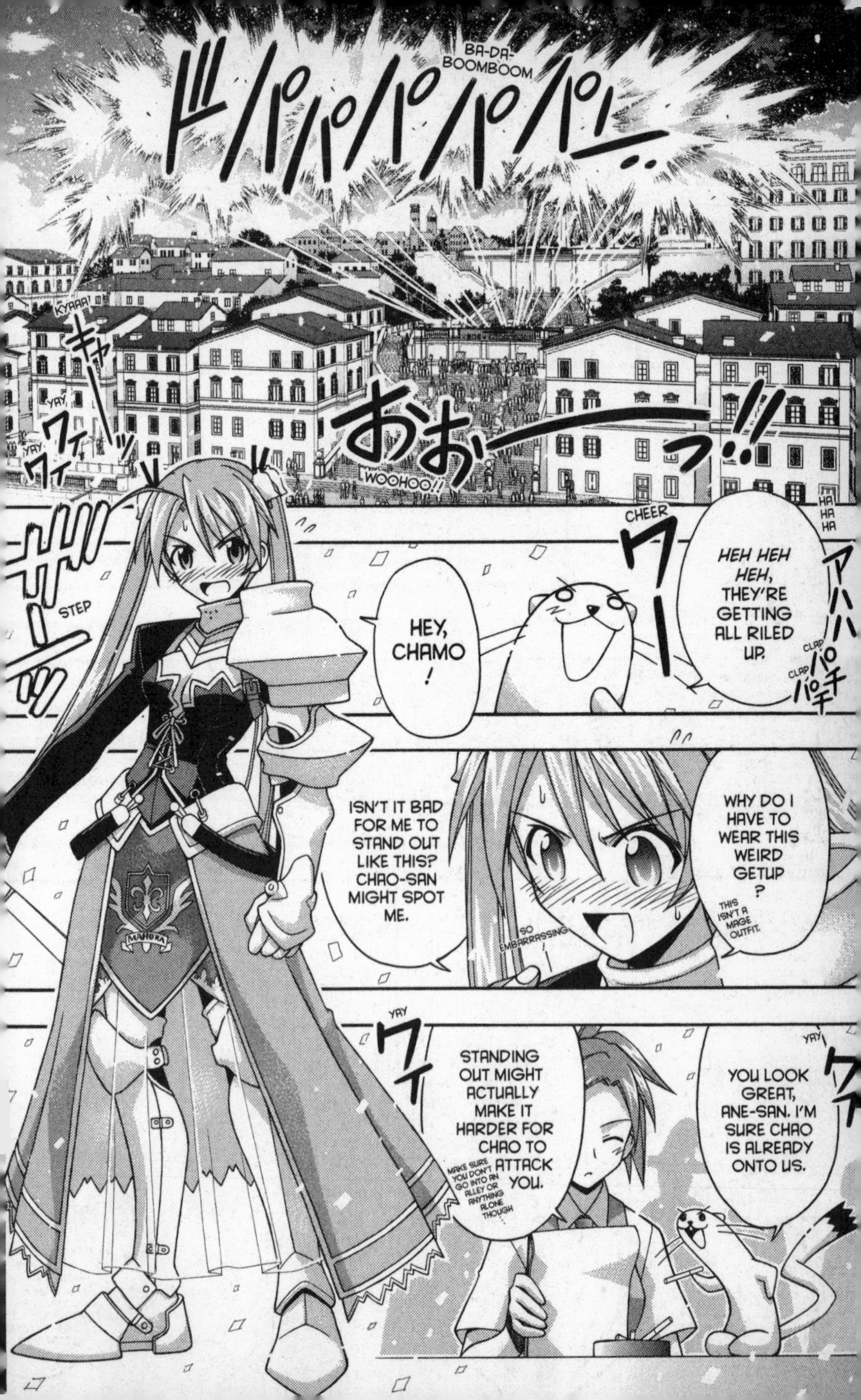

ドパパパパン
BA-DA-BOOMBOOM
あおーーっ!!
WOOHOO!!
キャーッ
KYAAA
ワイワイ
YAY
YAY
CHEER
ワー
HA HA HA
アハハ
HEH HEH HEH, THEY'RE GETTING ALL RILED UP.
CLAP
CLAP
パチパチ
HEY, CHAMO!
ザッ
STEP
WHY DO I HAVE TO WEAR THIS WEIRD GETUP?
THIS ISN'T A MAGE OUTFIT.
SO EMBARRASSING!
ISN'T IT BAD FOR ME TO STAND OUT LIKE THIS? CHAO-SAN MIGHT SPOT ME.
YAY
ワイ
YOU LOOK GREAT, ANE-SAN. I'M SURE CHAO IS ALREADY ONTO US.
STANDING OUT MIGHT ACTUALLY MAKE IT HARDER FOR CHAO TO ATTACK YOU.
MAKE SURE YOU DON'T GO INTO AN ALLEY OR ANYTHING ALONE THOUGH
YAY
ワイ

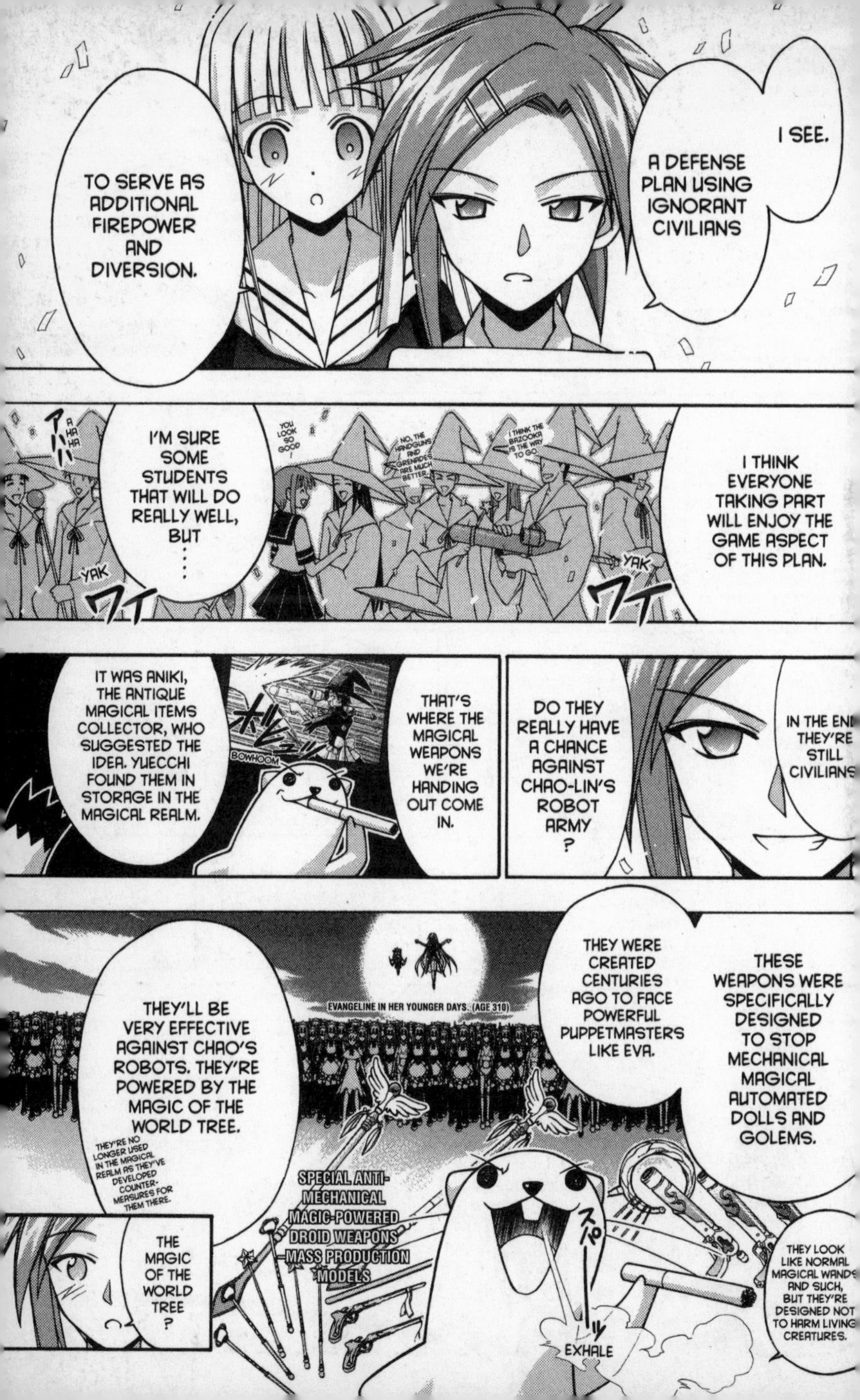
I SEE.
A DEFENSE PLAN USING IGNORANT CIVILIANS
TO SERVE AS ADDITIONAL FIREPOWER AND DIVERSION.
I THINK EVERYONE TAKING PART WILL ENJOY THE GAME ASPECT OF THIS PLAN.
YAK
I THINK THE BAZOOKA IS THE WAY TO GO.
NO, THE HANDGUNS AND GRENADES ARE MUCH BETTER.
YOU LOOK SO GOOD!
I'M SURE SOME STUDENTS THAT WILL DO REALLY WELL, BUT ....
A HA HA
YAK
IN THE EN THEY'RE STILL CIVILIANS
DO THEY REALLY HAVE A CHANCE AGAINST CHAO-LIN'S ROBOT ARMY ?
THAT'S WHERE THE MAGICAL WEAPONS WE'RE HANDING OUT COME IN.
BOWHOOM
IT WAS ANIKI, THE ANTIQUE MAGICAL ITEMS COLLECTOR, WHO SUGGESTED THE IDEA. YUECCHI FOUND THEM IN STORAGE IN THE MAGICAL REALM.
THESE WEAPONS WERE SPECIFICALLY DESIGNED TO STOP MECHANICAL MAGICAL AUTOMATED DOLLS AND GOLEMS.
THEY WERE CREATED CENTURIES AGO TO FACE POWERFUL PUPPETMASTERS LIKE EVA.
EVANGELINE IN HER YOUNGER DAYS. (AGE 310)
THEY'LL BE VERY EFFECTIVE AGAINST CHAO'S ROBOTS. THEY'RE POWERED BY THE MAGIC OF THE WORLD TREE.
THEY'RE NO LONGER USED IN THE MAGICAL REALM AS THEY'VE DEVELOPED COUNTER-MEASURES FOR THEM THERE.
THEY LOOK LIKE NORMAL MAGICAL WANDS AND SUCH, BUT THEY'RE DESIGNED NOT TO HARM LIVING CREATURES.
EXHALE
SPECIAL ANTI-MECHANICAL MAGIC-POWERED DROID WEAPONS MASS PRODUCTION MODELS
THE MAGIC OF THE WORLD TREE ?

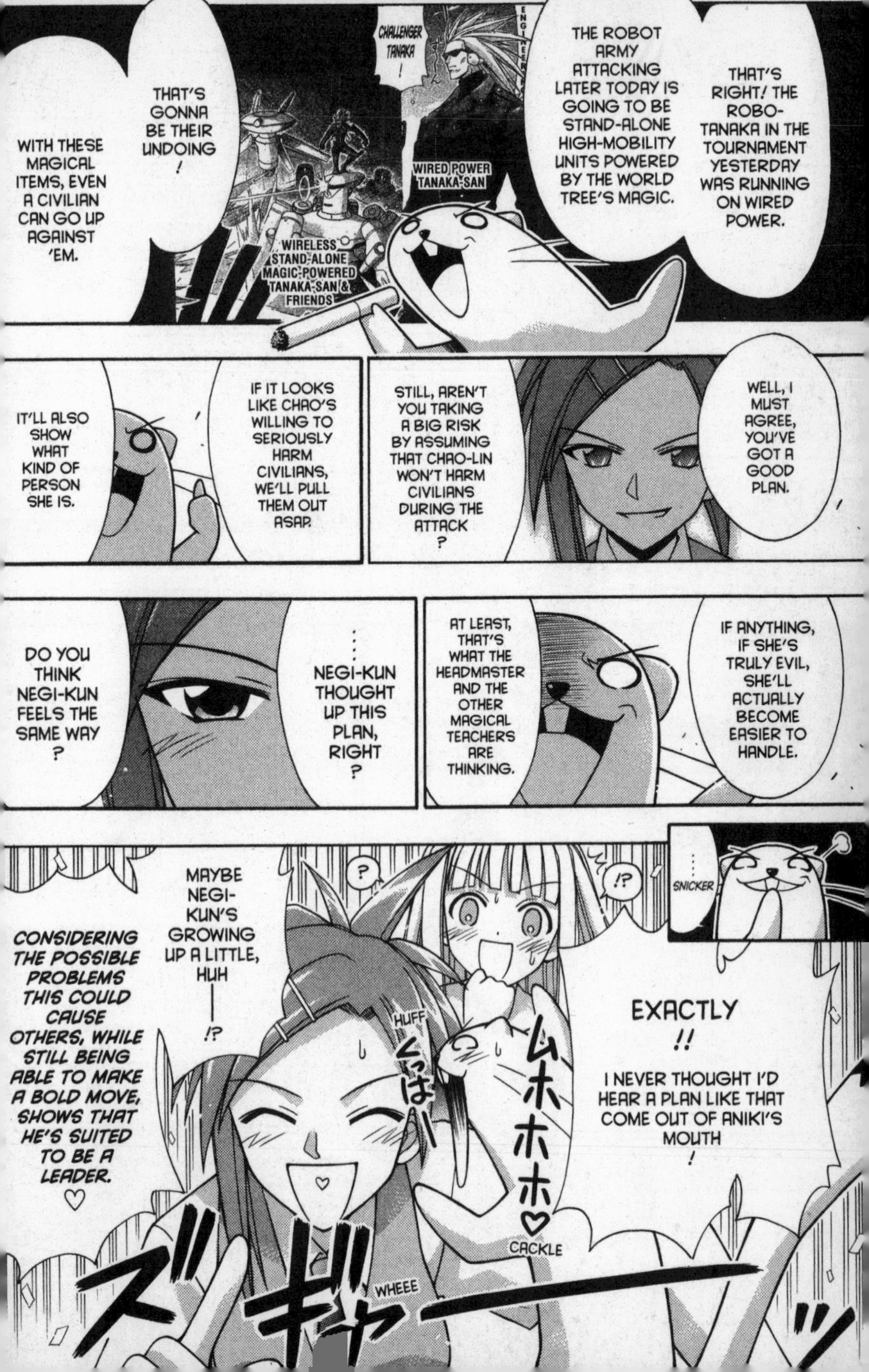
THAT'S RIGHT! THE ROBO-TANAKA IN THE TOURNAMENT YESTERDAY WAS RUNNING ON WIRED POWER.
THE ROBOT ARMY ATTACKING LATER TODAY IS GOING TO BE STAND-ALONE HIGH-MOBILITY UNITS POWERED BY THE WORLD TREE'S MAGIC.
ENGINEER
CHALLENGER TANAKA!
WIRED POWER TANAKA-SAN
WIRELESS STAND-ALONE MAGIC-POWERED TANAKA-SAN & FRIENDS
THAT'S GONNA BE THEIR UNDOING!
WITH THESE MAGICAL ITEMS, EVEN A CIVILIAN CAN GO UP AGAINST 'EM.
WELL, I MUST AGREE, YOU'VE GOT A GOOD PLAN.
STILL, AREN'T YOU TAKING A BIG RISK BY ASSUMING THAT CHAO-LIN WON'T HARM CIVILIANS DURING THE ATTACK?
IF IT LOOKS LIKE CHAO'S WILLING TO SERIOUSLY HARM CIVILIANS, WE'LL PULL THEM OUT ASAP.
IT'LL ALSO SHOW WHAT KIND OF PERSON SHE IS.
IF ANYTHING, IF SHE'S TRULY EVIL, SHE'LL ACTUALLY BECOME EASIER TO HANDLE.
AT LEAST, THAT'S WHAT THE HEADMASTER AND THE OTHER MAGICAL TEACHERS ARE THINKING.
...NEGI-KUN THOUGHT UP THIS PLAN, RIGHT?
DO YOU THINK NEGI-KUN FEELS THE SAME WAY?
...SNICKER
EXACTLY!!
I NEVER THOUGHT I'D HEAR A PLAN LIKE THAT COME OUT OF ANIKI'S MOUTH!
ムホホホ♡
CACKLE
!?
?
くっはー
HUFF
MAYBE NEGI-KUN'S GROWING UP A LITTLE, HUH—!?
CONSIDERING THE POSSIBLE PROBLEMS THIS COULD CAUSE OTHERS, WHILE STILL BEING ABLE TO MAKE A BOLD MOVE, SHOWS THAT HE'S SUITED TO BE A LEADER. ♡
ズギャーーッ
WHEEE

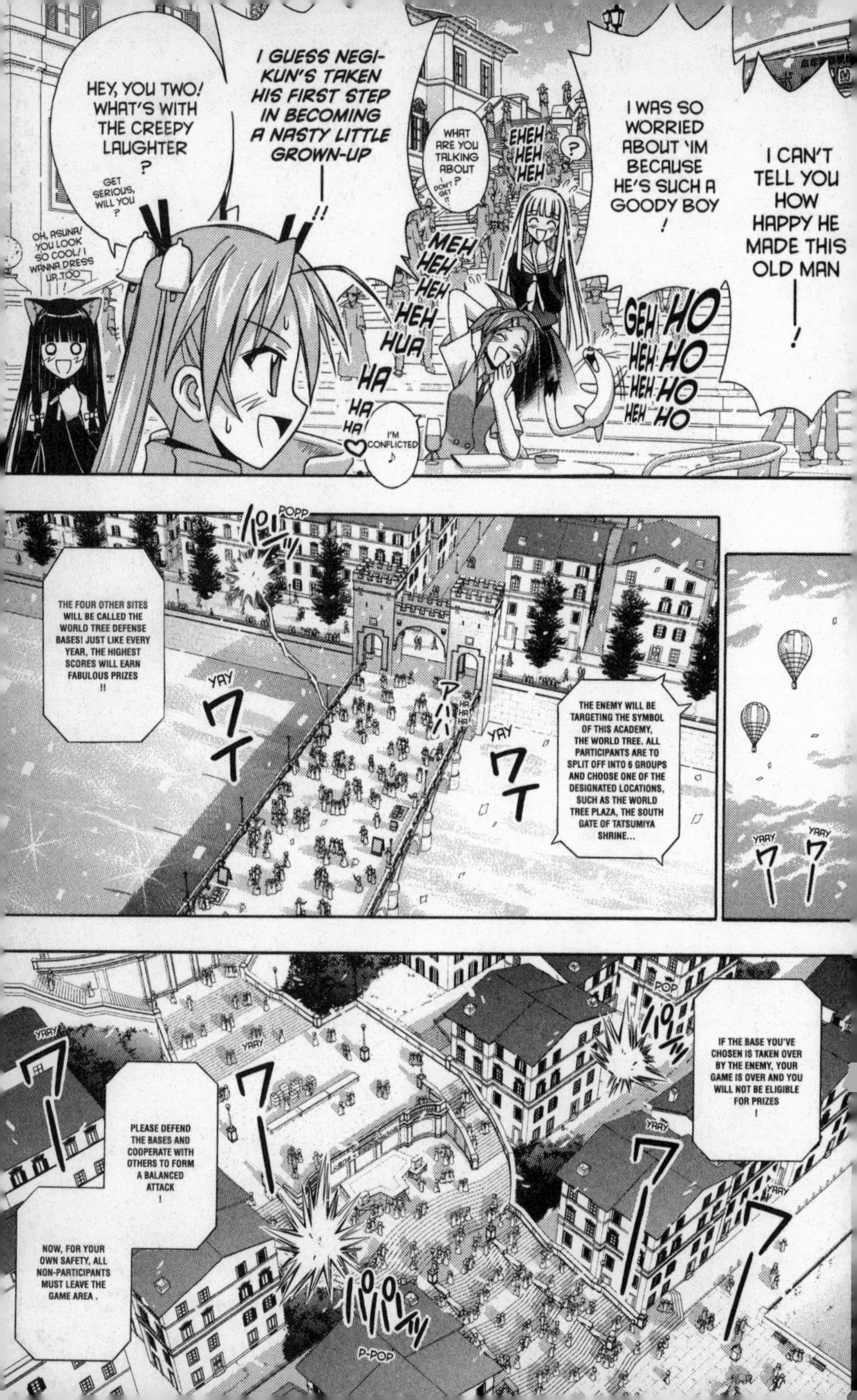

I CAN'T TELL YOU HOW HAPPY HE MADE THIS OLD MAN !
I WAS SO WORRIED ABOUT 'IM BECAUSE HE'S SUCH A GOODY BOY !
GEH HEH HEH HEH
HO HO HO HO
EHEH HEH HEH
?
WHAT ARE YOU TALKING ABOUT ?
I DON'T GET IT
I GUESS NEGI-KUN'S TAKEN HIS FIRST STEP IN BECOMING A NASTY LITTLE GROWN-UP !!
MEH HEH HEH HEH HUA HA HA HA
I'M CONFLICTED ♪
HEY, YOU TWO! WHAT'S WITH THE CREEPY LAUGHTER ?
GET SERIOUS, WILL YOU ?
OH, ASUNA! YOU LOOK SO COOL! I WANNA DRESS UP, TOO !
YAAY
YAAY
POPP
THE ENEMY WILL BE TARGETING THE SYMBOL OF THIS ACADEMY, THE WORLD TREE. ALL PARTICIPANTS ARE TO SPLIT OFF INTO 6 GROUPS AND CHOOSE ONE OF THE DESIGNATED LOCATIONS, SUCH AS THE WORLD TREE PLAZA, THE SOUTH GATE OF TATSUMIYA SHRINE...
HA HA HA
YAY
THE FOUR OTHER SITES WILL BE CALLED THE WORLD TREE DEFENSE BASES! JUST LIKE EVERY YEAR, THE HIGHEST SCORES WILL EARN FABULOUS PRIZES !!
YAY
IF THE BASE YOU'VE CHOSEN IS TAKEN OVER BY THE ENEMY, YOUR GAME IS OVER AND YOU WILL NOT BE ELIGIBLE FOR PRIZES !
POP
YAAY
YAAY
YAAY
PLEASE DEFEND THE BASES AND COOPERATE WITH OTHERS TO FORM A BALANCED ATTACK !
YAAY
NOW, FOR YOUR OWN SAFETY, ALL NON-PARTICIPANTS MUST LEAVE THE GAME AREA .
P-POP

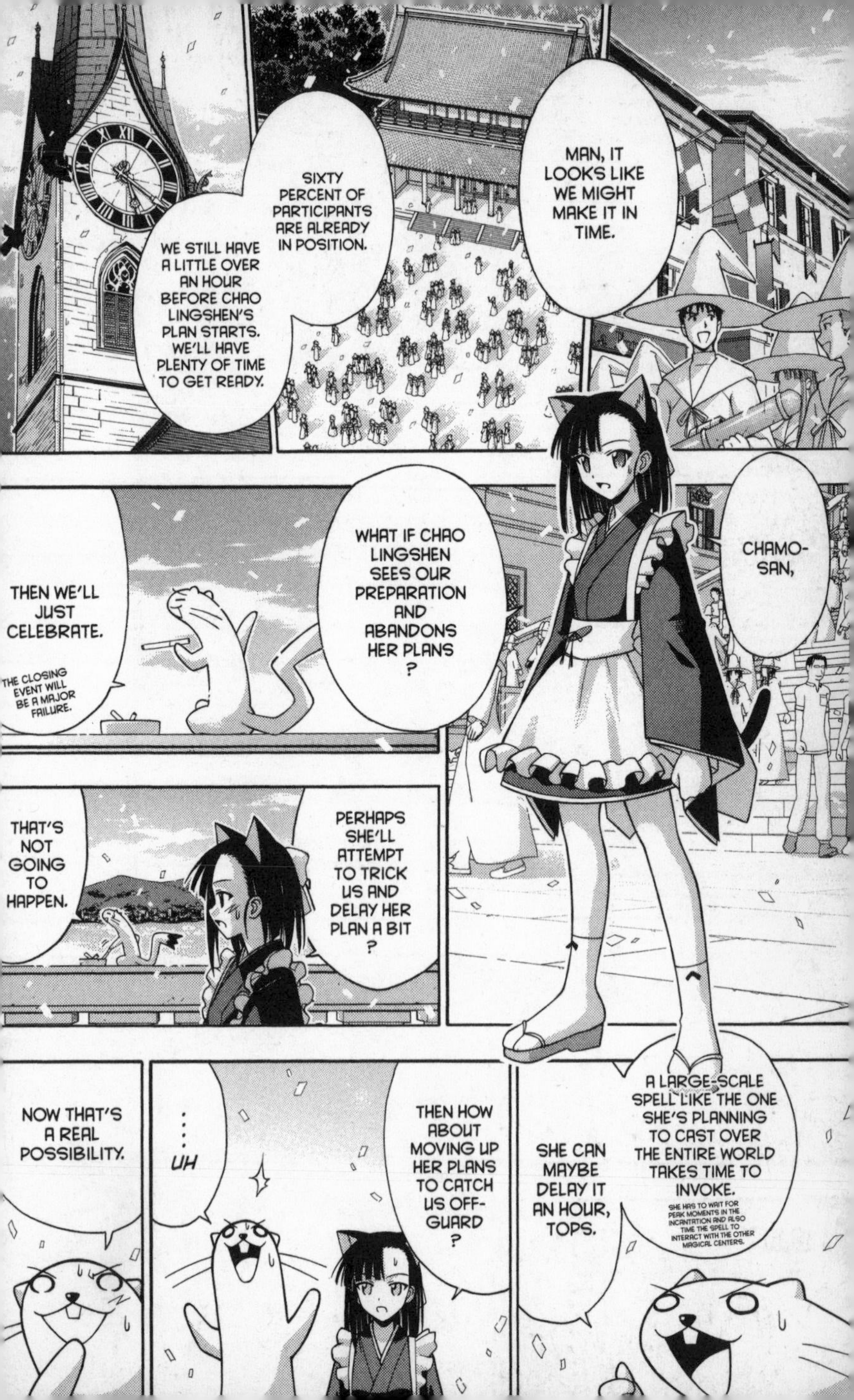
MAN, IT LOOKS LIKE WE MIGHT MAKE IT IN TIME.
SIXTY PERCENT OF PARTICIPANTS ARE ALREADY IN POSITION.
WE STILL HAVE A LITTLE OVER AN HOUR BEFORE CHAO LINGSHEN'S PLAN STARTS. WE'LL HAVE PLENTY OF TIME TO GET READY.
CHAMO-SAN,
WHAT IF CHAO LINGSHEN SEES OUR PREPARATION AND ABANDONS HER PLANS?
THEN WE'LL JUST CELEBRATE.
THE CLOSING EVENT WILL BE A MAJOR FAILURE.
PERHAPS SHE'LL ATTEMPT TO TRICK US AND DELAY HER PLAN A BIT?
THAT'S NOT GOING TO HAPPEN.
A LARGE-SCALE SPELL LIKE THE ONE SHE'S PLANNING TO CAST OVER THE ENTIRE WORLD TAKES TIME TO INVOKE.
SHE HAS TO WAIT FOR PEAK MOMENTS IN THE INCANTATION AND ALSO TIME THE SPELL TO INTERACT WITH THE OTHER MAGICAL CENTERS.
SHE CAN MAYBE DELAY IT AN HOUR, TOPS.
THEN HOW ABOUT MOVING UP HER PLANS TO CATCH US OFF-GUARD?
...UH
NOW THAT'S A REAL POSSIBILITY.

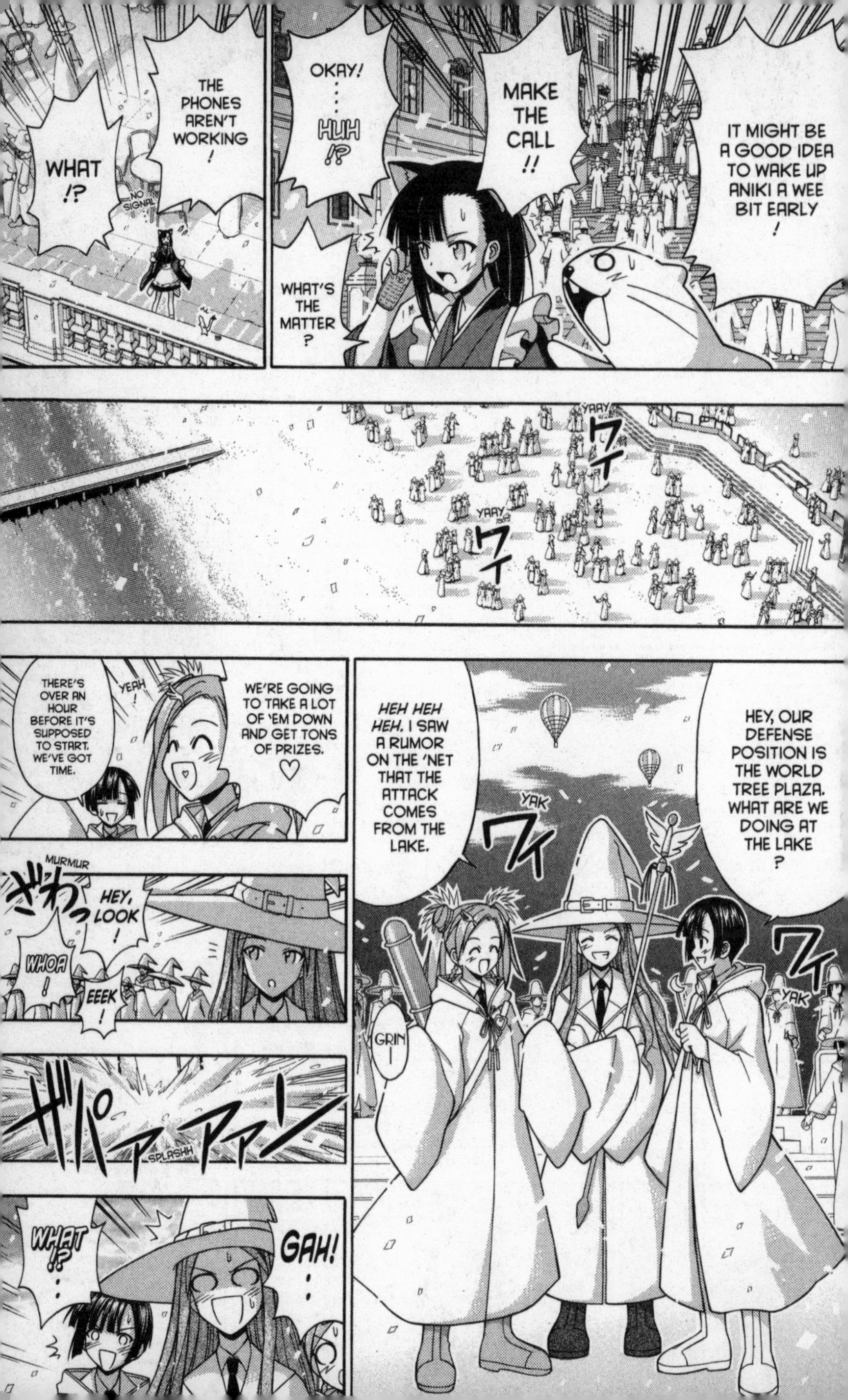
IT MIGHT BE A GOOD IDEA TO WAKE UP ANIKI A WEE BIT EARLY!
MAKE THE CALL!!
OKAY! ... HUH!?
WHAT'S THE MATTER?
THE PHONES AREN'T WORKING!
NO SIGNAL
WHAT!?
YAAY
YAAY
HEY, OUR DEFENSE POSITION IS THE WORLD TREE PLAZA. WHAT ARE WE DOING AT THE LAKE?
HEH HEH HEH. I SAW A RUMOR ON THE 'NET THAT THE ATTACK COMES FROM THE LAKE.
YAK
YAK
GRIN!
WE'RE GOING TO TAKE A LOT OF 'EM DOWN AND GET TONS OF PRIZES. ♡
YEAH!
THERE'S OVER AN HOUR BEFORE IT'S SUPPOSED TO START. WE'VE GOT TIME.
MURMUR
HEY, LOOK!
WHOA!
EEEK!
SPLASHH
GAH!
WHAT!?

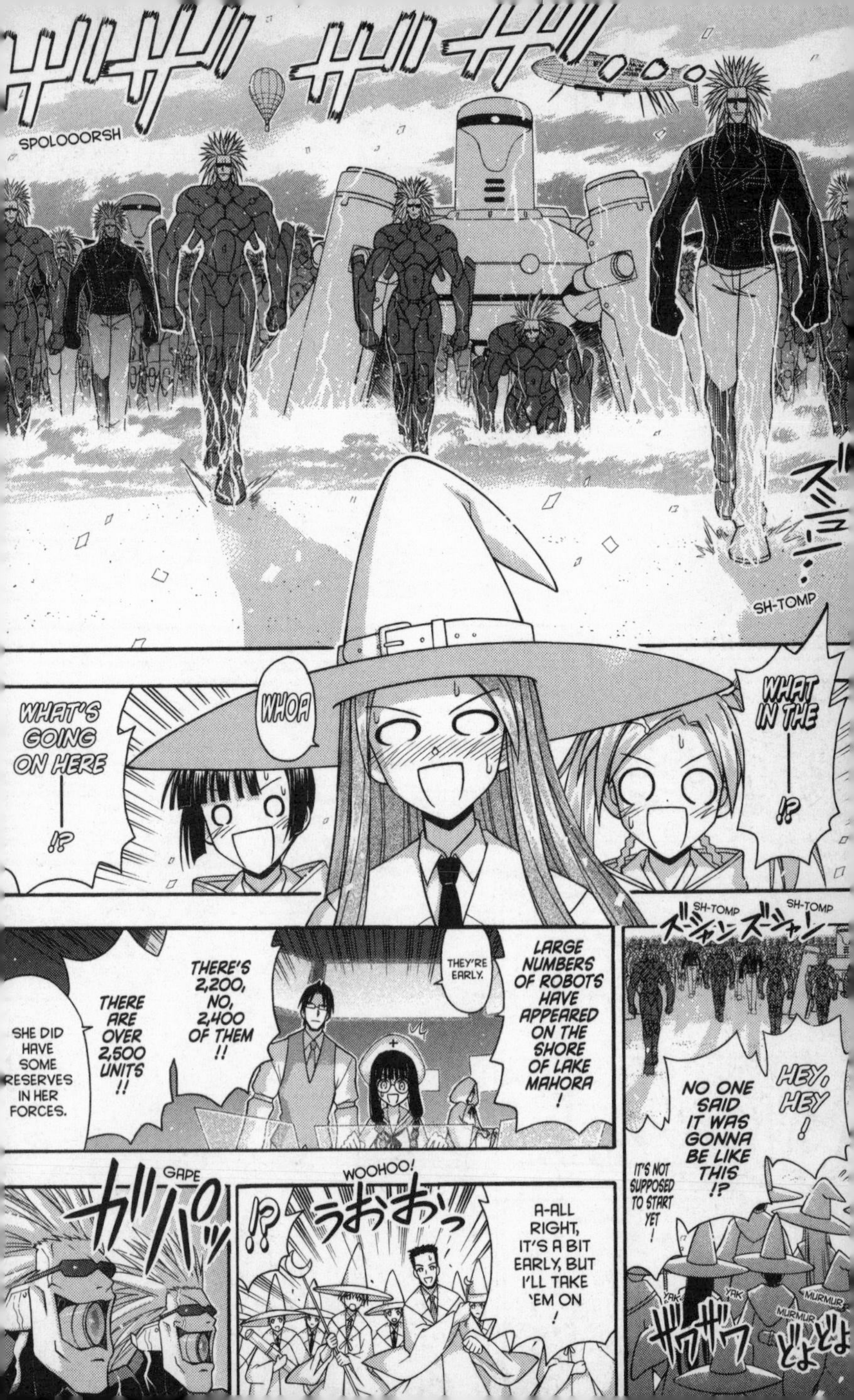
SPOLOOORSH
SH-TOMP
WHAT IN THE——!?
WHOA
WHAT'S GOING ON HERE——!?
SH-TOMP
SH-TOMP
HEY, HEY!
NO ONE SAID IT WAS GONNA BE LIKE THIS!?
IT'S NOT SUPPOSED TO START YET!
YAK
YAK
MURMUR
MURMUR
LARGE NUMBERS OF ROBOTS HAVE APPEARED ON THE SHORE OF LAKE MAHORA!
THEY'RE EARLY.
THERE'S 2,200, NO, 2,400 OF THEM!!
THERE ARE OVER 2,500 UNITS!!
SHE DID HAVE SOME RESERVES IN HER FORCES.
WOOHOO!
!?
A-ALL RIGHT, IT'S A BIT EARLY, BUT I'LL TAKE 'EM ON!
GAPE

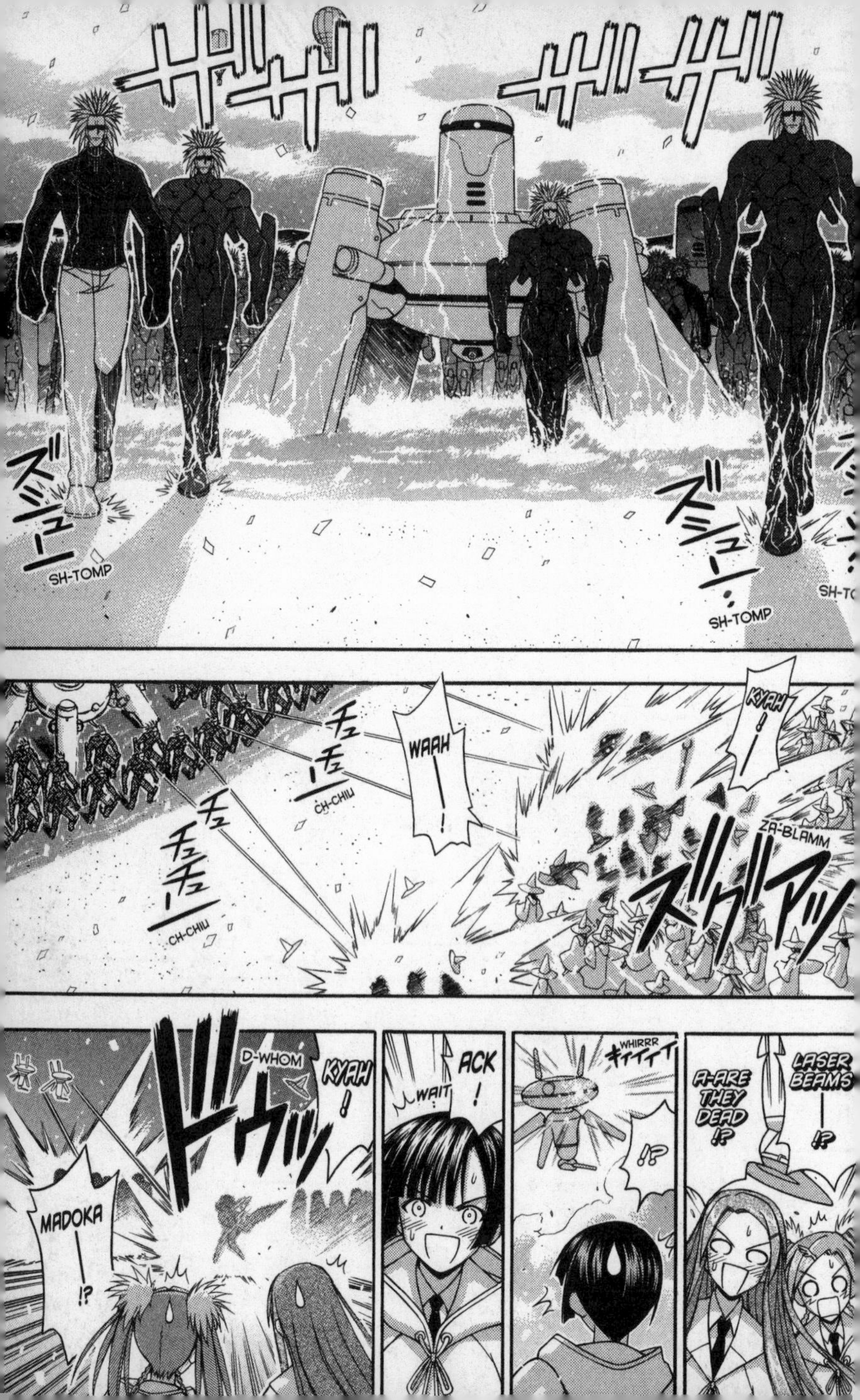

SH-TO
SH-TOMP
SH-TOMP
KYAH!
ZA-BLAMM
WAAH!
CH-CHIU
CH-CHIU
LASER BEAMS—!?
A-ARE THEY DEAD!?
WHIRRR
!?
ACK!
WAIT
KYAH!
D-WHOM
MADOKA—!?

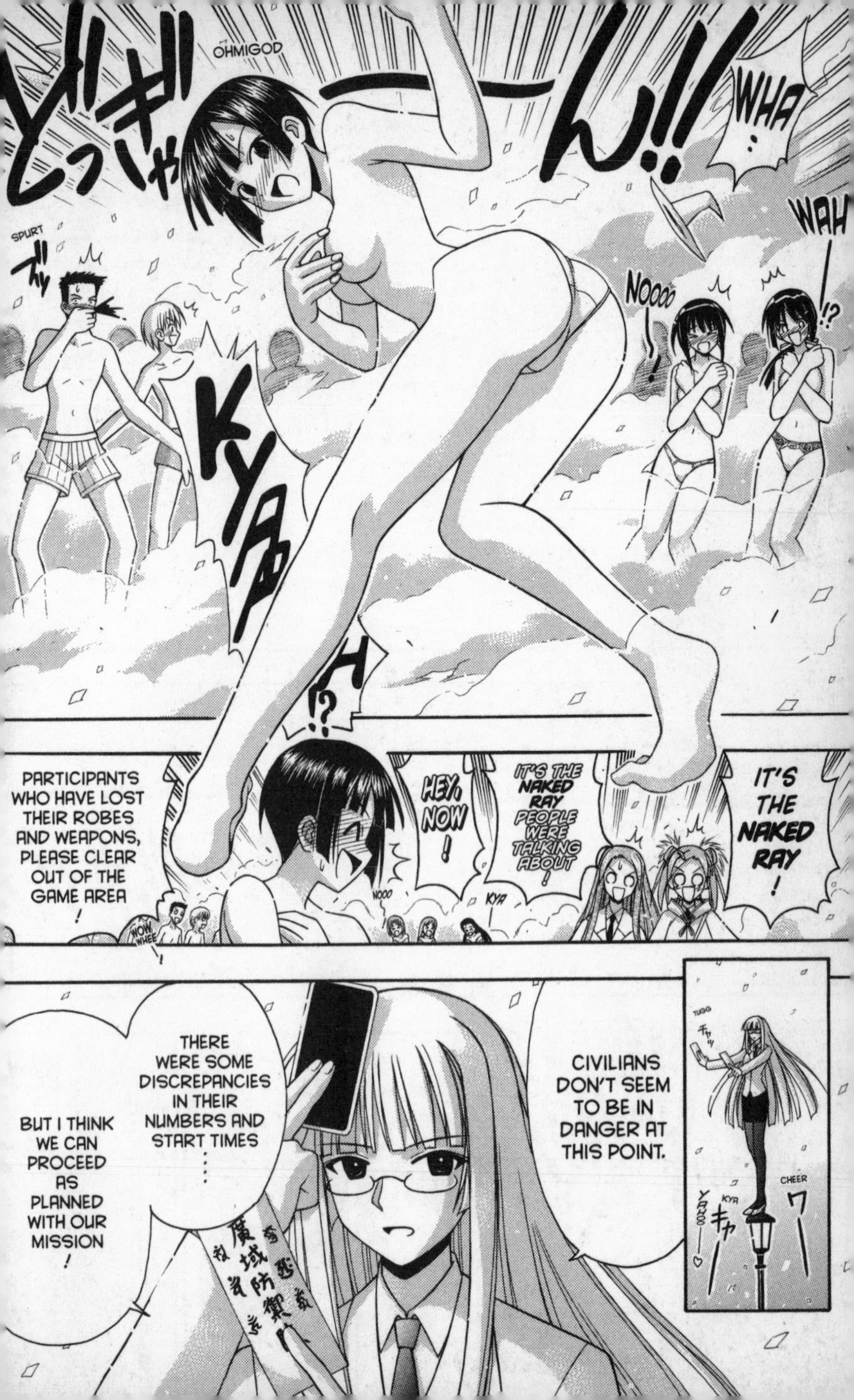
WHA...
WAH!!?
NOOOO!
OHMIGOD
KYAAAH!?
SPURT
IT'S THE NAKED RAY!
IT'S THE NAKED RAY PEOPLE WERE TALKING ABOUT!
HEY, NOW!
KYA
NOOO
PARTICIPANTS WHO HAVE LOST THEIR ROBES AND WEAPONS, PLEASE CLEAR OUT OF THE GAME AREA!
WOW WHEE!
TUGG
CHEER
KYA
YAHOO!
CIVILIANS DON'T SEEM TO BE IN DANGER AT THIS POINT.
THERE WERE SOME DISCREPANCIES IN THEIR NUMBERS AND START TIMES.....
BUT I THINK WE CAN PROCEED AS PLANNED WITH OUR MISSION!

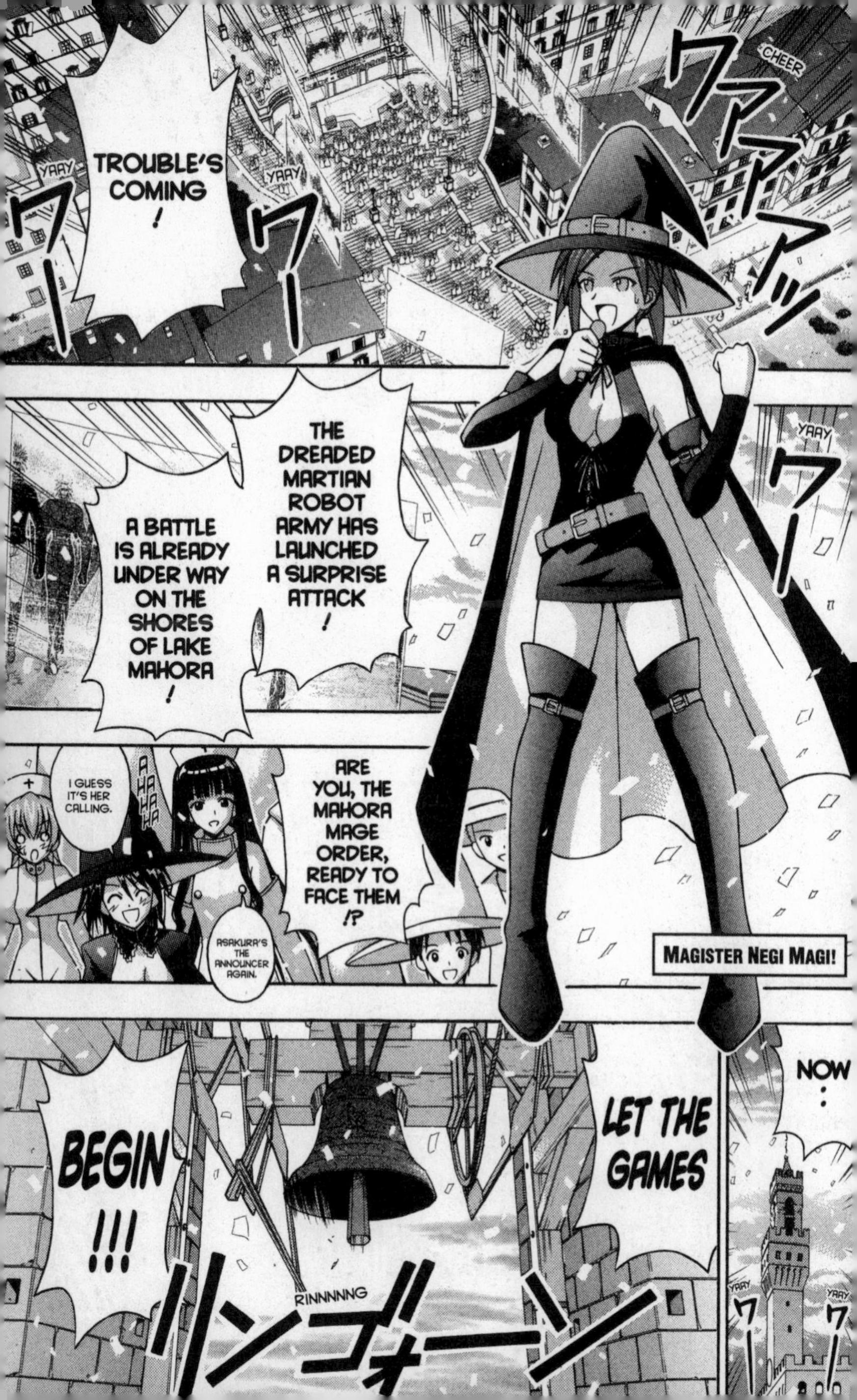
CHEER
YAAY
YAAY
TROUBLE'S COMING!
YAAY
THE DREADED MARTIAN ROBOT ARMY HAS LAUNCHED A SURPRISE ATTACK!
A BATTLE IS ALREADY UNDER WAY ON THE SHORES OF LAKE MAHORA!
ARE YOU, THE MAHORA MAGE ORDER, READY TO FACE THEM!?
I GUESS IT'S HER CALLING.
ASAKURA'S THE ANNOUNCER AGAIN.
MAGISTER NEGI MAGI!
NOW:
LET THE GAMES
BEGIN!!!
RINNNNNG
YAAY
YAAY

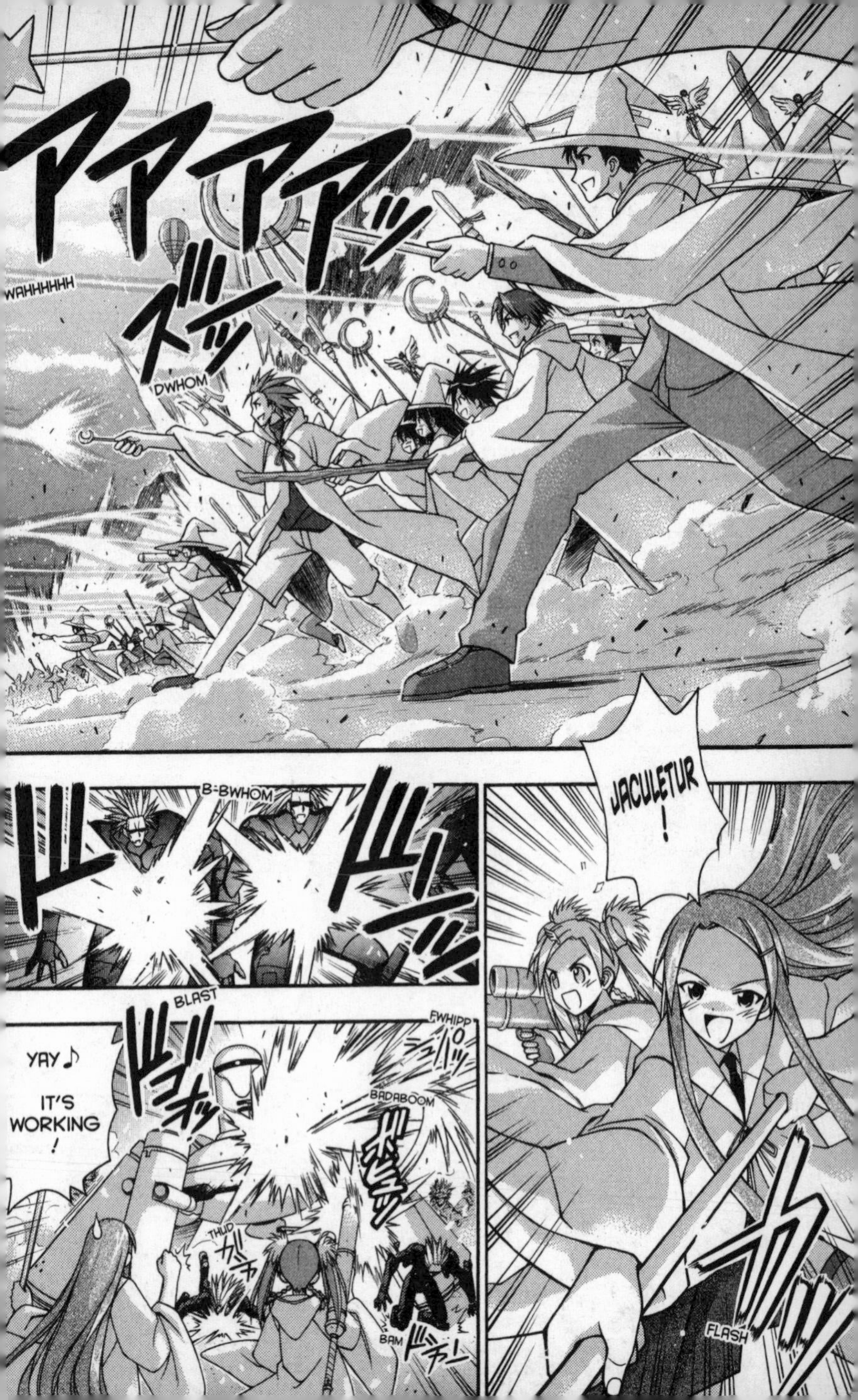
WAHHHHHH
DWHOM
JACULETUR!
FLASH
B-BWHOM
FWHIPP
BLAST
BADABOOM
YAY♪
IT'S WORKING!
THUD
BAM

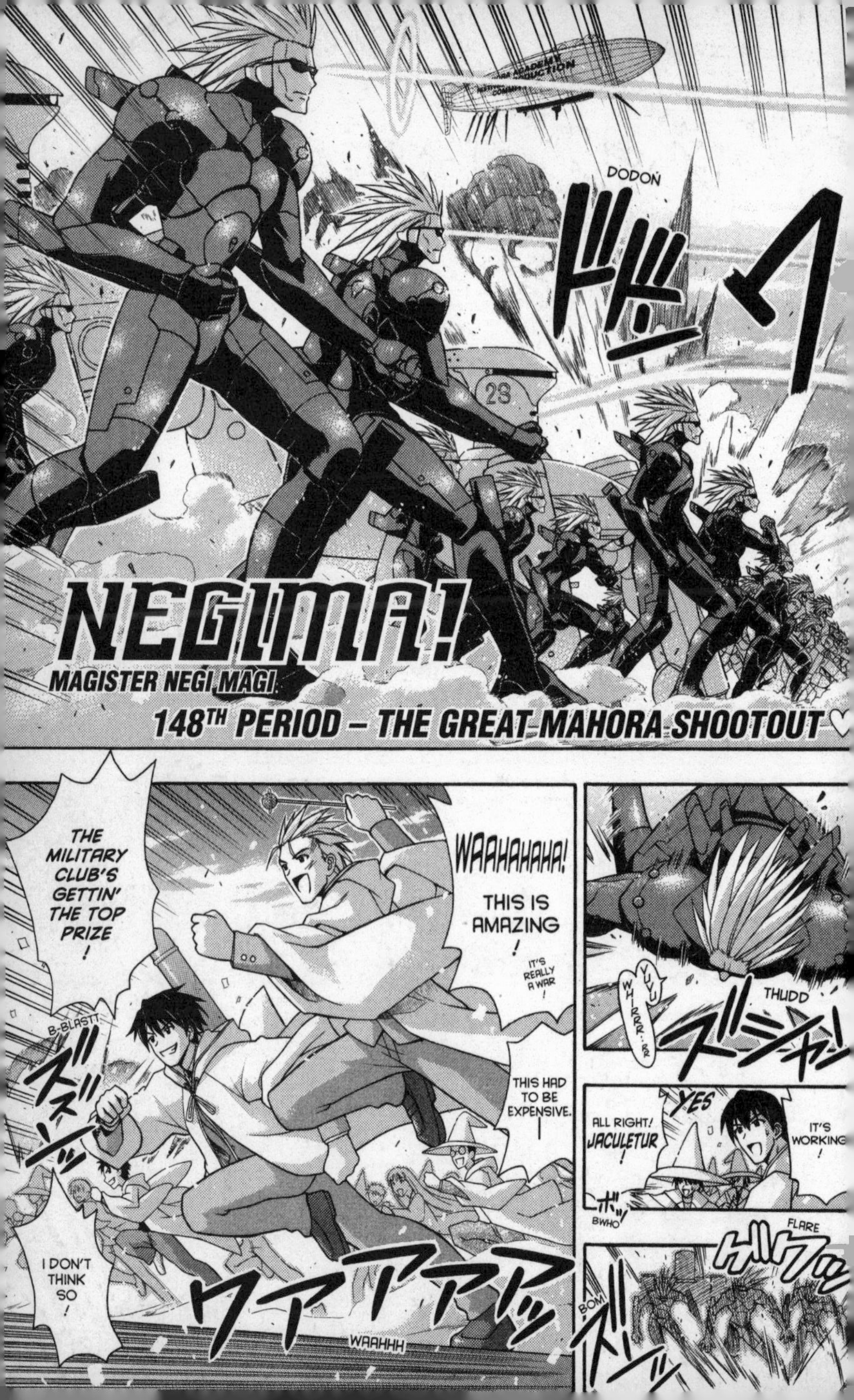
DODON
NEGIMA!
MAGISTER NEGI MAGI
148TH PERIOD – THE GREAT MAHORA SHOOTOUT♡
YUYU
WHIRRR...RR
THUDD
YES
ALL RIGHT! JACULETUR!
IT'S WORKING!
BWHO
FLARE
BOM!
THE MILITARY CLUB'S GETTIN' THE TOP PRIZE!
WAAHAHAHA!
THIS IS AMAZING!
IT'S REALLY A WAR!
THIS HAD TO BE EXPENSIVE.
B-BLASTT
I DON'T THINK SO!
WAAHHH

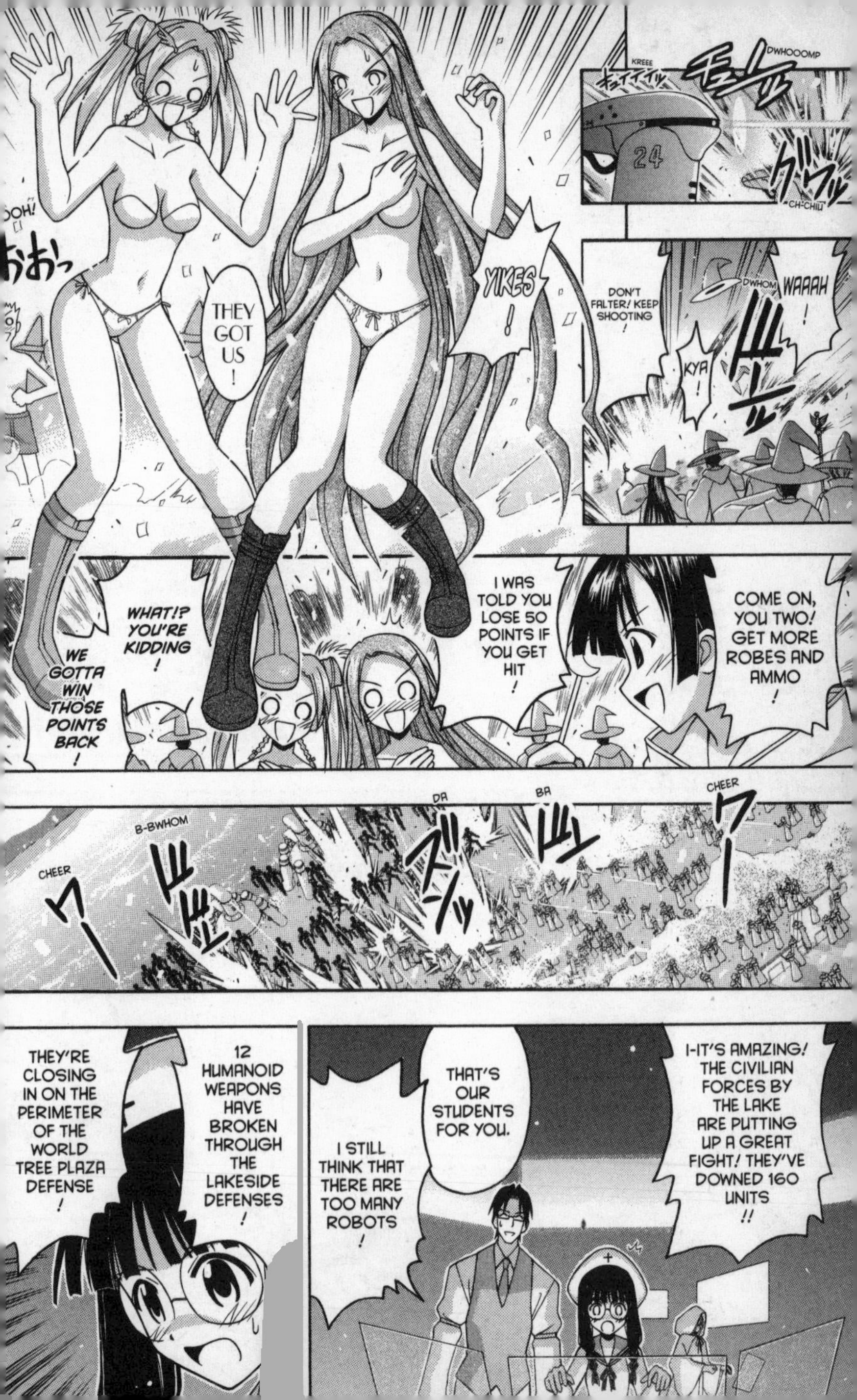
KREEE
DWHOOOMP
CH-CHIU
DON'T FALTER! KEEP SHOOTING!
DWHOM
WAAAH!
KYA!
OOH!
おおっ
THEY GOT US!
YIKES!
COME ON, YOU TWO! GET MORE ROBES AND AMMO!
I WAS TOLD YOU LOSE 50 POINTS IF YOU GET HIT!
WHAT!? YOU'RE KIDDING!
WE GOTTA WIN THOSE POINTS BACK!
CHEER
BA
DA
B-BWHOM
CHEER
I-IT'S AMAZING! THE CIVILIAN FORCES BY THE LAKE ARE PUTTING UP A GREAT FIGHT! THEY'VE DOWNED 160 UNITS!!
THAT'S OUR STUDENTS FOR YOU.
I STILL THINK THAT THERE ARE TOO MANY ROBOTS!
12 HUMANOID WEAPONS HAVE BROKEN THROUGH THE LAKESIDE DEFENSES!
THEY'RE CLOSING IN ON THE PERIMETER OF THE WORLD TREE PLAZA DEFENSE!

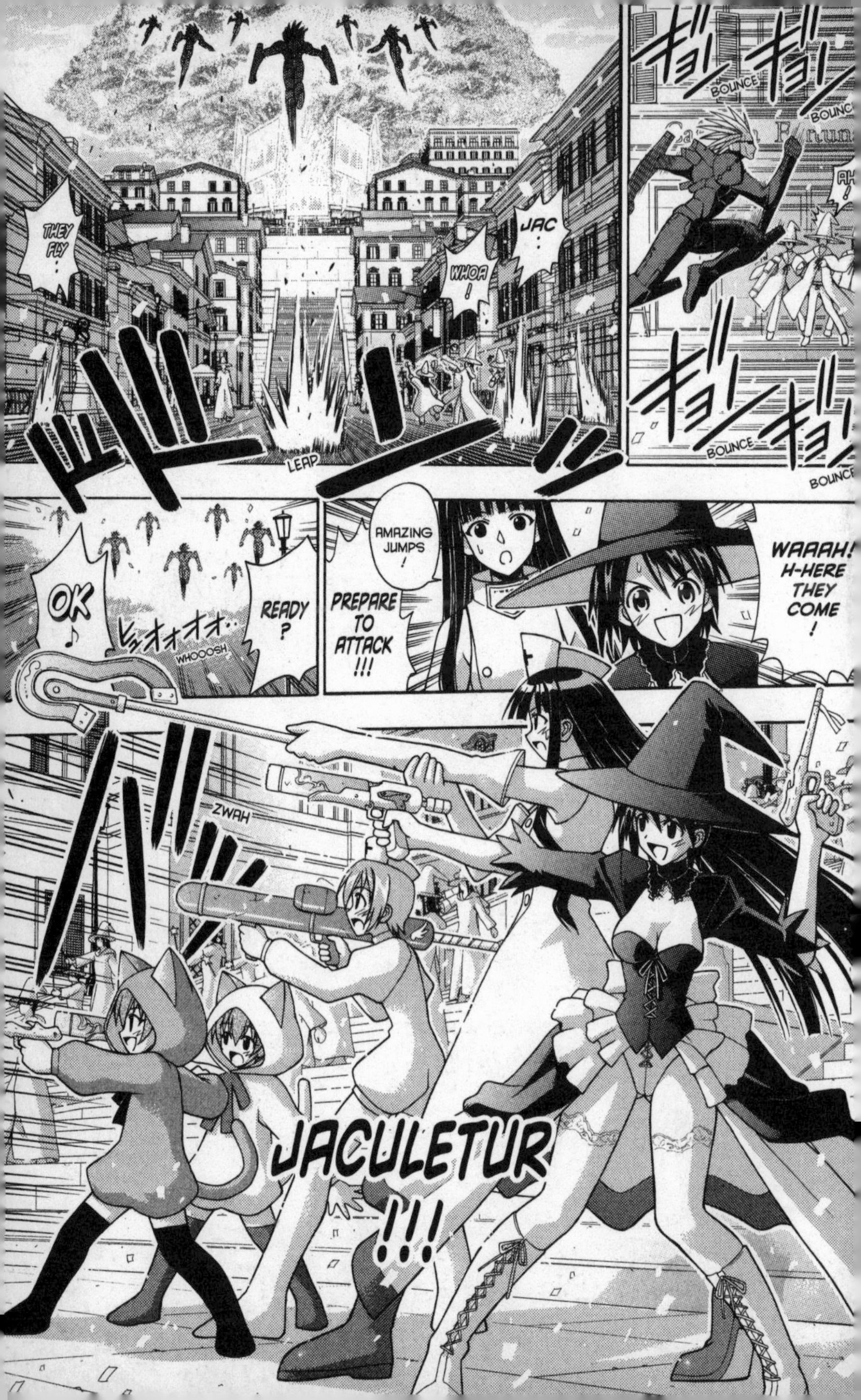
ギョン ギョン
BOUNCE
BOUNCE
AH!
ギョン ギョン
BOUNCE
BOUNCE
JAC...
WHOA!
THEY FLY...
ドドン
LEAP
WAAAH! H-HERE THEY COME!
AMAZING JUMPS!
PREPARE TO ATTACK!!!
READY?
ヒョオオオオ...
WHOOOSH
OK ♪
ZWAH
JACULETUR!!!

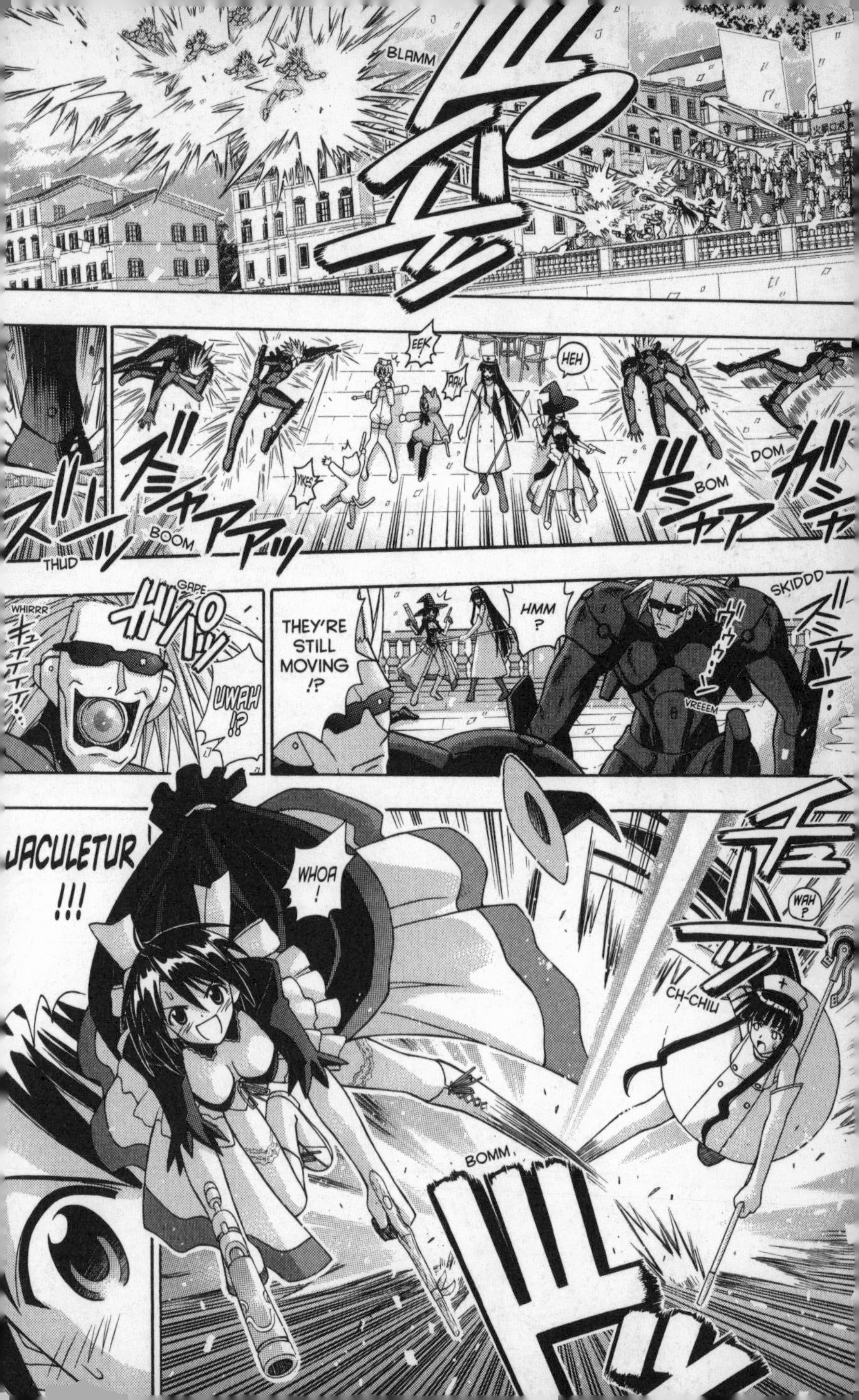
BLAMM
DOM
BOM
HEH
AAH
EEK !
YIKES
BOOM
THUD
SKIDDD
HMM ?
VREEEM
THEY'RE STILL MOVING !?
GAPE
WHIRRR
UWAH !?
WAH ?
CH-CHIU
WHOA !
JACULETUR !!!
BOMM

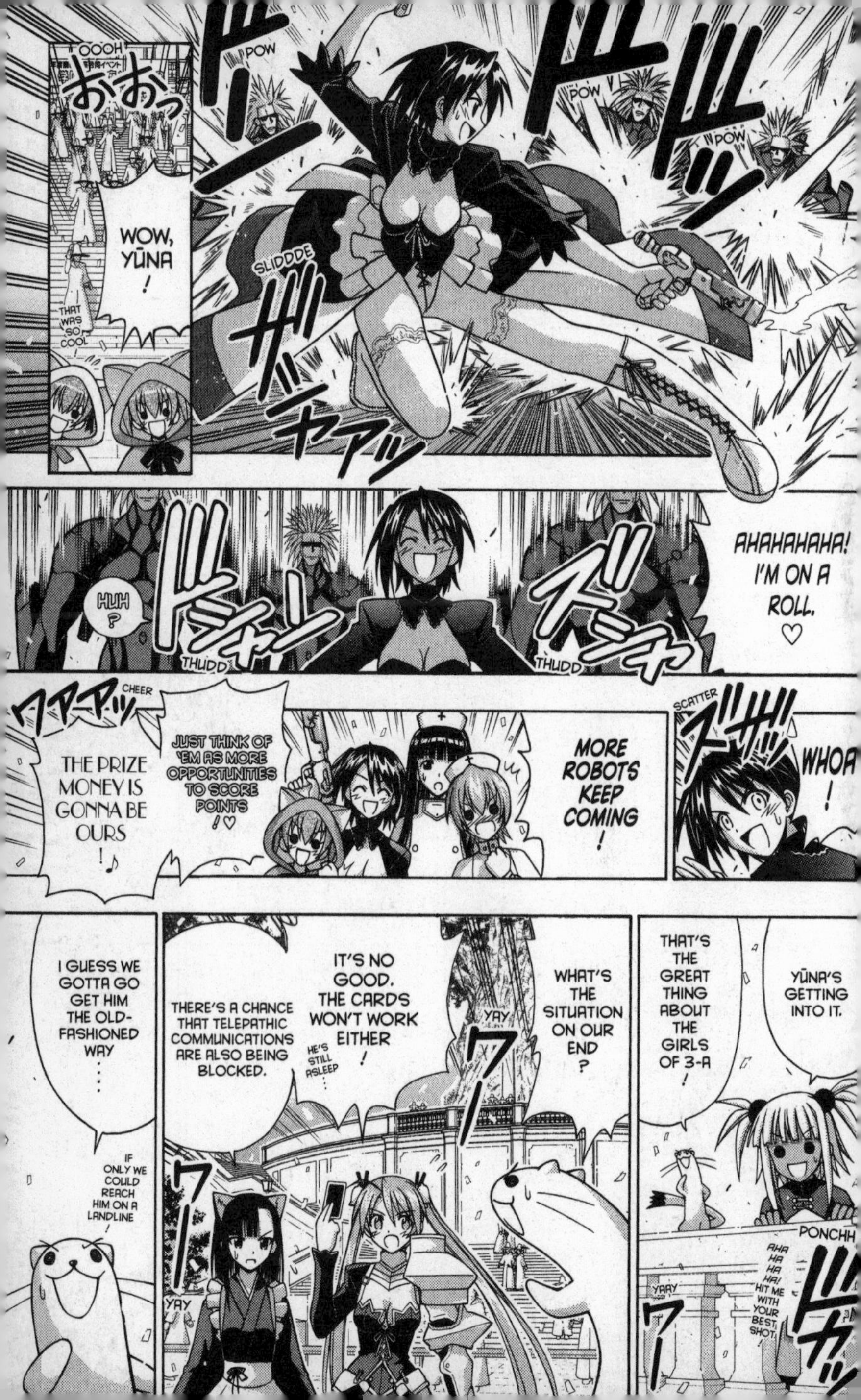
POW
POW
POW
SLIDDDE
OOOH
WOW, YŪNA!
THAT WAS SO COOL
AHAHAHAHA! I'M ON A ROLL. ♡
THUDD
HUH?
THUDD
SCATTER
WHOA!
MORE ROBOTS KEEP COMING!
JUST THINK OF 'EM AS MORE OPPORTUNITIES TO SCORE POINTS! ♡
CHEER
THE PRIZE MONEY IS GONNA BE OURS! ♪
YŪNA'S GETTING INTO IT.
THAT'S THE GREAT THING ABOUT THE GIRLS OF 3-A!
PONCHH
AHAHAHA! HIT ME WITH YOUR BEST SHOT.
YAAY
WHAT'S THE SITUATION ON OUR END?
YAY
IT'S NO GOOD. THE CARDS WON'T WORK EITHER!
HE'S STILL ASLEEP
THERE'S A CHANCE THAT TELEPATHIC COMMUNICATIONS ARE ALSO BEING BLOCKED.
YAY
I GUESS WE GOTTA GO GET HIM THE OLD-FASHIONED WAY......
IF ONLY WE COULD REACH HIM ON A LANDLINE!

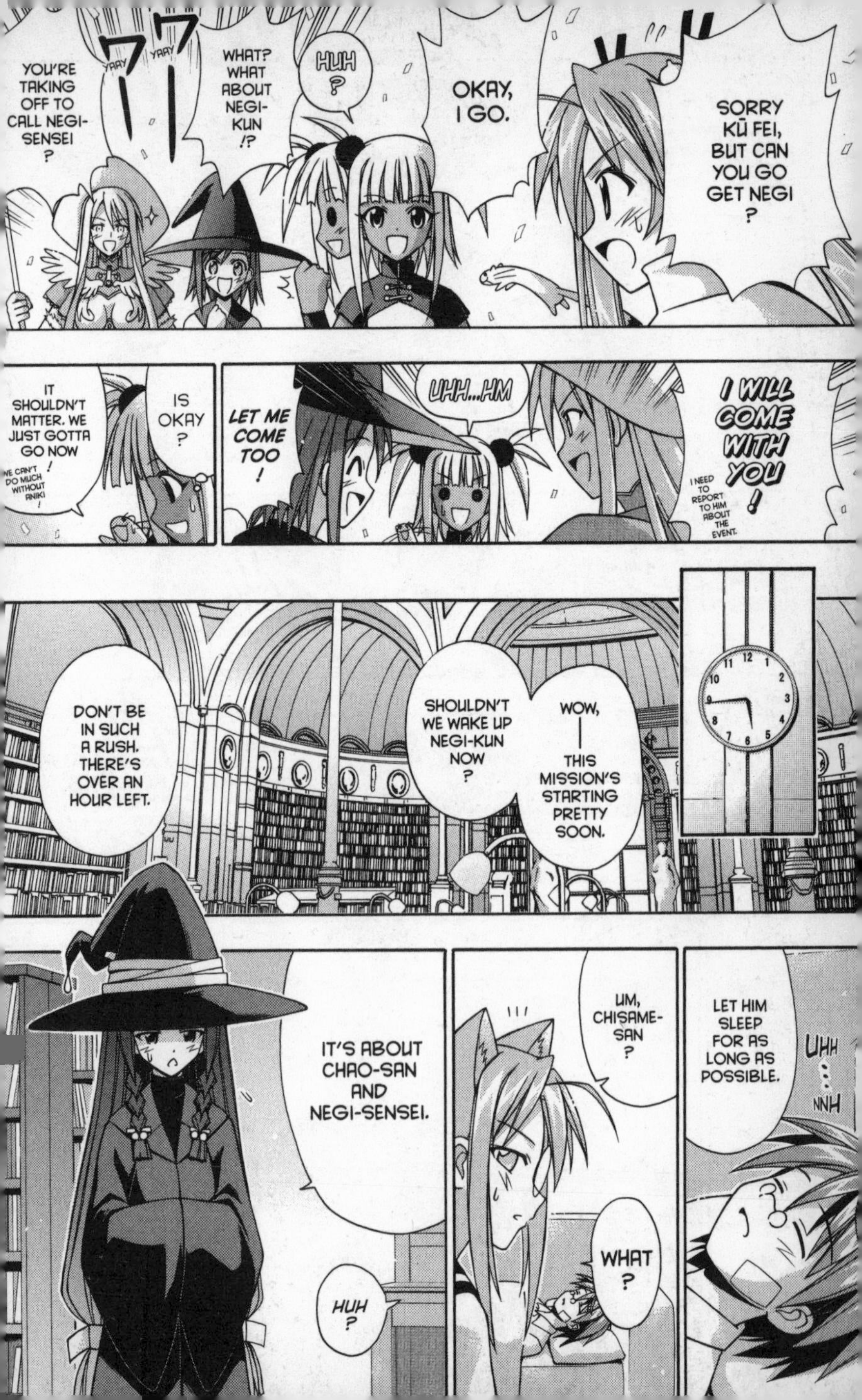
SORRY KŪ FEI, BUT CAN YOU GO GET NEGI?
OKAY, I GO.
HUH?
WHAT? WHAT ABOUT NEGI-KUN!?
YAAY YAAY
YOU'RE TAKING OFF TO CALL NEGI-SENSEI?
I WILL COME WITH YOU!
I NEED TO REPORT TO HIM ABOUT THE EVENT.
UHH...HM
LET ME COME TOO!
IS OKAY?
IT SHOULDN'T MATTER. WE JUST GOTTA GO NOW!
WE CAN'T DO MUCH WITHOUT ANIKI!
WOW, THIS MISSION'S STARTING PRETTY SOON.
SHOULDN'T WE WAKE UP NEGI-KUN NOW?
DON'T BE IN SUCH A RUSH. THERE'S OVER AN HOUR LEFT.
LET HIM SLEEP FOR AS LONG AS POSSIBLE.
UHH... NNH
UM, CHISAME-SAN?
WHAT?
IT'S ABOUT CHAO-SAN AND NEGI-SENSEI.
HUH?

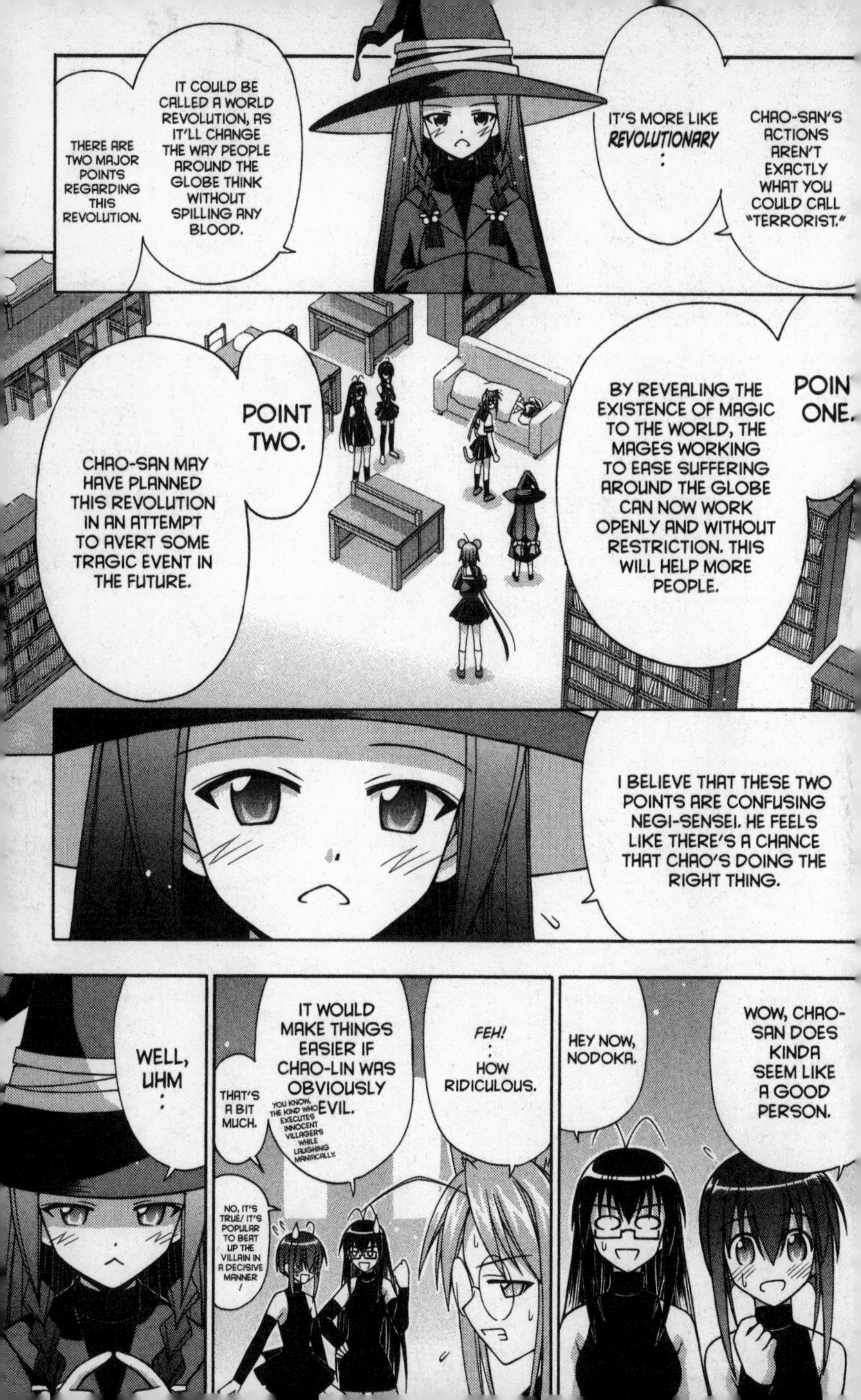
CHAO-SAN'S ACTIONS AREN'T EXACTLY WHAT YOU COULD CALL "TERRORIST."
IT'S MORE LIKE *REVOLUTIONARY* :
IT COULD BE CALLED A WORLD REVOLUTION, AS IT'LL CHANGE THE WAY PEOPLE AROUND THE GLOBE THINK WITHOUT SPILLING ANY BLOOD.
THERE ARE TWO MAJOR POINTS REGARDING THIS REVOLUTION.
POIN ONE.
BY REVEALING THE EXISTENCE OF MAGIC TO THE WORLD, THE MAGES WORKING TO EASE SUFFERING AROUND THE GLOBE CAN NOW WORK OPENLY AND WITHOUT RESTRICTION. THIS WILL HELP MORE PEOPLE.
POINT TWO.
CHAO-SAN MAY HAVE PLANNED THIS REVOLUTION IN AN ATTEMPT TO AVERT SOME TRAGIC EVENT IN THE FUTURE.
I BELIEVE THAT THESE TWO POINTS ARE CONFUSING NEGI-SENSEI. HE FEELS LIKE THERE'S A CHANCE THAT CHAO'S DOING THE RIGHT THING.
WOW, CHAO-SAN DOES KINDA SEEM LIKE A GOOD PERSON.
HEY NOW, NODOKA.
FEH! : HOW RIDICULOUS.
IT WOULD MAKE THINGS EASIER IF CHAO-LIN WAS OBVIOUSLY EVIL.
YOU KNOW, THE KIND WHO EXECUTES INNOCENT VILLAGERS WHILE LAUGHING MANIACALLY.
THAT'S A BIT MUCH.
NO, IT'S TRUE! IT'S POPULAR TO BEAT UP THE VILLAIN IN A DECISIVE MANNER!
WELL, UHM :

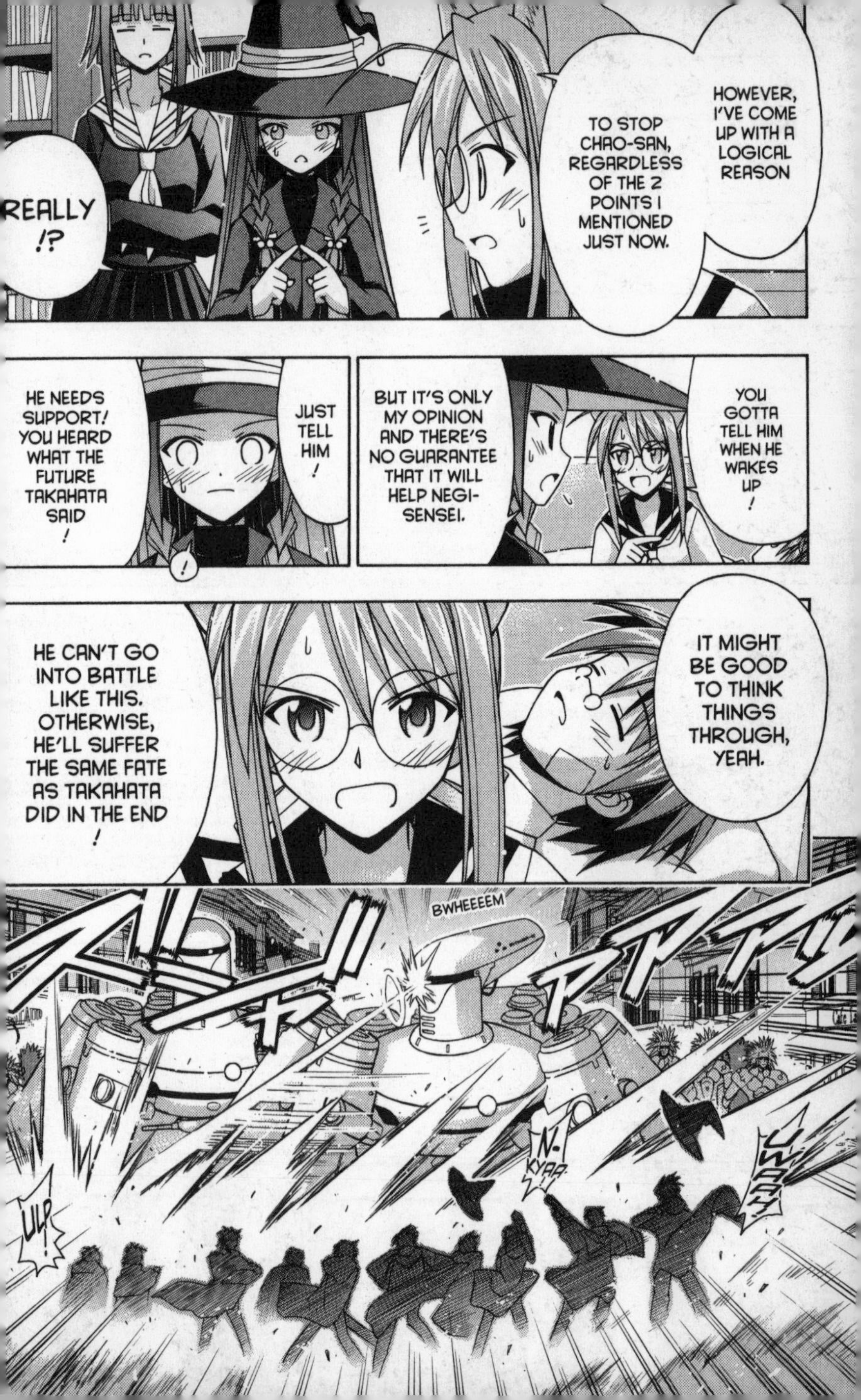
HOWEVER, I'VE COME UP WITH A LOGICAL REASON
TO STOP CHAO-SAN, REGARDLESS OF THE 2 POINTS I MENTIONED JUST NOW.
REALLY !?
YOU GOTTA TELL HIM WHEN HE WAKES UP !
BUT IT'S ONLY MY OPINION AND THERE'S NO GUARANTEE THAT IT WILL HELP NEGI-SENSEI.
JUST TELL HIM !
HE NEEDS SUPPORT! YOU HEARD WHAT THE FUTURE TAKAHATA SAID !
!
IT MIGHT BE GOOD TO THINK THINGS THROUGH, YEAH.
HE CAN'T GO INTO BATTLE LIKE THIS. OTHERWISE, HE'LL SUFFER THE SAME FATE AS TAKAHATA DID IN THE END !
BWHEEEEM
U-WAAH!
N-KYAA!
ULP!

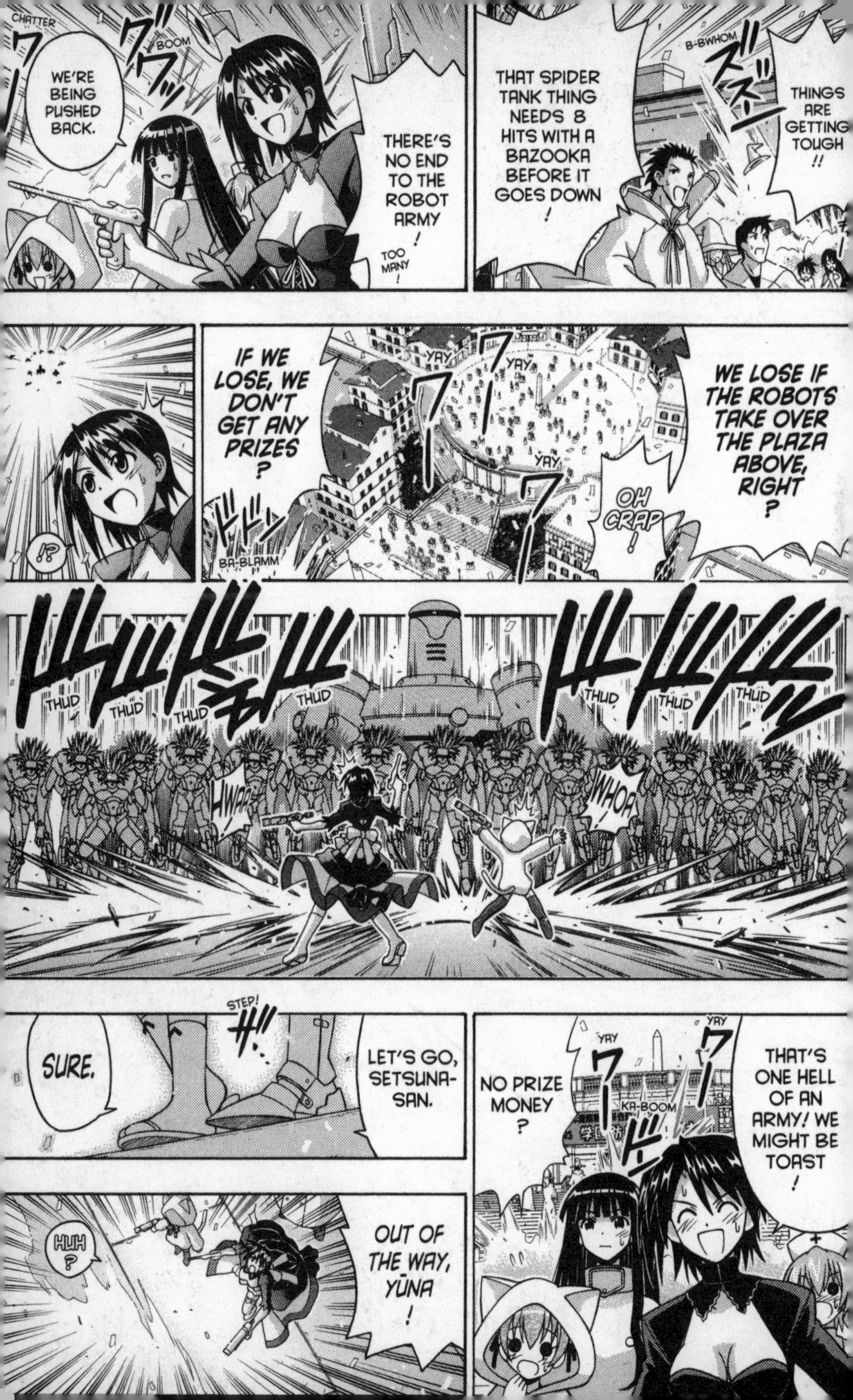
B-BWHOM
THINGS ARE GETTING TOUGH!!
THAT SPIDER TANK THING NEEDS 8 HITS WITH A BAZOOKA BEFORE IT GOES DOWN!
BOOM
THERE'S NO END TO THE ROBOT ARMY!
TOO MANY!
WE'RE BEING PUSHED BACK.
CHATTER
WE LOSE IF THE ROBOTS TAKE OVER THE PLAZA ABOVE, RIGHT?
OH CRAP!
YAY
YAY
YAY
IF WE LOSE, WE DON'T GET ANY PRIZES?
BA-BLAMM
!?
THUD
THUD
THUD
THUD
THUD
THUD
THUD
WHOA!
HWAA
YAY
THAT'S ONE HELL OF AN ARMY! WE MIGHT BE TOAST!
YAY
KA-BOOM
NO PRIZE MONEY?
LET'S GO, SETSUNA-SAN.
STEP!
SURE.
OUT OF THE WAY, YŪNA!
HUH?

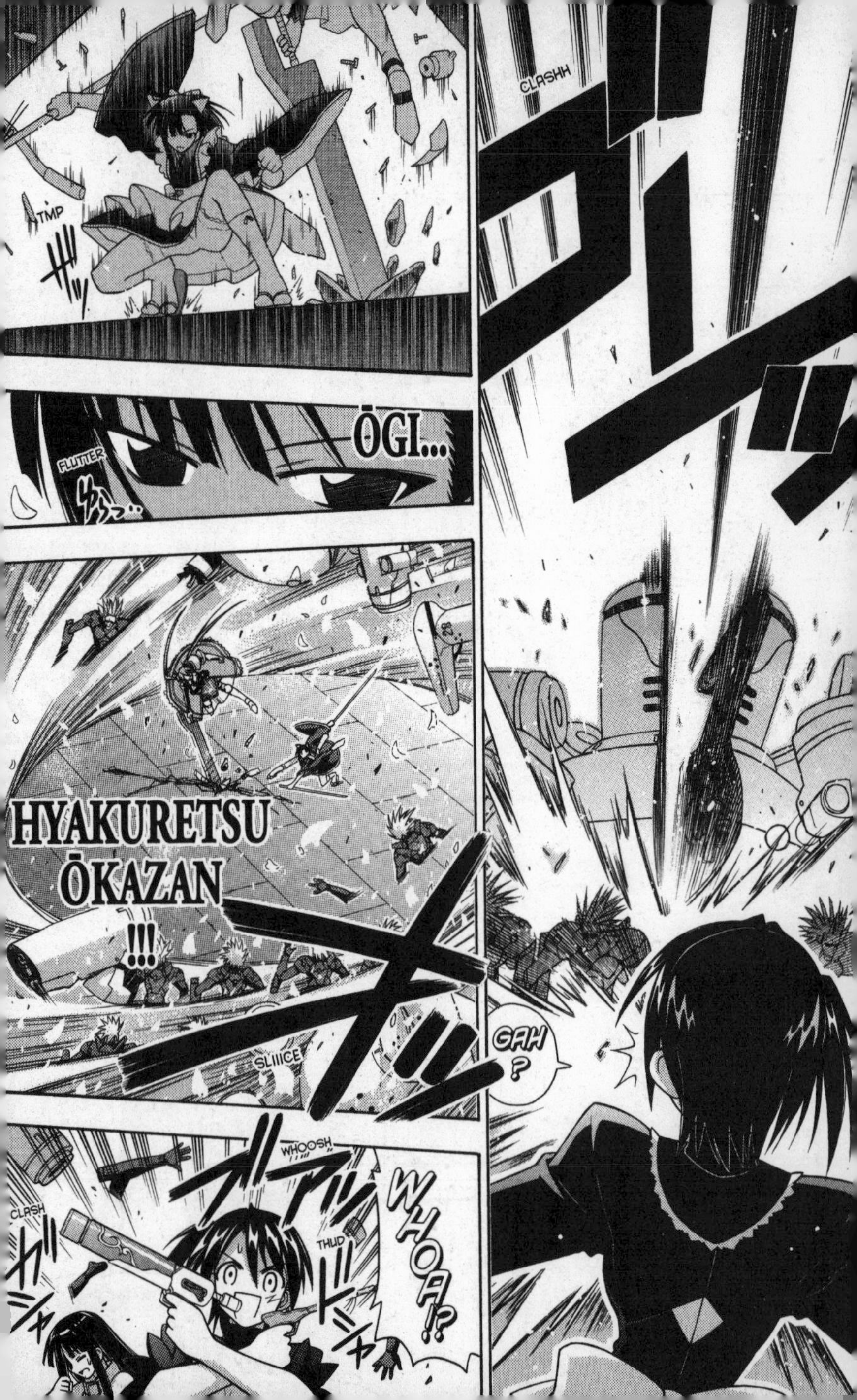
CLASHH
GAH?
TMP
ŌGI...
FLUTTER
HYAKURETSU ŌKAZAN!!!
SLIIICE
WHOOSH
WHOA!?
CLASH
THUD

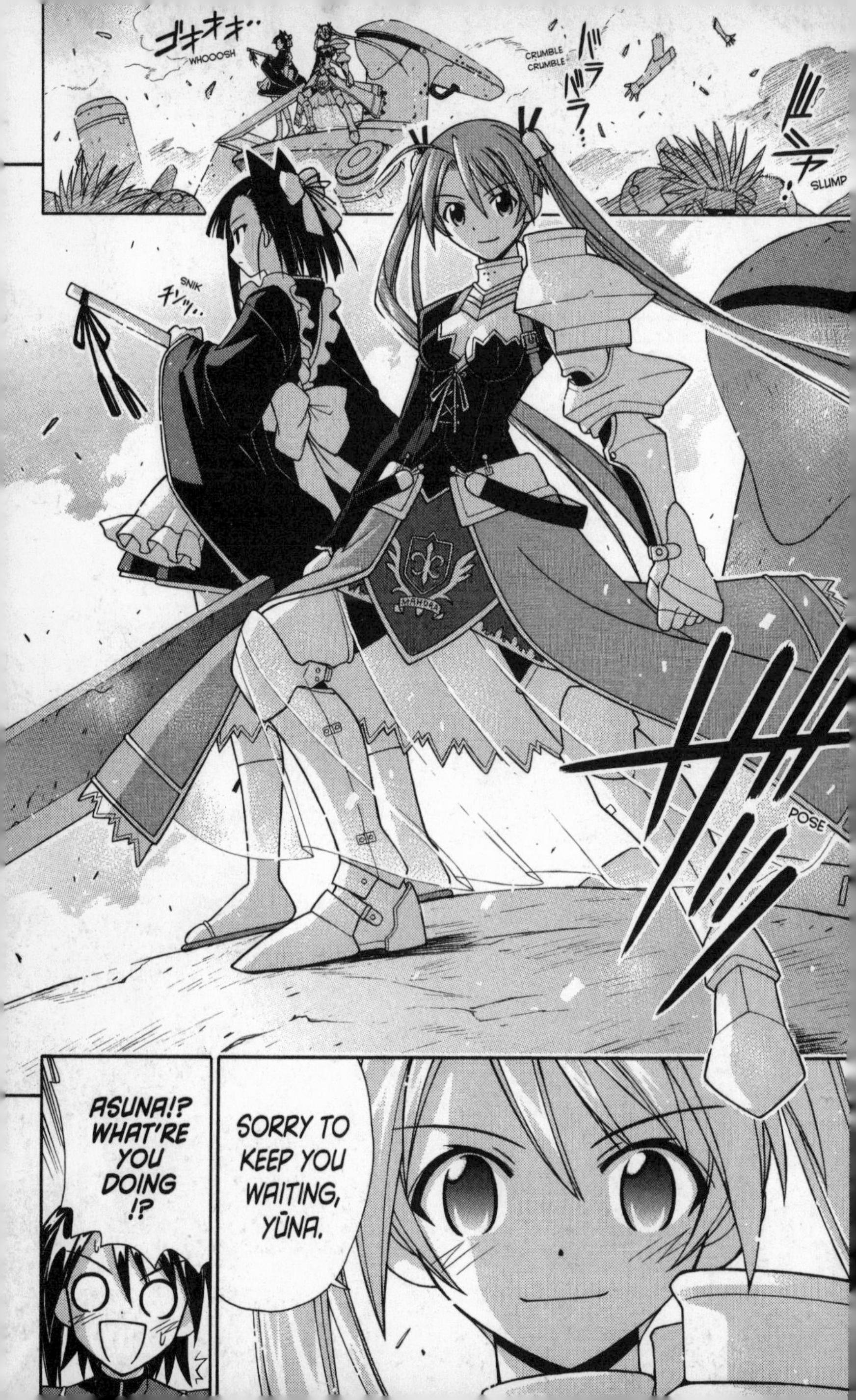
SLUMP
CRUMBLE CRUMBLE
WHOOOSH
POSE
SNIK
SORRY TO KEEP YOU WAITING, YŪNA.
ASUNA!? WHAT'RE YOU DOING!?

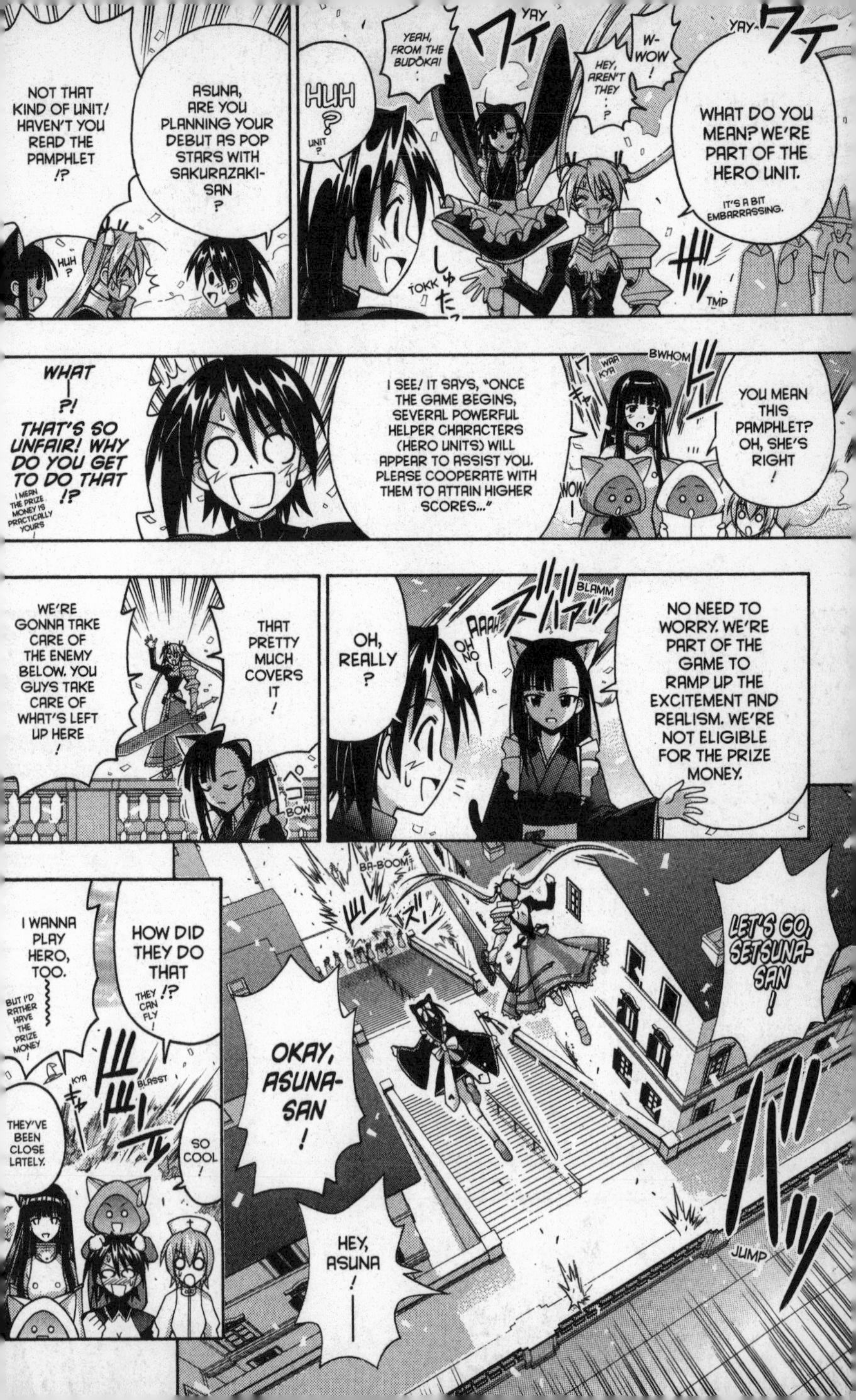
YAY
WHAT DO YOU MEAN? WE'RE PART OF THE HERO UNIT.
IT'S A BIT EMBARRASSING.
W-WOW!
HEY, AREN'T THEY...?
YAY
YEAH, FROM THE BUDŌKAI...
HUH? UNIT?
TMP
TOKK
ASUNA, ARE YOU PLANNING YOUR DEBUT AS POP STARS WITH SAKURAZAKI-SAN?
NOT THAT KIND OF UNIT! HAVEN'T YOU READ THE PAMPHLET!?
HUH?
YOU MEAN THIS PAMPHLET? OH, SHE'S RIGHT!
BWHOM
WAA KYA
WOW!
I SEE! IT SAYS, "ONCE THE GAME BEGINS, SEVERAL POWERFUL HELPER CHARACTERS (HERO UNITS) WILL APPEAR TO ASSIST YOU. PLEASE COOPERATE WITH THEM TO ATTAIN HIGHER SCORES..."
WHAT?! THAT'S SO UNFAIR! WHY DO YOU GET TO DO THAT!?
I MEAN THE PRIZE MONEY IS PRACTICALLY YOURS!
BLAMM
NO NEED TO WORRY. WE'RE PART OF THE GAME TO RAMP UP THE EXCITEMENT AND REALISM. WE'RE NOT ELIGIBLE FOR THE PRIZE MONEY.
AAAH!
OH NO!
OH, REALLY?
THAT PRETTY MUCH COVERS IT!
WE'RE GONNA TAKE CARE OF THE ENEMY BELOW. YOU GUYS TAKE CARE OF WHAT'S LEFT UP HERE!
BOW
LET'S GO, SETSUNA-SAN!
BA-BOOM
OKAY, ASUNA-SAN!
JUMP
HEY, ASUNA!
HOW DID THEY DO THAT!?
THEY CAN FLY
I WANNA PLAY HERO, TOO.
BUT I'D RATHER HAVE THE PRIZE MONEY
BLASST
KYA
SO COOL!
THEY'VE BEEN CLOSE LATELY.

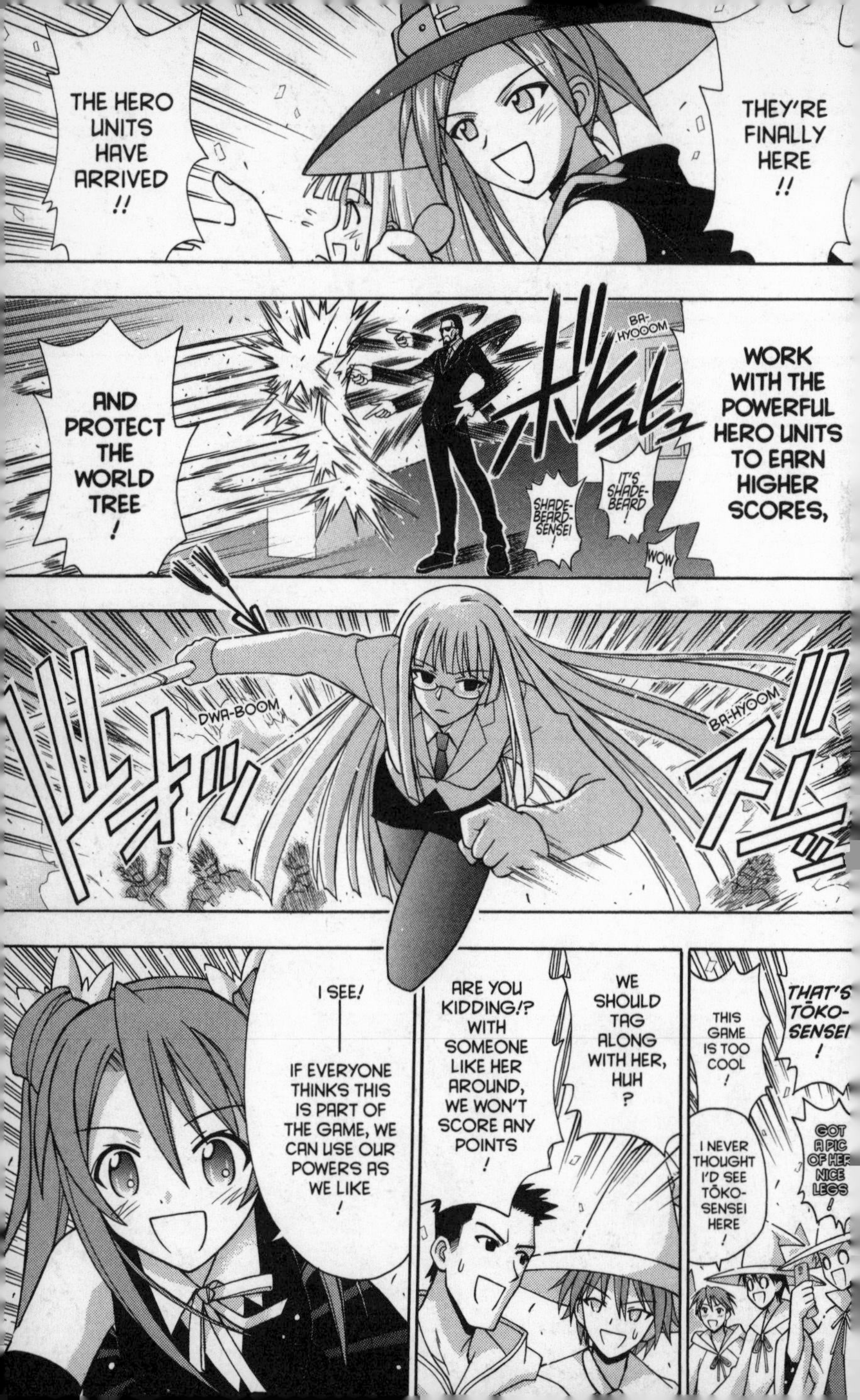
THEY'RE FINALLY HERE !!
THE HERO UNITS HAVE ARRIVED !!
WORK WITH THE POWERFUL HERO UNITS TO EARN HIGHER SCORES,
BA-HYOOOM
IT'S SHADE-BEARD !
SHADE-BEARD-SENSEI !
WOW !
AND PROTECT THE WORLD TREE !
BA-HYOOM
DWA-BOOM
THAT'S TŌKO-SENSEI !
THIS GAME IS TOO COOL !
GOT A PIC OF HER NICE LEGS !
I NEVER THOUGHT I'D SEE TŌKO-SENSEI HERE !
WE SHOULD TAG ALONG WITH HER, HUH ?
ARE YOU KIDDING!? WITH SOMEONE LIKE HER AROUND, WE WON'T SCORE ANY POINTS !
I SEE!
IF EVERYONE THINKS THIS IS PART OF THE GAME, WE CAN USE OUR POWERS AS WE LIKE !

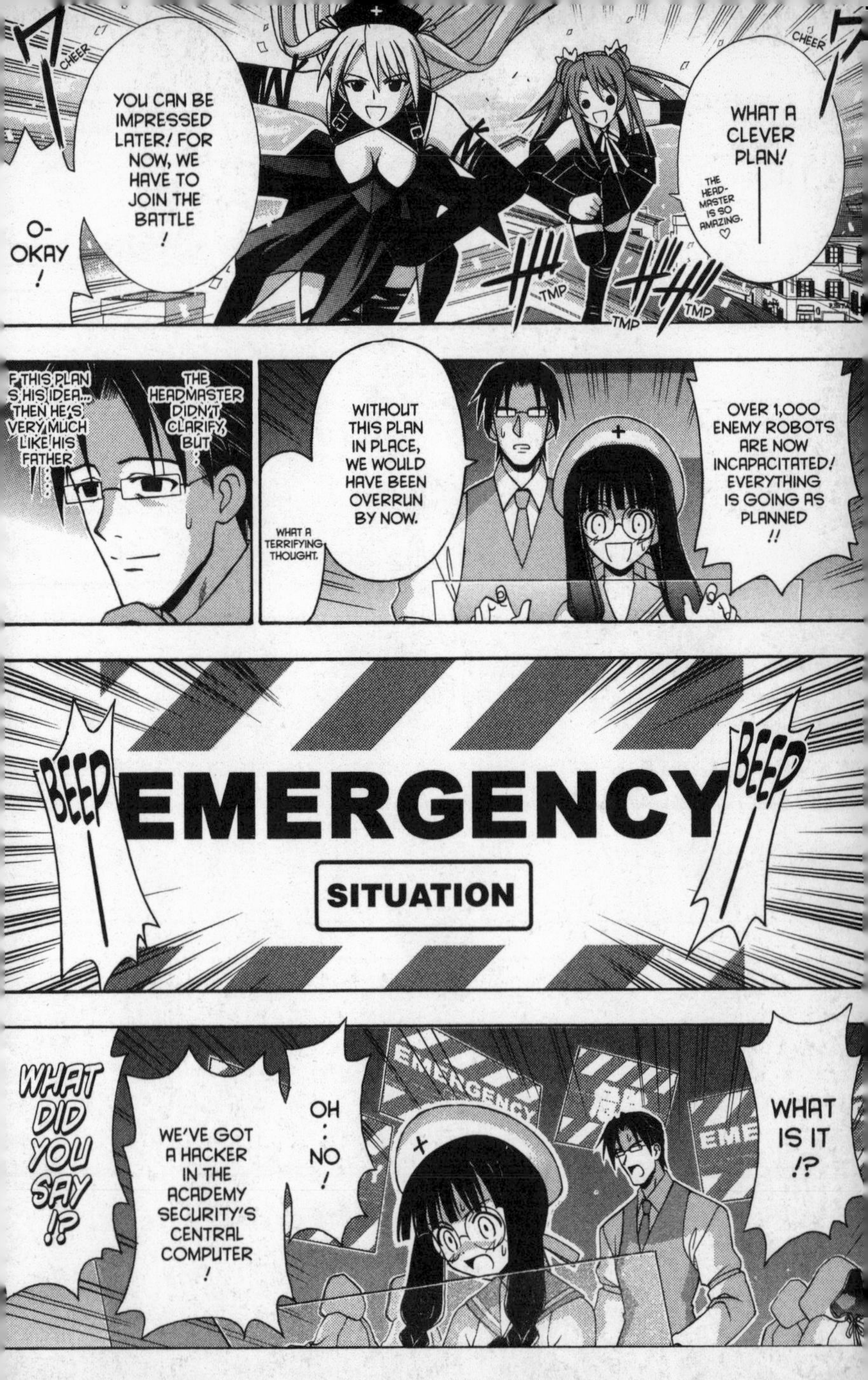
CHEER
WHAT A CLEVER PLAN!
THE HEADMASTER IS SO AMAZING. ♡
YOU CAN BE IMPRESSED LATER! FOR NOW, WE HAVE TO JOIN THE BATTLE!
CHEER
O-OKAY!
TMP
TMP
TMP
OVER 1,000 ENEMY ROBOTS ARE NOW INCAPACITATED! EVERYTHING IS GOING AS PLANNED!!
WITHOUT THIS PLAN IN PLACE, WE WOULD HAVE BEEN OVERRUN BY NOW.
WHAT A TERRIFYING THOUGHT.
THE HEADMASTER DIDN'T CLARIFY, BUT...
IF THIS PLAN IS HIS IDEA... THEN HE'S VERY MUCH LIKE HIS FATHER
BEEP
EMERGENCY
SITUATION
BEEP
WHAT IS IT!?
OH... NO!
WE'VE GOT A HACKER IN THE ACADEMY SECURITY'S CENTRAL COMPUTER!
WHAT DID YOU SAY!?

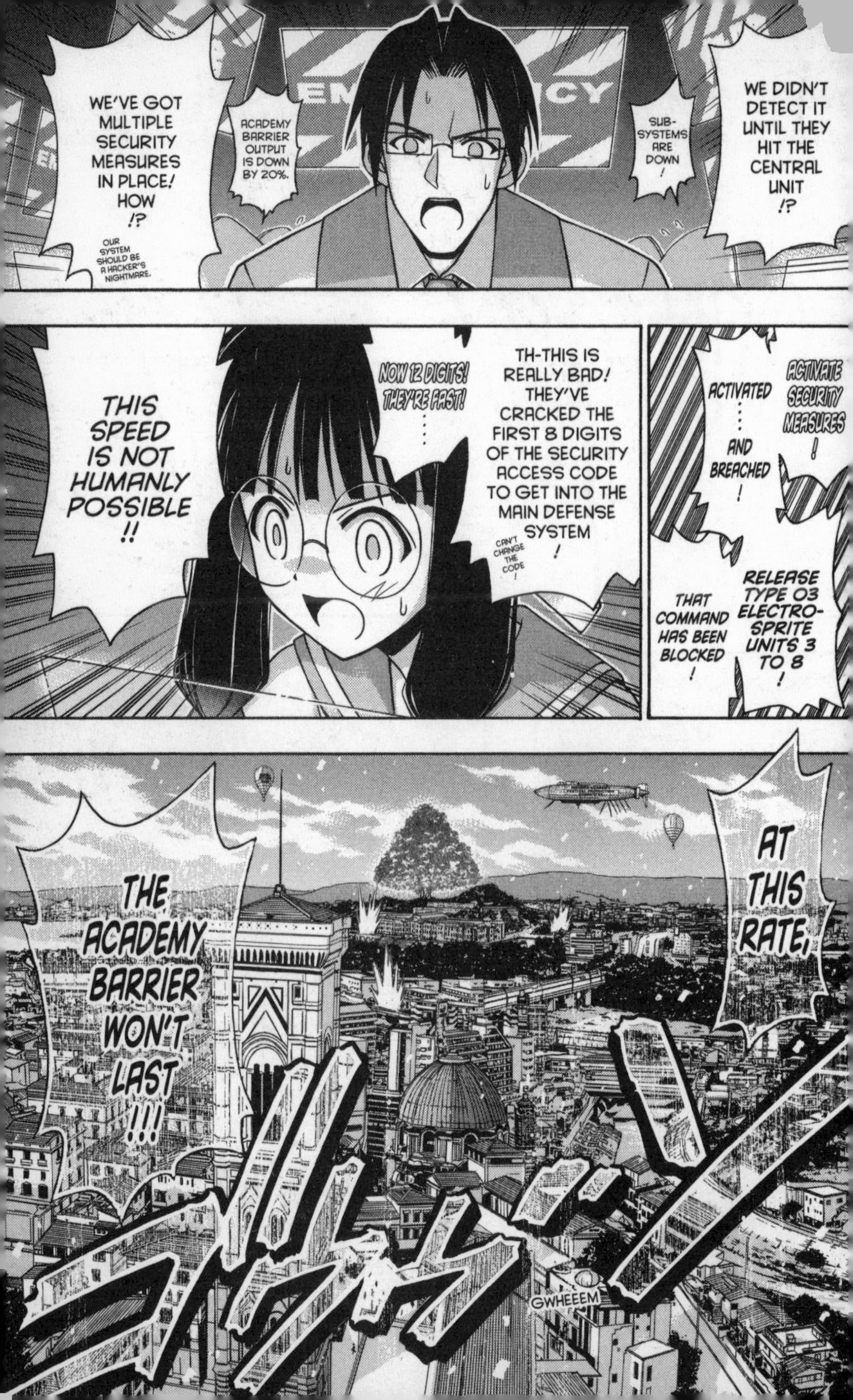
WE DIDN'T DETECT IT UNTIL THEY HIT THE CENTRAL UNIT !?
SUB-SYSTEMS ARE DOWN !
ACADEMY BARRIER OUTPUT IS DOWN BY 20%.
WE'VE GOT MULTIPLE SECURITY MEASURES IN PLACE! HOW !?
OUR SYSTEM SHOULD BE A HACKER'S NIGHTMARE.
ACTIVATE SECURITY MEASURES !
ACTIVATED ... AND BREACHED !
RELEASE TYPE 03 ELECTRO-SPRITE UNITS 3 TO 8 !
THAT COMMAND HAS BEEN BLOCKED !
TH-THIS IS REALLY BAD! THEY'VE CRACKED THE FIRST 8 DIGITS OF THE SECURITY ACCESS CODE TO GET INTO THE MAIN DEFENSE SYSTEM !
CAN'T CHANGE THE CODE !
NOW 12 DIGITS! THEY'RE FAST! ...
THIS SPEED IS NOT HUMANLY POSSIBLE !!
AT THIS RATE,
THE ACADEMY BARRIER WON'T LAST !!!
GWHEEEM

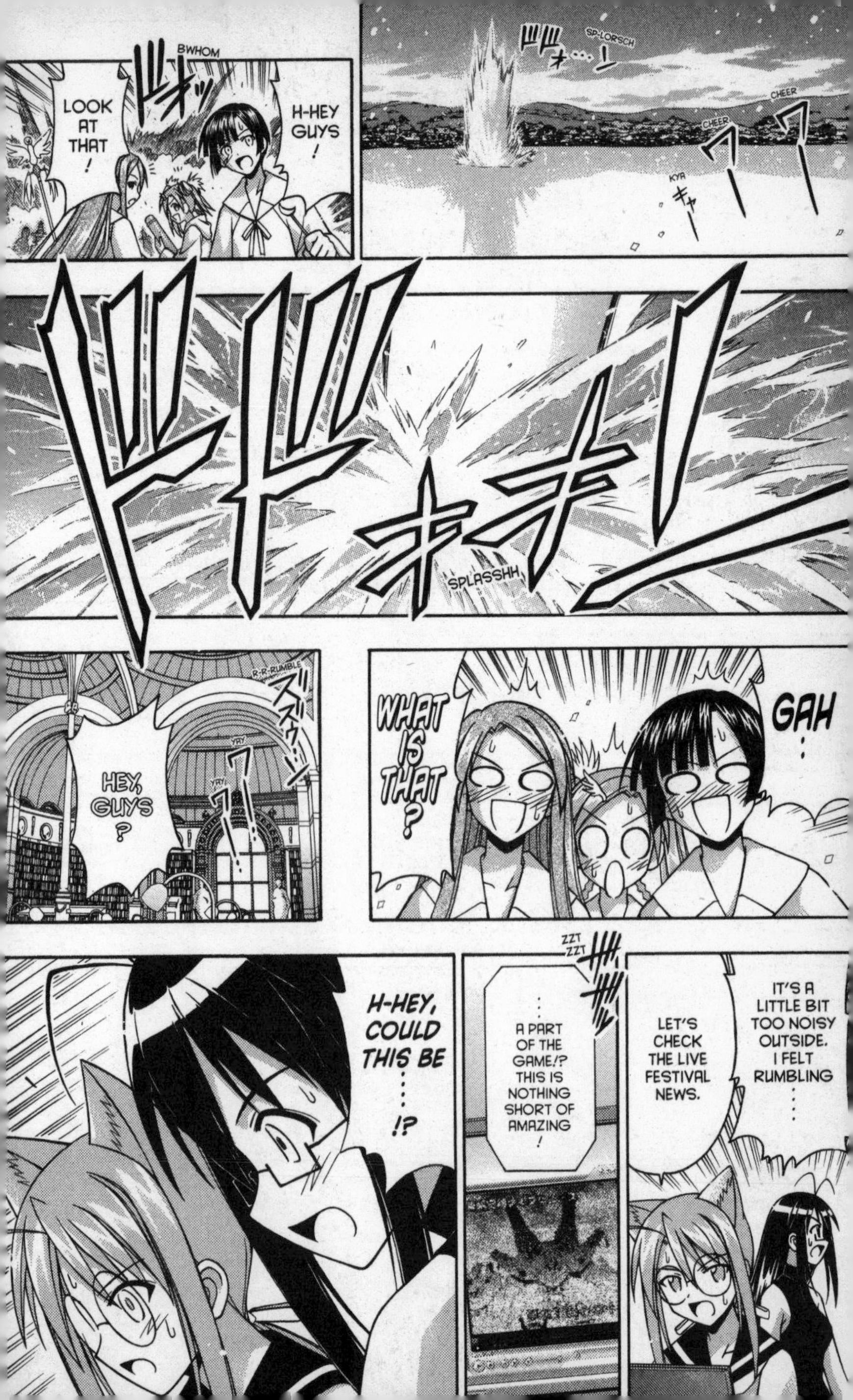
SP-LORSCH
CHEER
CHEER
KYA
BWHOM
H-HEY GUYS!
LOOK AT THAT!
SPLASSHH
GAH...
WHAT IS THAT?
R-R-RUMBLE
YAY
YAY
HEY, GUYS?
IT'S A LITTLE BIT TOO NOISY OUTSIDE. I FELT RUMBLING....
LET'S CHECK THE LIVE FESTIVAL NEWS.
ZZT ZZT
...A PART OF THE GAME!? THIS IS NOTHING SHORT OF AMAZING!
H-HEY, COULD THIS BE....!?

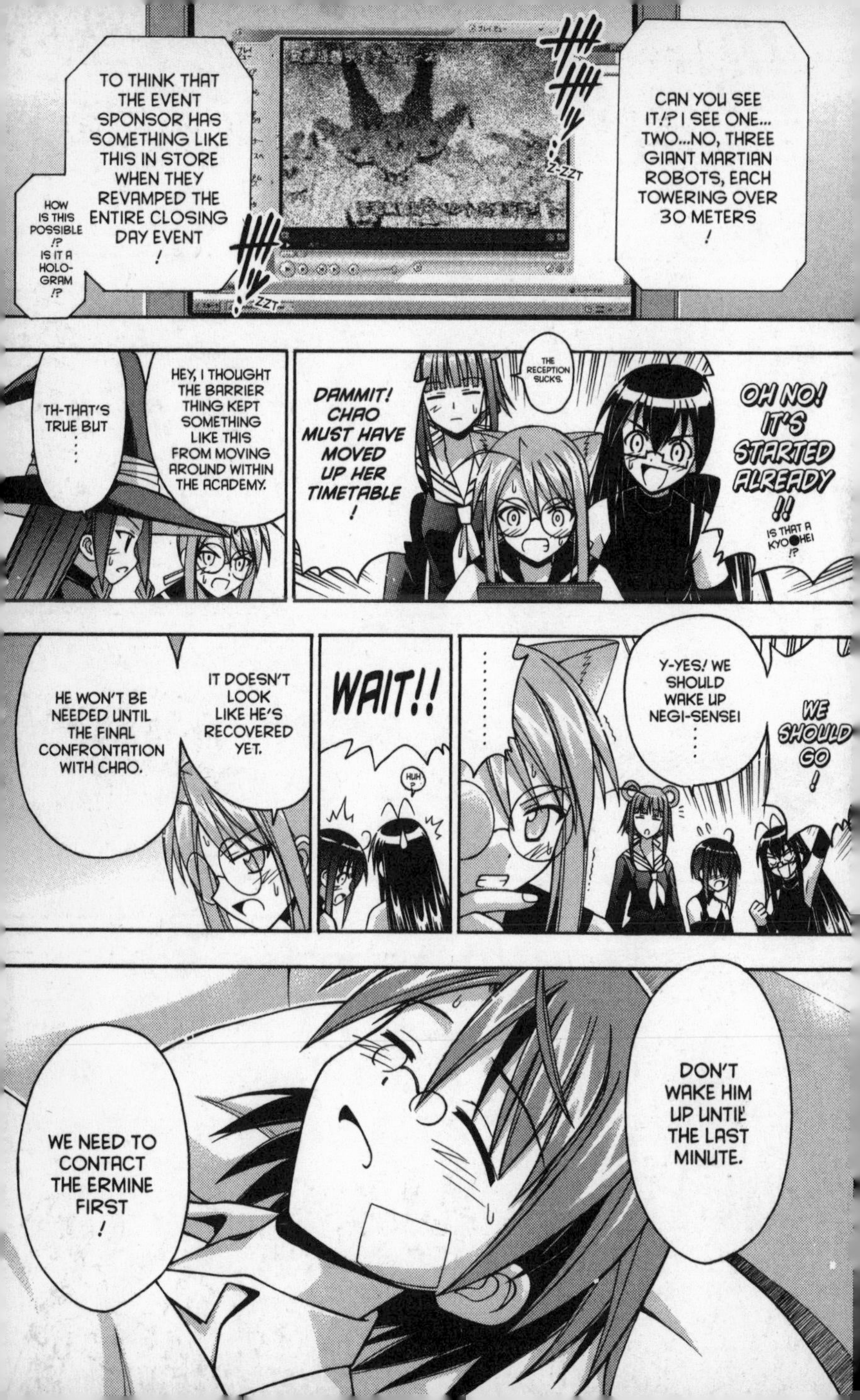
CAN YOU SEE IT!? I SEE ONE... TWO...NO, THREE GIANT MARTIAN ROBOTS, EACH TOWERING OVER 30 METERS!
Z-ZZT
TO THINK THAT THE EVENT SPONSOR HAS SOMETHING LIKE THIS IN STORE WHEN THEY REVAMPED THE ENTIRE CLOSING DAY EVENT!
HOW IS THIS POSSIBLE!? IS IT A HOLOGRAM!?
ZZT
OH NO! IT'S STARTED ALREADY!!
IS THAT A KYO●HEI!?
THE RECEPTION SUCKS.
DAMMIT! CHAO MUST HAVE MOVED UP HER TIMETABLE!
HEY, I THOUGHT THE BARRIER THING KEPT SOMETHING LIKE THIS FROM MOVING AROUND WITHIN THE ACADEMY.
TH-THAT'S TRUE BUT...
WE SHOULD GO!
Y-YES! WE SHOULD WAKE UP NEGI-SENSEI...
......
WAIT!!
HUH?
IT DOESN'T LOOK LIKE HE'S RECOVERED YET.
HE WON'T BE NEEDED UNTIL THE FINAL CONFRONTATION WITH CHAO.
DON'T WAKE HIM UP UNTIL THE LAST MINUTE.
WE NEED TO CONTACT THE ERMINE FIRST!

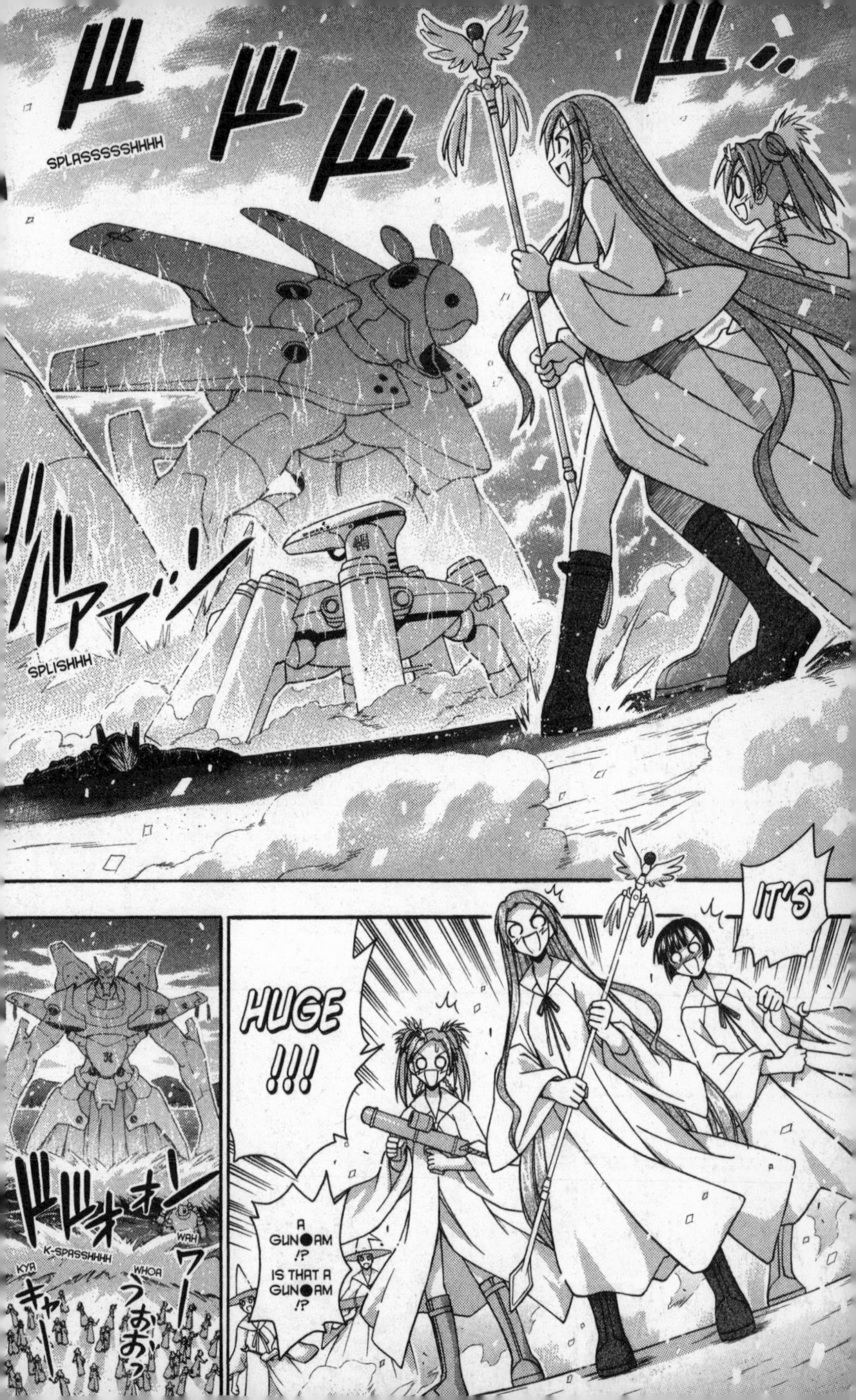
SPLASSSSSHHHH
SPLISHHH
IT'S
HUGE
!!!
A GUN●AM !?
IS THAT A GUN●AM !?
K-SPASSHHHH
WAH
ワー
WHOA
うおおっ
KYA
キャー!

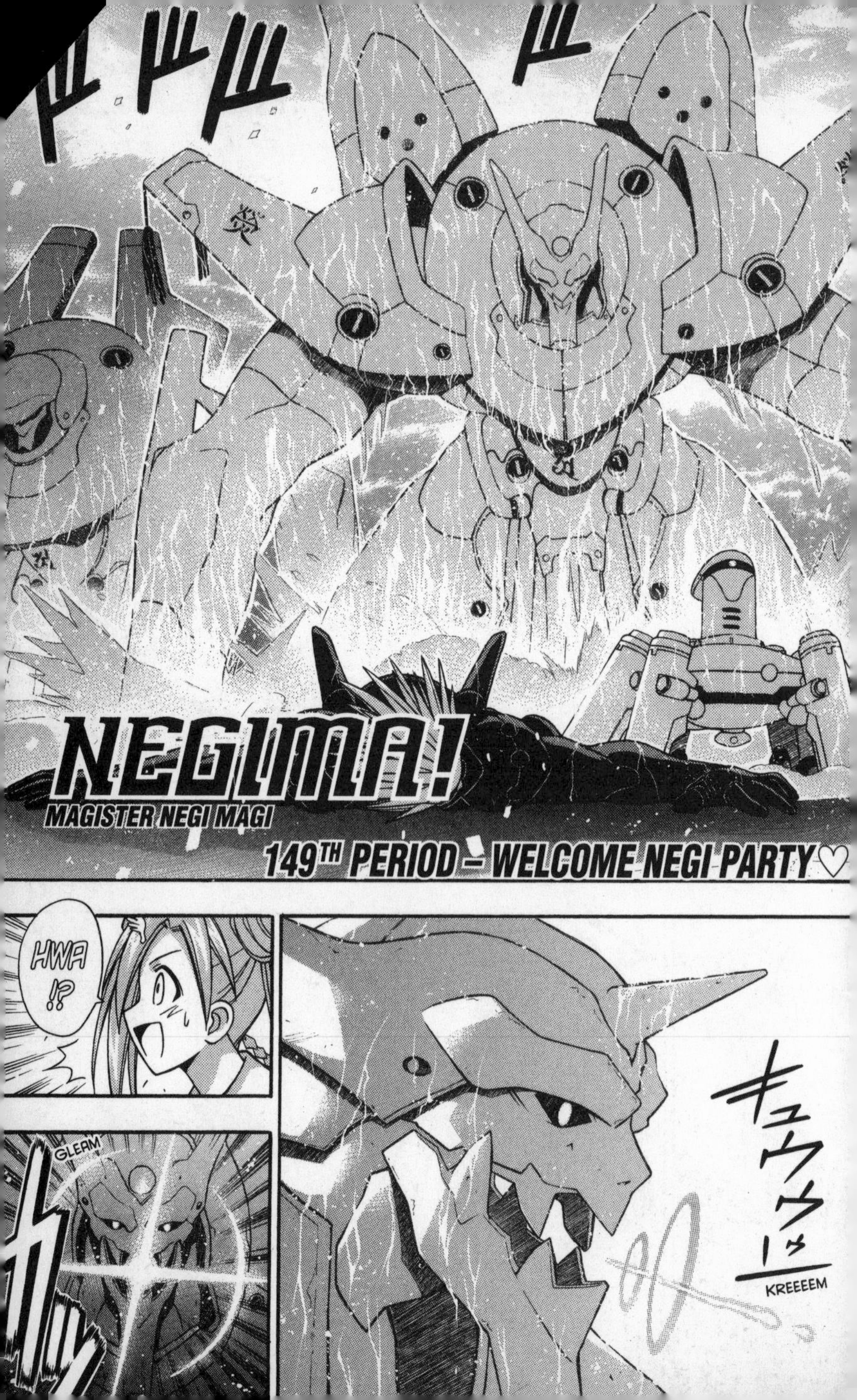
NEGIMA!
MAGISTER NEGI MAGI
149TH PERIOD – WELCOME NEGI PARTY♡
KREEEEM
HWA !?
GLEAM

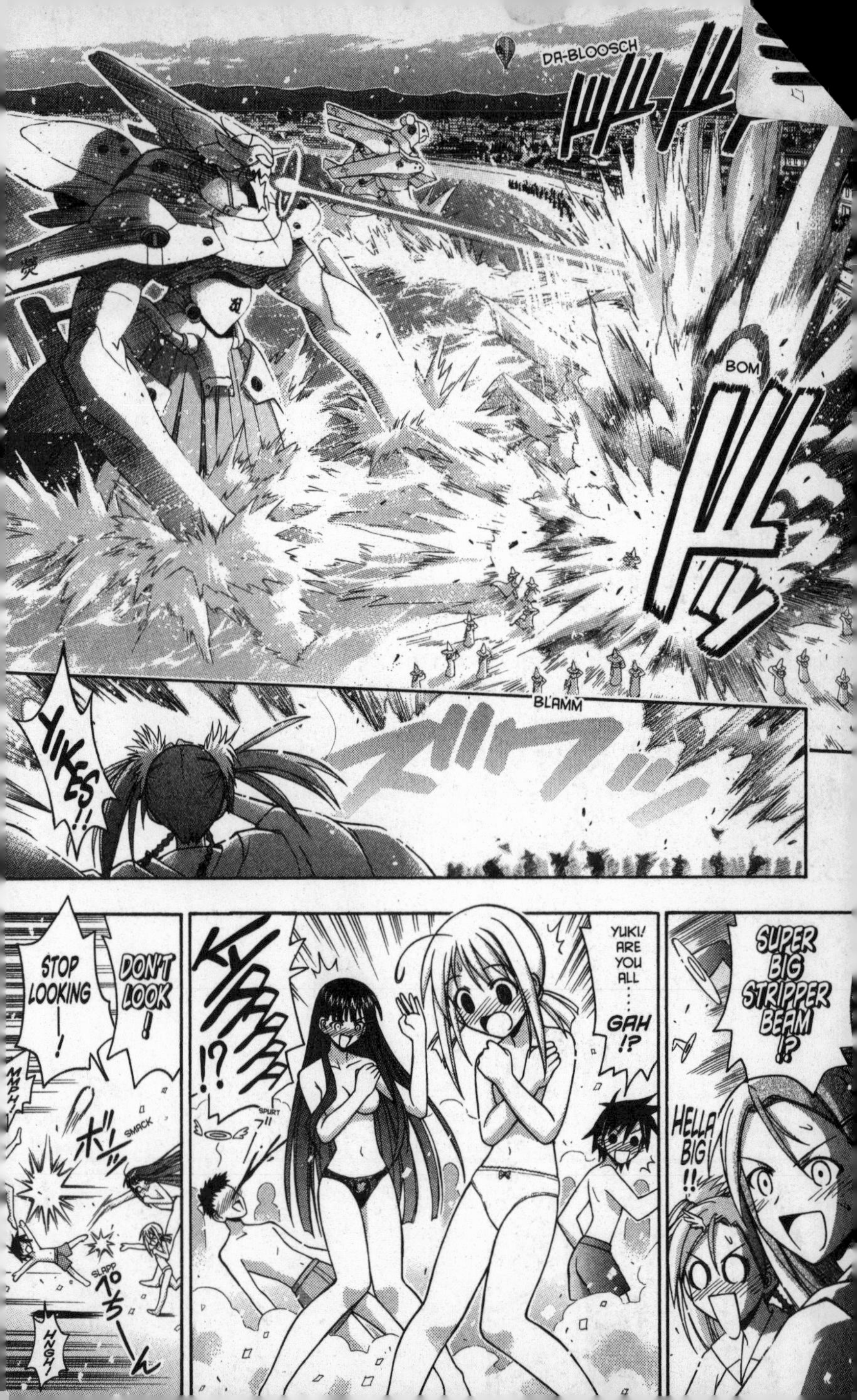
DA-BLOOSCH
BOM
BLAMM
YIKES!!
SUPER BIG STRIPPER BEAM!?
HELLA BIG!!
YUKI! ARE YOU ALL..... GAH!?
KYAAAAA!?
SPURT
DON'T LOOK!
STOP LOOKING!
MMPH!
SMACK
SLAPP
HNGH!

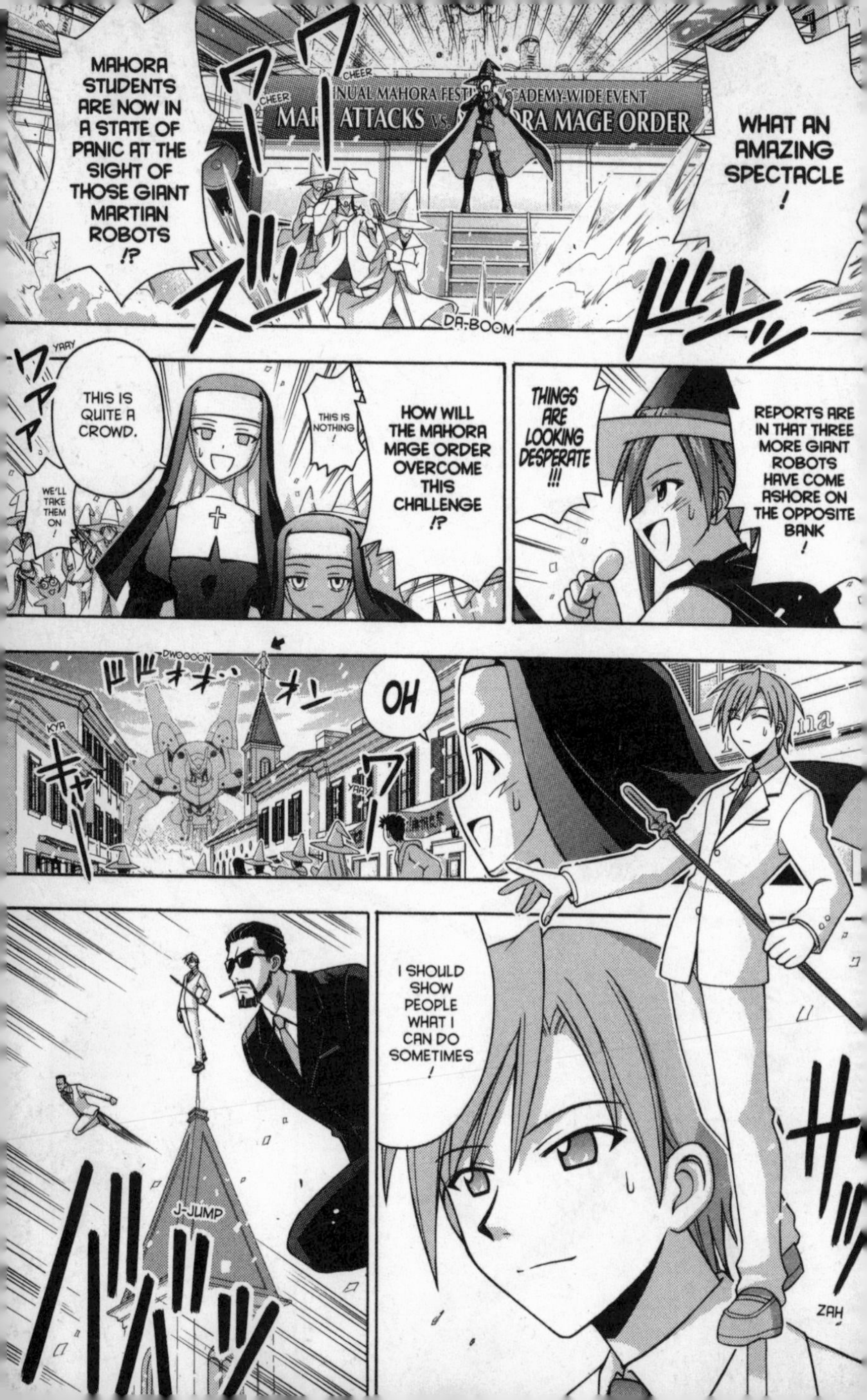
NUAL MAHORA FESTI ACADEMY-WIDE EVENT
MAR ATTACKS vs. ORA MAGE ORDER
CHEER
CHEER
WHAT AN AMAZING SPECTACLE!
MAHORA STUDENTS ARE NOW IN A STATE OF PANIC AT THE SIGHT OF THOSE GIANT MARTIAN ROBOTS!?
DA-BOOM
REPORTS ARE IN THAT THREE MORE GIANT ROBOTS HAVE COME ASHORE ON THE OPPOSITE BANK!
THINGS ARE LOOKING DESPERATE!!!
HOW WILL THE MAHORA MAGE ORDER OVERCOME THIS CHALLENGE!?
THIS IS NOTHING!
YAAY
THIS IS QUITE A CROWD.
WE'LL TAKE THEM ON!
OH
DWOOOON
YAAY
KYA
I SHOULD SHOW PEOPLE WHAT I CAN DO SOMETIMES!
ZAH
J-JUMP

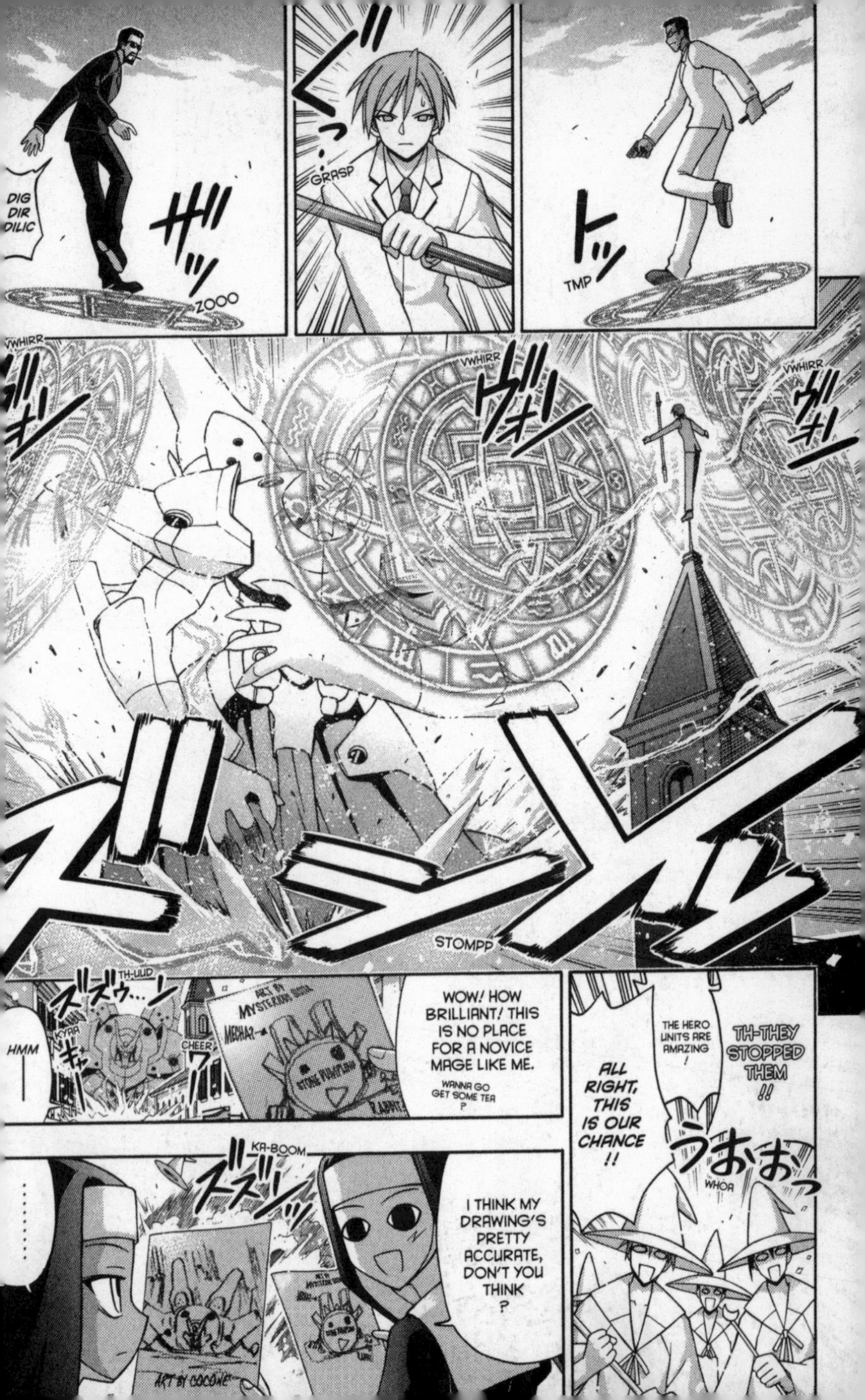
トッ
TMP
ぐっ
GRASP
ザッ
ZOOO
DIG DIR DILIC
VWHIRR
VWHIRR
VWHIRR
STOMPP
TH-THEY STOPPED THEM!!
THE HERO UNITS ARE AMAZING!
ALL RIGHT, THIS IS OUR CHANCE!!
うおおっ
WHOA
WOW! HOW BRILLIANT! THIS IS NO PLACE FOR A NOVICE MAGE LIKE ME.
WANNA GO GET SOME TEA?
MECHA?
CHEER
KYAA
TH-UUD
HMM
KA-BOOM
I THINK MY DRAWING'S PRETTY ACCURATE, DON'T YOU THINK?
ART BY COCONE
....

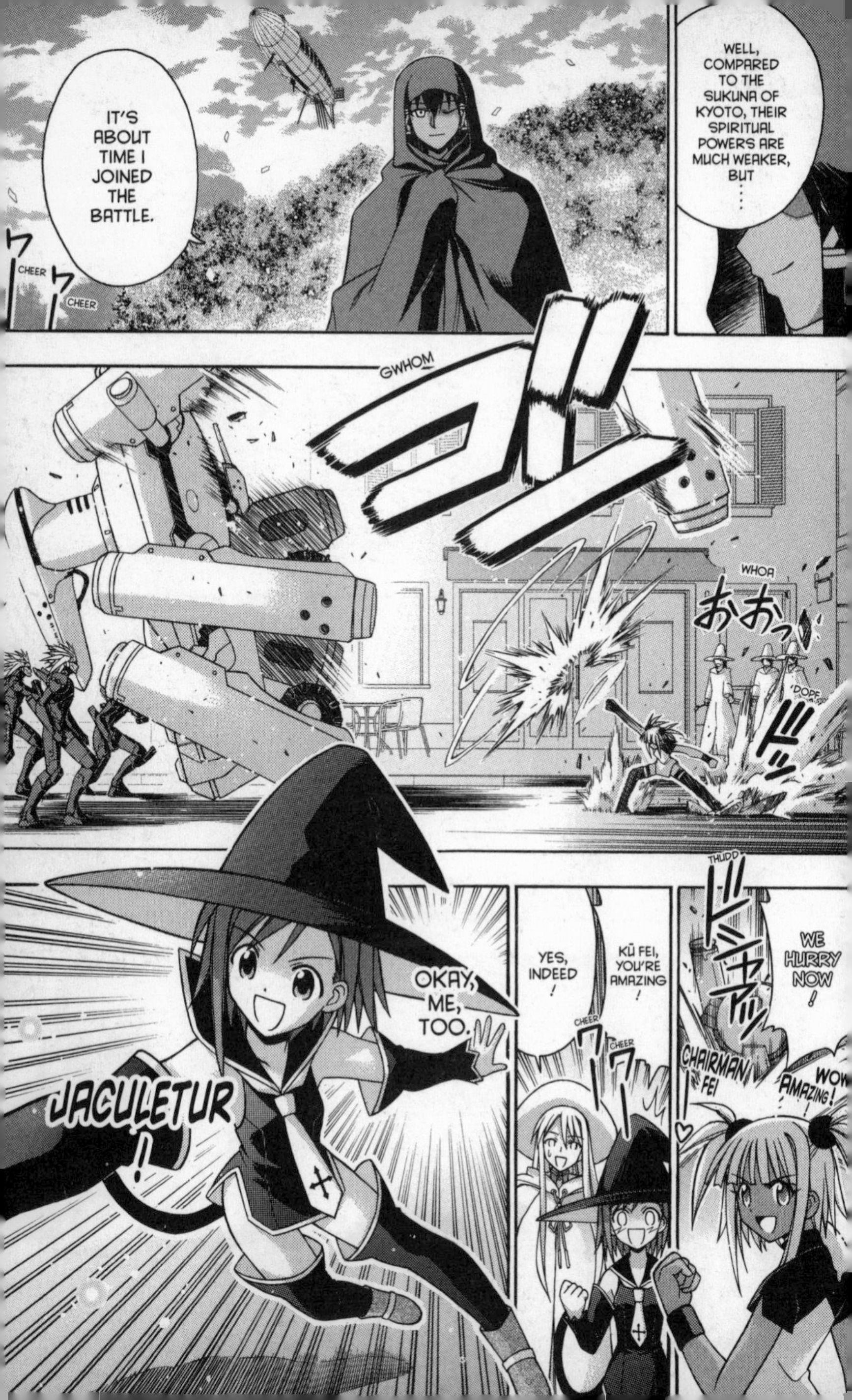
WELL, COMPARED TO THE SUKUNA OF KYOTO, THEIR SPIRITUAL POWERS ARE MUCH WEAKER, BUT . . .
IT'S ABOUT TIME I JOINED THE BATTLE.
CHEER
CHEER
GWHOM
WHOA
おおっ
DOPF
ドッ
THUDD
ドシャアッ
WE HURRY NOW!
CHAIRMAN FEI!
WOW AMAZING!
KŪ FEI, YOU'RE AMAZING!
YES, INDEED!
CHEER
CHEER
OKAY, ME, TOO.
JACULETUR!

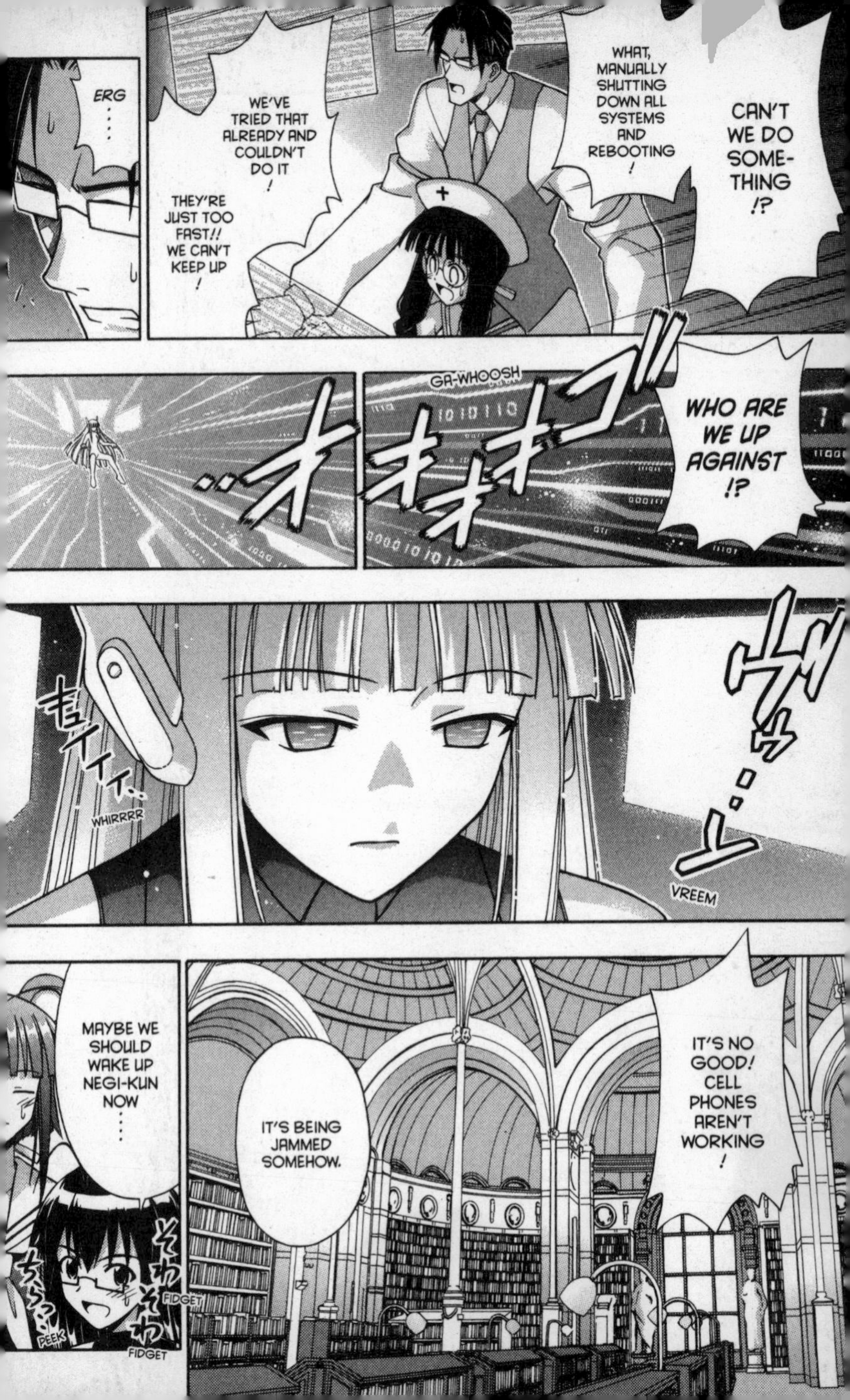
CAN'T WE DO SOME-THING!?
WHAT, MANUALLY SHUTTING DOWN ALL SYSTEMS AND REBOOTING!
WE'VE TRIED THAT ALREADY AND COULDN'T DO IT!
THEY'RE JUST TOO FAST!! WE CAN'T KEEP UP!
ERG...
WHO ARE WE UP AGAINST!?
GA-WHOOSH
VREEM
WHIRRRR
IT'S NO GOOD! CELL PHONES AREN'T WORKING!
IT'S BEING JAMMED SOMEHOW.
MAYBE WE SHOULD WAKE UP NEGI-KUN NOW...
FIDGET
FIDGET
PEEK

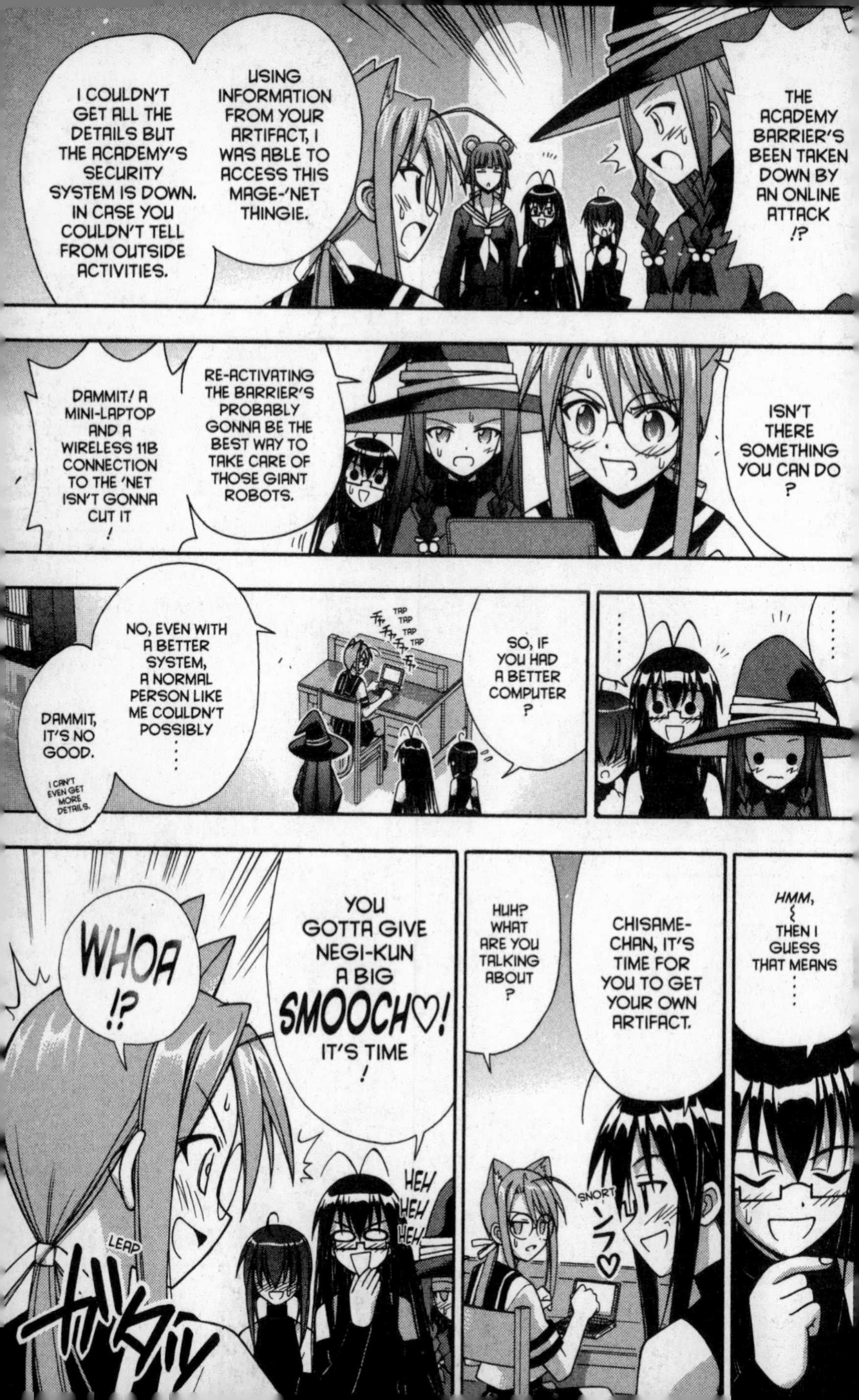
THE ACADEMY BARRIER'S BEEN TAKEN DOWN BY AN ONLINE ATTACK !?
USING INFORMATION FROM YOUR ARTIFACT, I WAS ABLE TO ACCESS THIS MAGE-'NET THINGIE.
I COULDN'T GET ALL THE DETAILS BUT THE ACADEMY'S SECURITY SYSTEM IS DOWN. IN CASE YOU COULDN'T TELL FROM OUTSIDE ACTIVITIES.
ISN'T THERE SOMETHING YOU CAN DO ?
RE-ACTIVATING THE BARRIER'S PROBABLY GONNA BE THE BEST WAY TO TAKE CARE OF THOSE GIANT ROBOTS.
DAMMIT! A MINI-LAPTOP AND A WIRELESS 11B CONNECTION TO THE 'NET ISN'T GONNA CUT IT !
......
......
SO, IF YOU HAD A BETTER COMPUTER ?
TAP TAP TAP TAP
NO, EVEN WITH A BETTER SYSTEM, A NORMAL PERSON LIKE ME COULDN'T POSSIBLY ....
DAMMIT, IT'S NO GOOD.
I CAN'T EVEN GET MORE DETAILS.
HMM, THEN I GUESS THAT MEANS ......
CHISAME-CHAN, IT'S TIME FOR YOU TO GET YOUR OWN ARTIFACT.
HUH? WHAT ARE YOU TALKING ABOUT ?
SNORT
YOU GOTTA GIVE NEGI-KUN A BIG SMOOCH♡! IT'S TIME !
HEH HEH HEH
WHOA !?
LEAP

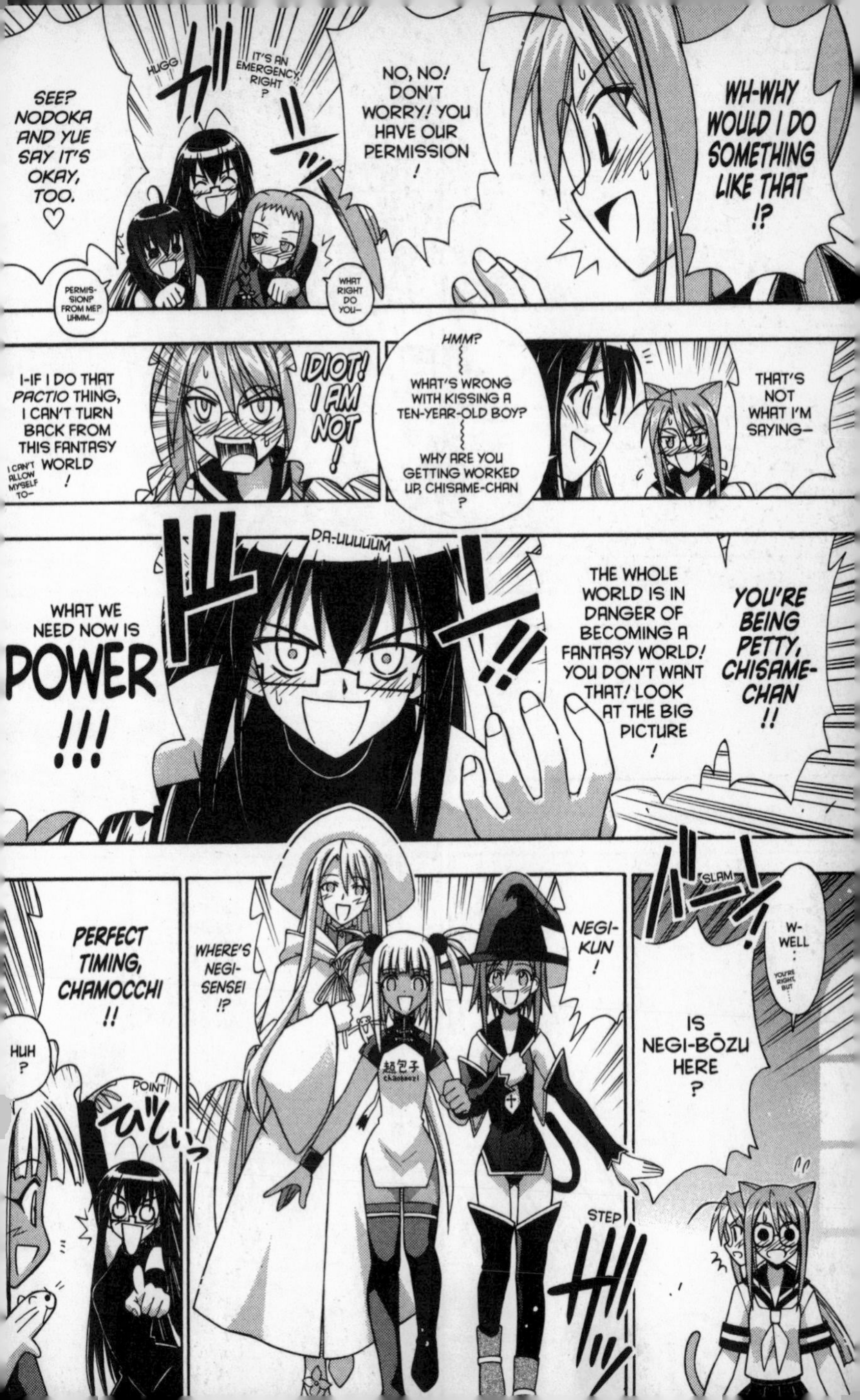
WH-WHY WOULD I DO SOMETHING LIKE THAT !?
NO, NO! DON'T WORRY! YOU HAVE OUR PERMISSION!
IT'S AN EMERGENCY, RIGHT?
HUGG
SEE? NODOKA AND YUE SAY IT'S OKAY, TOO. ♡
WHAT RIGHT DO YOU—
PERMISSION? FROM ME? UHMM...
THAT'S NOT WHAT I'M SAYING—
HMM? WHAT'S WRONG WITH KISSING A TEN-YEAR-OLD BOY? WHY ARE YOU GETTING WORKED UP, CHISAME-CHAN?
IDIOT! I AM NOT!
I-IF I DO THAT *PACTIO* THING, I CAN'T TURN BACK FROM THIS FANTASY WORLD!
I CAN'T ALLOW MYSELF TO—
YOU'RE BEING PETTY, CHISAME-CHAN!!
THE WHOLE WORLD IS IN DANGER OF BECOMING A FANTASY WORLD! YOU DON'T WANT THAT! LOOK AT THE BIG PICTURE!
DA-UUUUUM
WHAT WE NEED NOW IS POWER!!!
W-WELL...
YOU'RE RIGHT, BUT...
SLAM
IS NEGI-BŌZU HERE?
NEGI-KUN!
WHERE'S NEGI-SENSEI!?
超包子
STEP
PERFECT TIMING, CHAMOCCHI!!
POINT
HUH?

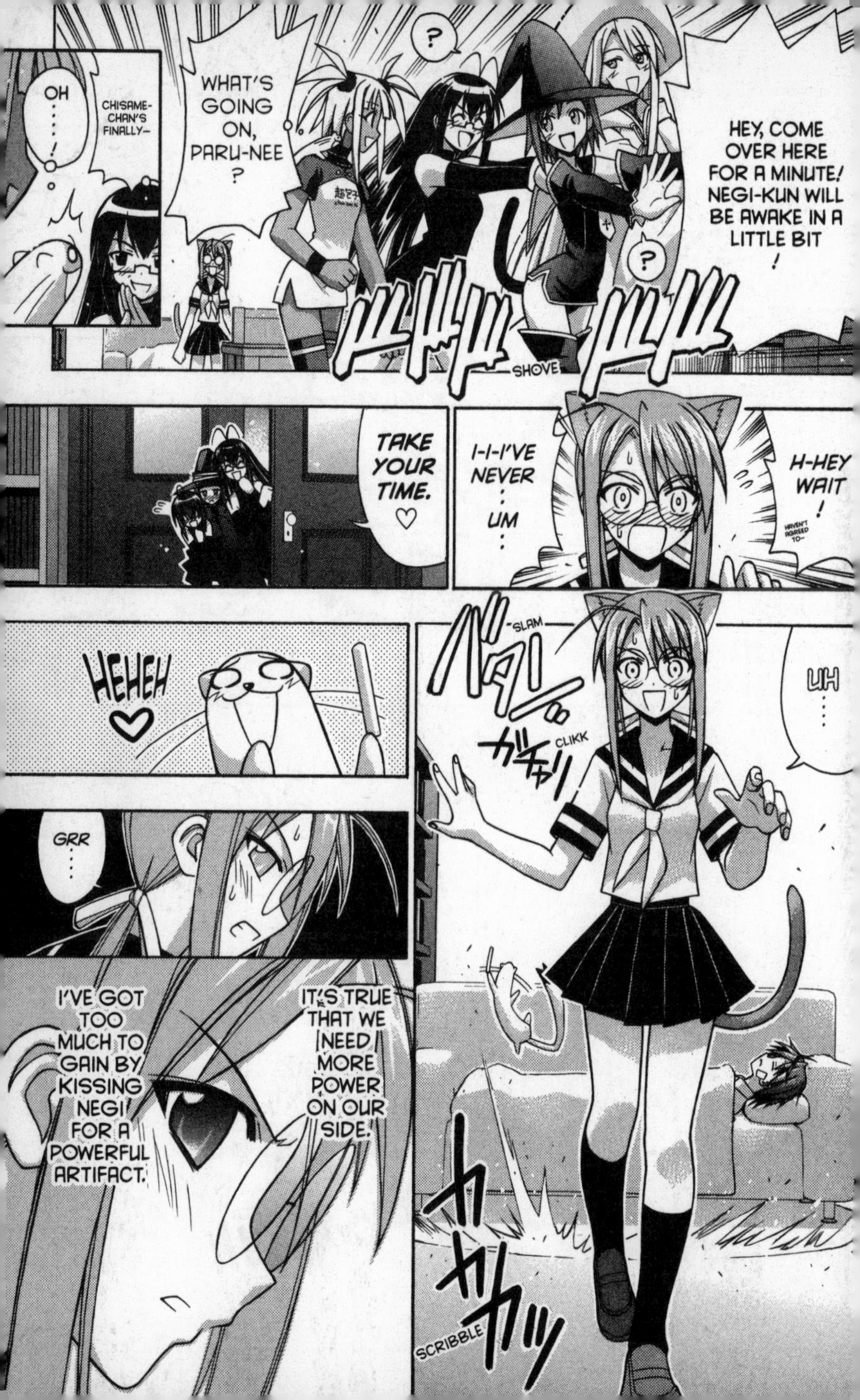
HEY, COME OVER HERE FOR A MINUTE! NEGI-KUN WILL BE AWAKE IN A LITTLE BIT!
?
?
WHAT'S GOING ON, PARU-NEE?
SHOVE
CHISAME-CHAN'S FINALLY—
OH.....!
H-HEY WAIT!
HAVEN'T AGREED TO—
I-I-I'VE NEVER... UM...
TAKE YOUR TIME. ♡
SLAM
CLIKK
UH....
SCRIBBLE
HEHEH ♡
GRR....
IT'S TRUE THAT WE NEED MORE POWER ON OUR SIDE.
I'VE GOT TOO MUCH TO GAIN BY KISSING NEGI FOR A POWERFUL ARTIFACT.

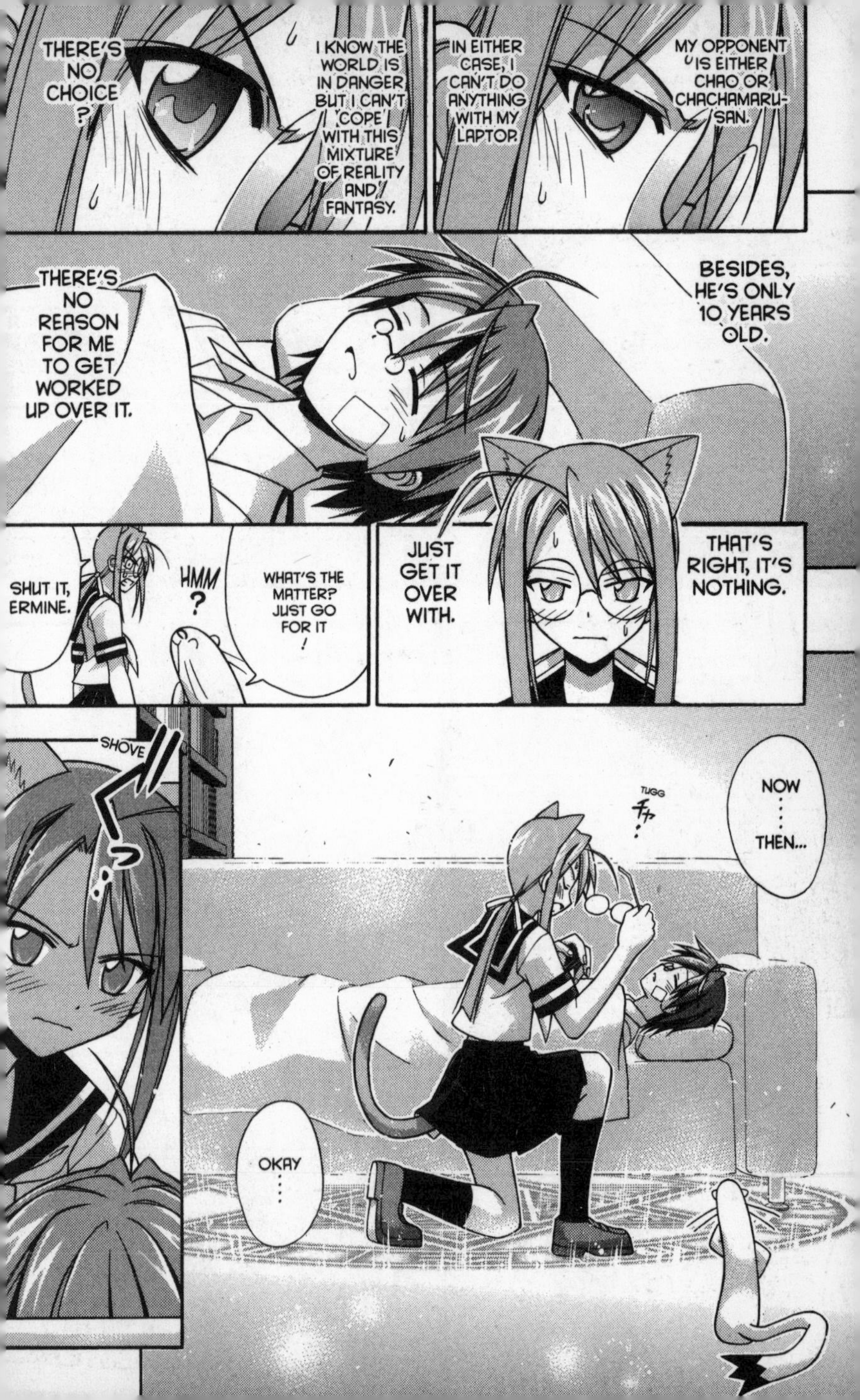
MY OPPONENT IS EITHER CHAO OR CHACHAMARU-SAN.
IN EITHER CASE, I CAN'T DO ANYTHING WITH MY LAPTOP.
I KNOW THE WORLD IS IN DANGER BUT I CAN'T COPE WITH THIS MIXTURE OF REALITY AND FANTASY.
THERE'S NO CHOICE?
BESIDES, HE'S ONLY 10 YEARS OLD.
THERE'S NO REASON FOR ME TO GET WORKED UP OVER IT.
THAT'S RIGHT, IT'S NOTHING.
JUST GET IT OVER WITH.
WHAT'S THE MATTER? JUST GO FOR IT!
HMM?
SHUT IT, ERMINE.
NOW... THEN...
TUGG
OKAY...
SHOVE

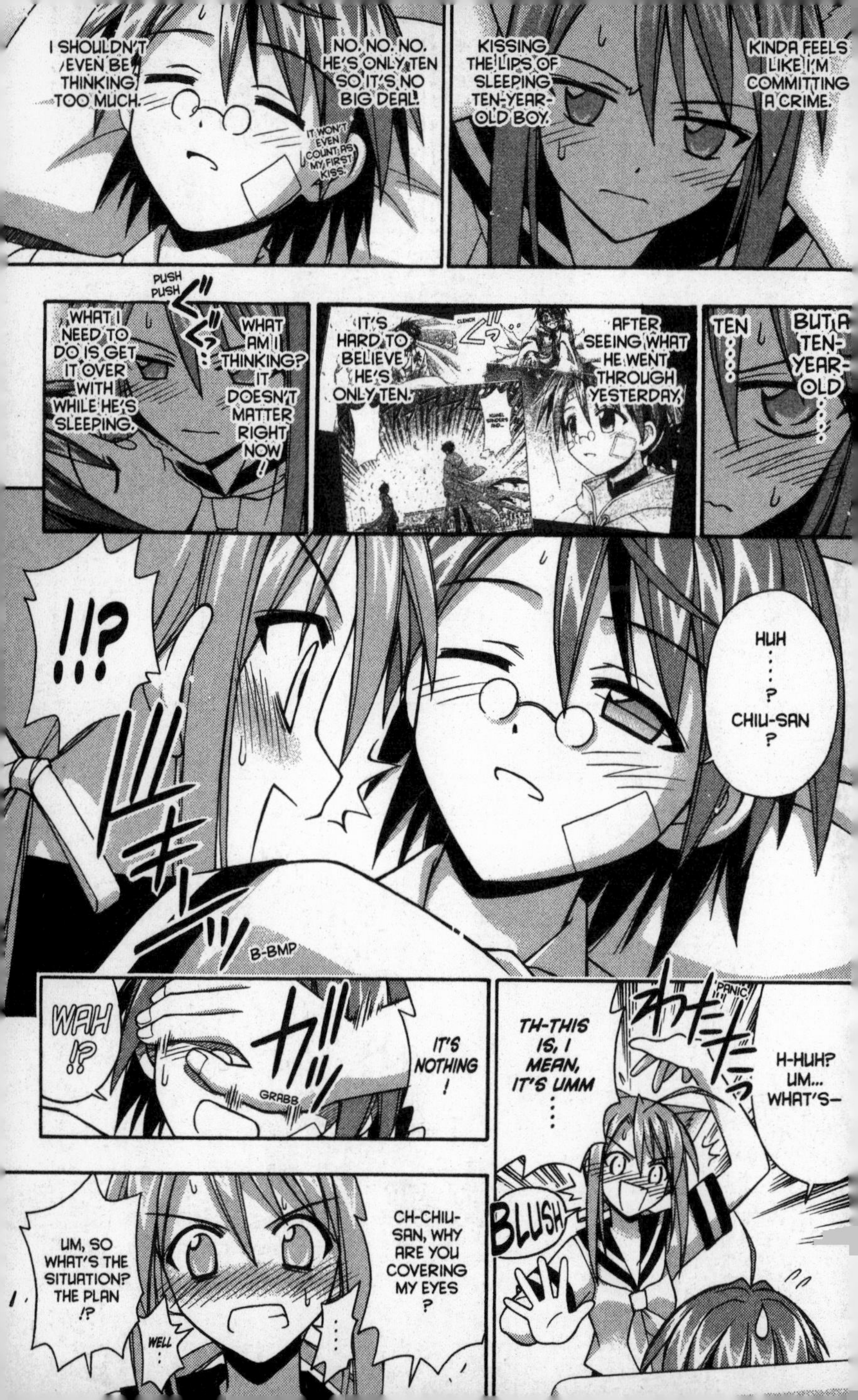
KINDA FEELS LIKE I'M COMMITTING A CRIME.
KISSING THE LIPS OF SLEEPING TEN-YEAR-OLD BOY.
NO, NO, NO. HE'S ONLY TEN SO IT'S NO BIG DEAL.
IT WON'T EVEN COUNT AS MY FIRST KISS.
I SHOULDN'T EVEN BE THINKING TOO MUCH.
BUT A TEN-YEAR-OLD......
TEN......
AFTER SEEING WHAT HE WENT THROUGH YESTERDAY,
CLENCH
IT'S HARD TO BELIEVE HE'S ONLY TEN.
PUSH PUSH
WHAT AM I THINKING? IT DOESN'T MATTER RIGHT NOW!
WHAT I NEED TO DO IS GET IT OVER WITH WHILE HE'S SLEEPING.
HUH...? CHIU-SAN?
!!?
B-BMP
PANIC
H-HUH? UM... WHAT'S—
TH-THIS IS, I MEAN, IT'S UMM...
BLUSH
IT'S NOTHING!
GRABB
WAH!?
CH-CHIU-SAN, WHY ARE YOU COVERING MY EYES?
UM, SO WHAT'S THE SITUATION? THE PLAN!?
WELL...

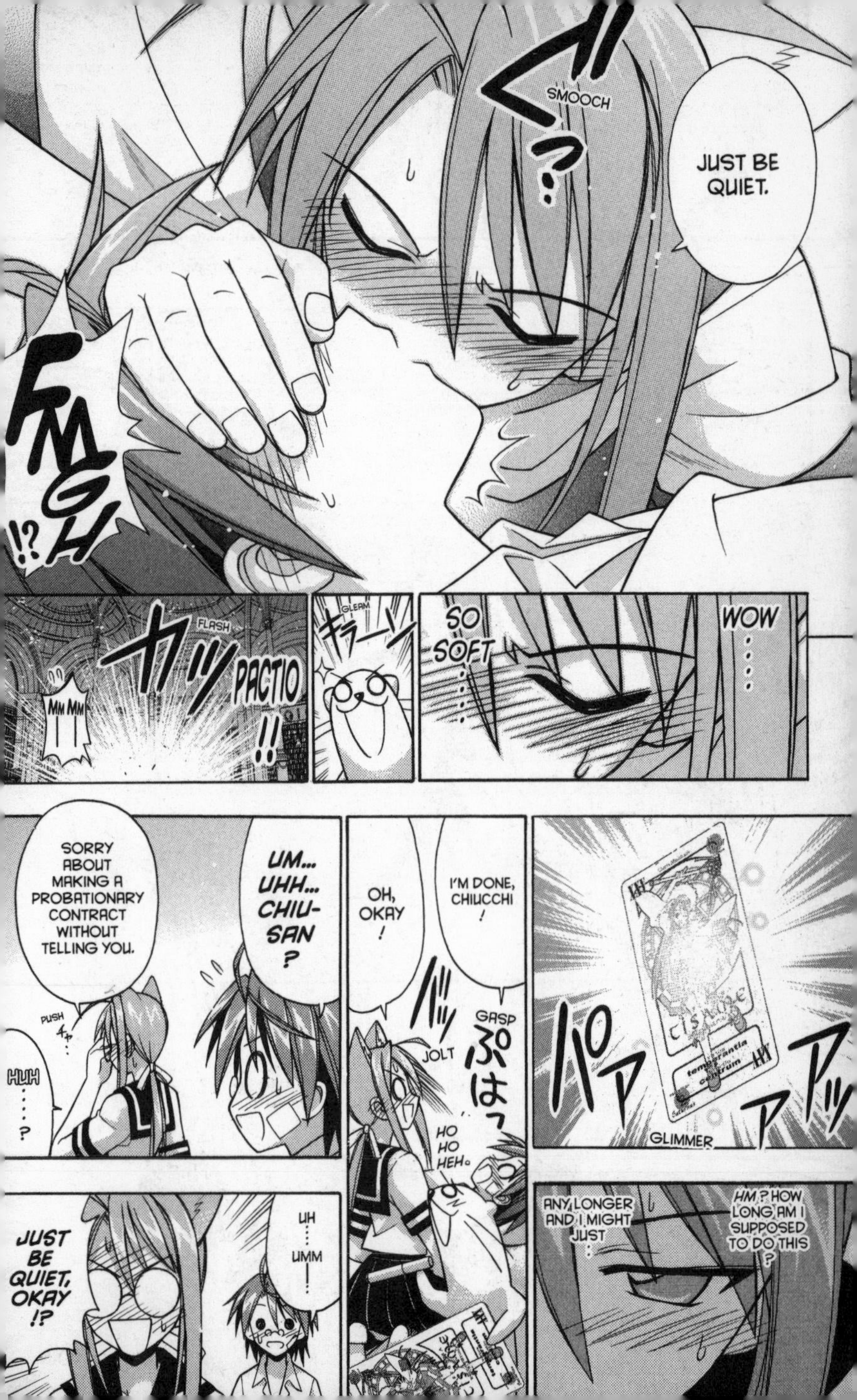
JUST BE QUIET.
SMOOCH
FMGH!?
WOW.....
SO SOFT.....
GLEAM
FLASH
PACTIO!!
MM MM
GLIMMER
I'M DONE, CHIUCCHI!
OH, OKAY!
GASP
ぷはっ
JOLT
HO HO HEH.
UM... UHH... CHIU-SAN?
SORRY ABOUT MAKING A PROBATIONARY CONTRACT WITHOUT TELLING YOU.
PUSH
HUH.....?
HM? HOW LONG AM I SUPPOSED TO DO THIS?
ANY LONGER AND I MIGHT JUST...
UH..... UMM!
JUST BE QUIET, OKAY!?

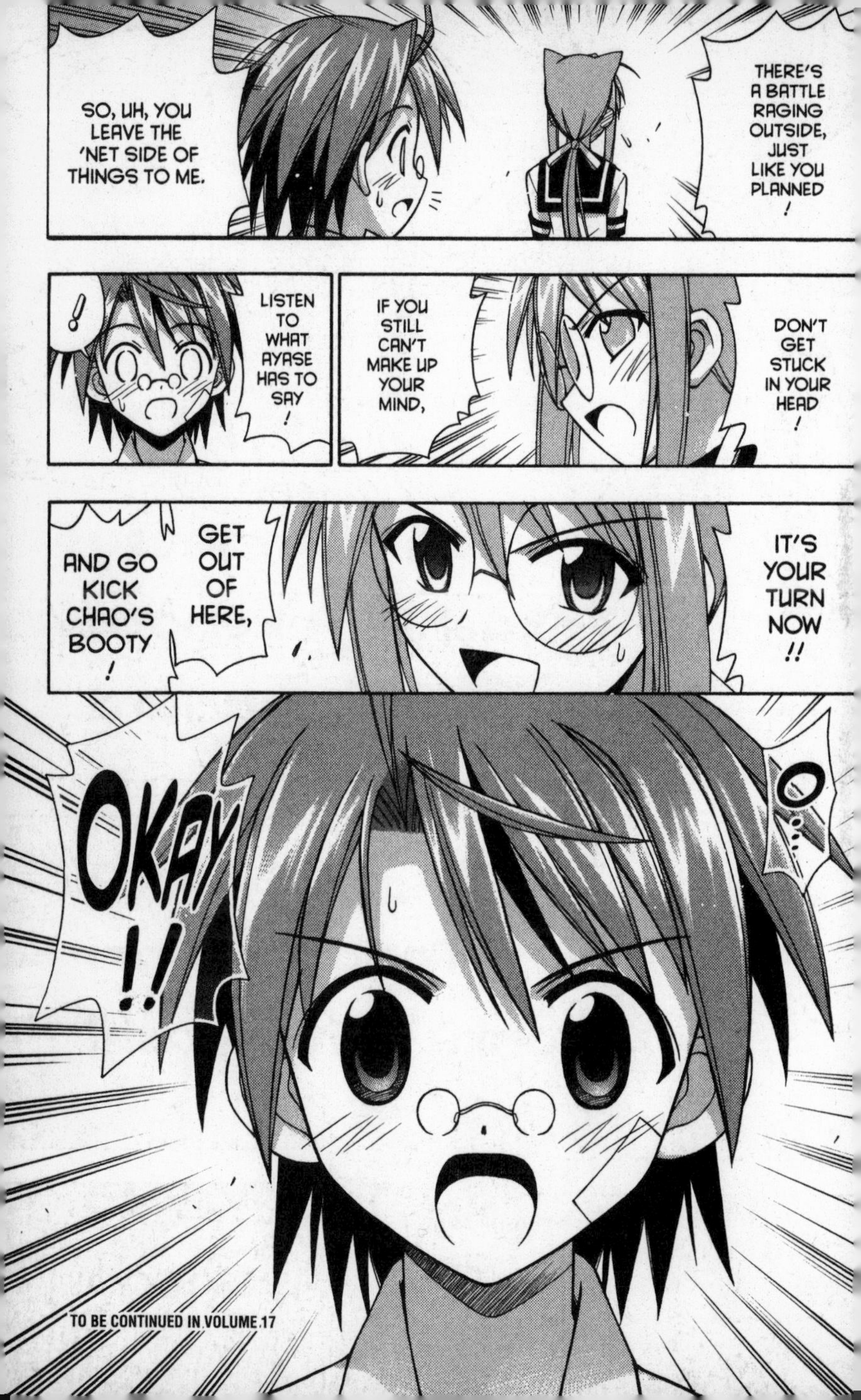
THERE'S A BATTLE RAGING OUTSIDE, JUST LIKE YOU PLANNED!
SO, UH, YOU LEAVE THE 'NET SIDE OF THINGS TO ME.
DON'T GET STUCK IN YOUR HEAD!
IF YOU STILL CAN'T MAKE UP YOUR MIND,
LISTEN TO WHAT AYASE HAS TO SAY!
!
IT'S YOUR TURN NOW!!
GET OUT OF HERE,
AND GO KICK CHAO'S BOOTY!
O...
OKAY!!
TO BE CONTINUED IN VOLUME 17

-STAFF-

Ken Akamatsu

Takashi Takemoto

Kenichi Nakamura

Masaki Ohyama

Keiichi Yamashita

Tadashi Maki

Tohru Mitsuhashi

Thanks to

Ran Ayanaga

LEXICON NEGIMARIUM
DE CANTU ET ARTIFACTO

[140th Period]

■ dig dir dilic Volholl

This magic activation key belongs to the Magical Teacher who looks like a Secret Service agent, with his dark sunglasses and black suit. In the casting of an unincanted spell, it is possible to start an incanted spell while the first is still in progress. However, casting an unincanted spell during the incantation of a spell is very difficult, as the caster needs to activate the spell in his heart/mind while speaking the incantation, unless it is one the caster can cast almost unconsciously.

■ vertatur tempestas aestiva, illis carcarem circumvertentem

(Let the Summer Storm Turn! Send a Tornado Prison upon Them! Blusterous Tornado Prison!)

A spell that creates a powerful tornado that surrounds the target in the middle of the tempest. Those trapped inside are safe from harm, unless they try to escape through the tornado.

[141st Period]

■ rap tjap la tjap ragpur

The magic activation key of Mahora Arts University, Junior High School second-year student Nutmeg (real name: Megumi Natsume).

■ Ex somno exsitat, exundans Undina, inimicum immergrat in alveum.VINCTUS AQUARIUS

(Let the Wave-Tossed Undine Appear from Sleep and Submerge the Enemy into the Riverbed! Water Binder!)

This spell creates a column of water and binds the target within it. The conjured column of water is very rich in oxygen and allows living things without gills to breathe. The oxygen can also be cut off to drown the target inside.

This spell utilizes alliteration in its incantation pattern: *Ex somno exsitat, exundans Undina, inimicum immergrat in alveum.*

■ Undina

These are water spirits or elementals from German mythology. The word *undina* (the English spelling is *undine*) comes from the Latin word *unda,* which means "an ocean wave." By adding the feminine ending *–ina* to it, the word comes to mean "virgin of the ocean waves." In T.P.A.B. Paracelsus's *Liber de Nymphis, Sylphis, Pygmaeis et Salamandris et de Caeteris Spiritibus* (sometimes called the *Book of Fairies*), he writes, "In water there are nymphs, in the wind there are sylphs, in the earth are *pygmae,* and in fire there are salamanders. Now, these beings do not have proper names. ... Truth be told, the water beings are the *undina,* the wind beings are *sylvester,* the mountain beings are *gnomus,* and the name of the fire beings are *vulcanos.*" (Tractatus II)

According to Paracelsus, these four races are both *Geist* (spirits) and *Mensch* (human) but, at the same time, neither. These are special beings that have spirit bodies but are not immortal. However, unlike human beings, they lack a *Seele** (soul). But even so, they can talk like humans and even laugh. (Tractatus I Caput II) Of the four races, the *undina* look the most human, as seen in the passage: "Male and female water beings act and move about like normal humans." (Tractatus II)

The fact that *undina* and humans could marry was well-known, and Paracelsus wrote that "By marrying a human, an *undine* female can bear children. By having a child with the descendant of Adam, the child will resemble the father and the child will have a soul. And since it has a soul, the child will be truly human." (Tractatus III)

■ Ex somno exsitat, exurens Salamandra, inimicum involvat igne. CAPTUS FLAMMEUS

(Everything Burning with the Flame of Purification, Lord of Destruction and Sign of Rebirth, Residing in My Hand! Let It Eat the Enemy! Red Blaze!)

This spell creates a ring of fire and binds the target within it. As the column of fire is in a ring form, the target inside is not burned by the fire but does suffer saunalike conditions. The flames themselves are shielded, so in order to break out of the confinement, one must employ magic. Prolonged exposure to the spell can cause circulatory damage from the heat and heat stroke.

This spell also utilizes alliteration in its incantation pattern: *Ex somno exsitat, exurens Salamndara, inimicum involvat igne.*

■ Salamandra

An elemental of fire from the Greek/Roman mythology. Its form is that of a lizard. *Salamandra* means "lizard" in ancient Greek and in Latin. According to Paracelsus, "*Salamandra* are long, narrow

---

*This translation uses the ancient German spelling *Seele* rather than the modern *Seel.*

and very thin." (Tractatus II) The ending formation of the word *salamandra*, according to dictionaries such as Lewis & Short, is feminine, but Paracelsus uses it as a masculine noun.

In Aristotle's *History of Animals, salamandra* are described as animals that can live in fire. He goes on to say, "Now the *salamandra* is a clear case in point, to show us that animals do actually exist that fire cannot destroy; for this creature, so the story goes, not only walks through the fire but puts it out in doing so." (552b15–17)

■ favor purgandi
(*Osōi Daisuki*—I love to clean/sweep)

By the power of the Pactio with a mage, Mei Sakura is awarded a magical broom. As touched upon in the story, this broom is standard issue to the Order of the Mage Knights in the Magical Realm. It is a superior magical item with many possible uses. How it is determined what artifact each *ministra* receives is unknown, but as with Negi's *ministra,* it is believed that the person's inner being and desires for their future play a role in the selection of the artifact.

■ Ad Summam Exarmatio
(Total Disarmament)

A spell that disarms everyone in its area of operation. It affects anyone in the area, including one's allies. However, that can aid in the laying down of arms for all parties involved.

■ Sagitta Magica Series Ignis
(Magic Arrow, Fire Series)

A magic arrow spell with the element of fire as its basis. A line of fire attacks the enemy. As it's a flaming arrow, it can set the target ablaze. Because of this, it is one of the most attack-oriented and damaging of the magic arrow spells.

Mei is able to launch three arrows unincanted, showing her level of skill with the spell. Should Mei have faced off with Negi when he first arrived at the academy, Negi would not have lasted long in that battle!

[142nd Period]

■ Cerberus
(Κέρβερος)

The three-headed canine guardian of Hades in Greek mythology. The description that Nodoka gives, with the mane of snakes, comes from Virgil's (70–19 BC) *Aeneid,* "Grim Cerberus, who soon began to rear/His crested snakes, and armed his bristling hair/The prudent Sibyl had before prepared a sop, in honey steeped, to charm the guard;/which,

mixed with powerful drugs, she cast before his greedy, grinning jaws."
(*Aeneid*, Book 6, 417–421)

On the other hand, in *Thogeny* by Hesiod (700? BC) it is written,
"and then again she bare a second, a monster not to be overcome and
that may not be described, Cerberus who eats raw flesh, the brazen-
voiced hound of Hades, fifty-headed, relentless and strong" (310–
312), which shows that in older legends it had fifty heads.

However, the common image of Cerberus having three heads with
a mane of snakes came from the tragedy *Hercules* written by Euripides
(485?–406? BC), "I passed through a herd of countless other toils
besides and came to the dead to fetch to the light at the bidding of
Eurystheus the three-headed hound, hell's porter." (1277–1278)
Furthermore, the Jar of Cairéa found in Etruria depicts Hercules with
a three-headed and snake-maned Cerberus.

[143rd Period]

■ se dissolvent circumstantial falsa
(Let the False World Dissolve Itself!)

A spell utilizing the power of the artifact being wielded by Asuna
Kagurazaka, a *ministra* of Negi. A spell is not a keyword that is uttered
to activate some supernatural power. As written by Virgil, "Songs can
even draw the moon down from heaven" (*Eclogue* VIII.69)—there
is power in words. So the power of a spell comes from the power
contained in its words. Even the words of an ordinary person can
have a certain level of magic contained within them. Yue, as she is
not yet well trained in the ways of magic, did not have the ability
to activate the spell. So by using her words along with the power of
Asuna's artifact, she was able to break the illusion. Using a tool to
amplify the power of words is a very popular manner in which to cast
spells. For example, words did not have much power until they were
inscribed on stone tablets. In the Middle Ages, the jongleur (minstrels)
gained recognition by adding words to their music. Even today,
unaccompanied singing is said to be a way of using tools to increase
the power of words.

[144th Period]

■ Hippogriff (or Hippogryph)
(ιππογυψ)

The word roots for Hippogriff come from the amalgamation of the
ancient Greek words for horse (ιππος) and griffin (γρυψ). Generally
speaking, a hippogriff is a monster with the body of a horse and
the head and wings of a hawk. It is said to be the hybrid offspring
of a mare and griffin. The Latin term *gryps* is most often translated

as griffin, but one theory says that the creature is closer to a dragon in appearance, so in reality, no one really knows what a hippogriff is supposed to look like.

[145th Period]

■ limes aerialis
(Boundary Wall of Air)

A spell that creates a mid-level magical barrier by using air currents. It's especially suited for protecting against fire, cold, poison gas, and other air-related attacks. Of the air-based spells, it is a fairly basic one compared to others that can block physical attacks, such as the *Deflectio* and *Flans Paries Aeriales*.

[147th Period]

■ jaculetur
(assail the enemy)

As said in a previous entry, even the words of a common person can hold magical power—a little or a lot. Makie and the others use the tools attained by the Headmaster to cast the spells, but as Kakizaki joked about pretending to be Magical Girls, it is undoubtedly the power within each person's words that exerts the magic for the spell.

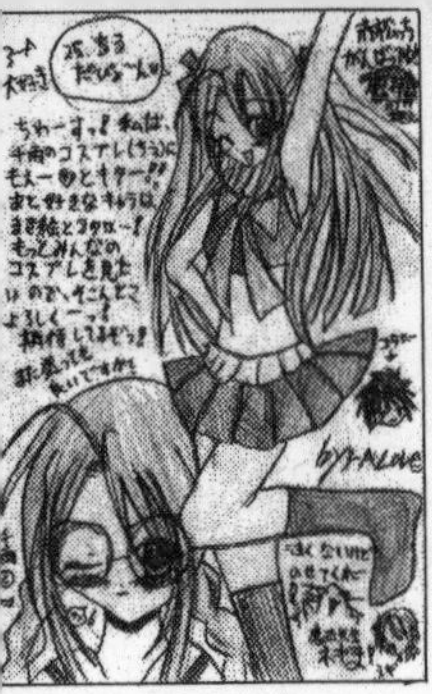
WE LOVE THE COSTUME!

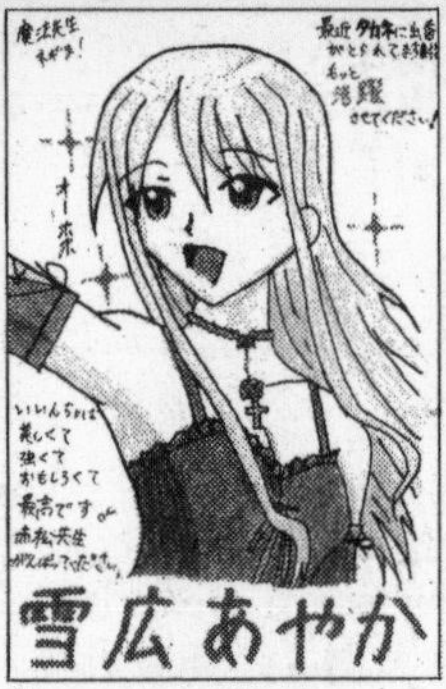
雪広あやか
WE DON'T GET VERY MANY PICTURES OF AYAKA LATELY...

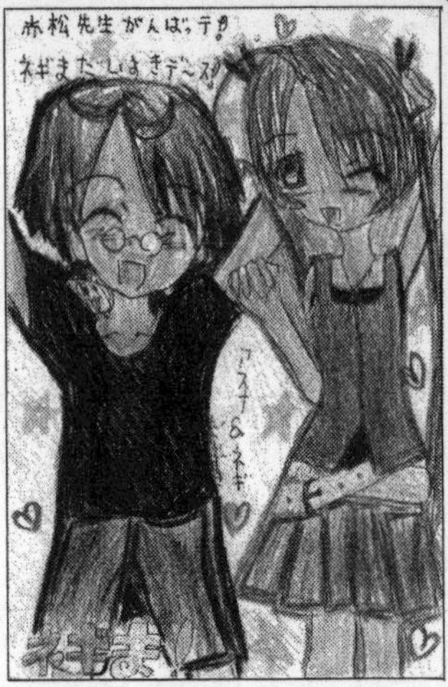
赤松先生がんばってー!
ネギまだいすきデース!
THESE TWO LOOK VERY HAPPY!

NEGIMA! FAN ART CORNER

IN THIS VOLUME, WE'LL CONTINUE TO PRESENT TO YOU A SMALL SELECTION OF ALL THE ILLUSTRATIONS THAT WE RECEIVE. (^^;) WE ALL THANK YOU FOR ALL THE ART AND THE SUPPORT YOU HAVE BEEN SHOWING US! WE LOOK FORWARD TO SEEING MORE OF YOUR ILLUSTRATIONS!

YOU CAN SEND YOUR ILLUSTRATIONS TO THE EDITORIAL OFFICES OF KODANSHA COMICS.

TEXT BY ASSISTANT MAX

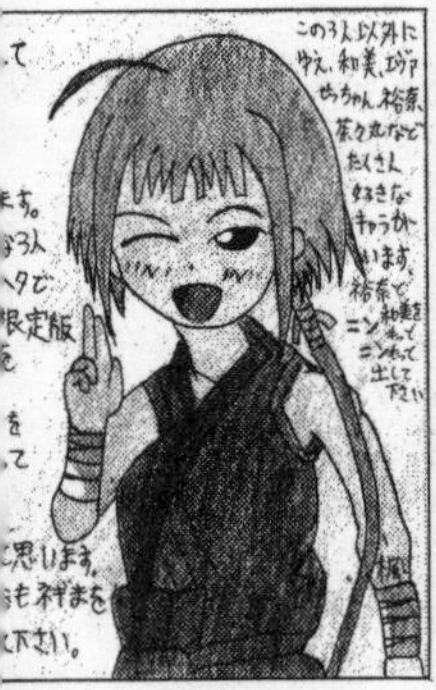
HERE'S A NICE ONE OF KAEDE ★

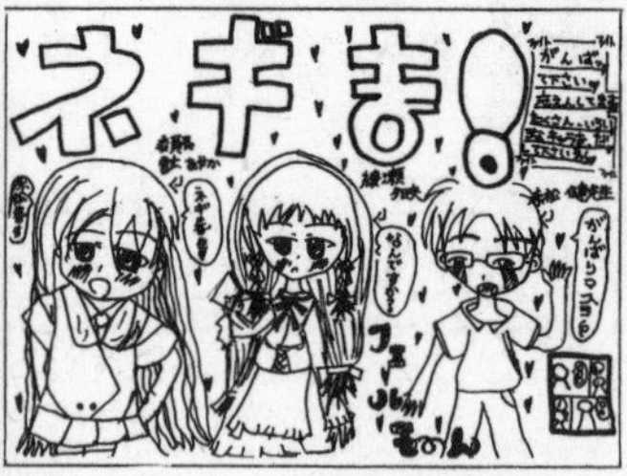
ネギま!
AKAMATSU-SAN IS CRYING TEARS OF BLOOD! (LAUGHS)

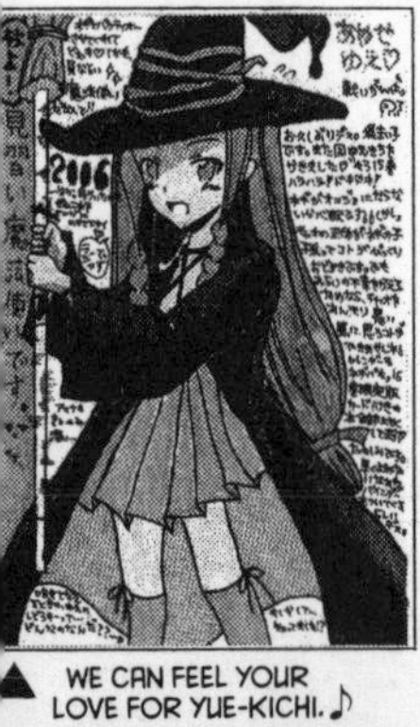
WE CAN FEEL YOUR LOVE FOR YUE-KICHI.♪

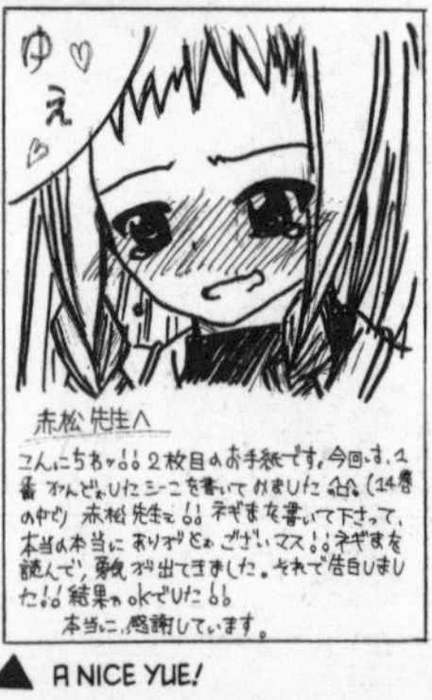
ゆえ
赤松先生へ
A NICE YUE!

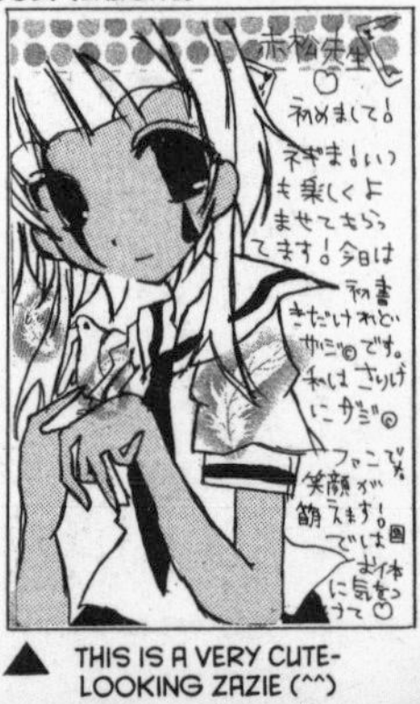
赤松先生
初めまして。
ネギま!いつも楽しくよませてもらってます!
THIS IS A VERY CUTE-LOOKING ZAZIE (^^)

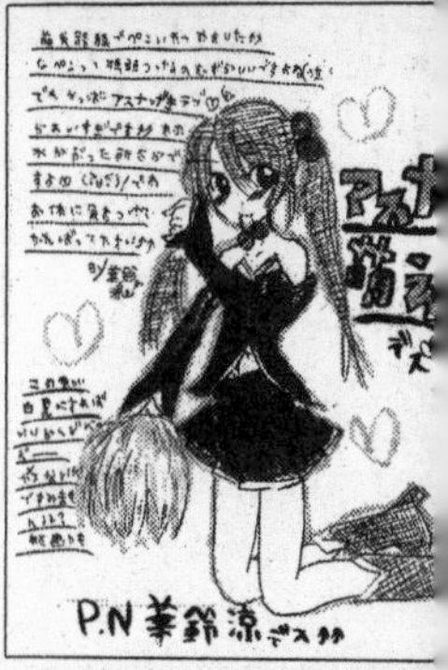
P.N 華鈴涼デス

▲ THIS ONE IS OVERFLOWING WITH CUTE.

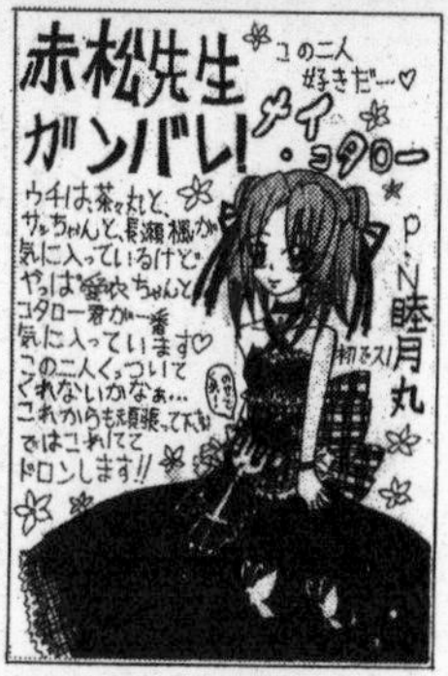
赤松先生 ガンバレ!
この二人好きだ…♡
メイ・コタロー
ウチは茶々丸と、サッちゃんと、長瀬楓が気に入っているけど、やっぱ夏美ちゃんとコタロー君が一番気に入っています♡
この二人くっついてくれないかなぁ…
これからも頑張って下さい
ではこれにてドロンします!!
P.N 睦月丸

▲ WE LOVE THE KŌTARO DOLL! (LAUGHS)

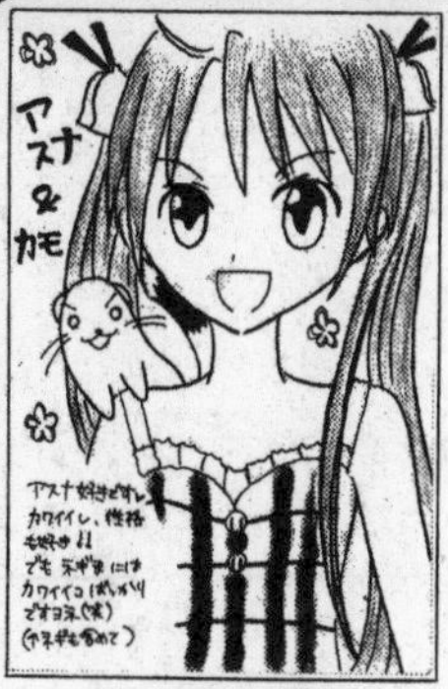
アスナ & カモ

▲ ASUNA LOOKS VERY FEMININE HERE.

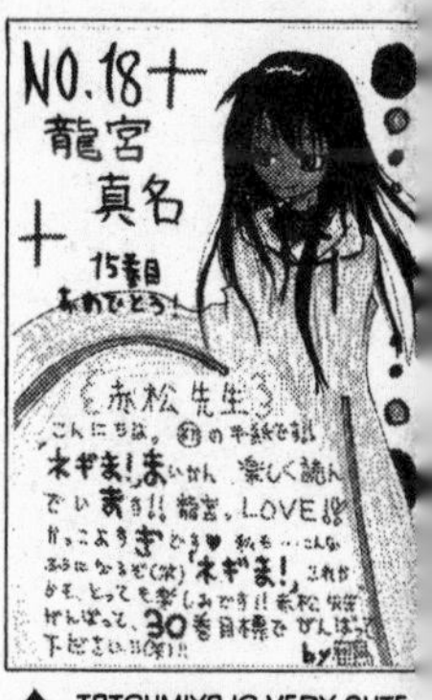
NO.18 龍宮 真名
15巻目 おめでとう!
赤松先生
龍宮、LOVE!!

▲ TATSUMIYA IS VERY CUTE IN THIS ONE!

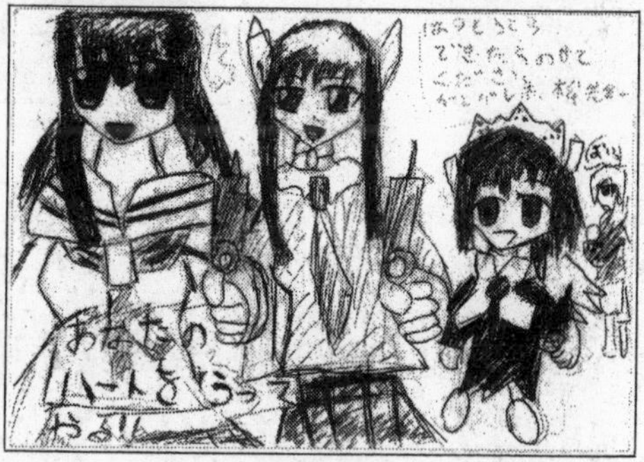

▲ EVERYONE SMILE!♪

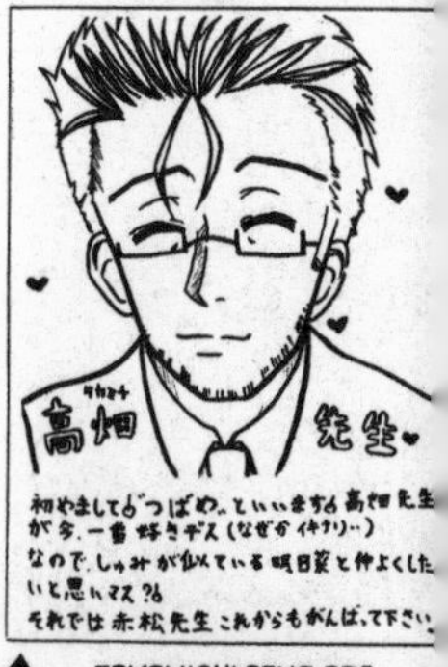
高畑 先生
初めましてつばめ。といいます。高畑先生が今、一番好きデス (なぜかイキナリ…)
それでは赤松先生これからもがんばって下さい。

▲ TAKAMICHI FANS ARE VERY PRECIOUS!

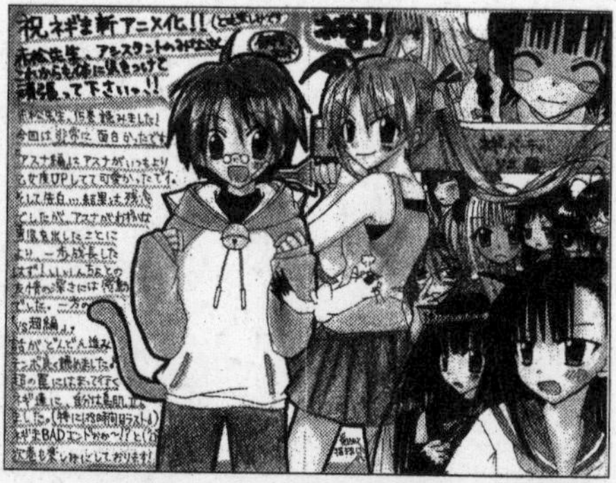
祝ネギま新アニメ化!!

▲ WE CAN FEEL YOUR DETERMINATION FROM THIS PICTURE!

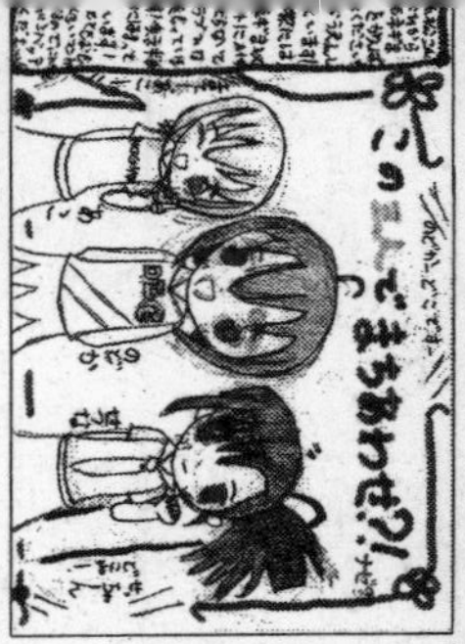

ARE THESE THREE OUT SHOPPING?

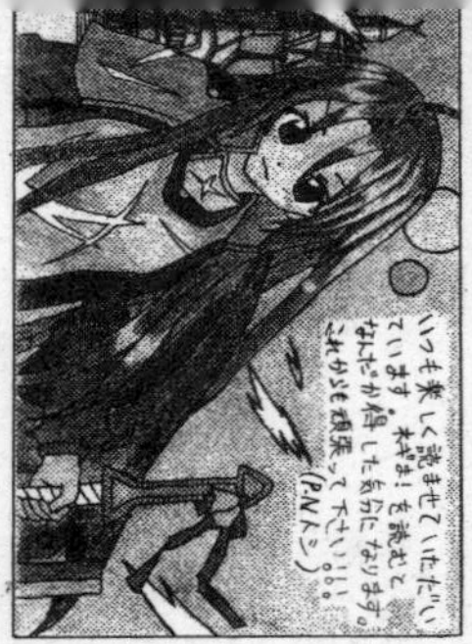

ASUNA LOOKS REALLY TOUGH IN THIS ONE.

A VERY NICE WEDDING DRESS!

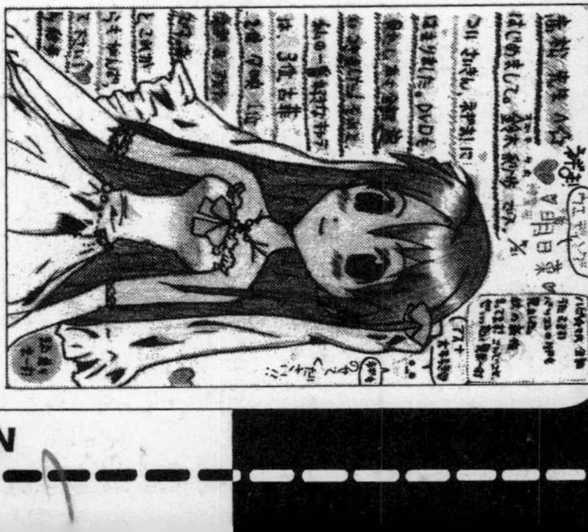

THE USE OF RED IN THIS PICTURE OF ASAKURA WAS NICE!

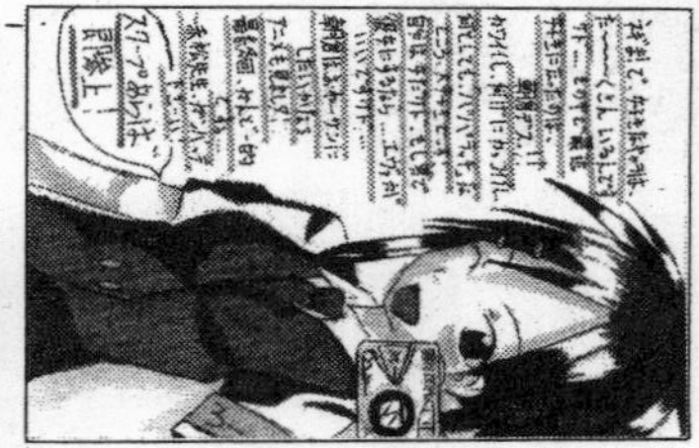

PARU MANAGES TO APPEAR A LOT LATELY!

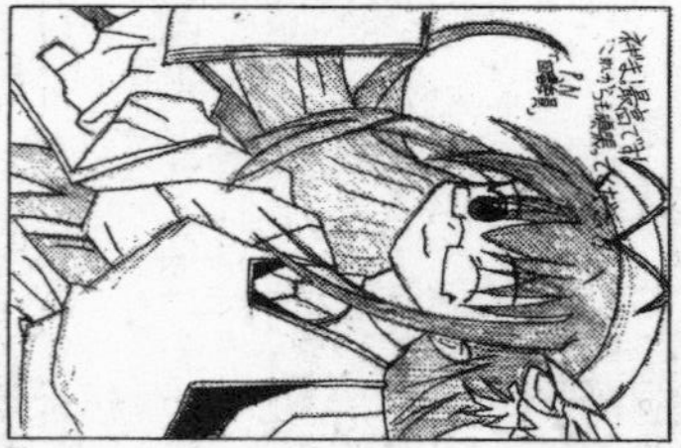

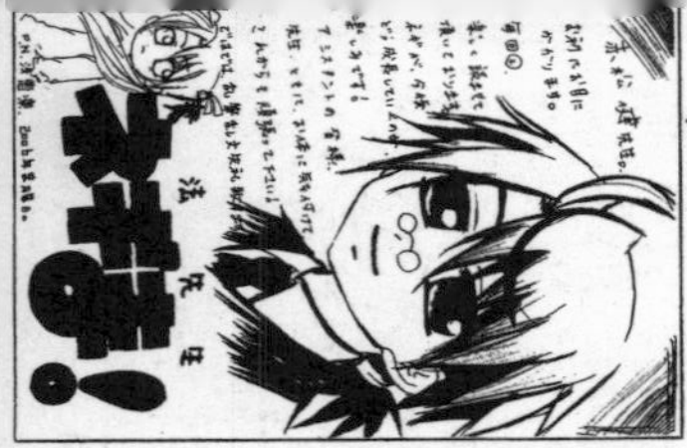

NEGI LOOKS VERY CALM AND COOL IN THIS PICTURE!

TTHIS IS A VERY COMFORTING PICTURE.

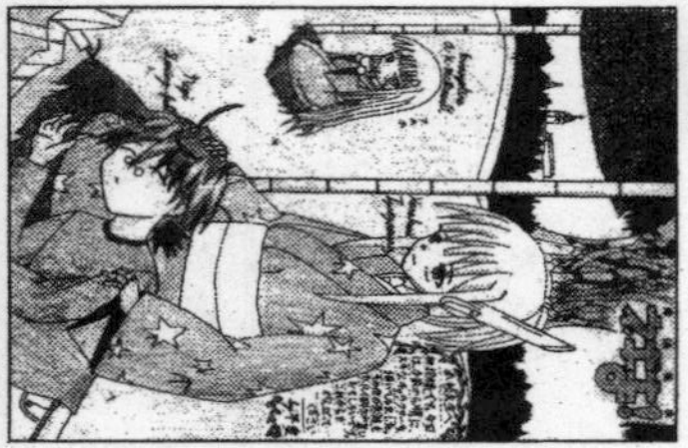

THE TWINS LOOK VERY CLOSE IN THIS PICTURE. ★

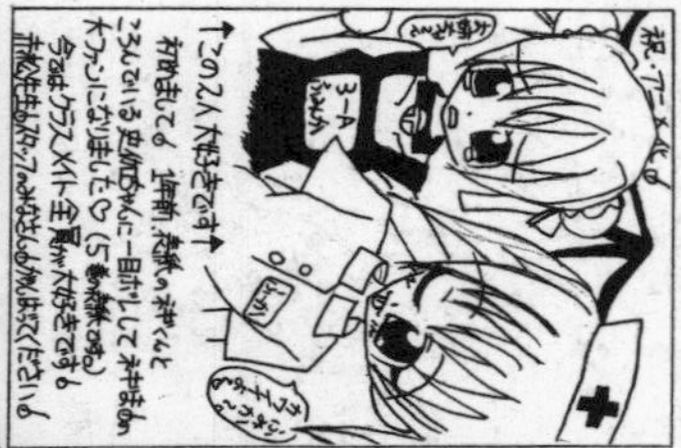

NEGI MA!

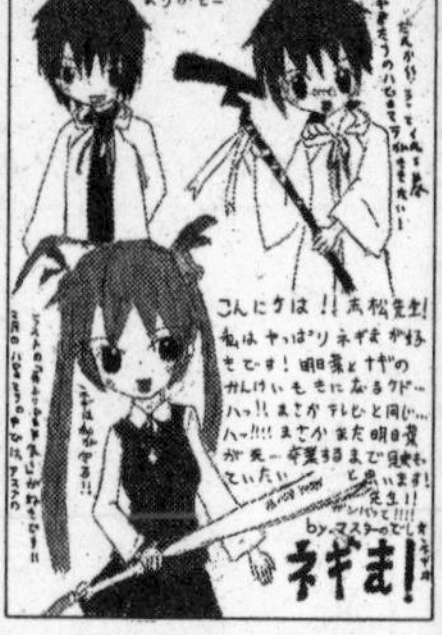
ネギま!

NAGI LOOKS VERY CUTE!

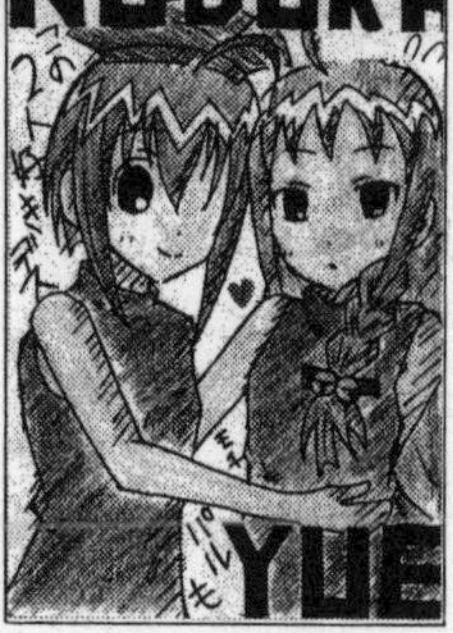
NODOKA
YUE

YOU CAN ALMOST FEEL THE WARMTH COMING FROM THE PICTURE!

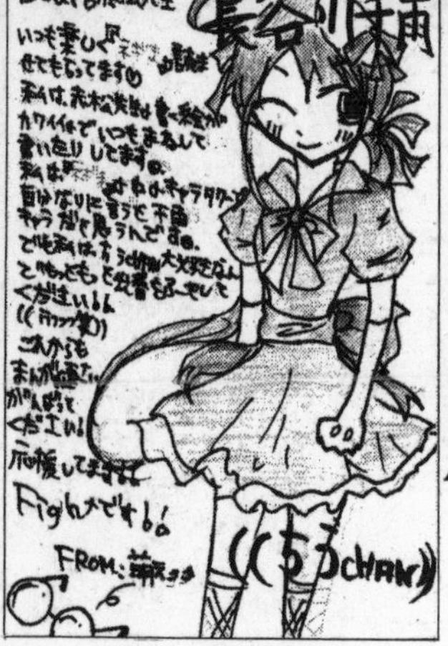
Dear 赤松先生
長谷川千雨
Fightです!!
FROM:

CHIU LOOKS KIND OF RAMBUNCTIOUS IN THIS ONE!

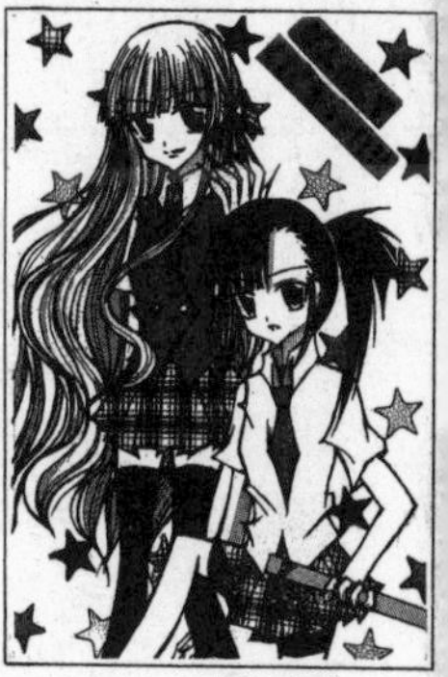

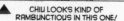

IF EVA AND SETSUNA WERE TO TEAM UP, THEY'D BE UNSTOPPABLE! ★

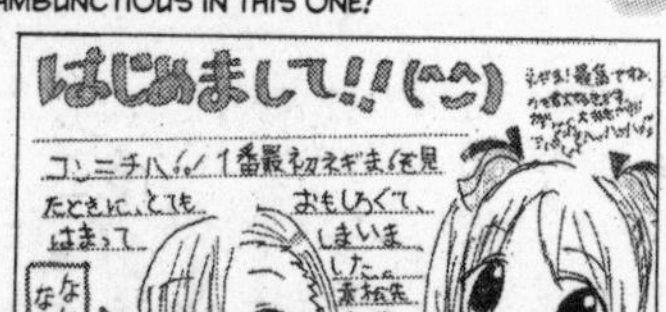
はじめまして!!(^-^)

BOTH ASUNA AND SETSUNA LOOK CUTE! ♪

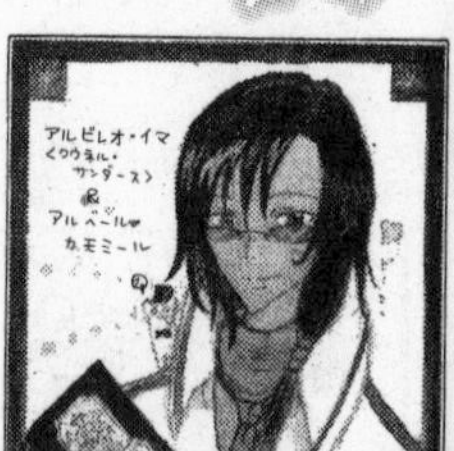
エロコンビ 結成!?!!?

IT'S THE AL & AL COMBO TEAM.

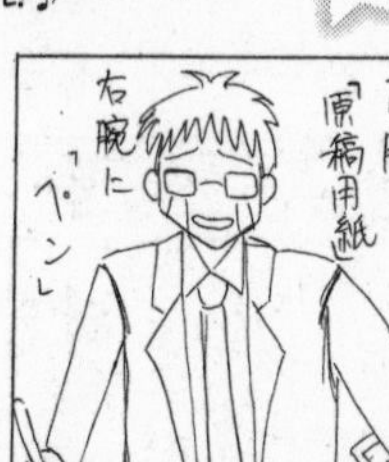
左腕に「原稿用紙」
右腕に「ペン」
ネギま!

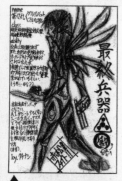

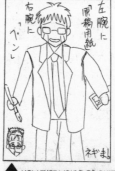

NOW THAT WOULD BE QUITE THE *KANKAHŌ* (LAUGHS)

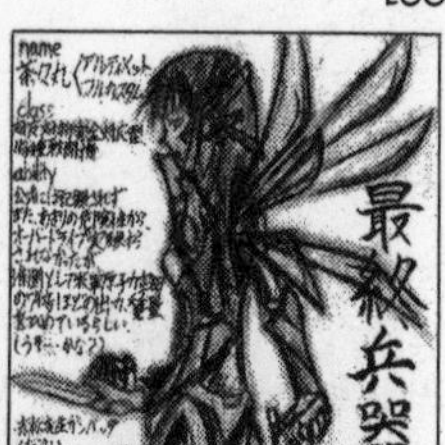
最終兵器

THIS CHACHAMARU LOOKS VERY POWERFUL INDEED! ★

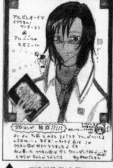

3-D BACKGROUNDS EXPLANATION CORNER

AS THE VOLUMES INCREASE IN NUMBER, SO DO THE NUMBER
OF 3-D BACKGROUNDS. WE'LL FEATURE THE 3-D BACKGROUNDS
FROM VOLUME 15 AS WELL AS ONES FROM THIS BOOK.

• EVANGELINE'S HOUSE
SCENE NAME: EVA'S HOUSE
POLYGON COUNT: 37,604

AT THE BEGINNING OF THIS VOLUME, IT WAS THE SCENE OF THE BATTLE WITH THE MAGICAL TEACHERS. A 3-D VERSION OF THE HOUSE WAS CREATED. IN AN ACTION SEQUENCE, IT'S VERY HELPFUL TO BE ABLE TO FREELY ADJUST THE ANGLES FROM PANEL TO PANEL. WE'RE REALLY HAPPY WITH THE FACT THAT IT STILL LOOKS HAND-DRAWN!

ALTHOUGH, AS I'M SURE A FEW EAGLE-EYED READERS HAVE ALREADY NOTICED, THE NUMBER AND SIZE OF THE WINDOWS ARE DIFFERENT FROM THE ONES YOU SEE ON THE INSIDE. (^^;)

A GOOD EXCUSE WOULD BE TO SAY THAT EVA USES MAGIC AND ILLUSIONS TO CAMOUFLAGE THE OUTSIDE OF HER HOUSE. YES, MAGIC IS A POWERFUL TOOL INDEED. (LAUGHS)

• EVANGELINE'S RESORT (INTERIOR)
SCENE NAME: DINNER ROOM
POLYGON COUNT: 106,487

EVA'S RESORT HAS BEEN FEATURED BEFORE, BUT THE INTERIOR OF THE RESORT MADE ITS FIRST APPEARANCE IN VOLUME 15. WE WANTED TO KEEP THE EXOTIC "ASIAN BEACH RESORT" FEEL BY CREATING THIS LARGE OPEN ROOM WITH A BEACH VIEW AND A BIG INDOOR SWIMMING POOL.

BUT AGAIN, IF YOU TRY TO FIND THIS LOCATION FROM THE OUTSIDE SHOTS OF THE RESORT, YOU WON'T BE ABLE TO. PERHAPS THIS TOO IS HIDDEN BY MAGIC. (LAUGHS) THEN AGAIN, IF WE START POINTING THESE THINGS OUT, THERE WOULD BE NO END TO IT! (^^;)

• STONE CASTLE
SCENE NAME: STONE CASTLE
POLYGON COUNT: 13,334

THIS IS THE CASTLELIKE BUILDING THAT ASUNA AND TAKAHATA VISITED DURING THEIR DATE IN VOL. 15. IT'S NORMALLY USED AS A MUSEUM AND A REGIONAL REFERENCE LIBRARY. THE UNADORNED ARCHITECTURE GIVES THE BUILDING A MEDIEVAL FEEL, BUT BECAUSE OF THE SPECTACULAR VIEWS FROM THE ROOF, IT'S BECOME A VERY POPULAR DATE SPOT.

PART OF THE DESIGN IS BASED ON WARWICK CASTLE IN THE UNITED KINGDOM.

• CITY HALL AND PLAZA

SCENE NAME: CITY HALL
POLYGON COUNT: 775,446

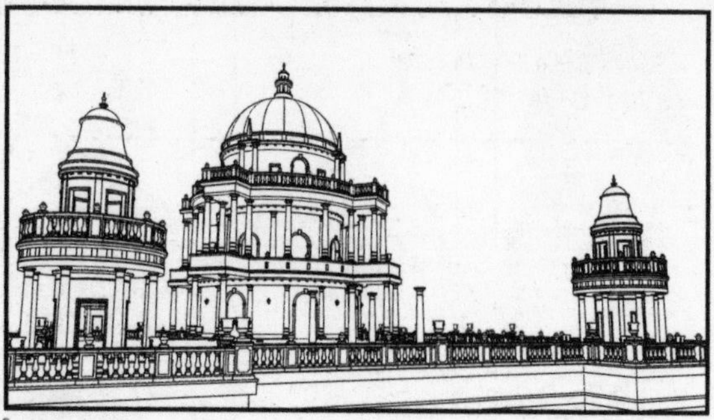

THIS IS THE BUILDING AND THE PLAZA WHERE NEGI FOUGHT CHAO IN VOL. 15. THE CITY HALL IS OFTEN USED FOR EVENTS AND AS A POPULAR MEETING PLACE AND IS THE CENTER OF THE CITY'S ECONOMIC ACTIVITY. THE DECORATIVE ARCHITECTURE IS AN EXAMPLE OF THE CITY'S ELEGANCE.

THE BUILDING IS PARTIALLY BASED ON THE CITY HALL IN BELFAST, IRELAND.

• UNDERGROUND WORLD TREE ALTAR

SCENE NAME: LARGE ALTAR
POLYGON COUNT: 97,485

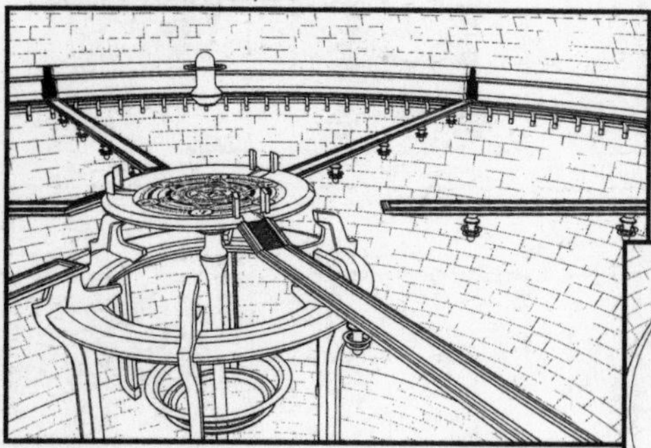

THE MYSTERIOUS RUINS FOUND AT THE DEEPEST DEPTHS BENEATH THE WORLD TREE. ONE THEORY SAYS THAT THE MAGES OF OLD HAD USED THIS PLACE TO COLLECT THE MAGIC OF THE WORLD TREE IN ORDER TO PERFORM SOME KIND OF GREAT RITUAL.

AT THE CENTER OF THE LARGE CAVERN IS A MAGIC CIRCLE THAT DEPICTS THE BEGINNINGS OF ALL LIVING AND NON-LIVING THINGS.

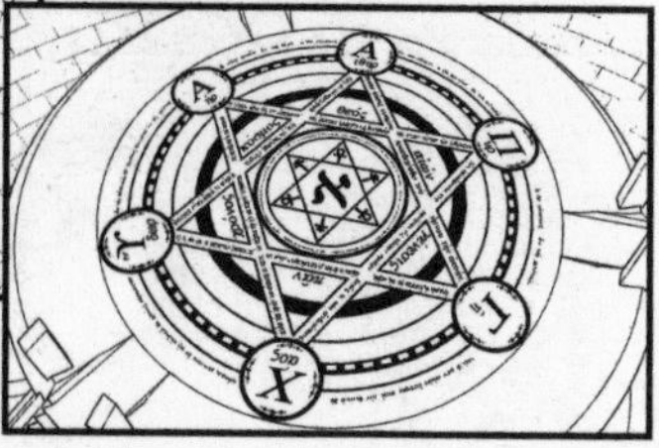

- BONUS -

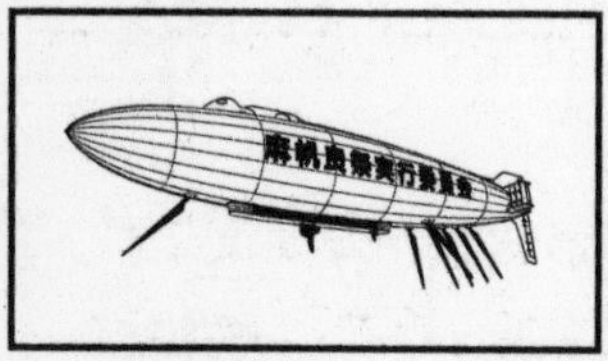

• AIRSHIP

THIS WAS MADE INTO A 3-D OBJECT FOR VOL. 16. YOU'LL SEE IT FLYING AROUND EVERYWHERE.

• MYSTERIOUS STONE SCULPTURES

WHY THESE THINGS ARE AROUND IS AN EVEN BIGGER MYSTERY. (LAUGHS)

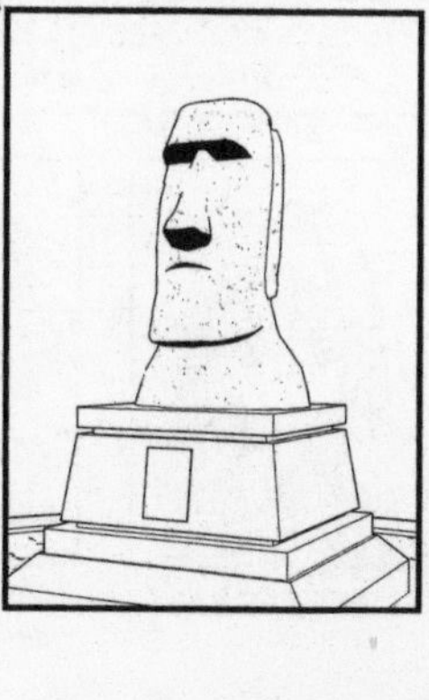

• POLY-MEN MAGE VERSION

THESE WERE A MUST AND A SAVING GRACE FOR MOB SCENES. SEEING THEM LIKE THIS, THEY LOOK MORE LIKE VIDEO-GAME CHARACTERS. (LAUGHS)

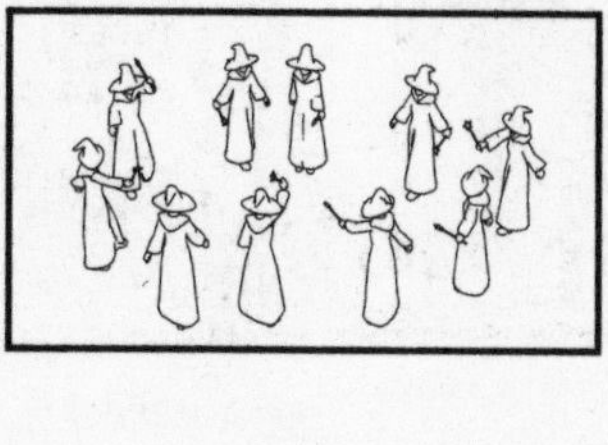

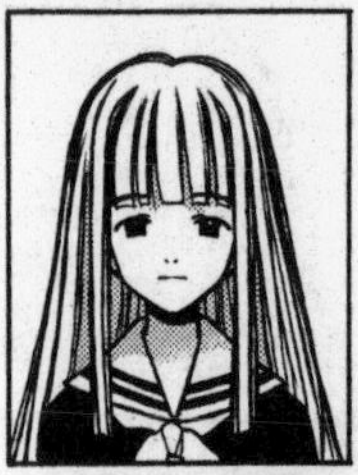

1. SAYO AISAKA

1940~
DON'T CHANGE HER SEATING

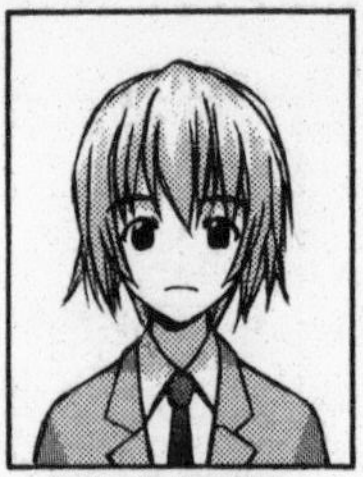

5. AKO IZUMI
NURSE'S OFFICE AIDE
SOCCER TEAM
(NON-SCHOOL ACTIVITY)

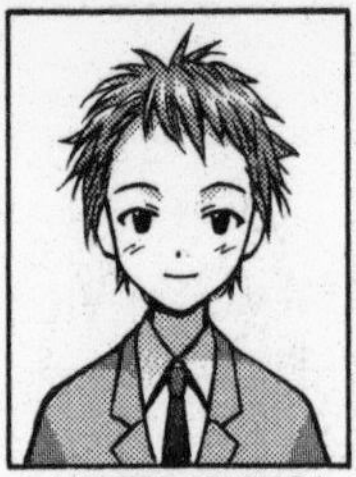

9. MISORA KASUGA
TRACK & FIELD

GRANDDAUGHTER OF SCHOOL DEAN

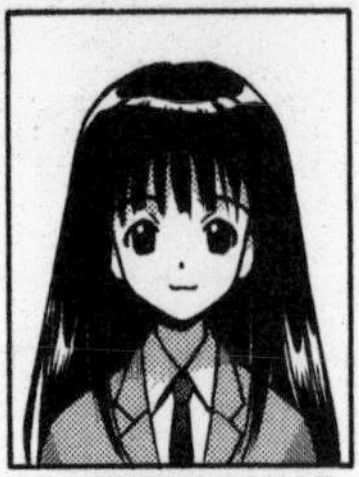

13. KONOKA KONOE
SECRETARY
FORTUNE-TELLING CLUB
LIBRARY EXPLORATION CLUB

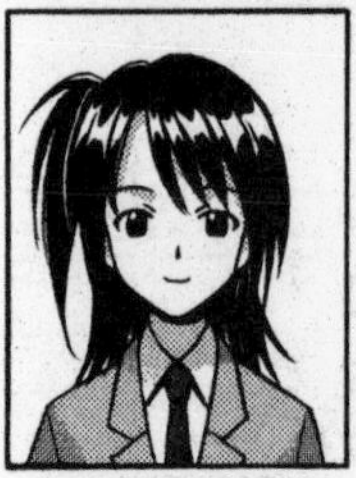

2. YUNA AKASHI
BASKETBALL TEAM

PROFESSOR AKASHI'S DAUGHTER

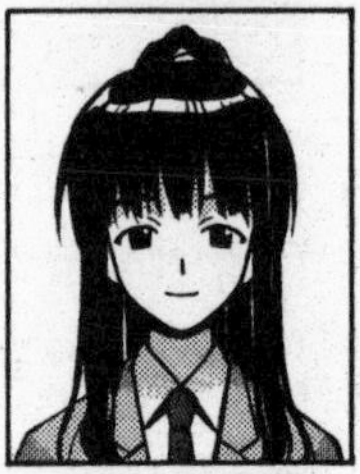

6. AKIRA OKOCHI
SWIM TEAM

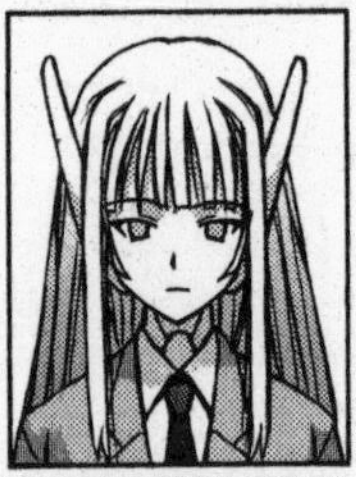

10. CHACHAMARU KARAKURI
TEA CEREMONY CLUB
GO CLUB

CALL ENGINEERING (ext. A08-7796) IN CASE OF EMERGENCY

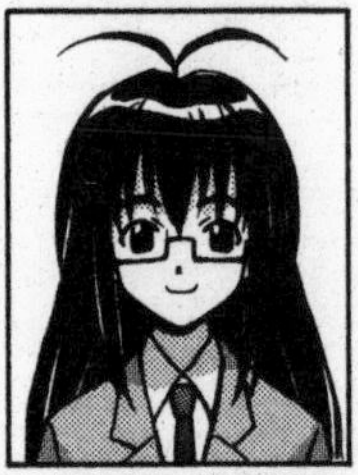

14. HARUNA SAOTOME
MANGA CLUB
LIBRARY EXPLORATION CLUB

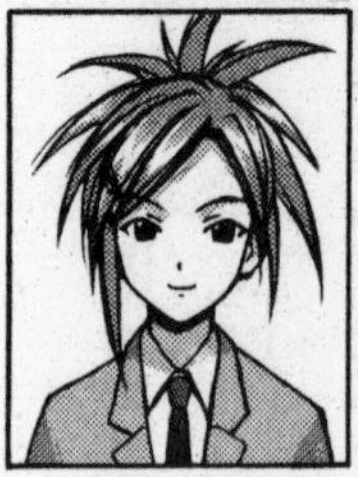

3. KAZUMI ASAKURA
SCHOOL NEWSPAPER

MAHORA NEWS (ext. B09-3780)

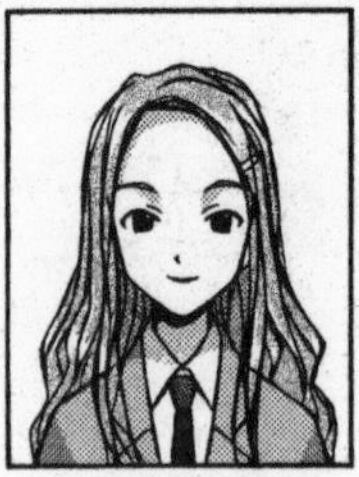

7. MISA KAKIZAKI
CHEERLEADER
CHORUS

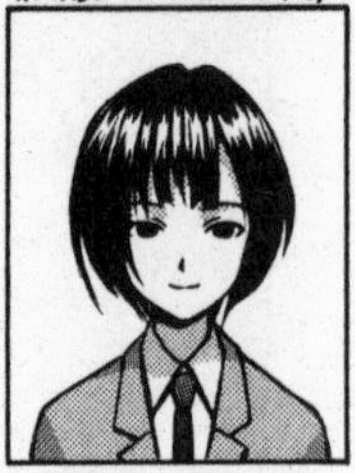

11. MADOKA KUGIMIYA
CHEERLEADER

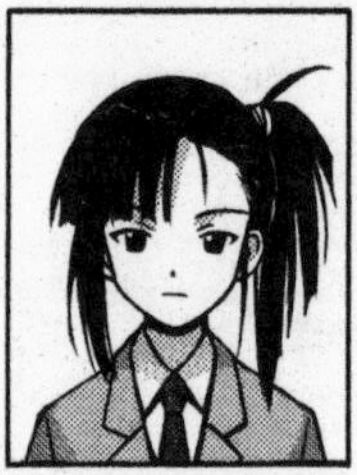

15 SETSUNA SAKURAZAKI
KENDO CLUB

KYOTO SHINMEI STYLE

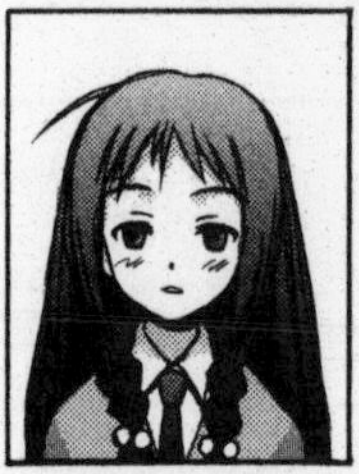

4. YUE AYASE
KIDS' LIT CLUB
PHILOSOPHY CLUB
LIBRARY EXPLORATION CLUB

A GOOD PERSON JUST AS I THOUGHT.

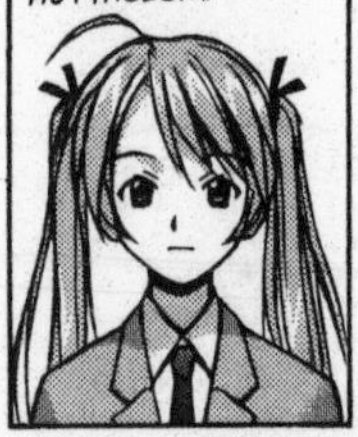

8. ASUNA KAGURAZAKA
ART CLUB
HAS A TERRIBLE KICK

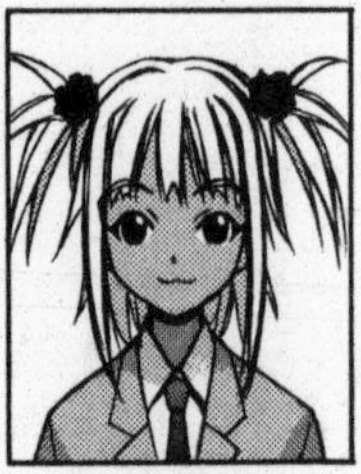

12. KŪ FEI
CHINESE MARTIAL ARTS CLUB

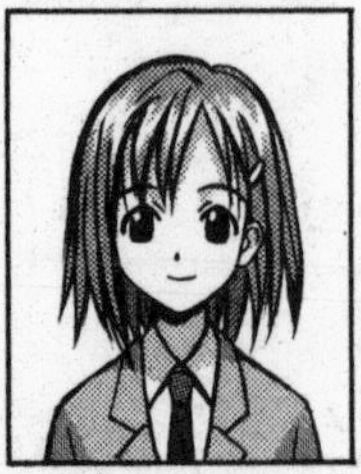

16. MAKIE SASAKI
GYMNASTICS

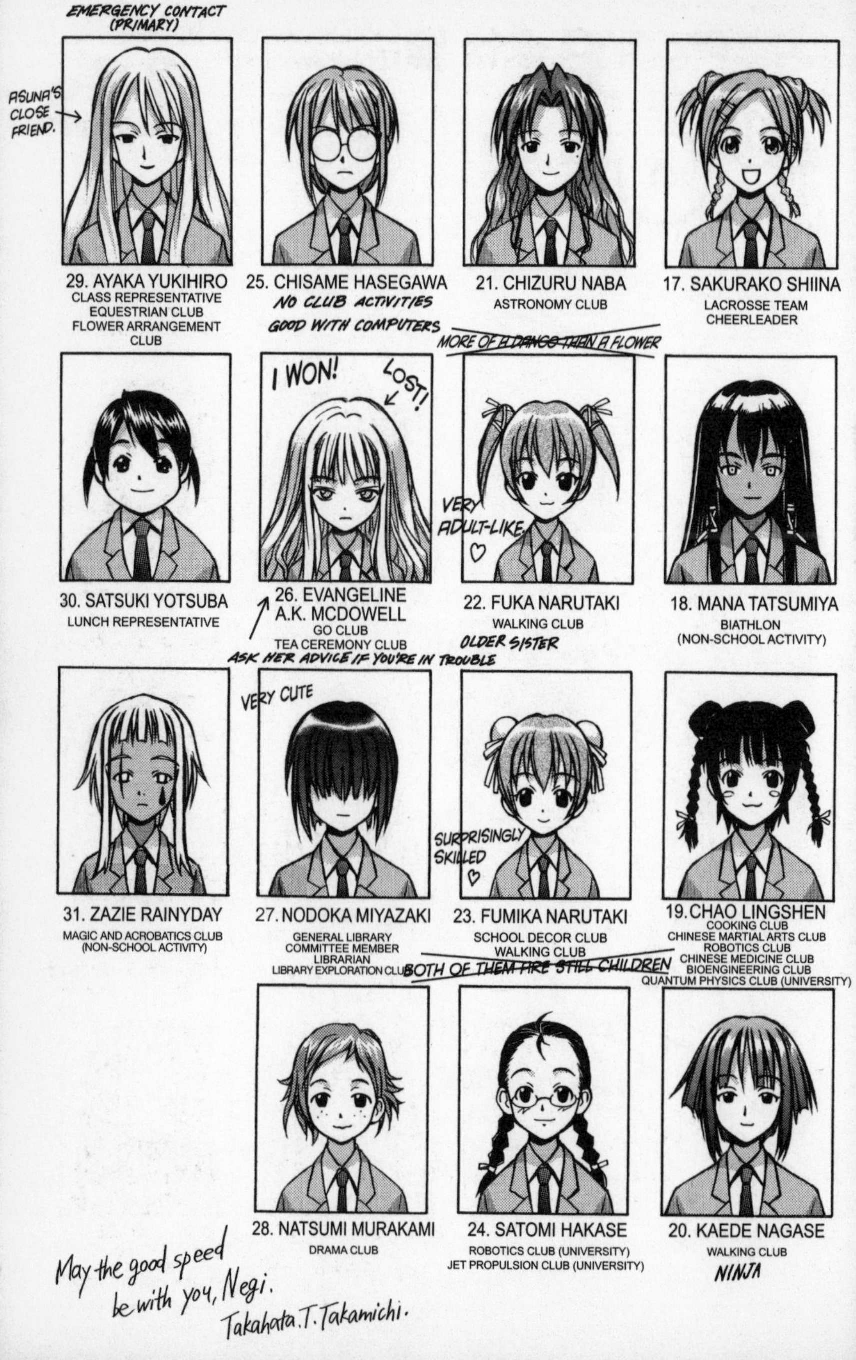
17. SAKURAKO SHIINA
LACROSSE TEAM
CHEERLEADER
21. CHIZURU NABA
ASTRONOMY CLUB
MORE OF A DANGO THAN A FLOWER
25. CHISAME HASEGAWA
NO CLUB ACTIVITIES
GOOD WITH COMPUTERS
EMERGENCY CONTACT (PRIMARY)
ASUNA'S CLOSE FRIEND.
29. AYAKA YUKIHIRO
CLASS REPRESENTATIVE
EQUESTRIAN CLUB
FLOWER ARRANGEMENT CLUB
18. MANA TATSUMIYA
BIATHLON
(NON-SCHOOL ACTIVITY)
VERY ADULT-LIKE
22. FUKA NARUTAKI
WALKING CLUB
OLDER SISTER
I WON!
LOST!
26. EVANGELINE A.K. MCDOWELL
GO CLUB
TEA CEREMONY CLUB
ASK HER ADVICE IF YOU'RE IN TROUBLE
30. SATSUKI YOTSUBA
LUNCH REPRESENTATIVE
19. CHAO LINGSHEN
COOKING CLUB
CHINESE MARTIAL ARTS CLUB
ROBOTICS CLUB
CHINESE MEDICINE CLUB
BIOENGINEERING CLUB
QUANTUM PHYSICS CLUB (UNIVERSITY)
SURPRISINGLY SKILLED
23. FUMIKA NARUTAKI
SCHOOL DECOR CLUB
WALKING CLUB
BOTH OF THEM ARE STILL CHILDREN
VERY CUTE
27. NODOKA MIYAZAKI
GENERAL LIBRARY COMMITTEE MEMBER
LIBRARIAN
LIBRARY EXPLORATION CLUB
31. ZAZIE RAINYDAY
MAGIC AND ACROBATICS CLUB
(NON-SCHOOL ACTIVITY)
20. KAEDE NAGASE
WALKING CLUB
NINJA
24. SATOMI HAKASE
ROBOTICS CLUB (UNIVERSITY)
JET PROPULSION CLUB (UNIVERSITY)
28. NATSUMI MURAKAMI
DRAMA CLUB
May the good speed be with you, Negi.
Takahata.T.Takamichi.

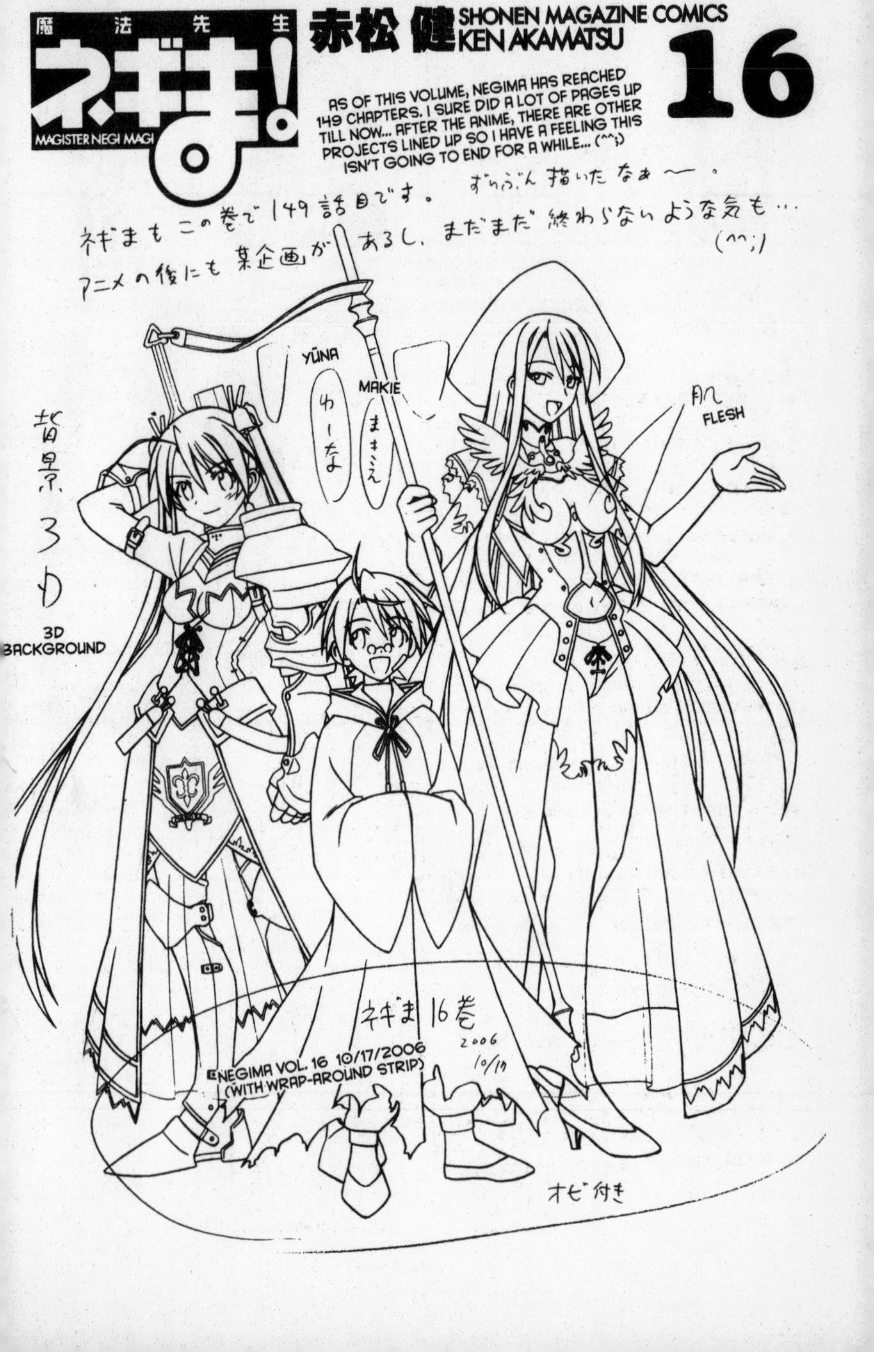

魔法先生
ネギま!
MAGISTER NEGI MAGI
赤松 健
SHONEN MAGAZINE COMICS
KEN AKAMATSU
16
AS OF THIS VOLUME, NEGIMA HAS REACHED 149 CHAPTERS. I SURE DID A LOT OF PAGES UP TILL NOW... AFTER THE ANIME, THERE ARE OTHER PROJECTS LINED UP SO I HAVE A FEELING THIS ISN'T GOING TO END FOR A WHILE... (^^;)
ネギまも この巻で 149話目です。 ずいぶん 描いたなぁ〜。
アニメの後にも 某企画が あるし、まだまだ 終わらないような気も…
(^^;)
背景3D
3D BACKGROUND
YŪNA
ゆーな
MAKIE
まきえ
肌
FLESH
ネギま16巻
2006 10/17
NEGIMA VOL. 16 10/17/2006 (WITH WRAP-AROUND STRIP)
オビ付き

キャラ解説
CHARACTER PROFILE

② 明石 裕奈　ムネが
② YŪNA AKASHI

最近めっきり成長してきた 裕奈
RECENTLY, YUNA HAS BEEN GROWING A LOT (←IN
ですが。そんな彼女の好きなものは
BREAST SIZE). AND HER FAVORITE PERSON HAPPENS
お父さん」。一体 今後、どんなドキドキ
TO BE HER FATHER. I WONDER WHAT KIND OF
エピソードが 待っているのでしょうか?! (^^;)
EXCITING STORY LINES AWAIT HER IN THE FUTURE!? (^^;)

運動神経は 良い方で、この16～17巻でも
SHE IS VERY ATHLETICALLY COORDINATED AND WILL BE
かなり活躍しています。
DOING A LOT IN VOL 16 & 17.

13話目で髪の結びを逆に
TO THIS DATE, I'M STILL HAUNTED BY THE FACT
描いてしまったのが、今でも
THAT I PUT THE KNOT ON HER HAIR ON THE
心残りです。(笑)
WRONG SIDE IN 13TH PERIOD. (LAUGHS)

CVは、今イチオシの
HER VOICE ACTOR IS THE UP-AND-
木村まどか さん。
COMING MADOKA KIMURA.

ショートの あわあわ 妹系
WITH HER SHORT HAIR AND FLUSTERED
キャラで、かわいいんですよ♡
LITTLE SISTER-LIKE PERSONALITY YUNA
IS REALLY CUTE. ♡

麻帆良祭も、次巻でいよいよ クライマックスです。
THE MAHORA FESTIVAL WILL REACH ITS CLIMAX IN THE NEXT VOLUME.
もうしばらく おつきあい下さいませ。
PLEASE BEAR WITH ME A LITTLE BIT LONGER.

赤松
AKAMATSU

About the Creator

Negima! is only Ken Akamatsu's third manga, although he started working in the field in 1994 with *AI Ga Tomaranai* (released in the United States with the title *A.I. Love You*). Like all of Akamatsu's work to date, it was published in Kodansha's *Shonen Magazine*. *AI Ga Tomaranai* ran for five years before concluding in 1999. In 1998, however, Akamatsu began the work that would make him one of the most popular manga artists in Japan: *Love Hina. Love Hina* ran for four years, and before its conclusion in 2002, it would cause Akamatsu to be granted the prestigious Manga of the Year award from Kodansha, as well as going on to become one of the bestselling manga in the United States.

Translation Notes

Japanese is a tricky language for most westerners, and translation is often more an art than a science. For your edification and reading pleasure, here are notes on some of the places where we could have gone in a different direction, or where a Japanese cultural reference is used.

Bad ending, page 5

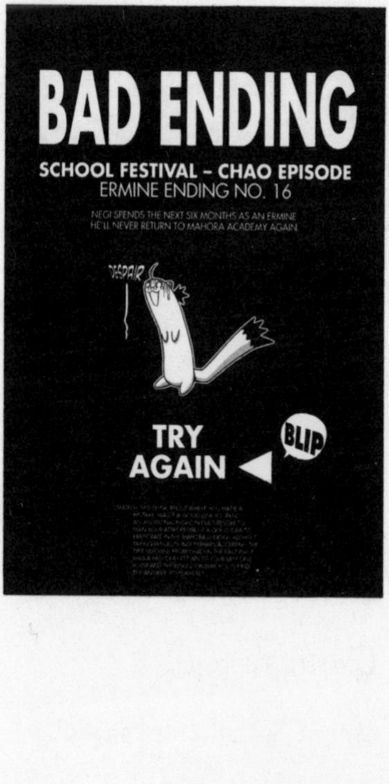
BAD ENDING
SCHOOL FESTIVAL – CHAO EPISODE
ERMINE ENDING NO. 16
NEGI SPENDS THE NEXT SIX MONTHS AS AN ERMINE
HE'LL NEVER RETURN TO MAHORA ACADEMY AGAIN
DESPAIR
TRY AGAIN
BLIP

One may come across this in some simulation video games when you make the wrong choices. Dating and mystery games typically have more than one outcome. A bad ending occurs when the main character didn't improve his parameters enough in a game (for example, getting to know a girl well enough in a dating game or missing important clues in a mystery game).

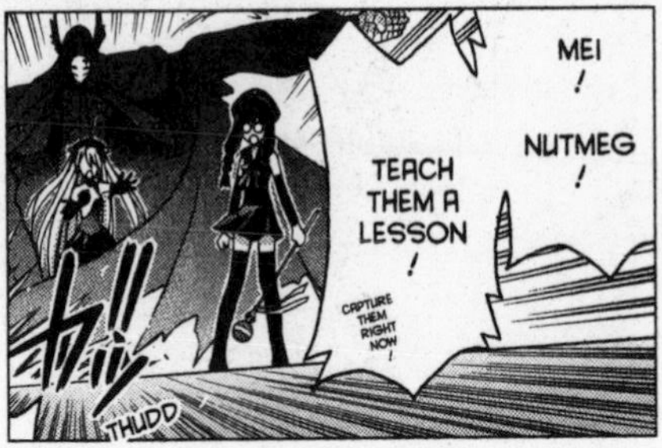
MEI!
NUTMEG!
TEACH THEM A LESSON!
CAPTURE THEM RIGHT NOW!
THUDD

Nutmeg, page 25

In the original Japanese text, Takane calls Megumi Natsume "Natsu Megu," a nickname that is not only a cute abbreviation of her full name but roughly translates to "nutmeg."

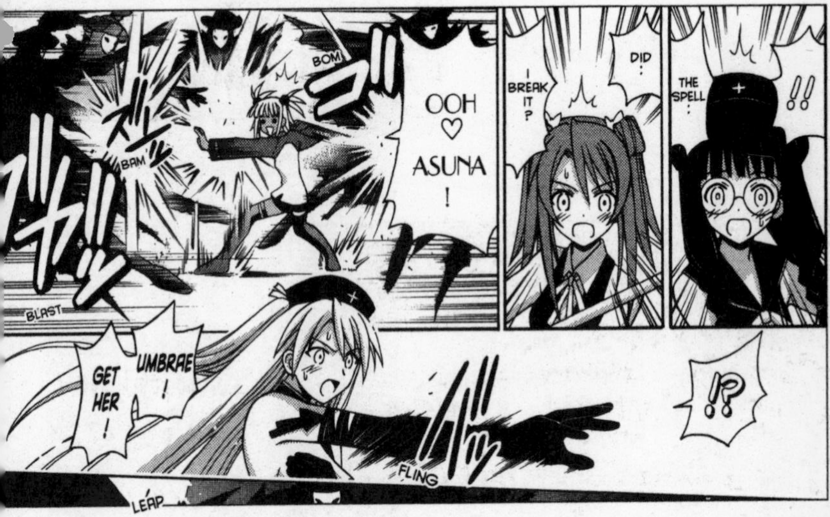
THE SPELL...
!!
DID I BREAK IT?
OOH ♡ ASUNA!
BOM
BAM
BLAST
!?
UMBRAE!
GET HER!
FLING
LEAP

Umbrae, page 27

Umbrae is Latin for "shadows."

Mei Sakura artifact, page 28

The Japanese name for this artifact is *Osoji Daisuki*, which means something like "I love to clean" or "I love to sweep."

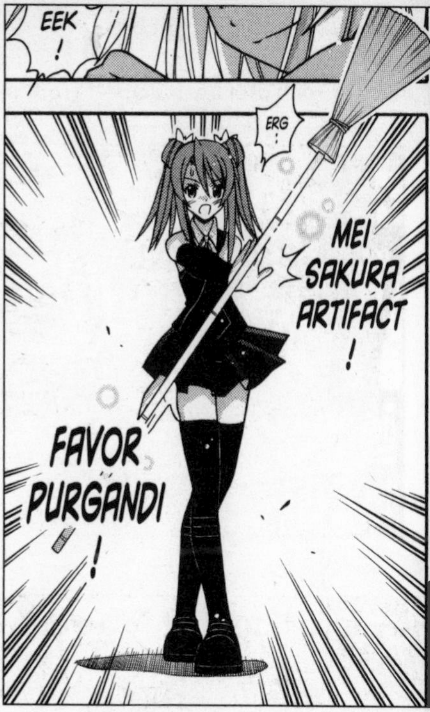
EEK !
ERG !
MEI SAKURA ARTIFACT !
FAVOR PURGANDI !

Tsurugi no Tan, page 67

The name of this attack translates to "Goddess of the Sword" in English.

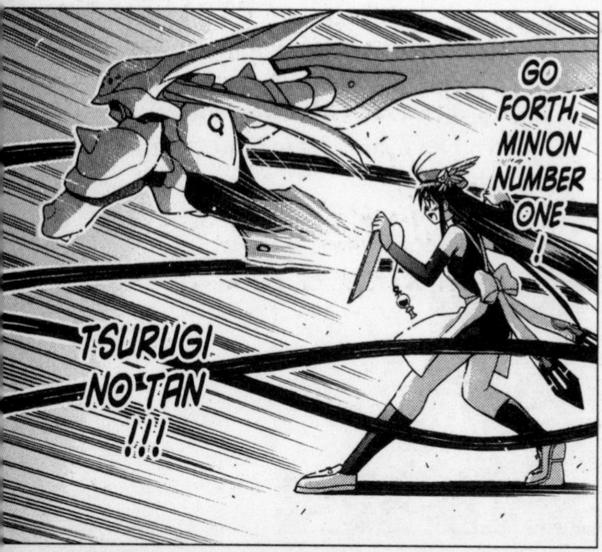
GO FORTH, MINION NUMBER ONE !
TSURUGI NO TAN !!!

Vente Nos, page 112

Negi's spell literally means "Wind, protect us

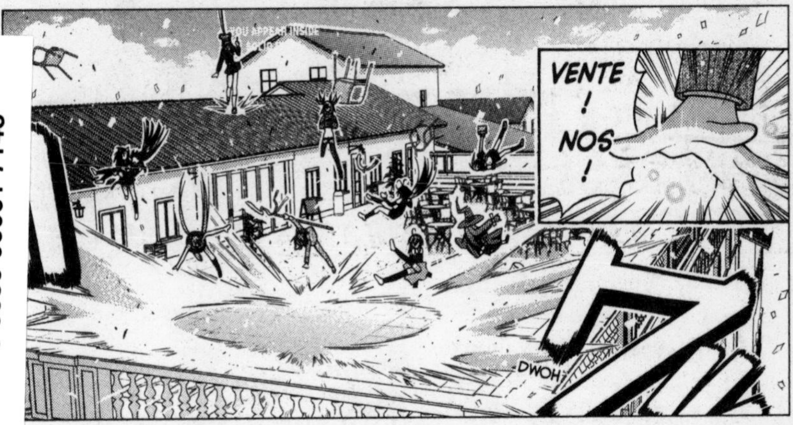
VENTE
!
NOS
!
DWOH

Appearing inside a rock, page 113

The original Japanese phrase was made famous by the Japanese version of the classic 1980s computer game series Wizardry, by Andrew C. Greenberg and Robert Woodhead (who later went on to found one of the first anime companies in the U.S., AnimEigo). It was a basic adventure game in which a group traveled through a multilevel dungeon. Along the way, the player would learn the Malor spell, which allowed the party to travel to any location simply by punching in its coordinates. However, if you put in the wrong coordinates, you could end up materializing inside a rock, instantly killing your entire party.

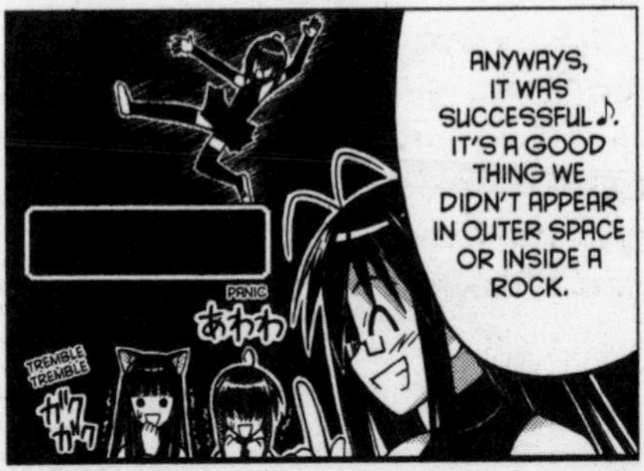
ANYWAYS, IT WAS SUCCESSFUL♪. IT'S A GOOD THING WE DIDN'T APPEAR IN OUTER SPACE OR INSIDE A ROCK.
PANIC
あわわ
TREMBLE TREMBLE

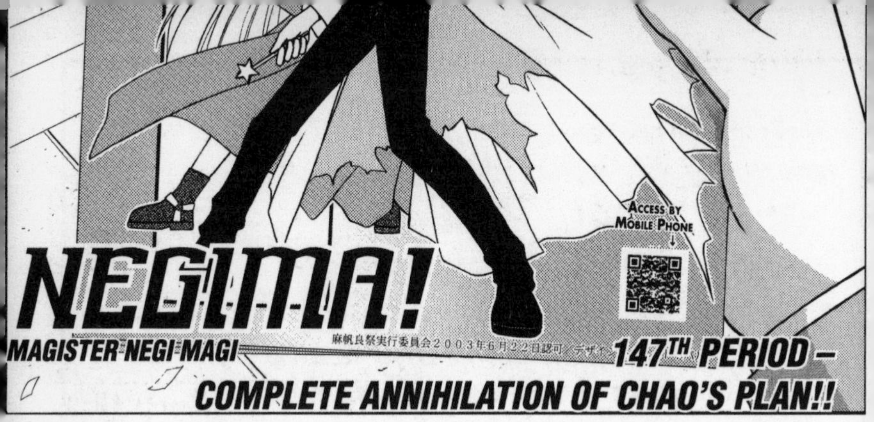
ACCESS BY
MOBILE PHONE
NEGIMA!
MAGISTER NEGI MAGI
麻帆良祭実行委員会２００３年６月２２日認可 デザイ
147TH PERIOD –
COMPLETE ANNIHILATION OF CHAO'S PLAN!!

QR codes, page 128

The squares you see on the corners of Japanese ads are actually a matrix code (two-dimensional bar codes) that were created by the Denso Wave Corporation of Japan in 1994. QR stands for Quick Response, which was developed so that information could be decoded quickly. As cell phones gained popularity and technological advances took place, camera phones in Japan became equipped with a QR decoder. By pointing the camera at the QR code, one can go directly to a URL. These days, many Japanese business cards incorporate QR code technology so that information can quickly be entered into a PDA or cell phone.

Kyo●hei and Gun●am, pages 163 and 164

The first word with the blacked-out character in the middle is probably Kyoshinhei, or God-Soldier, from Hayao Miyazaki's *Nausicäa of the Valley of the Wind*. On the next page, Sakurako name-checks the popular Gundam series of giant-robot anime and manga sagas.

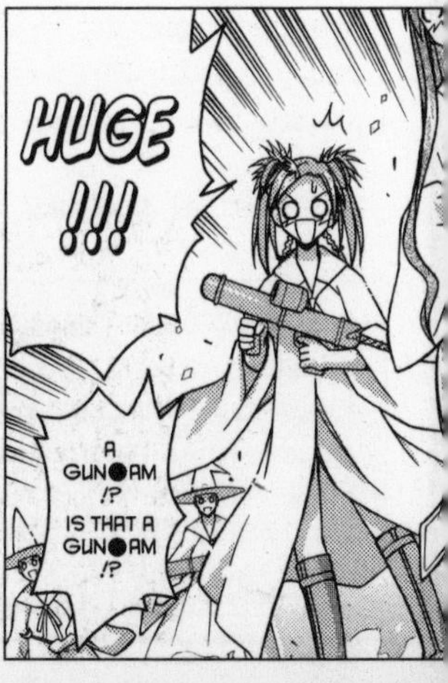
HUGE
!!!
A GUN●AM !?
IS THAT A GUN●AM !?

SHIN MIDORIKAWA

NEVER STOP BELIEVING

Since ancient days, the Gaius School of Witchcraft and Wizardry has trained the fiercest swordsmen and the most powerful wizards.

Now one boy could become the greatest of them all. If he studies hard. If he is true to his friends. If he believes.

And if he survives . . .

Special extras in each volume! Read them all!

TOMARE!

[STOP!]

You're going the wrong way!

Manga is a completely different type of reading experience.

To start at the *beginning*, go to the *end*!

That's right! Authentic manga is read the traditional Japanese way—from right to left, exactly the *opposite* of how American books are read. It's easy to follow: Just go to the other end of the book, and read each page—and each panel—from right side to left side, starting at the top right. Now you're experiencing manga as it was meant to be.